COVERING THE UNITED STATES SUPREME COURT IN THE DIGITAL AGE

The U.S. Supreme Court seeks to withhold information about its deliberations, while the press's job is to report and disseminate this information. These two objectives conflict and create tension between the justices and the reporters who cover them; add to that the increasing demands for transparency in the digital age and the result is an interesting dynamic between an institution that seeks to preserve its opaqueness and a press corps that demands greater transparency. This volume examines the relationship between justices and the press through chapters that discuss such facets as coverage of the institution, the media's approach to the docket, and the effects of news coverage on public opinion. Additionally, two journalists who cover the Court offer insights into the profession of reporting today, while two biographers of Supreme Court justices share the perspectives of those justices regarding the press.

Richard Davis is a professor of political science and director of the Office of Civic Engagement at Brigham Young University. He holds a PhD in political science from Syracuse University. He is the author of several books on the role of the media in American politics. He is past chair of the political communication section of the American Political Science Association.

Covering the United States Supreme Court in the Digital Age

Edited by
RICHARD DAVIS
Brigham Young University

CAMBRIDGE
UNIVERSITY PRESS

CAMBRIDGE
UNIVERSITY PRESS

University Printing House, Cambridge CB2 8BS, United Kingdom

Cambridge University Press is part of the University of Cambridge.

It furthers the University's mission by disseminating knowledge in the pursuit of education, learning and research at the highest international levels of excellence.

www.cambridge.org
Information on this title: www.cambridge.org/9781107642492

First published 2014
First paperback edition 2016

A catalogue record for this publication is available from the British Library

Library of Congress Cataloguing in Publication data
Covering the United States Supreme Court in the digital age / edited by Richard Davis.
pages cm
ISBN 978-1-107-05245-1 (Hardback)
1. United States. Supreme Court–Press coverage. 2. Courts of last resort–Press coverage–United States. 3. Mass media–Law and legislation–United States.
I. Davis, Richard, editor of compilation.
KF8742.C679 2014
070.4′493477326–dc23 2014003454

ISBN 978-1-107-05245-1 Hardback
ISBN 978-1-107-64249-2 Paperback

To the reporters of the United States Supreme Court press corps

Contents

About the Contributors

Bill Barnhart is a Chicago-based journalist and former financial columnist for the *Chicago Tribune*. He is the coauthor of biographies of Justice John Paul Stevens and former Illinois Governor Otto Kerner.

Rosalee A. Clawson is a professor of political science at Purdue University. Her research focuses on public opinion, mass media, and the politics of race, class, and gender. Her work has been published in the *American Political Science Review*, *Journal of Black Studies*, *Judicature*, and *Public Opinion Quarterly*. She is the coauthor of *Legacy and Legitimacy: Black Americans and the Supreme Court* and *Public Opinion: Democratic Ideals, Democratic Practice*.

Richard Davis is a professor of political science at Brigham Young University. He is the author of *Decisions and Images: The Supreme Court and the Press*, *Electing Justice: Fixing the Supreme Court Nomination Process*, and *Justices and Journalists: The U.S. Supreme Court and the Media*.

Valerie Hoekstra is an associate professor of political science in the School of Politics and Global Studies at Arizona State University. Her research focuses on the Supreme Court and public opinion, judicial independence in state courts of last resort, judicial decision making, and the diversity of high courts globally.

Tyler Johnson is an assistant professor in the Department of Political Science at the University of Oklahoma. His research interests lie at the intersection of American political behavior and institutions, using elite activity and norms to explain media coverage and public opinion. His work has appeared in *Political Behavior*, *American Politics Research*, *Politics & Policy*, *Social Science Quarterly*, and the *Journal of Integrated Social Sciences*. He holds a PhD in political science from Texas A&M University.

Nicholas LaRowe received his PhD in 2010 from Arizona State University and is an assistant professor of political science at the University of Southern

Indiana. His research focuses on the interrelation of courts, legitimacy, and public opinion; he is currently looking at the impact of *Citizens United versus FEC* on judicial elections.

Dahlia Lithwick is a senior editor at *Slate*. Her work has appeared in the *New York Times*, *Harper's*, *The New Yorker*, *The Washington Post*, and *Commentary*, among other places. She won a 2013 National Magazine Award for her columns on the Affordable Care Act. She has received two Online Journalism Awards for her legal commentary. She also is the first online journalist invited to be on the Reporters Committee for the Freedom of the Press.

Phil Marcin is a college lecturer at the University of Akron. He is pursuing his PhD from the University of Georgia. His research focuses on judicial selection methods and media attention to the Supreme Court.

Laura Moyer is an assistant professor of political science at the University of Louisville. She graduated summa cum laude from Emory University and earned her Master of Public Administration and PhD in political science from the University of Georgia. Her research examines judicial behavior and identity politics and has appeared in numerous political science journals.

David G. Savage has covered the Supreme Court for the *Los Angeles Times* since 1986. He also writes about national legal issues and reports for the *Chicago Tribune*, the *Baltimore Sun*, and the other Tribune papers. He is the author of *Turning Right: The Making of the Rehnquist Supreme Court*, which describes the increasingly conservative court in the early 1990s. More recently, he revised and rewrote the two-volume *Guide to the U.S. Supreme Court*.

Rorie Spill Solberg is an associate professor in the School of Public Policy at Oregon State University. She is widely published in journals such as *Political Research Quarterly*, *Social Science Quarterly*, *Policy Studies Quarterly*, and the *Journal of Empirical Legal Studies*. In 2011, she was selected to edit *Judicature*, the journal of the American Judicature Society. She received her PhD in American politics from The Ohio State University in 1997.

Seth Stern is coauthor, with Stephen Wermiel, of *Justice Brennan: Liberal Champion*, a biography of Justice William J. Brennan Jr. published in 2010. He is an editor at Bloomberg BNA and previously was a reporter for Bloomberg News, the *Christian Science Monitor*, and *Congressional Quarterly*. He is a graduate of Harvard Law School, the Kennedy School of Government at Harvard University, and Cornell University.

Vincent James Strickler lives in Valdosta, Georgia, with his wife and seven children. He is an assistant professor of political science at Valdosta State University. He earned a PhD from Stanford University and a JD from the J. Reuben Clark Law School at Brigham Young University. His work has appeared in the edited volumes *Freedom and the Rule of Law* and *Media Power, Media Politics*, in the *Georgia Law Review*, and in the *International Journal of Press/Politics*.

Matthew Thornton is an assistant professor of convergence media and chair of the Division of Media and Communication at Louisiana College. His research focuses on political communication and campaigns. Dr. Thornton has authored or coauthored numerous conference papers. Additionally, his work has been published in the *Journal of Politics*.

Terri L. Towner received her PhD from Purdue University and is an associate professor in the Department of Political Science at Oakland University in Michigan. Towner's research focuses on American politics, public opinion, media coverage of elections and political institutions, and the politics of race and class. Her research has been published as chapters and journal articles in outlets such as the *Journal of Political Marketing*, *Social Science Computer Review*, and *New Media & Society*.

Joseph Daniel Ura is an associate professor of political science at Texas A&M University. His research addresses the dynamic interactions between the United States Supreme Court and public opinion as well as other issues of macropolitical responsiveness and representation. He teaches courses on American national government, judicial politics, and constitutional law.

Richard L. Vining, Jr., received his PhD from Emory University in 2008. He is an associate professor of political science in the School of Public and International Affairs at the University of Georgia. His research interests include judicial selection and departures, judicial decision making, interbranch politics, and media coverage of American courts. His work has appeared in academic journals including the *Journal of Politics*, *Political Research Quarterly*, *American Politics Research*, and *Social Science Quarterly*.

Eric N. Waltenburg is an associate professor of political science at Purdue University. He is the author or coauthor of three books on judicial politics and the United States Supreme Court.

Introduction

The U.S. Supreme Court is one of the most secretive and yet one of the most public institutions in American government. It is remarkably effective in shielding its decision-making process from the public's view, while its products, the opinions themselves, are lengthy tomes filled with detail about the justices' decisions and the rationales behind them. Ironically, the justices are the most verbose of public officials, while also acting as the most sheltered from public attention.

In recent years, however, that tightrope act of publicizing the product but masking the decision-making process behind it has become more difficult for the Court. The justices have become objects of press attention from their role in deciding a presidential election to their decision regarding a president's signature legislative reform. Their own actions have contributed to this higher profile. Unlike their predecessors, most justices give news media interviews. Moreover, these interviews appear not only in legal publications. For example, Justice Ginsburg has given interviews to *USA Today*, *Oprah* magazine, and the *New York Times*. Justice Scalia has been interviewed by *CBS Evening News*, the *Laura Ingraham Show*, and BBC radio. In addition, Justice Breyer has appeared on many media outlets, including *Larry King Live*, the *NBC Nightly News*, and FOX News.

At the same time, the Court has not altered the secrecy of its decision-making process. A press report in 2012 that Chief Justice John Roberts may have switched his vote in the case of *National Federation of Independent Business et al v. Sebelius* may suggest the shroud around decision making is being lifted. However, such breaches of the Court's secrecy have occurred in the past, albeit rarely. Indeed, it is the rarity of such disclosures, even in the face of extensive media coverage of high profile cases and enhanced coverage of the Court and justices generally, that suggests the Court remains successful in its media strategy of directing the public's attention to its product and not to its decision-making process.

How does the Court achieve its press goals, particularly in an age of increased transparency, 24-hour cable news coverage, and the plethora of Internet news and information? What are the routines of press reporting on the Court in the Internet age? As justices have become more visible, has press coverage focused more on individual justices? How has the Court's role in high profile social issues affected its press coverage and public image? How is new communication technology affecting the Court?

These are all questions that political science, communication, and legal scholars seek to answer. Scholars have addressed these questions in various formats such as law reviews, as well as political science and communications journals. This volume brings together scholarly and journalistic perspectives on these questions. The purpose of this book is to illuminate the relationship between the Court and the press by examining the nature of press coverage of the Court and its effects on public opinion, the functioning of the Court, and the Court's interaction with its various public constituencies. It accomplishes that purpose by organizing aspects of the relationship between the Court and the press and then presenting new research by academics describing and explaining those aspects. Additionally, it offers journalistic perspectives, primarily from current members of the U.S. Supreme Court press corps, on the job of covering the Court.

The volume begins with a brief overview of the historical relationship between the Court and the press while also emphasizing developments in national politics, the Court, and the press occurring in the twentieth century that heightened the relationship. Next, we turn to the nature of media coverage of the institution. Tyler Johnson discusses the type of media coverage devoted to the Supreme Court today and addresses the causes of the Court's media portrayal.

News coverage of the docket is the subject of the following three chapters. Terri Towner and Rosalee Clawson discuss which cases receive more attention from the press and specifically focus on one type of case – civil rights – to analyze media framing of these cases. Vincent James Strickler compares coverage of two cases two decades apart to show the changes in press coverage of the Court caused by the Internet. He also speculates on how these developments will affect the future of news media coverage and what they mean for how citizens will acquire news about the Court. Richard Vining and Phil Marcin investigate intermedia coverage of decisions to determine the factors that affect a wide array of media coverage despite audience fragmentation.

Then, Eric N. Waltenburg and Rorie Spill Solberg focus on media coverage of one particular justice, Harry Blackmun. Through their extensive analysis of *New York Times* coverage of Blackmun, they offer insights into how a medium reports on the various facets of a justice's public work – from Blackmun's role in oral arguments to his opinions to his personal life.

Two chapters shift to the Court, news media, and public opinion and examine the Court from two different perspectives in that relationship. Nicholas LaRowe and Valerie Hoekstra examine the role of media coverage in shaping diffuse support for the Court as well as public opinion towards specific Court actions. Joseph Ura examines how the Court has shaped the issue attention of national media outlets through its decisions. He demonstrates how *Brown v. Board of Education* served as a catalyst to public discussion of desegregation.

Then we move to the view from the pressroom. *Los Angeles Times* reporter David Savage, a twenty-eight-year veteran of the Supreme Court press corps, explains how new media such as the Internet and blogs have affected reporter routines. Then, Dahlia Lithwick, former Supreme Court reporter for *Slate*, describes the Court's struggles to adapt to or resist new media changes, as well as the difficulties of new media reporters in covering an institution wedded to traditionalism.

Finally, we get the justices' perspectives on their relationship with the press. Laura Moyer and Matthew Thornton review justices' public statements about the press corps that reveal their attitudes about press coverage while expressing their willingness to engage the press. Additionally, two biographers of justices relate views about the press as gleaned from personal interviews with the justices while they served on the Court. Seth Stern recounts Justice William Brennan's ambivalence toward a press he championed in opinions, but whom he derided personally due to his negative experiences with some reporters. John Paul Stevens' biographer Bill Barnhart describes Stevens' distance from, but not complete disinterest, in the press – both in terms of the cases Stevens handled as well as his personal interactions with reporters. Both chapters provide readers with an inside look at justices' views about the press corps that covered them.

1

The Symbiotic Relationship Between the U.S. Supreme Court and the Press

RICHARD DAVIS

INTRODUCTION

Soon after the U.S. Supreme Court ruled that the Affordable Care Act passed by Congress in 2010 was constitutional, CBS News reporter Jan Crawford aired a story claiming that Chief Justice John Roberts had switched his vote. Crawford reported that Roberts had changed while he was writing an opinion for the majority of conservative justices, and that Justice Anthony Kennedy led the effort to redeem Roberts' vote with the conservatives. The story was unusual because Crawford cited "two sources with specific knowledge" about the incident. That suggested the justices themselves might have been sources. While one of the references was to an unidentified source the other was explicitly, although perhaps indirectly, attributed to a justice: "And so the conservatives handed him their own message which, as one justice put it, essentially translated into, 'You're on your own.'" CBS News anchor Scott Pelly termed the story a "rare insight."[1]

Indeed, such a story is rare. As scholars of the Court know, inside information about the process of decision making for a specific case does not reach the public, except in unusual circumstances. Typically, the Court's norm has been to maintain the secrecy of the decision-making process.

Nevertheless, there are indications that such stories may become more common. U.S. Supreme Court justices have become public in a way that would have been unimaginable even thirty years ago. Moreover, the press has undergone an evolution in its approach to the Court. Reporters have become less willing to view the justices as above political scrutiny, personalize Court

[1] Jan Crawford, "Roberts Switched Views to Uphold Health Care Law," *CBS News*, July 1, 2012, at /www.cbsnews.com/8301-3460_162-57464549/roberts-switched-views-to-uphold-health-care-law/.

coverage, and cover the Court with less formality than in the past. What has led to this change in the relationship between justices and the press?

The thesis of this chapter is that the justices and the press operate within a symbiotic relationship that is marked by public tension, but also by frequent accommodation of each other. That relationship is defined and examples of accommodation on the part of the press towards the Court and the Court towards the press are described. Finally, three recent developments affecting the relationship are discussed. These are more extensive interaction between justices and journalists, increasing scrutiny by the press, and greater judicial acceptance of press norms.

SYMBIOSIS

With the possible exception of the federal bureaucracy, the conventional wisdom is that there is no national institution needing the press less than the Supreme Court. The justices serve life terms, do not stand for re-election, and often issue decisions that are blatantly countermajoritarian. Similarly, the press should be disinterested in the Court because the justices fail to abide by press norms, such as routinely making themselves available for interviews, speaking on the record, holding press conferences, or writing brief decisions stripped of legalese (perhaps in the form of press releases).

It is true that the justices are the least visible of national policymakers and the Court as an institution is the least covered of the three branches of government, which would suggest the absence of much of a relationship between justices and journalists. Nevertheless, the institution possesses certain incentives to interact with the press that Alexander Hamilton realized when he predicted that the Court would lack the power of enforcement: "It may truly be said to have neither Force nor will, but merely judgment."[2] The power of that judgment would depend on the acceptance by other political players – the executive, Congress, and the public. Another power the Court lacked was a mechanism to communicate to those players in order to gain deference to the Court. The Court's ability to communicate that judgment, and therefore build respect for it, also would be dependent upon other players, particularly the press. The Court, then, possessed a strong incentive to utilize the press to convey certain images that reinforced the significance of its role in the minds of others with power over the Court's role.

[2] Federalist no. 78.

Many individual justices also have reason to pursue press relations. These include influencing their colleagues, shaping public attitudes about legal issues, or writing their own historical records. In addition to autobiographies, biographies (some written by journalists), and, of course, their own written opinions, some justices use interviews with reporters to achieve their own individual aims.

In addition, the press itself has powerful incentives to forge a relationship with the Court. The Court is an influential decision maker in public policy with the capability to shape the agendas, attitudes, and behavior of the president, the Congress, the bureaucracy, interest groups, and the public. Moreover, the Court occasionally addresses high profile issues that reporters cover and the public thinks and talks about. Decisions about controversial issues such as health care reform, gay marriage, gun control, and abortion affect ordinary Americans, but also correspond to existing media and public agendas.

Publicly, the symbiotic relationship between the Court and the press is marked by tension. Justices often describe their distance from the press and occasionally criticize press coverage as shallow and incapable of reporting effectively on Court action. Simultaneously, journalists complain about that distance and their inability to cover the Court as they do other beats. The press often describes the justices as inflexible and unwilling to satisfy press demands for greater transparency and accessibility. In reality, the relationship is marked by accommodation on both sides.

Press Accommodation to the Court

The approach to the Court by the press is dissimilar from the press's treatment of other beats because the justices themselves are unique among national governmental players in their norms, practices, and traditions. In order to cover the Court, news organizations must recognize and adapt to the Court's institutional peculiarities. That is what they have done, even though these norms fly in the face of traditional newsgathering approaches.

One example of accommodation is adherence to the unique rules of the Court. One of those is press access to the decision makers – the justices who possess information reporters want. Unlike other institutions, the Court severely limits press access to those individuals – the justices – who, in another setting, such as Congress, would have frequent interaction with reporters.

Limitations on press access are not unique to the Court. For example, White House reporters understand where they can and cannot go in the White House. Journalists covering Congress are not allowed on the floor of the House or Senate or in congressional cloakrooms.

However, Supreme Court rules are more restrictive. Even physical proximity to the justices is more limited than for other institutions. Reporters covering Congress move freely among congressional offices and committee rooms. White House reporters see the president at photo-ops and press briefings where they can ask questions, and usually are able to walk around in the White House Press Secretary's office. But at the Supreme Court, reporters are not allowed to visit the floors where the justices work, unless they have an appointment with a specific justice, and their only regular contact with the justices is in the courtroom, where they obviously cannot ask questions.

In addition, the White House press corps has potential sources both in and out of the White House to obtain information about White House activities and processes. Moreover, leaks are common and even officially sanctioned. None of that is true for the Court. There is no sanctioned leak process. Most interactions with the press are off the record, not even on background. Moreover, justices' clerks are prohibited from releasing information and could well lose their jobs if they did so.

Reporters rarely chafe against the rules of the Court. They typically do not seek to violate those rules to uncover scoops about the Court. Rather, they rely on the official information provided by the Public Information Office and on what they observe in the courtroom. For example, when Tim O'Brien, an ABC News reporter, picked up a piece of paper from the ashes of the fireplace in the conference room during a photo shoot there, the justices discussed in a subsequent conference what action to take against O'Brien. One wanted O'Brien banned from the building. However, Justice John Paul Stevens suggested that O'Brien would not use any material he had obtained because he "will decide that the news value of what he may have seen is not worth the loss of our good will..."[3]

Stevens was right. O'Brien did not use the material, whatever it was. The good will of the justices is a carrot that encourages accommodation, rather than journalistic entrepreneurship, by reporters who might be inclined to follow their journalistic instincts to get a good story.

Breaking the rules is uncommon because members of the Supreme Court press corps generally have accepted the Court's practice of concentrating attention on the opinions of the justices rather than the justices themselves or the processes by which they reach those decisions. Adherence to the Court's norms may have diminished somewhat in the wake of the Thomas nomination, but reporters still are careful about shifting their focus to the

[3] Quoted in Davis, *Justices and Journalists*, p. 136.

individual justice, even when it is an attractive story. For example, one broadcast reporter confidentially related to the author that his producers had asked him to investigate the sexual life of one of the justices because of rumors about homosexuality. This request came in the wake of the Bork and Thomas nominations when judicial nominees' private lives became part of the public record. The reporter replied that he was uncomfortable doing so because he felt he should not report on the justices' private lives. His producers backed off when he expressed his reluctance to pursue such a story.

Reporters who cover the Court also accommodate to the Court by changing basic journalistic routines. Since on-record interviews are rarely available, reporters rely on documents to write stories. Stories about cases and decisions are typically about the legal principles of the case more than the personalities of the parties. That may be changing, particularly on television, but reporters covering the Court must adapt to their inability to use the standard journalistic tools of interviewing and observation of decision-making processes to understand and explain what the Court is doing. Instead, they must be willing to pore over stacks of legal documents in the form of writs, oral argument transcripts, and written opinions.

New York Times reporter Linda Greenhouse once described the difference between her previous beat covering New York state government and the Supreme Court this way: "Compared with the frenzied drama of the New York Legislature, the quiet of the Supreme Court press room was the silence of the tomb. In place of the easy banter with politicians that had made the Albany beat so engaging, there was an almost suffocating paper flow."[4]

Still another type of accommodation is news organizations' reliance on specialists to cover the Court. For most of the Court's history, reporters who covered the Court had no specialized training beyond journalism. In the 1950s, Justice Felix Frankfurter urged the *New York Times* to hire reporters with legal training. Frankfurter reportedly told a *New York Times* editor that the *Times* would not consider assigning a reporter to cover a New York Yankees game with as little understanding of baseball as *Times* reporters had about the Court. As a result, *Times* executives sent Anthony Lewis to law school for a year and then assigned him to cover the Court.[5]

Today, such legal training or even a law degree is more common in the Supreme Court press corps. Recent or current Supreme Court correspondents

[4] Linda Greenhouse, "2,691 Decisions," *New York Times*, July 13, 2008, at www.nytimes.com/2008/07/13/weekinreview/13linda.html?pagewanted=all&_r=0.

[5] David L. Grey, *The Supreme Court and the Media*, Evanston, IL: Northwestern University Press, pp. 52–53.

with law degrees have included Adam Liptak (*New York Times*), Jess Bravin (*Wall Street Journal*), Dahlia Lithwick (*Slate*), Tim O'Brien (ABC News), Marcia Coyle (*Legal Times*), and Jan Crawford (CBS News).

Not all reporters approve of the trend. Some reporters believe a legal background has the potential of increasing deference to the Court. SCOTUSblog reporter Lyle Denniston suggested, "If a reporter hangs around judges and lawyers too long he begins to smell like them. A journalist has his own smell and he should never trade that aroma for someone else's."[6] Nevertheless, journalists with legal training, such as Jan Crawford Greenburg, Adam Liptak, Dahlia Lithwick, and Jess Bravin, write critically of the justices.

The press has adapted its practices to align with the culture of the Court. It has done so in order to report on the Court's decisions more accurately and effectively. In the case of the use of legal specialists, it did so as a direct result of a justice's suggestion. In other cases, the press corps has accepted the Court's norms in order to maintain access to the Court as an institution and to the justices individually, but also due to a sense of protectiveness toward the Court in its constitutionally-assigned role. Regardless of the reason, the press has accommodated to the Court as well as the Court to the press.

Pressure to alter the press corps' approach to the Court has tested such accommodation. *Washington Post* reporter Bob Woodward urged the Supreme Court press corps to cover the "courts as a political institution" in line with a critical analysis approach to political institutions that emerged with "new journalism" in the 1960s.[7]

At first, coverage of the Supreme Court was unaffected by this analytical approach. Then, *The Brethren* appeared. An account of the court then headed by Chief Justice Warren Burger, *The Brethren* was an inside look at an institution that rarely received inside looks. The fact that the book's coauthor was Bob Woodward, an icon in American journalism who had uncovered Watergate, made it all the more compelling. The book, which appeared in 1979, followed the justices as they decided controversial cases from 1969 to 1974. Those years were pivotal in the Court's jurisprudence, as they decided cases regarding executive power, abortion, school busing, and freedom of the press.

The Brethren was not the first book-length attempt to humanize the justices. *The Nine Old Men*, a 1936 book by Drew Pearson and Robert Sharon Allen, treated the justices with a mix of humor and derision during

[6] Quoted in Mitchell J. Tropin, "What, Exactly, Is the Court Saying?" *The Barrister* (Winter 1984): 14.

[7] Quoted in David Shaw, *Media Watch*, New York: MacMillan, 1984, p. 120.

the New Deal era.[8] However, *The Brethren* was more substantial in its treatment of individual decision-making processes. Unlike the vast majority of prior books about the Court, *The Brethren* treated the highest court as primarily a political institution and the justices themselves as individuals adopting political methods to achieve their goals.

Through anonymous sources, Woodward and his coauthor, Scott Armstrong, revealed the justices' attempts to lobby one another, their personal animosities towards each other, and the influences of current events and public opinion on their decisions. It was a rare examination of a secretive institution and exposed the justices as political players, as much as legal arbiters. Woodward and Armstrong purposely sought to portray the justices as human beings who, despite the official public image of the Court, were driven by personal passions and strong political considerations.

The aim of *The Brethren* was not entirely new. William O. Douglas once admitted, "We all have subconscious parts, we're not entirely rational in our decisions."[9] But such candor was rare. Woodward sought to make transparent that to which Douglas alluded. He also encouraged other journalists to do the same. In fact, he publicly chastised the press for not being aggressive enough in covering the Court. Woodward hoped to shape future coverage of the Court by asserting, "The courts are a political institution and we [the press] don't cover them as such."[10]

Like *All the President's Men*, *The Brethren* had a significant impact on journalists. Following Woodward's lead, some other reporters began to view the Court as an institution full of individuals with political goals. At the *New York Times*, Stuart Taylor paid close attention to the justices' speeches, not just their decisions. Similarly, ABC News reporter Tim O'Brien sought to scoop his peers by digging for unreleased information he could report. Richard Carelli, an Associated Press reporter, felt that the personal context of a justice's opinion was important for the public to understand: "When Justice Stevens writes an opinion about parental rights, we can put in the story that this author is himself the adoptive parent of two children. It adds something for the readers, an appreciation of where this guy is coming from."[11]

Not all reporters shared the Woodward and Armstrong approach. Some believed that even if they received a draft of an opinion before it was

8 Drew Pearson and Robert S. Allen, *The Nine Old Men*, New York: Doubleday, Doran, and Co., 1936.

9 Transcript, Knight-Ridder interview, October 29, 1973, Box 621, William O. Douglas Papers, Manuscript Division, Library of Congress, Washington, D.C.

10 Quoted in David Shaw, *Media Watch*, New York: MacMillan, 1984, p. 120.

11 Quoted in Davis, *Decisions and Images*, p. 103.

circulated, they should not use it. Nor would they go out of their way to obtain such information.[12] Still other reporters saw such investigative behavior as unnecessary. Justice Lewis Powell referred to this camp of Supreme Court reporters when he commented that they "deserve a great deal of credit for not making efforts to ascertain information that would be very easy to obtain if one put his or her hand to doing so..."[13]

But journalism had changed. Recent exposes about the Court have updated *The Brethren*. Jeffrey Toobin and Jan Crawford Greenberg have offered recent book-length insider glimpses of the Court. Toobin had remarkable access to the justices to describe the interplay among the justices, particularly during the Court's consideration *of Bush v Gore*. Greenberg's discussion of the relationship between Scalia and Thomas countered the conventional wisdom of Scalia's dominance of Thomas.[14]

In the twenty-first century, the blogosphere clearly is following Woodward's lead. [15] The justices, the nomination process, and the Court itself have all become regular blog topics. Some of the leading bloggers are attorneys, such as John Hindraker and Scott Johnson of Powerline, or law school professors such as Glenn Reynolds, Instapundit; Hugh Hewitt; and Eugene Volokh, The Volokh Conspiracy. In addition, other bloggers specializing in the Supreme Court have acquired a niche within the blogger community. Their approaches focus more on personalities than in the past, although coverage of cases is still more likely to predominate. One example is SCOTUSblog, which offers texts of cert petitions and opinions, transcripts of oral arguments, as well as extensive discussion of judicial selection. It also occasionally discusses the personalities on the bench. Dahlia Lithwick at *Slate* goes even further in focusing on individual justices, such as commenting on Alito's, Roberts', and Scalia's new vigor in oral argument questioning, calling John Paul Stevens the "court's last negotiator and bridge builder," and noting that Antonin Scalia's "hide is tougher than a rhino's."[16]

[12] Davis, *Decisions and Images*, pp. 103–104.

[13] Transcript of Lewis Powell press conference, June 26, 1987, Box 575, Thurgood Marshall Papers, Manuscript Division, Library of Congress, Washington, D.C.

[14] Jeffrey Toobin, *The Nine: Inside the Secret World of the Supreme Court*, New York: Random House, 2008; and Jan Crawford Greenberg, *Supreme Conflict: The Inside Story of the Struggle for the Control of the United States Supreme Court*, New York: Penguin, 2007.

[15] For a discussion of the political blogosphere, see Matthew Hindman, *The Myth of Digital Democracy*, Princeton, NJ: Princeton University Press, 2009; and Richard Davis, *Typing Politics: The Role of Politics in American Blogs*, New York: Oxford University Press, 2009.

[16] "Holding Court: Dahlia Lithwick Dishes with Readers on the Supremes and the Start of a New Term," *Slate*, October 4, 2007, at /www.slate.com/id/2175318/; and Dahlia Lithwick, "A Supreme Court Case That Puts Scalia and Gay Rights Advocates on the Same Side," *Slate*, April 28, 2010, at /www.slate.com/id/2252251/.

Even though more news stories may be emerging with this more analytical approach to the justices' personalities, the coverage still primarily focuses on the actual public products and activities of the Court – oral arguments and written opinions. That description not only fits editors' expectations and journalists' self-perception of their primary role, but also corresponds to how the institution operates in providing minimal opportunities for personal exposure but lengthy written decisions that focus attention on products. Moreover, the reporters who regularly cover the Court lack the ability to analyze when faced with intense pressure to read an opinion, determine its outcome, and then write a story within a few minutes of the announcement of a decision.

Court accommodation to the press

Accommodation has not been a one-way street. While the press has accommodated to Court norms, the Court similarly has accommodated itself to the press. Journalists often suggest there is little or no accommodation from the justices to their requests. For example, journalists have called on the Court to open its public sessions to television cameras and provide early release of opinions to aid reporters in reporting on them, both of which the Court has refused to do.

However, the Court has a history of adjusting to the needs of the press, while attempting to avoid the appearance of doing so. One area is distribution of opinions. For many years, the Court did not provide the texts of announced opinions. Only after press demands, and instances of inaccuracy in reporting, did the justices release full texts of opinions when they announced them. The press also had urged the Court to spread out decision days to avoid dumping many decisions on the press in one day. In response, the Court moved decision days beyond Mondays and subsequently announced what days decisions would be released, although not which decisions would come on which days. The Court did not explain why it had changed. However, one scholar concluded that the Court "does not like to be placed in a position of letting press pressure result in procedural changes."[17]

The Court also began providing a headnote at the beginning of each Court opinion when it was released in order to help journalists understand quickly what the Court has decided. Previously, the headnote was written after the opinion was released, which did not help journalists seeking to understand

[17] David L. Grey, *The Supreme Court and the News Media*, Evanston, IL: Northwestern University Press, 1968, pp. 35–37; and Davis, *Decisions and Images*, pp. 36–37.

the opinion.[18] The press section in the Courtroom itself has been enlarged to seat more journalists. More recently, the Court has been willing to use electronic dissemination rather than rely on the old-fashioned method of distributing printed copies of the opinions to the press. In addition, it uses a website to house information for easy reference such as orders lists, oral argument calendars, press releases, and texts of speeches by the justices. The Court also has moved gradually to release more information concerning high profile cases. The Court has allowed same-day release of transcripts of oral arguments on the Court's website and then same-day release of audio recording.[19]

Why some accommodations and not others? The Court is accommodating to press imperatives when such modification meets the Court's own needs and does not limit the autonomy of the justices. The justices understand that high profile cases on issues such as abortion, same-sex marriage, affirmative action, and First Amendment are magnets for press coverage. The press's coverage of those cases will affect public attitudes about the Court. Thus, in those cases, the justices have a stake in increasing public understanding of the specific decision, as well as enhancing diffuse support for the Court.

However, the justices have rejected other press initiatives when they perceived that they would negatively affect them and not further the institution's imperatives. Television coverage is one example. The current justices have concluded that video coverage of their proceedings would damage the Court by altering the behavior of the participants, including themselves. Justice Anthony Kennedy has expressed his fear that "one of my colleagues on the bench is asking a question just because a camera is there. I don't want that insidious dynamic between me and my colleagues." The judges also were concerned about being taken out of context and thus becoming reluctant to pose questions, fearing they will be misconstrued in television reporting. Justice Stephen Breyer told a congressional committee that he has been told that once he saw his oral argument questions taken out of context in broadcast coverage "the next day you will watch what you say."[20]

[18] Grey, *The Supreme Court and the News Media*, pp. 142–143.

[19] Edward L. Carter, "Supreme Court Oral Argument Video: A Review of Media Effects Research and Suggestions for Study," *Brigham Young University Law Review*, (December 2012): 1719–1721.

[20] "Supreme Court Watch: Justices Note Continued Reservations Over Cameras in the Supreme Court," *Federal Evidence Review*, March 15, 2013, at federalevidence.com/blog/2013/march/justices-note-reservations-about-cameras-supreme-court; and "Justices Testify on Budget, Cameras, Minority Clerks," *The BLT: The Blog of Legal Times*, March 14, 2013, at legaltimes.typepad.com/blt/2013/03/justices-testify-on-budget-cameras-minority-clerks.html.

Not only would the justices be careful in their questioning for fear of being misquoted; they also would be under more intense scrutiny as individuals. They fear it could harm their images. One reporter speculated they worry the public "would find out. . . These are people like you. Some of them are getting old and some of them are known to doze off on the bench."[21]

The justices have taken a similar approach to early release of opinions to the press. Court rules allow a justice to withdraw an opinion up to the point it is announced in the courtroom. Early release to the press would diminish that right since a justice would be constrained once the opinion had been handed out to reporters.

Perhaps the most important adjustment has been the justices' willingness to "go public." Historical comparison best illustrates the extent of the change. In 1968, Justice Hugo Black gave an on-camera interview with CBS News correspondents Eric Sevareid and Martin Agronsky. The appearance was a major event because of its rarity. Justices at that time avoided television and on-record interviews with the press. The Black interview and one other interview, an appearance by William O. Douglas on an interview program with Mike Wallace in 1958, were the only two instances of justices appearing on television for interviews over a three-decade period after television became a mass medium.

The first major shift in open access came in the 1980s when the justices agreed to participate in Constitution bicentennial education programs. Several sat for on-camera interviews with Bill Moyers for a documentary series titled "In Search of the Constitution." During the 1990s, the justices gradually became more comfortable with C-SPAN. They sat for interviews with founder Brian Lamb and allowed their speeches to be broadcast on the network.

Since 2000, justices have moved even further in accepting invitations to appear on television news and interview programs. The list of appearances has ranged from the staid *Charlie Rose Show* on PBS to programs such as *Piers Morgan* (CNN), *Larry King Live* (CNN), *Nightline* (ABC), *CBS Evening News*, and the *NBC Nightly News*.[22] Talk radio hosts, including Sean Hannity and Rush Limbaugh, have interviewed Clarence Thomas.[23]

[21] Davis, *Decisions and Images*, p.151.

[22] For samples, see "Justice Breyer Speaks," *First Read on NBC News*, September 13, 2010, at firstread.nbcnews.com/_news/2010/09/13/5102686-justice-breyer-speaks?lite; See www.charlierose.com; and "Nightline Online: Chief Justice," *ABC News Nightline*, November 14, 2006, at abcnews.go.com/Nightline/video?id=2651301.

[23] Robert Barnes, Michael A. Fletcher, and Kevin Merida, "Justice Thomas Lashes Out in Memoir," *Washington Post*, September 29, 2007, at www.washingtonpost.com/wp-dyn/content/article/2007/09/28/AR2007092801634.html; "Cable Exclusive: Justice Clarence Thomas Sits Down with Sean Hannity," FOX News, October 3, 2007, at www.foxnews.com/story/0,

In a rare session, Justices Scalia, Breyer, and O'Connor participated in a televised "constitutional conversation" at the National Archives three months before O'Connor retired in 2005. During the session, the three justices sparred genially over constitutional interpretation. Breyer and Scalia also have appeared together in several settings, including at a televised forum at the Supreme Court building. The two justices used that occasion to express their differences on interpreting the Constitution and the proper approach to judging.[24]

Second, televised interviews have become more common as well. Television appearances by the justices seem to have increased in the 1980s and the 1990s. Those appearances usually occurred on C-SPAN, which provided a respectful venue for the justices, overriding their fear of undesirable publicity. In the 1990s, and early 2000s, Brian Lamb was able to persuade several justices, including William Rehnquist, Antonin Scalia, and Sandra Day O'Connor, to sit for interviews on the cable network.[25]

In 2009, C-SPAN interviewed all of the then-current justices of the Supreme Court and posted the video and transcripts of the interviews on the network's website. The interviews avoided discussion of cases then before the Court. However, the justices did offer personal perspectives on such matters as their first day at the Court, their childhoods, and their feelings about serving on the Court. Justice Ruth Bader Ginsburg, talking about her mother's death on the day she graduated from high school, revealed that her mother's death "was one of the most trying times in my life, but I knew that she wanted me to study hard and get good grades and succeed in life so that's what I did."[26] Antonin Scalia admitted that cert petitions are the most uninteresting part of a justice's job and that he hates Fourth Amendment cases.[27]

2933,298923,00.html; and "Book Parties and Festivals: Clarence Thomas, 'My Grandfather's Son'" C-SPAN, October 3, 2007, at www.booktv.org/Program/8744/Clarence+Thomas+My+Grandfathers+Son.aspx.

[24] Joan Biskupic, *Sandra Day O'Connor: How the First Woman on the Supreme Court Became its Most Influential Justice*, New York: Harper Perennial, 2005, pp. 332–333; and Tony Mauro, "Breyer and Scalia Take Their Road Show Inside," *The National Law Journal*, March 24, 2010, at www.law.com/jsp/scm/PubArticleSCM.jsp?id=1202446761287&Breyer_and_Scalia_Take_Their_Road_Show_Inside.

[25] Davis, *Justices and Journalists*, Chapter 5.

[26] "Interview with Justice Ruth Bader Ginsburg," July 1, 2009, C-SPAN, at supremecourt.c-span.org/assets/pdf/RBGinsburg.pdf. "Supreme Court Justice Stephen Breyer Interview," CNN *Larry King Live*, November 23, 2005, at transcripts.cnn.com/TRANSCRIPTS/0511/23/lkl.01.html

[27] "Interview with Justice Antonin Scalia," June 19, 2009, C-SPAN, at supremecourt.c-span.org/assets/pdf/AScalia.pdf.

Not only has there been more access to television, but also to print media. Before leaving the Court, Justice John Paul Stevens sat for a series of interviews with the *Washington Post*, the *New York Times Magazine*, and the *New Yorker*. In recent years, Justice Ginsburg has given interviews with the *New York Times Magazine*, *USA Today*, and Reuters.[28]

The justices also have been increasingly willing to allow the press to be present at their speeches and to allow televised coverage of the speeches. Those speeches sometimes have become newsworthy, particularly during the Q&A sessions, a fact that is not likely to have escaped most of the justices when writing speeches or answering questions. For example, Chief Justice Roberts gave a speech soon after President Barack Obama chided the justices in a State of the Union address for their *Citizens United* decision. Roberts used the public opportunity (with C-SPAN cameras running) to characterize the president's remarks as "one branch of government standing up, literally surrounding the Supreme Court, cheering and hollering while the court – according to the requirements of protocol – has to sit there expressionless."[29]

The justices use these media forums to promote new books. Clarence Thomas and Sandra Day O'Connor both wrote autobiographies while serving on the Court and gave media interviews to discuss their respective books. Antonin Scalia and Stephen Breyer wrote books on judging that were accompanied by press appearances.

Justices Breyer and Scalia have used press interviews to explain judicial philosophies. Under the rubric of a book tour, Justice Breyer discussed his rejection of originalism with reporters and trumpeted a "prudent and

[28] Robert Barnes, "After Years as Justice, John Paul Stevens Wants What's 'Best for the Court,'" *Washington Post*, April 4, 2010, at http://www.washingtonpost.com/wp-dyn/content/article/2010/04/03/AR2010040301693.html; Jeffrey Rosen, "Interview Transcript: Justice John Paul Stevens," *New York Times Magazine*, April 12, 2010, at www.nytimes.com/2010/04/12/magazine/12stevens-interview.html?pagewanted=all; Jeffrey Toobin, "After Stevens: What Will the Supreme Court be Like Without Its Liberal Leader," *The New Yorker*, March 22, 2010, at www.newyorker.com/reporting/2010/03/22/100322fa_fact_toobin; Emily Bazelon, " The Place of Women on the Court," *New York Times Magazine*, July 7, 2009, at www.nytimes.com/2009/07/12/magazine/12ginsburg-t.html?pagewanted=all&_r=0; "Ginsburg: Court Needs Another Woman," *USA Today*, May 5, 2009, at usatoday30.usatoday.com/news/washington/judicial/2009-05-05-ruthginsburg_N.htm; *and* Joan Biskupic, "Exclusive: Justice Ginsburg Shrugs Off Rib Injury," *Reuters*, August 8, 2012, at www.reuters.com/article/2012/08/09/us-usa-court-ginsburg-idUSBRE87801920120809.

[29] Robert Barnes, "High Court: Justices Increasingly Speaking Outside the Classroom," *Washington Post*, April 5, 2010, at www.washingtonpost.com/wp-dyn/content/article/2010/04/04/AR2010040402464.html?nav=rss_politics.

pragmatic" approach to judging. Also on book tours, Justice Scalia articulates originalism and criticizes the "living constitution" approach to interpretation.[30]

At times, the press is a vehicle for continuing debate over a case, particularly one in which the majority does not share the justice's position. In an interview with National Public Radio in 2010, Justice Breyer described the rationale of the minority, which he had joined, in a recently decided case on gun control. Similarly, Justice Scalia criticized the health care decision in 2012 arguing on FOX News "there is no way to regard this penalty as a tax."[31]

The justices' publicity roles also may not just be individual-oriented; they may intend to further institutional objectives as well. Ironically, the justices are becoming more public at a time when news media coverage of the Court generally is shrinking and fewer cases are being covered.[32] Perhaps the justices are seeking to retain attention to the Court by using television's emphasis on personality.

Interviews can become a tool for the justices to promote greater understanding of the Court, and forums such as C- SPAN and PBS have become venues for explaining the institution. The justices use interviews to explain how the Court's processes work, how individual justices decide cases, and the place of the judiciary in a democratic society. However, there also is the danger that the statements of individual justices may undermine the public's perception of the justices as capable of impartially arbitrating conflicts. When the justices enter the political fray through public battles with others, they run the risk of diminishing an aura of being above politics. In response to criticism by Judge

[30] See, for instance, "Transcript: Justice Stephen Breyer Sits Down with 'FOX News Sunday'," FOX News, December 3, 2006, at www.foxnews.com/story/0,2933,234068,00.html; Tony Mauro, "Justice Breyer on Originalism, the Media, and the Court," *National Law Journal*, October 8, 2010, at www.law.com/jsp/article.jsp?id=1202473052552&Justice_Breyer_on_Originalism_the_Media_and_the_Court&slreturn=20130428175157; Chris Wallace, "Justice Antonin Scalia on Issues Facing SCOTUS and the Country," FOX News, July 29, 2012, at www.foxnews.com/on-air/fox-news-sunday-chris-wallace/2012/07/29/justice-antonin-scalia-issues-facing-scotus-and-country#p//v/1760654457001; and *Piers Morgan Tonight*: Interview with Antonin Scalia, CNN, July 18, 2012, at /transcripts.cnn.com/TRANSCRIPTS/1207/18/pmt.01.html.

[31] "Justice Breyer: The Court, The Cases and Conflicts," National Public Radio, September 14, 2010, at www.npr.org/templates/story/story.php?storyId=129831688; and "Justice Scalia Steps Up Criticism of Healthcare Ruling," Reuters, July 29, 2012, at www.reuters.com/article/2012/07/29/us-usa-court-scalia-idUSBRE86S0OR20120729.

[32] Richard Davis, *Justices and Journalists: The U.S. Supreme Court and the Media*, New York: Cambridge University Press, 2011, pp. 155–169; and Todd A. Collins and Christopher A. Cooper, "Case Salience and Media Coverage of Supreme Court Decisions – Toward a New Measure," *Political Research Quarterly*, 65 (June 2012): 396–407.

Richard Posner that Scalia's written opinion in a case was political, Justice Scalia criticized Posner as merely an appeals court judge who "doesn't sit in judgment of my opinions as far as I'm concerned." The justice defended his counterattack, explaining, "When Richard Posner comes out with a statement like that, I should fire back a statement equally provocative." That act of firing back is precisely what justices refrained from doing in the past because it dragged them into political tit for tat.

Justices may become commentators on current events, much like other public figures interviewed by the media. FOX News host Chris Wallace interviewed Justice Scalia in July 2012. In the interview, Wallace asked Scalia about originalism, the Affordable Care Act decision, gun control and the Heller case, whether the Court is political, and when Scalia would retire and whether he would like to have his successor appointed by a Democratic or Republican president. In the interview, Wallace encouraged Scalia to reveal the internal conference deliberations, which Scalia refused to do.[33]

Does this more public approach not only increase interaction with the press, particularly with journalists who are not covering the Court and focusing on legal decisions, but also place the justices in a position of commenting on issues that could come before the Court or opining on issues of the day in a manner that potentially undermines diffuse support for the Court? Will they make statements off the bench that raise questions about their ability to judge on the bench? For example, in September 2010, when Justice Stephen Breyer appeared on *Larry King Live*, King took the opportunity to ask whether a Florida pastor who threatened to publicly burn the Quran had the right to do so. Breyer answered, "Yeah." However, two days earlier Breyer had appeared on *ABC News This Week* with George Stephanopoulos and admitted that the Court could address the case.[34]

It is not surprising that in a media culture dominated by conflict as a news value, the justices have been prodded to publicly criticize other officials, particularly the president. Asked by a reporter to respond to President Barack Obama's criticism of the Court, Justice Scalia responded: "What can he do to me? Or to any of us? We have life tenure and we have it precisely so that

[33] "Justice Antonin Scalia on Issues Facing SCOTUS and the Country," FOX News, July 29, 2012, at www.foxnews.com/on-air/fox-news-sunday/2012/07/29/justice-antonin-scalia-issues-facing-scotus-and-country#p//v/1760654457001.

[34] Josh Gerstein, "Obama v. Breyer v. Breyer on Quran Burning & the Law," *Politico*, September 16, 2010, at www.politico.com/blogs/joshgerstein/0910/Obama_v_Breyer_v_Breyer_on_Koran_burning__the_law.html.

we will not be influenced by politics, by threats from anybody." Clarence Thomas criticized President Obama as being president only because he was "approved by the elites and the media," which prompted a law professor to conclude, "Thomas seems more interested in becoming a FOX commentator than preserving the integrity of the Court."[35]

Such discussion of future cases, inside gossip, or overt criticism is still rare. Justices use television interviews primarily to do other things. According to a study by Colin Glennon, the justices explain their judicial philosophies, describe Court procedures, or analyze landmark cases of the past.[36] This finding demonstrates that the justices are using interviews for both institutional and, to some extent, individual purposes.

The fact that they view press interviews as a means to accomplish those ends, versus background and off-the-record interviews of the past, suggests a continued interest in using the press for their own purposes rather than merely accommodating press interests. That interest in using yet another medium beyond the previous type of interview (off the record ones) and the written opinion itself has drawn the Court more tightly into a relationship with the press. The public interaction with journalists is more frequent than in the past as the justices make themselves more available to the press. Justices incorporate the press into their strategies to influence public opinion. Indeed, justices use press coverage to "make news."

The justices' decisions about how to relate to the press are based on whether accommodations to press interests also serve the justices' own interests. When those interests merge, then the Court accommodates. When the justices perceive they do not merge, such as a press lock-down in advance of opinion release, televised coverage of Court sessions, or announcement of the date a decision will be released that limits the ability to withdraw decisions at the last minute, press accommodation does not occur. The key factor in decision making is what benefits the Court. So far, the press has been unable to pressure the Court to oppose the Court's own perception of its interests.

35 Al Kamen, "Justice Scalia Fires Back at Judge Richard Posner," *Washington Post*, August 2, 2012, at www.washingtonpost.com/blogs/in-the-loop; "Justice Scalia Steps Up Criticism of Healthcare Ruling," Reuters, July 29, 2012, at /www.reuters.com/article/2012/07/29/us-usa-court-scalia-idUSBRE86S0OR20120729; and Nick Wing, "Clarence Thomas: Obama Only President Because He's What 'Elites' Expect 'From a Black Person,'" *The Huffington Post*, May 3, 2013, at /www.huffingtonpost.com/2013/05/03/clarence-thomas-obama_n_3210224.html.

36 Colin Glennon, "Protecting Legitimacy or Hiding Politics? A Textual Analysis of Supreme Court Justice Television Interviews," paper presented at the annual meeting of the Midwest Political Science Association, Chicago, Ill., April 11–14, 2013

External forces also are pushing the justices to "go public." Justices today are selected through a confirmation process that is longer, more controversial, and more public than ever before. The justices live in a celebrity culture that emphasizes personalities, including those in politics. Additionally, they face the demands of television to make themselves more visible to the public, even though they continue to resist applying that change to their formal roles. Journalistic approaches to the Court have shifted toward covering the justices as individuals and the Court itself as more of a political institution. All of these have placed pressure on the justices to become more open to the press and the public, and to develop external relations strategies that will help them navigate a political and social environment affected by media.

Clearly, the increased attention justices have received, and may even solicit, is not comparable to that accorded the president or congressional leaders. Justices still do infrequently what the president, presidential candidates, members of Congress, governors, and other politicians do constantly – hold press conferences, sit for on-the-record interviews, issues dozens of press releases, hire press relations staff, and so forth. Moreover, it is necessary to emphasize that not all recent justices have abandoned the traditional avoidance of extra-judicial attention. For the vast majority of his time on the Court, John Paul Stevens eschewed on-the-record interviews, public forums, or controversial speeches. Again, David Souter was a recluse compared to some of his colleagues. However, both of those justices have retired and their replacements have been more public than they were. Whether there will continue to be a recluse among the justices in the future is an open question.

Antonin Scalia explained in a television interview why he had altered his approach to publicity:

> [T]hat's one reason I've sort of come out of the closet and – in recent months – done more interviews and allowed my talks to be televised more than I did formerly. I've sort of come to the conclusion that the old common law tradition of judges not making public spectacles of themselves and hiding in the grass has just broken down. It's no use, I'm going to be a public spectacle whether I come out of the closet or not...[37]

The culture of the justice as remote from the press and the public has diminished, which has unleashed the justices to accept interviews more readily. However, the greater access is not simply for accommodation's sake. This shift is in accordance with the objectives of individual justices.

[37] "Justice Antonin Scalia," *CSPAN*, May 4, 2008, at /www.q-and-a.org/Transcript/?ProgramID=1178.

CONCLUSION

The Court and the press function in a relationship that is marked by public tension. Journalists who cover the Court complain about the lack of access and transparency by the Court. Broadcast media organizations repeatedly have lobbied the Court for cameras in the courtroom during Court sessions and as often have been rebuffed. Justices also have been vocal, particularly recently, about the shortcomings of media coverage.

At the same time, that interaction also has resulted in gradual accommodation by each towards the other. The image of the justices as immune to media change is inaccurate. The justices are aware of the impact of media culture changes (television, Internet, and the constant news cycle) on political communication. They seek to avoid being considered anachronistic in an age of Facebook and Twitter, while still acting as the custodians of the Court's potentially fragile image. Simultaneously, the press has accommodated itself to the particular routines of the Court, and to its culture of legal specialization and protection of the institution's unique role in American governance.

Such adaptation is not the stuff of public discussion about the relationship between the Court and the press, where both justices and reporters express adversarial views towards each other. Explanation of accommodation may serve neither side's interests, as it would suggest reporters are bending their practices to satisfy the Court and justices care about news coverage enough to make life easier for the reporters who cover them. Nevertheless, it is the way both sides of the relationship have been able to function, particularly in a changing media and political environment.

The next question is the extent of future accommodation. The most significant would be the justices' attitudes towards television cameras. Will the Court succumb to public, media, and policymaker pressure and allow cameras during oral arguments and the announcement of decisions? Will the justices accept television coverage as the next step in press accommodation? The justices have been successful in resisting such pressure in the past because it has not been particularly intense. The public is not concerned about the issue, and the press is weak as a persuasive force. Congress could compel the justices to allow cameras, but it is not a fight worth waging beyond rhetoric. The answer, then, lies in whether the justices perceive that they can make this accommodation work while preserving themselves and their institution. Changing that perception likely will require changing the personnel on the Court, which will happen gradually.

Yet, other accommodations could have larger impacts. For example, acceptance of a lock-up process where reporters receive decisions one hour before announcement in the Court could reduce mistakes by reporters when they are under pressure to read, comprehend, and report within a matter of seconds after a major decision announcement. This is particular true when the Court's decision is complex and requires far more than a quick glance at which party won the case. Press reporting on *NFIB v. Sebelius* (Affordable Care Act decision) in 2012 is a case study in failure to report accurately the Court's decision due to time pressures. Had there been time for reporters to analyze the decision before they were expected to explain it, those mistakes likely would not have happened.

That accommodation could preserve the Court's image. Indeed, it could enhance the Court's communication with the public because mistakes would be rarer. Public misperceptions could be reduced.

Another area is social media. Will justices, or the Court as a whole, use social media to communicate the Court's messages or their own? Will they be forced to adapt to the culture of social media? Are they willing to make such adjustments to the Court's culture to "fit" within the culture of social media?

Similarly, will the press accommodate? For example, if the Court adopted the lock-up process, it would be a major accommodation by the press since reporters would be required to agree to remain in a room for one hour even though they may be anxious to report on a decision long before that time. Would they agree to do so?

Since both the justices and the press have demonstrated a disposition to adapt to each other, it is likely future accommodation will occur as well. This is particularly true as the personnel on the Court changes from the David Souters and John Paul Stevens to newer and younger justices who experienced media-oriented nomination processes and feel comfortable with newer media outlets. Nevertheless, the form such accommodation will take and the impact it will have on the relationship remains to be seen.

2

How and Why the Supreme Court Remains Undercovered

TYLER JOHNSON

On the morning of June 26, 2013, the final decision day of its 2012 term, the Supreme Court handed down rulings in three cases: *Hollingsworth v. Perry* (a case dealing with same-sex marriage, ballot initiatives, and constitutional amendments in California), *United States v. Windsor* (a case involving the federal Defense of Marriage Act), and *Sekhar v. United States* (a case involving extortion). That evening, *ABC Evening News* led their newscast with nine minutes of coverage on the *Windsor* and *Hollingsworth* cases. This coverage quoted directly from both the majority and dissenting opinion in *Windsor*, interviewed parties directly involved in both of the cases as well as legislators with thoughts on the decisions rendered, and more generally discussed the current state of same-sex marriage in the United States. Stories on the *Windsor* and *Hollingsworth* cases could also be found the next morning on the front pages of the *New York Times*, *USA Today*, the *Los Angeles Times*, and the *Boston Globe* (to name just a few of the many newspapers who made similar choices). The *Sekhar* case, on the other hand, made no network newscasts the evening the Court made its decision public. It received no front-page attention from the *New York Times* or the *Washington Post* either; in fact, it received no attention whatsoever from either elite newspaper.

The media's reaction to the Supreme Court's actions that final week in June of 2013 serves as a microcosm of how the press treats the Supreme Court in modern times. Some cases are deemed newsworthy and receive coverage, while others are labeled unworthy and receive no coverage. Some cases lead newscasts and make headlines on front pages while others are lucky to get thirty seconds in the middle of a program or are buried within the front section of the newspaper. The Supreme Court has been described as a "remote and mysterious oracle" made up of nine justices who, to many Americans, are "essentially faceless" (Greenhouse 1996, 1538). This remoteness may build a mystique of sorts for the Court, but it also keeps the justices and their judgments separate from the public (Graber 2010). The media can make the Court less remote, less mysterious, and put a face on those nine individuals previously deemed faceless. However, this depends entirely on the extent to which the media choose to cover the Court, as well as on the content of the stories the press tells. So long as coverage remains scattershot, the Court risks remaining "the branch of government about which most Americans are decidedly uninformed" (Slotnick 1991, 28).

Media coverage of the Supreme Court is essential for maintaining a path by which the public can, if they so choose, remain up-to-date on what this branch of government is doing and what it means for life as an American citizen. It is not just the public, however, that needs this coverage to exist. The media cover the Court because they hope the stories they tell will attract readers and viewers and allow themselves to maintain and build upon a foothold in an increasingly competitive marketplace. It has been argued that the Supreme Court also needs the media to serve as a conduit of information to the general public in order to maintain both its power and its positive image and reinforce deference to the decisions it hands down (Davis 1994; Davis and Strickler 2000). However, this conduit is undoubtedly undermined by the way in which the Court does business, the modern state of journalism, and the public's interest (or lack thereof) in media output related to the Court. In this chapter, I will discuss all three of these shortcomings as well as what actually ends up comprising media coverage of the Supreme Court. First, however, a quick look at the extent to which the media cover (and have covered) the Court is required.

THE STATE OF COVERAGE (OR UNDERCOVERAGE)

There is no denying the reality that the Supreme Court is, as Graber (2010, 259) puts it, "sparsely covered" by the American media. This low level of coverage leaves the public with only a partial look at the workload the Court takes on from one year to the next (O'Callaghan and Dukes 1992). This reality might have been even worse if the Court over the past few decades did not trade in contentious social issues such as abortion, gay rights, or the right to die (Davis 2011). Statistics bolstering the reality of this paucity of coverage are just as grim (and perhaps even more so) as they were decades ago. This tradition of under-coverage also holds true across multiple types of media (newspaper, television, and newsmagazine, to be specific).

Examinations of newspaper coverage of the Court have found wide variation from one paper to the next in terms of volume of Court stories (Ericson 1977; Collins and Cooper 2012). Reporting on the Court, according to Ericson, is inadequate across the board, even in elite newspapers such as the *New York Times*. An examination of forty-six major newspapers found that the average newspaper covers eight decisions per Court term, but that average is affected by a handful of papers that covered only one to two decisions (Spill and Oxley 2003). The lack of attention paid to the Court by newspapers may also be becoming more of an issue in recent years. Johnson and Socker (2012) examined Associated Press coverage from the late 1970s through 2006 and discovered a decline in the volume of coverage from the mid-1990s onward (a pattern only broken when the Court undergoes the process of replacing a member who has left the bench). Collins and Cooper (2012), looking at Court coverage in the *Washington Post*, the *Chicago Tribune*, the *Los Angeles Times*, and the *New York Times*, found a similar decline over time. Not only do newspapers often fail to cover the Court, but when they do, coverage is generally less than comprehensive. In newspapers, Court stories tend to be short stories; over one-third of them are finished in ten sentences or less (Spill and Oxley 2003). There has also been some research examining the lack of attention newsmagazines give the Supreme Court (Tarpley 1984; Bowles and Bromley 1992). Tarpley generally notes that most decisions get no coverage, while Bowles and Bromley discover one in ten Supreme Court cases were covered between 1981 and 1988 (and that this number was down from one in six in the years leading up to the Reagan administration).

Television should prove to be a strong medium for covering the Supreme Court, in that the decisions the Court renders could be married with human interest-related audio and visuals that make the weight of the rulings hit home for viewers. Just because this potential exists, however, does not mean it has come to fruition. Slotnick and Segal, (1998), in their comprehensive look at the relationship between television news and the Supreme Court, state that TV's treatment of the Court ranges "from very poor to, at best, adequate" (8). Court stories on television are brief, often timing in at thirty seconds or less (Slotnick and Segal 1998); in terms of sentences, they are typically half as long as those found in newspapers (Spill and Oxley 2003). They also are not likely to lead newscasts, and break through these barriers typically only when dealing with sensitive issues. Unlike the variations found from one newspaper to the next, though, it appears as if all major television networks cover the Court fairly similarly in terms of overall volume (Katsh 1983).

Several scholars have attempted to quantify these minimal levels of attention afforded the Court by television news. Franklin and Kosaki (1995), examining television coverage of the Court on networks from 1989 through mid-1990, found that the Court received, on average, 0.25 stories per day. The probability of an individual not seeing a Supreme Court story in any given week was 39 percent. Graber (2010) examined coverage from March 2008 through March 2009 and discovered that reporting on the Court comprised a single hour of news time on NBC. She also found that, in terms of coverage of the three branches of the federal government, coverage of the Supreme Court accounted for 6 percent of storytelling. Regarding the percentage of individual cases that received attention from television news, Katsh (1983), looking at coverage from the mid-1970s through the early 1980s, found that only 20 percent of cases received reporting. Much of this television coverage is about the docket of cases the Court chooses to hear. Slotnick and Segal (1998) estimate that three-fourths to five-sixths of Court stories are case stories.

Coverage levels may be boosted based on variables such as case geography and Court calendars. Hoekstra (2003) notes that a case should receive more coverage from media sources headquartered in the location in which it originated. Sill, Metzgar, and Rouse (2013) concur, finding that cases originated in New York received significantly more coverage in the *New York Times*; similarly, cases originating in Washington D.C. received significantly more coverage from the *Washington Post*. Haider-Markel, Allen, and Johansen (2006), in their look at media coverage of the *Lawrence v. Texas* decision, note that not only should the geographic origin of the case potentially see higher coverage, but also that locations where the case might impact existing laws might experience more stories told about the Court's ruling as well. In terms of the Court's calendar, Johnson and Socker (2012) find seasonal variations in coverage; unsurprisingly, the first half of a year (with both oral arguments and decisions) brings with it a noticeably higher volume of Court stories than the second half of a year.

The bulk of research on the extent to which the Court is under-covered is research that looks solely at major newspapers, network newscasts, and newsmagazines as a barometer for how well the media is doing its job in the judicial realm. This approach may underestimate the degree to which the press pays attention to the highest court in the land. O'Brien (1983) points out that, at least in terms of ABC's approach to the Court, programs like *Nightline* and *Good Morning America* as well as Sunday morning news shows were just as likely if not more so than weekday evening newscasts to address the Court's output. Such programs also might attract audiences that differ from those who tend to watch evening newscasts, meaning that Court stories might be reaching a larger (and more diverse) set of individuals than we think.

Today, journalists and scholars alike take for granted that media coverage of the Supreme Court will pale in comparison to the attention afforded the president or Congress. It is important to note, however, that this has not always been the case. Davis (2011) discusses how the Supreme Court at the time of the nation's founding was the focus of a great deal of press attention. This attention sprung from the extent to which the reach of government power was still fluid and up for interpretation; the early Court set precedents in a way that the modern Court simply does not. This modern Court may also, through the choices it makes as to when and how to conduct its business in the courtroom and with the press, diminish the extent to which the media find decisions worthy of being reported.

IS THE COURT TO BLAME?

Many explanations for why the Court fails to receive the attention that other branches of government do are inextricably linked to how the Court does its business. For the media, the nature of when and how the Court issues its decisions often points to potentially problematic operating procedures by the Court. June has become the premier month for Supreme Court decision announcements. In some years, the Court has saved more than 40 percent of its rulings for the last few weeks of its term (Wasby 1978). This calendar is a slight improvement over the way the Court used to do business; Grey (1968) notes that prior to 1965, the Court's release of its opinions took place on so-called Decision Mondays and led to points at which anywhere from five to fifteen decisions might be handed down within a few hours. Rulings are not spread evenly across these final weeks though (Slotnick and Segal 1998); Mondays in June are still popular for heavy decision activity and multiple rulings on Wednesdays or Thursdays have become increasingly commonplace as well. On days when the Court issues several rulings, journalists may have tough calls to make, forced to pick and choose which cases they think are most newsworthy, leading to a situation in which not all rulings are covered. Some have suggested spreading out decision days even further; this would diminish the need for journalists to prioritize some cases over others and increase the odds of more cases receiving at least a little attention (Dennis 1975). Eliminating the arbitrary deadline of producing all decisions by the end of June might also boost the Court's media profile (O'Brien 1983).

It has been argued that the Supreme Court "speaks on complex issues … and then remains silent" (Grey 1968, 2). This complexity, both in the opinions the Court issues and the cases the Court chooses to take on, may undermine the ability of the media to easily cover the Court. Supreme Court rulings can be difficult to understand in general. Decisions are often technical (Graber 2010). The process of understanding may be further complicated by multiple dissenting and concurring opinions in addition to the majority opinion. The very essence of a Supreme Court decision itself, the language used by justices in writing opinions, might dampen the ability of the press to produce content on the Court. Much of what the Court produces can only be interpreted by "specialists who speak a language that the average American does not" Slotnick and Segal (1998, 4). Slotnick (1991) goes so far as to argue that this use of complicated language might be deliberate on the part of some justices. Moreover, journalists cannot ask members of the Court to clarify what a decision or opinion does or does not mean. Paperwork related to the cases the Court hears is available, but many in the media feel the Court does little to shape what it is within that paperwork that might be worth covering. Another potential explanation for the lack of coverage of the Court might lie in the choices the Court makes about which cases to hear and which to reject. Slotnick and Segal (1998) claim that the modern Court trades in decision making that is less interesting than in the past. The Court fails to "strike out boldly in new and controversial policy directions" (62).

The Supreme Court might also make for a less attractive story to journalists because the Court beat is atypical in comparison to many other beats journalists cover. The Supreme Court does not have inside sources like those that we would see with Congress, the White House, state and local governments, or bureaucratic agencies. There is very little breaking of stories when it comes to the Court (Slotnick and Segal 1998). Reporters assigned to the Court feel like they are on the "fringes" of Court activity (Davis and Strickler 2000, 87). Covering the Court is, for many, about sitting back and waiting for scheduled events like oral arguments or decisions to be handed down. Moreover, the Court's workload does not lead journalists to do a great deal of investigating. The briefs submitted to the Court are public record. So too are the arguments made in and questions asked during oral arguments. Reporters can "cover the institution without even being there" (19). The job is, as Greenhouse (1995, 1540) describes it, "almost entirely paper-dependent, defined by the endless flow of conference lists, order lists, petitions for certiorari, and opinions." This information is not constantly coming at a reporter day after day, as it might for a journalist assigned to the president or to Congress. The Court beat is undoubtedly sporadic in nature.

Over time, the Court has taken some steps to attempt to meet the changing needs (and even some specific requests) of the press. The Court created a Public Information Office in the mid-1930s and appointed an officer to run the PIO full time in the late 1940s (Davis 1994). The office distributes opinions as well as other important materials such as schedules detailing when oral arguments will take place and when the Court will hand down decisions.

Such materials were not always available to reporters; originally, the press had to interpret decisions as they were being read instead of having access to copies of the opinions themselves (Slotnick 1991).

This office should not be mistaken for a public relations office, however (Newland 1964). It does not assist the media in interpreting the output of the Court (Graber 2010). The office is more about conveyance (Davis 1994) and has been characterized as passive in the execution of its duties (Dennis 1975). Since the PIO is so passive and fails to interpret decisions for the media, some like Grey (1968) have argued that the Court would provide a great service to journalists if it employed a legal expert whose skill in deciphering "legalese" could help them understand what justices may or may not mean in the opinions they hand down. Greenhouse (1996) goes so far as to say that the Court, in the past, has stood in the way of technological advancements outside the courtroom itself that would make the job of reporters covering oral arguments easier. In her time covering the Court for the *New York Times*, Greenhouse was made aware of an offer from the company that transcribes oral argument sessions to provide transcripts the day the arguments were held (instead of two weeks later, as had been tradition). Reporters wrote to the Chief Justice at the time asking if such a service could be made available and explaining the tangible benefits of having said transcripts expediently. According to Greenhouse, reporters were later told that their proposal was rejected and were given no explanation as to why. It is no wonder that, as Greenhouse (1996, 1559) put it, reporters feel they are "groping along in the dark, trying to make sense out of the shadows on the cave wall" without further assistance from justices (themselves or via a public relations arm). They have been able to raise concerns with standard operating procedure at the Court, but have consistently faced "a strange mix of accommodation on the one hand and aloofness on the other" (Wermiel 1997, 1069).

Traditionally, the relationship between Supreme Court justices, the media, and the public is characterized by remoteness; justices have not been known to take part in interviews and news conferences like politicians (Slotnick 1991; Graber 2010). Supreme Court justices, for the most part, are not interested in opening themselves up in any way (O'Brien 1983). Many take part in what Grey (1968, 15) calls "deliberate isolation." Nevertheless, this often-icy relationship between those on the Court and those in the media may be showing some signs of thawing. Some justices are more aggressive in pursuing relationships with media members, while others still choose to shrink from the potential spotlight (Davis 1994). A handful of justices have seemed slightly more willing in recent years to become public figures; Davis (2011) notes that that number of television appearances of justices on C-SPAN went up in the 1980s and 1990s and that justices were appearing in forums and allowing their speeches to be recorded.

However, this minimal move toward openness by some justices still has not translated into having cameras in the courtroom for oral arguments or decision announcements, avenues by which more stories about the Court might be reported by the media. At a minimum, such a move would mean footage would exist that would provide pictures for the front pages of newspapers or audiovisual fodder appealing to those setting the agenda of television news. The decision-making processes that take place between justices after the oral arguments are not open to outsiders as well. Piccus (1992) argues that were the Court more open to cameras, the emotions, issues, personalities, and clashes of theories would provide natural fodder for the media to cover and for the public to ingest. Moreover, the personalities of the justices themselves might prove worth watching to Americans. It seems as if, as MacKenzie wrote decades ago, "certain things about the Supreme Court will remain unknowable" (1979, 354). Newland (1964, 34) cautions those naysayers of the Court's efforts (or lack thereof) when it comes to outreach, stating, "Their chief responsibility is to their work itself." The onus might lie on reporters to make the best of what they are given. According to some critics, journalists fail to do so.

BLAME THE MEDIA?

For decades, conventional wisdom has also held that the shortcomings of journalists who cover the Court, and of American media in general, might affect coverage of the Supreme Court. The lack of resources media outlets allocate to the Court beat might also drive under-coverage. The number of reporters who cover the Supreme Court is small; both Slotnick and Segal (1998) and Davis and Strickler (2000) put the total at approximately fifty, but only one-quarter of those are devoted to the Court on a full-time basis. The press corps on the Court beat is a mix of experience and inexperience in terms of time devoted to covering the Court as well as background before covering the Court. Half of reporters covering the Court have been doing so for more than six years; this longevity may add to their reporting, given that the Court faces many of the same issues from year to year. Still, it appears many reporters covering the Court are somewhat new to the beat. This might in some ways affect the quality of reporting of Supreme Court decision making.

More than four decades ago, Grey (1968) lamented the fact that many of those assigned to cover the Court do not seem to know much about how the legal system works. There is a belief that many reporters assigned to the Court have a superficial understanding of the Court and its processes (MacKenzie 1979). Shaw (1981) points out that the professionalism of those covering the Court has improved over time, but many who report on the Court lack any sort of legal background. Some reporters have legal training and some do not; the former group may have an advantage in that they might better understand how the legal system works and can speak the language spoken by legal experts (Davis and Strickler 2000). At times, television networks fail even to take advantage of the legal experts they employ to cover the Court. Katsh (1983) notes that relying on such correspondents is incredibly rare in television reporting on the Court.

Some of these shortcomings on the Court beat might exist, to some extent, because of the changing nature of what it means to cover the Court. Greenhouse (1996) argues that there is a broader movement within newsrooms writ large to shrink the extent to which an individual reporter covers the Supreme Court full time. Instead of having a single beat consisting of the Court, many journalists cover not just the Court, but other legal beats as well. These beats might include the Department of Justice, other courts, the Senate Judiciary Committee, and legal developments throughout government at multiple levels. Such a divided beat might undermine the extent to which a Supreme Court reporter could do the homework necessary to understand the cases the Court takes on, the parties on either side, the motivation behind the arguments made orally, and the scope of the decisions the Court hands down.

On the other hand, this mix of journalists, some of whom cover the Court full time and some of whom cover it part time, some of whom have legal experience and some of whom do not, may actually provide an informational benefit to the public. Diversity within the press corps on the Court beat may lead to a broader variety of stories told about the Court as well as in themes within said stories. Jamieson (1998) suggests that we see "specialist reporters" and "generalist reporters" on the Court beat. Specialists are more likely to produce stories on the Court that utilize legal language and discuss opinions in terms of precedents. Reporters who cover the Court full time or those who have a legal background often deliver this type of output. Generalist reporters, on the other hand, boil down a case into the elements that will attract the average reader. Such reporters are more likely to report decisions in terms of how the case fits within well-known extrajudicial philosophies (linking outcomes to ideologies, political parties, or prominent leaders) or why the case matters to the average American. The different methods by which journalists cover the Court may affirm or undermine existing perceptions of the Court; Jamieson sees a sort of reverence for the bench in the work of specialists, while generalists seem to want to remove the mystery from Court activity and make case outcomes much more accessible to the everyday public. Changes in the financial structure supporting media may also diminish Court reporting. Editors and producers face increasing pressures to run stories that will return profits. Such pressures push reporters to differentiate themselves from their fellow members of the press, and one way to do so is through being the first to report a story (Graber 2010). This pressure inherent in modern media may also affect the quality of reporting on the Supreme Court. Often in journalism in general, an emphasis on speed creates the potential for misunderstandings (Sobel 1970). One such example in the judicial realm came when journalists and pundits scrambled (on air, in some cases) on June 28, 2012 to interpret the Court's ruling on the constitutionality of the Patient Protection and Affordable Care Act (so-called Obamacare) in *National Federation of Independent Business v. Sebelius*. Famously, CNN and FOX News erroneously announced that the Court had overturned the law's individual mandate before being forced to later correct their statements. This imperative to report breaking news as quickly as possible has affected Supreme Court reporting for decades; Shaw (1981) notes that in June 1978, NBC went live with coverage of the decision in the Bakke affirmative action case ninety seconds after the decision was handed down by the Court. As the pressure to differentiate one's reporting from that of other newspapers or networks increases, so too may the quality of reporting on the Court increasingly suffer. Many have argued that the nature of what the Court does simply does not lend itself to quick and simple discussion. Newspaper reporters may not face entirely the same pressures in that, while they have filing deadlines that might affect story writing (Jamieson 1998), such deadlines pale in comparison to the need to get on air immediately faced by television journalists. The rise of the Internet as a news source for many Americans (coming to rival television or newspapers) may also create new pressures for print journalists to get their story on their publication's website well before the story shows up in the newspaper the next morning.

There is also a belief that Supreme Court reporting tends to be laden with inaccuracies beyond those created by getting things wrong due to telling a story too quickly. One such common inaccuracy lies in the media's attempts to cover denials of cert. According to Slotnick and Segal (1994), when the media report on the Court's refusals to hear a case, journalists often read more into these refusals than they should. This might cause the public to believe the Court took a stronger, clearer position than it actually did. Reporting on denials of cert often erroneously claim that the Court took a stand on the merits of what a lower court declared. Slotnick and Segal, in an analysis of such stories, found that the media were likely to characterize the refusal of the Court to hear a case as refusing to overturn a decision, upholding a decision, or rejecting a challenge. But in reality, the Court's refusal to hear a case can be due to a multitude of reasons, most of which do not meet the extremity of the language that journalists use in attempting to read into the motivations of the Court's decision. In general, Court coverage is often criticized for sacrificing accuracy for a more concise version of the story (Slotnick and Segal 1998); such journalistic choices often mean that the nuance of what the justices have actually stated is omitted from reporting due to its complicated nature. Supreme Court reporting also faces criticism for the extent to which it is more of a play-by-play of what happened and less a discussion of what a Court decision means. Grey (1968), for example, complains that media coverage of the Supreme Court lacks true analysis.

The common production strategy of attempting to condense as much news as possible into the modern newscast also hampers television coverage of the Supreme Court. Instead of trying to cover three or four longer stories, many newscasts attempt to report short stories in bulk. This choice frustrates television reporters on the Court beat, who know how difficult it will be to condense what justices say into sound bites for 30-second stories (Davis 1987). They realize, given that all reporters have equal access to the documents related to a case, the time a newscast's producer grants them to report a story might determine what separates a more comprehensive and illuminating story from one that seems like a rote play-by-play of what happened. Reporters also know that, at any point, editors and producers might trim their stories even further; such processes further damage the ability of a journalist to tell a detailed, nuanced story about the Court (Sobel 1970).

In her analysis of the *New York Times* Supreme Court coverage, Larson (1985) cautions those who criticize the media's efforts, claiming that the existing literature that tends to excoriate journalism for its lack of attention to the Supreme Court often fails to consider things from the perspective of reporters and editors. Not all decisions might be of the same importance to readers. Nor might all decisions have the same impact on the lives of individuals or on history (or, more specifically, legal history). Editors and reporters factor these variables into the process of deciding what ends up in a newscast or in a newspaper and what does not. Moreover, media coverage of other branches of government (such as Congress) fails to receive criticism for not covering every vote. Why then should Court coverage be chastised for failing to tell the story of every case? Just as those who cover Congress choose which bills or committee hearings or press conferences should receive the spotlight, so too do those who cover the Court take part in the process of assessing the newsworthiness of decisions, oral arguments, and cert decisions.

BLAME THE PUBLIC?

Others have argued that the public's lack of interest in the Supreme Court shapes the media's agenda. Therefore, the explanation of the traditional under-coverage of the Court lies at the preferences of the consumer. The public maintains, as Caldeira (1986, 1211) puts it, a "relatively shallow reservoir of knowledge" when it comes to the Court. Authors like Delli Carpini and Keeter (1996) have chronicled the public's lack of knowledge of the Supreme Court over the second half of the twentieth century. Survey research reveals the inability of many Americans to describe the substance of key decisions like *Brown v. Board of Education*, *Miranda v. Arizona*, or *Roe v. Wade*. Equally worrisome to those concerned with the state of civic education is the extent to which some are unaware of basic Court functions like determining the constitutionality of laws or major Court players such as the Chief Justice or nominees for the bench. It is no wonder, given survey findings like these, that authors like Slotnick (1991, 128) are able to call the American public "decidedly uninformed" when it comes to the Supreme Court.

What is less clear, however, is why many Americans fail to keep up to date with what the Court does and what that means for everyday life. Is it because they do not encounter enough Court stories to keep the "shallow reservoir" replenished? Or are they encountering Court stories and finding them not salient enough to commit to memory? Either way, if the Court is dependent on citizen awareness to maintain positive reviews and high levels of esteem and reverence, justices should feel concerned that their shunning of the press might be leading to a shunning from the public. The Supreme Court is distinctly different from the executive and the legislative branches because voters do not choose its members, so they cannot be held accountable through elections (Slotnick and Segal 1998). The Court is seen as more neutral in its decision making than the president or Congress (Clawson and Oxley 2013). These attitudes held by many Americans insulate the Court from the pressure and scrutiny faced daily by the president, senators, and representatives. However, this distance between justices and the public also might make it difficult for the Court to motivate citizens (as well as elected officials) to defer to the Court's power and then support and enforce its decisions. As Caldeira (1986, 1209) put it, the Court depends on "the confidence, or at least the acquiescence" of individuals. Media coverage of decisions could help bridge this gap between the public and the Court while at the same time keeping the distance necessary for the Court to maintain its historic independence.

The media should also take note of such survey findings on American ignorance when it comes to the judicial branch and question why their stories on the Court do not seem to be hitting home for readers and viewers. Could coverage of the Court change so that such stories are more interesting and memorable to readers or viewers? Given the low levels of knowledge about the Court, does reporting on the institution demand more simplicity than reporting on more well-known facets of government? It is possible, though, that such survey results could be read an entirely different way, as justification to continue diminishing coverage of the Court since Court stories may not attract viewers and readers and the details of Court storytelling do not appear newsworthy enough for citizens to remember.

WHAT STORIES ARE TOLD?

Scholars examining the content of Supreme Court coverage have discovered that there are several points at which stories about the Court are traditionally told. Some of these points are directly linked to the cases the Court hears (or doesn't hear), such as the petitioning for cert, the oral argument, and the rendering of a decision (Davis and Strickler 2000). Other stories might be told on the rare occasions when justices step down from the Court and the president must undertake the process of selecting a replacement (who then will face what have become increasingly newsworthy confirmation processes). As discussed earlier, another rare type of Court story involves the justices themselves making public appearances where they give speeches, participate in roundtables, or subject themselves to interviews by the press (although such interviews are increasing in frequency in comparison to the behavior of past justices).

Decisions provide the most fodder for Supreme Court reporting. This is not surprising, given that decisions are the points at which the power of a case heard by the Supreme Court might finally be felt by the legal community, lawmakers, and the average American (Slotnick and Segal 1998). Reporters may not know what the decision will be, but they can prepare for the decision by getting to know the arguments made by each side and the broader history of the case as well. These decision stories often fall short of the ideal described by Davis (1987). He stated that such stories should let the individual know the key issues in a case, use language directly from the justices' opinions, talk about the impact of the decision, discuss the decision in the context of existing opinions, and elicit reactions from those most interested in the outcome as well as practitioners and scholars. Davis notes that stories with this degree of depth are rarely seen. This especially seems true in the world of television coverage, which at times constricts storytelling to thirty seconds or less.

A handful of general case characteristics have been statistically linked to predicting which types of decisions will receive media attention, and which will not. Sill, Metzgar, and Rouse (2013), in a statistical analysis of cases the *New York Times* covered over multiple decades, identified variables that were significant predictors of media attention. Such predictive variables include multiple legal provisions, high levels of salience (as measured through the number of amicus curiae briefs filed), and high-profile case participants (such as the presence of the solicitor general). On the other hand, other predictors—whether the case altered precedent, whether the case reversed a lower court's decision, if the case's issue area was related to economics, and whether the case's participants were linked with business, interest groups, state governments, or national government – had no significant bearing on the *New York Times*' coverage. Johnson and Socker (2012), in their examination of Associated Press reporting on the Court, found coverage in general to be driven by decision characteristics summed over time. One such decision characteristic was liberal decision making; when the Court handed down rulings that proved to be victories for liberal positions, coverage of the Court increased. The same study also noted that Court actions also shaped specific types of frames within coverage. Declaring laws unconstitutional led to greater discussion of politics in Court coverage and less discussion of the law. Factionalism in decision making (that is, a preponderance of close decisions) led to less discussion of the law as well. Finally, Court retirements spurred the media to talk about how politics related to the Court.

Rarely do we see stories about moments before decisions (Davis 1987). At times, we see stories about the process of granting or denying cert. These stories are often brief and not prominently featured by the media (Slotnick and Segal 1994). When these stories are told, more often than not they concern the denial of cert rather than the granting of cert. As Slotnick and Segal (1994) point out in their analysis of cert stories run by television networks during the Supreme Court's 1989 and 1990 terms, only about 1 percent of cert denials became television stories. The ones that did, unsurprisingly, related to the Court's refusal to hear potentially contentious equal protection, privacy, abortion, and First Amendment cases.

Oral arguments also become the core of stories journalists report on the Supreme Court. They would clearly make for even better stories for television if cameras were allowed in the courtroom, but the potential still exists within oral arguments for reporters to make known the crux of the conflict between the two parties at hand. Reporters also use oral arguments as a jumping-off point to tell the story of the issue up for debate and deciding (Davis 1994). The translation of oral arguments into copy for newspaper articles or visuals for television reporting is undermined not just by the lack of access to footage of the arguments, but also by the fact that this stage of the judicial process at times can come off "technical and dry" (Davis and Strickler 2000, 88). More than thirty years ago, television networks covered, on average, five oral arguments per year (Katsh 1983); given general trends in coverage of the Court, we might expect that this amount has decreased since then.

Another way to look at the question of what types of Supreme Court stories are told is to look at whose stories are told in media coverage. The justices themselves place "a premium on secrecy" (Slotnick and Segal 1998, 35) and speak primarily through the choices to grant or deny cert. Therefore, the questions they ask at oral arguments, and the words they use in their decisions, provide many opportunities for journalists to include the perspectives of those outside the Court in stories. Court coverage can be more about reactions (national, state, or local) to decisions than the content of decisions themselves (Newland 1964). At times, Court stories rely on the perspectives of the parties directly involved in the case or the attorneys making the arguments before the justices. Reporting on cases might also incorporate academic and legal experts with knowledge about the issue, the case history, legal precedent, or the Court itself.

Interest groups step into the void created by the Court's unwillingness to publicly interpret its decisions after they are issued (Slotnick and Segal 1998). These organizations become "surrogate press secretaries" (Jamieson 1998, 10) of sorts, attempting to affect information dissemination on a decision as well as public opinion about a decision in the hours and days following the Court's verdict. Coverage of the actions taken by justices may be apolitical in tone (Baird and Gangl 2006), but political perspectives often seep into stories via the viewpoints of outsiders. Clearly, these groups take on this role not just to educate, but also for self-serving reasons (to gain publicity, to move citizens toward a favorable reaction to what the Court has just done, or to shape the policy process moving forward in the wake of the decision just rendered). As such, journalists have to be careful in incorporating such information into their reporting. As Slotnick and Segal (1998) point out, this interest group spin can be an important element of the story (the reactions of relevant parties might add color to existing content), but reporters cannot allow themselves to be spun and turned into mouthpieces for the needs and wants of outsiders.

Critics also seem to find their way into the stories journalists write about what the Court has done (Dennis 1975). These critics might question the Court's decisions in general, the extent to which the Court may have used its power (be that use under-reaching or overreaching), or the justifications the majority or minority opinions offer to underpin the conclusions drawn from a case. Critics recognize that the media often look for opposing perspectives in the aftermath of a decision; this stems from the broader media norm of "indexing," wherein journalists attempt to give widely held dissenting viewpoints time to state their case (Graber 2010). Critics must strike quickly, though, in providing that dissenting perspective, since coverage of decisions is often fleeting. Whereas the Court "speaks once and is silent," critics of the Court "seldom cease speaking" (Newland 1964, 35). The media allow that criticism to reach a broader audience.

Court coverage is not always about the cases themselves, but sometimes also about broader themes that develop across a Court's term (or even across multiple terms). Stories about the Court are often linked with analysis of changes on the Court (if there has been a retirement from the Court or an appointment of a new member), whether the Court seems activist, and the hardening or softening of ideological blocs over time (Slotnick and Segal 1998). Much is made by the media of whether so-called liberal or conservative justices hold together with like-minded members of the Court to create split decisions, come together to create unanimous rulings, or at times mix to create surprising and noteworthy alliances. Conflict (between litigants, political parties, branches of government, interest groups, levels of government, or even the philosophies of the justices themselves) is also often at the crux of reporting on the Court from one case to the next or one term to the next (Jamieson 1998).

WHAT QUESTIONS ABOUT COVERAGE REMAIN?

Much has been written about how the Supreme Court suffers from a lack of coverage; why the Court, the media, and the public might be to blame; and what constitutes the little coverage the Court does receive. Several questions about Supreme Court coverage do remain largely unanswered, though. We have seen a paucity of research grappling with how changes in the media affect coverage of the Supreme Court. Much of the scholarship discussed in this chapter analyzes forms of media (newspapers, television, newsmagazines) that, over the past decade or two, have begun to lose their grip on consumers of information. Newspaper readership is down. Network news ratings have slipped as well. Newsmagazines have seen subscriber rates plummet and some have gone to online-only models to attempt to adapt to the modern world of media consumption. In a world in which media ownership models increasingly value their media entities telling stories that attract the public and turn a profit, will reporting on the Court suffer further? Or will certain types of Court stories, the ones with the most potential to attract attention, survive and thrive? Such changes have the potential to affect the extent to which Americans are learning about the Court in the future as well. It is possible, given these changes across the broader media landscape, that new media may pick up some of the slack when it comes to information dissemination related to the Court. Xenos' (2008) work on the blogosphere's effects on public deliberation of the Alito nomination is one such step in this direction. But little has been made of how Court stories are reported on websites, how independent blogs and opinion sites cover the Supreme Court, how the public uses technology to discuss the Court, or if and how stories about the Court make their way across social media venues like Facebook and Twitter.

Another worthwhile question scholars should be asking relates to the content of Court coverage given the Court's changing workload. Conditions for Court reporters should theoretically have improved over time, given the noticeable decreases from term to term in the number of cases the Supreme Court chooses to take on (Slotnick and Segal 1998). Whereas the Court used to grant cert to hundreds of cases per term, these days the Court is more likely to grapple with less than 100 cases in a given year. Journalists have fewer cases to cover and therefore should be able to devote more time to each one. There is little, if any, evidence that the quantity or quality of reporting on the Court has gone up as the Court's workload has gone down. This should lead us to wonder why such shifts have failed to come to fruition (or if any shifts exist within the stories told over recent years).

Finally, it is apparent that much of the scholarship on media coverage of the Supreme Court examines questions through the perspective of the reporter or the justice. In fact, journalists themselves have written many works in this area. More could be done to investigate the topic through the eyes of the media consumer. Where are people getting their Court news today? What draws an individual into a story on the Court (or what repels an individual from a story)? Could changes be made in Court reporting to make it more palatable? Would undertaking such changes undermine the quality of coverage? It appears there is much room to take such questions on from an individual-level, survey-driven perspective.

WORKS CITED

Baird, Vanessa A. and Amy Gangl. "Shattering the Myth of Legality: The Impact of the Media's Framing of Supreme Court Procedures on Perceptions of Fairness." *Political Psychology* 27, (2006): 597–614.

Bowles, Dorothy A. and Rebekah V. Bromley. "Newsmagazine Coverage of the Supreme Court during the Reagan Administration." *Journalism & Mass Communication Quarterly* 69, (1992): 948–959.

Caldeira, Gregory. "Neither the Purse Not the Sword: Dynamics of Public Confidence in the Supreme Court." *American Political Science Review* 80, (1986): 1209–1226.

Clawson, Rosalee A. and Zoe M. Oxley. *Public Opinion: Democratic Ideals, Democratic Practice*. Washington, DC: CQ Press, 2013.

Collins, Todd A. and Christopher A. Cooper. "Case Salience and Media Coverage of Supreme Court Decisions: Toward a New Measure." *Political Research Quarterly* 65, (2012): 396–407.

Davis, Richard. "Lifting the Shroud: News Media Portrayal of the U.S. Supreme Court." *Communications and the Law* 9, (1987): 43–59.

Decisions and Images: The Supreme Court and the Press. Englewood Cliffs, NJ: Prentice-Hall, 1994.

Justices and Journalists: The U.S. Supreme Court and the Media. New York: Cambridge University Press, 2011.

Davis, Richard and Vincent James Strickler. "The Invisible Dance: The Supreme Court and the Press." *Perspectives on Political Science* 29, (2000): 85–92.

Delli Carpini, Michael X. and Scott Keeter. *What Americans Know About Politics and Why It Matters*. New Haven, CT: Yale University Press, 1996.

Dennis, Everette E. "Another Look at Press Coverage of the Supreme Court." *Villanova Law Review* 20, (1975): 765–799.

Ericson, David. "Newspaper Coverage of the Supreme Court: A Case Study." *Journalism Quarterly*, 54, (1977): 605–607.

Franklin, Charles H. and Liane C. Kosaki. "Media, Knowledge, and Public Evaluations of the Supreme Court." In *Contemplating Courts*, edited by Lee Epstein, 352–375. Washington, DC: CQ Press, 1995.

Graber, Doris L. *Mass Media and American Politics, 8th edition*. Washington, DC: CQ Press, 2010.

Greenhouse, Linda. "Telling the Court's Story: Justice and Journalism at the Supreme Court." *Yale Law Journal* 105, (1996): 1537–1539.

Grey, David L. *The Supreme Court and the News Media*. Evanston, IL: Northwestern University Press, 1968.

Haider-Markel, Donald P., Mahalley D. Allen, and Morgen Johansen. "Understanding Variations in Media Coverage of U.S. Supreme Court Decisions: Comparing Media Outlets in Their Coverage of Lawrence v. Texas." *The International Journal of Press/Politics* 11, (2006): 64–85.

Hoekstra, Valerie J. *Public Reaction to Supreme Court Decisions*. New York: Cambridge University Press, 2003.

Jamieson, Paul W. "Lost in Translation: Civic Journalism's Applicability to Newspaper Coverage of the U.S. Supreme Court." *Communications and the Law* 20, (1998): 1–36.

Johnson, Tyler and Erica Socker. "Actions, Factions, and Interactions: Newsworthy Influences on Supreme Court Coverage." *Social Science Quarterly* 93, (2012): 434–463.
Katsh, Ethan. "Law in the Lens: An Interview with Tim O'Brien, ABC News." *ALSA Forum* 5, (1980): 31–46.
"The Supreme Court Beat: How Television Covers the U.S. Supreme Court." *Judicature* 67, (1983): 6–11.
Larson, Stephanie Greco. "How the *New York Times* Covered Discrimination Cases." *Journalism Quarterly* 33, (1985): 363–71.
MacKenzie, John P. "The Supreme Court and the Press." In *The Mass Media and the Supreme Court, 2nd edition*, edited by Kenneth S. Devol, 353–359. New York: Hastings House, 1979.
Newland, Chester A. "Press Coverage of the United States Supreme Court." *The Western Political Quarterly* 17, (1964): 15–36.
O'Brien, Tim. "Yes, but…" *Judicature* 67, (1983): 12.
O'Callaghan, Jerome and James O. Dukes. "Media Coverage of the Supreme Court's Caseload." *Journalism & Mass Communication Quarterly* 69, (1992): 195–203.
Piccus, Todd. "Demystifying the Least Understood Branch: Opening the Supreme Court to Broadcast Media." *Texas Law Review* 71, (1992): 1053–1098.
Shaw, David. "Media Coverage of the Courts: Improving but Still Not Adequate." *Judicature* 65, (1981): 18–24.
Sill, Kaitlyn L., Emily T. Metzgar, and Stella M. Rouse. "Media Coverage of the U.S. Supreme Court: How Do Journalists Assess the Importance of Court Decisions?" *Political Communication* 30, (2013): 58–80.
Slotnick, Elliot E. "Media Coverage of Supreme Court Decision Making: Problems and Prospects." *Judicature* 75, (1991): 128–142.
Slotnick, Elliot E. and Jennifer A. Segal. "The Supreme Court Decided Today…or did it?" *Judicature* 78, (1994): 89–95.
Television News and the Supreme Court: All the News That's Fit to Air? New York: Cambridge University Press, 1998.
Sobel, Lionel S. "News Coverage of the Supreme Court." *American Bar Association Journal* 56, (1970): 547–551.
Spill, Rorie L. and Zoe M. Oxley. "Philosopher Kings or Political Actors: How the Media Portray the Supreme Court." *Judicature* 87, (2003): 22–29.
Tarpley, J. Douglas. "American Newsmagazine Coverage of the Supreme Court, 1978–81." *Journalism Quarterly* 61, (1984): 801–826.
Wasby, Stephen L. *The Supreme Court in the Federal Judicial System*. New York: Holt, Rinehart, and Winston, 1978.
Wermiel, Stephen J. "News Media Coverage of the United States Supreme Court." *St. Louis University Law Journal* 42, (1997): 1059–1078.
Xenos, Michael. "New Mediated Deliberation: Blog and Press Coverage of the Alito Nomination." *Journal of Computer-Mediated Communication* 13, (2008): 485–503.

3

News Coverage of the Supreme Court Docket

TERRI L. TOWNER AND ROSALEE A. CLAWSON[1]

INTRODUCTION

In the United States, the Supreme Court has a substantial influence on policymaking, and its rulings shape attitudes toward important, often highly controversial, issues. Therefore, it is critical for citizens to understand decisions handed down by the Court. Unlike presidents and members of Congress, however, Supreme Court justices do not hold press conferences or regularly discuss their positions with the public. There is tantalizing evidence that justices reach out to journalists and the public more often today than in the past (see Davis 2011), but justices still primarily communicate their views through written opinions. In turn, journalists, who serve as a fundamental link to the public, report these opinions, or at least a subset of them. Citizens depend on the news media to decipher, interpret, and convey Supreme Court rulings.

In this chapter, we examine media coverage of the Supreme Court docket. We discuss which cases receive the most attention and consider the quality of that coverage. We make distinctions among types of media – newspaper versus television, local versus national, mainstream versus specialized press – and compare news coverage of the Supreme Court's docket to coverage of decisions of state supreme courts. Finally, given the news media's attention to civil rights cases, we review how the media frame affirmative action rulings and present a case study of the media's coverage of the *Ricci v. DeStefano* affirmative action case.

[1] We thank Eric Waltenburg for his many contributions to our research. A portion of this study was prepared for presentation at the G.E. Hendricks Symposium on Inequality in the Age of Obama sponsored by the Department of Political Science at the University of Nebraska – Lincoln, November 3–5, 2010. The authors would like to thank Victoria Martinuzzi for providing able research assistance on this paper. The Oakland University Department of Political Science supported this research.

COVERAGE OF SUPREME COURT CASES IN NATIONAL NEWS OUTLETS

One of the most important aspects of media coverage of the Supreme Court is its episodic nature. Much of what the Supreme Court does is in private, and the institution has strong norms in place to ensure information about negotiation and decision making is not revealed to the media or the public. Oral arguments occur in open court, of course, as do rulings, yet even then cameras and recording devices are not allowed in the courtroom, making it impossible for television reporters to use visuals from inside the Court. Instead, television reporters rely on visuals of the parties involved to craft compelling stories for their visual medium (Slotnick and Segal 1998).

The good news is that the Court receives some coverage at the beginning of its term in October when oral arguments occur and even more coverage in June when the Court hands down many decisions. Franklin and Kosaki (1995, 358) conclude, "The Court is often ignored and invisible, but at times it becomes quite visible indeed. Thus, citizens may know little about the Court in general, yet be exposed to quite a lot of news about it in a short period of time." The bad news, however, is that television news coverage of the Supreme Court is declining dramatically (Slotnick and Segal 1998, Ch. 5; Spill and Oxley 2003). Indeed, a recent study of media coverage of Supreme Court cases does not analyze television network news because so few cases are covered (Collins and Cooper 2012). A study of national and regional newspapers between 1986 and 2004 shows that print coverage of Supreme Court cases is also decreasing (Collins and Cooper 2012). In 2004 the *New York Times* covered more than 50 percent of the cases orally argued that year, but the *Washington Post*, the *Chicago Tribune*, and the *Los Angeles Times* covered fewer than 40 percent of the cases (Collins and Cooper 2012).

Given the compressed nature of the Court's public activities and limited news space, journalists and editors must make strategic decisions about which cases should receive coverage. Furthermore, these journalistic choices must be made quickly when several cases are handed down on the same day. This brings us to a key question: which Supreme Court cases garner the most attention from the news media? Several studies examining different time periods and a variety of media outlets find that First Amendment and civil rights cases receive disproportionate coverage compared to their share of the docket (O'Callaghan and Dukes 1992; Davis 1994; Slotnick and Segal 1998; Spill and Oxley 2003; Collins and Cooper 2012). This emphasis on First Amendment and civil rights cases limits media coverage of economic cases (O'Callaghan and Dukes 1992; Epstein and Segal 2000; Collins and Cooper

2012). Scholars have also found that criminal procedure cases receive more coverage than would be expected by their share of the docket (Slotnick and Segal 1998; Spill and Oxley 2003; Collins and Cooper 2012).

Whether the media report a case depends on a number of factors, including how many other decisions came down on the same day (Slotnick and Segal 1998). A court reporter's job becomes very difficult when several important rulings are handed down simultaneously (Davis 1994; Slotnick and Segal 1998), forcing tough choices about how to allocate precious news space. Cases that attract more attention from interest groups, as evidenced by the number of amicus briefs filed, garner more coverage than other cases (Slotnick and Segal 1998). Cases involving constitutional questions (Epstein and Segal 2000; Collins and Cooper 2012), and especially those declaring a law unconstitutional (Johnson and Socker 2012), receive greater attention.

The limited amount of media coverage of the Supreme Court docket negatively influences the quality of the coverage. News stories are often short, especially on television, putting severe constraints on how well journalists can explain and discuss cases (Slotnick and Segal 1998; Spill and Oxley 2003). In fact, television news coverage of the Court's decisions is often flawed and sometimes inaccurate (Slotnick and Segal 1998). Newspapers, however, provide greater breadth and context than stories on television, and in general, Court reporters do a better job covering cases than non-Court reporters. For example, as experts on the judicial branch and the law, Court reporters are more likely to cite justifications provided by the justices than other reporters (Spill and Oxley 2003).

COVERAGE OF SUPREME COURT CASES IN LOCAL AND SPECIALIZED NEWS OUTLETS

It is also important to examine local media coverage of Supreme Court cases. Some cases do not resonate as much with a national audience, and national media outlets cover them less, or even ignore them. Yet, these cases may be of great interest to people in a particular geographical area and thus garner significant local media attention. For example, Hoekstra (2003) analyzes media coverage of a civil liberties case dealing with the creation of a special school district for a Hasidic Jewish community in Monroe Township, New York. The dispute was part of a long-standing, highly contentious conflict between the Hasidic Jewish Community and other citizens in the township, and therefore stimulated a lot of interest in the local area. The case received some attention in the national media, but attracted extensive coverage in the local *Times-Herald Record* (Hoekstra 2003, 61). In addition to the Monroe case, Hoekstra examines coverage of three other cases in the national media and in relevant local outlets, finding that "coverage by the local media is always at least twice as large as in any of the other [national] newspapers" (2003, 58). Moreover, the quality of this local coverage was quite good, and in many cases rivaled or surpassed the quality of coverage in national papers of record. In Hoekstra's words, "The local media did their job admirably" (Hoekstra 2003, 72). As a result, citizens in the immediate area had higher levels of awareness about the cases than did others.

Similarly, Franklin and Kosaki (1995) examine media coverage of a controversial 1989 case originating in Missouri, *Webster v. Reproductive Health Services*, which upheld restrictions on state-funded abortions. The *St. Louis Dispatch* dedicated an "extraordinarily high" level of coverage to the case (Franklin and Kosaki 1995, 359), which resulted in large numbers of citizens in St. Louis knowing about the case. *Webster* also received significant attention among national media with network television news dedicating substantial airtime to the decision (Franklin and Kosaki 1995; also see Slotnick and Segal 1998). Likewise, the *Lawrence v. Texas* sodomy case received extensive coverage in the state capital newspaper, the *Austin-American Statesman*, and in national newspapers (Haider-Markel, Allen, and Johansen 2006). With their focus on women's rights and gay rights, these cases captured the attention of both national and local journalists.

Taking a different approach to understanding news coverage of Court decisions, Davis (1994) interviews reporters to gain their perspective on the "dance" between Supreme Court justices and the press corps. Davis documents that journalists take into account audience characteristics when deciding which cases should receive attention. For example, regional reporters are cognizant of those cases originating in their geographic area and prioritize coverage of those decisions because they think their audience will be particularly interested in those rulings (Davis 1994, 71). Likewise, reporters for specialized news outlets pay particular attention to certain cases. Not surprisingly, *Wall Street Journal* reporters are especially interested in business cases (Davis 1994, 71). Similarly, Towner, Clawson, and Waltenburg (2006) interview reporters who work for specialized presses, namely black and Latino outlets, about their coverage of the University of Michigan affirmative action cases. These minority journalists "were consciously aware of their audience and focused on presenting their Michigan coverage in a manner that appealed to readers who were directly affected by changes in affirmative action policies" (Towner, Clawson, and Waltenburg 2006, 124).

MEDIA COVERAGE OF STATE SUPREME COURT DECISIONS

In recent years, scholars have also examined media coverage of the decisions of state supreme courts. Vining and Wilhelm (2011) analyze articles on state supreme courts between 1995 and 1998 in the most-circulated newspaper in each of the fifty states. First, they find a mere 1.46 percent of cases in the Brace-Hall State Supreme Court Data Archive are covered on the front page of the state's newspaper on the day after a decision. In general, the rulings of state supreme courts are not considered front-page news, thus leaving citizens largely uninformed of judicial branch activities close to home. Second, three types of cases make up most of the docket, and those cases receive the bulk of the front-page coverage; however, the proportion of media coverage for each type of case is not always similar to its proportion on the docket. Despite making up just one-third of all decisions, almost 45 percent of the front-page cases are "civil government" disputes, such as elections, the First Amendment, government regulation, and privacy. In contrast, "civil private" cases, involving disputes over such things as estates and private contracts and torts, are under-represented at about 22 percent of the cases covered, although they are more than one-third of the docket. Nearly 30 percent of the front-page cases fall into the category of "criminal appeals," consistent with their proportion on the docket.

Similar to coverage of the U.S. Supreme Court, state supreme court rulings addressing constitutional questions are disproportionately covered on the front page of the most-circulated newspapers (Vining and Wilhelm 2011; Yanus 2009). Less than 5 percent of cases before the state supreme courts between 1995 and 1998 involved constitutional issues, but about 22 percent of the front-page stories focused on constitutional cases. A large majority of those cases receiving coverage dealt with state constitutional questions rather than federal ones, suggesting the editors and journalists believe those cases are most relevant to their audience and most important due to state supreme courts having the final say on state constitutional issues (Vining and Wilhelm 2011). Furthermore, using a multivariate analysis to explain the variation in media coverage of state supreme court cases, Vining and Wilhelm (2010) find that rulings declaring a law unconstitutional are more likely to hit the front page than other cases. In addition, articles on state supreme court cases involving hotly contested issues, such as privacy and the death penalty, are significantly more likely to land on the front page (also see Yanus 2009). In sum, local newspapers do not report on the vast majority of state supreme cases, and their coverage disproportionately focuses on civil government cases and cases dealing with state constitutional issues.

MEDIA COVERAGE OF AFFIRMATIVE ACTION CASES

We turn now to an in-depth look at media coverage of affirmative action cases. Coverage of affirmative action cases is especially important to study for three reasons. First, because civil rights cases receive significant attention from reporters, it is critical to understand how they are presented to the public. Second, because of racial divisions among the American public, civil rights rulings are the types of decisions we would expect to generate substantially different coverage from different outlets. Finally, Supreme Court rulings have played a central role in determining public policy in the area of affirmative action. Since *Bakke*, Court decisions largely have driven affirmative action policy in education and employment, making it imperative to understand how the media portray those cases.

Affirmative Action Frames

We analyze a specific aspect of coverage of affirmative action cases by examining how the media frame cases. Framing is part and parcel of policy making in the United States (Gamson 1992; Nelson and Kinder 1996). As policies are proposed and debated, elites attempt to shape public opinion by casting the relevant issue in terms most favorable to their own objectives. This framing process is an indispensable rhetorical weapon. Frames are "story lines" or constructions of an issue. They order the developments germane to an issue and in the process determine the issue's essence (Entman 1993; Gamson and Lasch 1983; Gamson and Modigliani 1987). The successful issue construction becomes the consensus understanding of the matter and often yields the accepted recommendation regarding what should be done about it (Nelson and Kinder 1996).

Most of our systematic understanding of the framing of affirmative action traces its origins to the influential work of Gamson and Modigliani (1987). Relying on primary sources of elite political thought, such as speeches by government officials, Supreme Court opinions, political cartoons, and editorials, Gamson and Modigliani (1987) identified and defined a "core frame" of images, metaphors, and symbols individuals use to make sense of affirmative action. They then traced the frames' "political career," charting their ebb and flow and marking the forces that produced abrupt shifts in the dominant frame. To a large degree, the perturbations they uncovered were the product of significant events whose newsworthiness and public salience provided political elites with the opportunity to reshape the terms of debate in a way most favorable to their cause.

Gamson and Modigliani (1987) specifically examined elite discourse surrounding affirmative action from 1969 to 1984 and identified seven frames, two of which eventually dominated the discourse – Remedial Action and its No Preferential Treatment counterpart. The Remedial Action frame focuses on affirmative action as a policy necessary "to redress the continuing effects of a history of racial discrimination" (Gamson and Modigliani 1987, 148). It is premised on the notion that government is obligated to offer proactive assistance to black Americans because of the historical legacy of racial apartheid in this country. The No Preferential Treatment frame, on the other hand, presents affirmative action as inimical to basic constitutional values of equality. Consequently, all race-based programs and policies are unjust. Gamson and Modigliani (1987) show that these frames vary over time. The Remedial Action frame dominated the early years of their time series, but by 1984, the No Preferential Treatment frame was used more often.

Subsequent research confirmed the variability in the prominence of particular affirmative action frames, with new frames coming to the fore and established frames continuing to recede. Entman (1997, 35), for example, reported results that suggest the emergence of a new diversity frame. This frame turns on the notion that affirmative action furthers an important societal objective, and it is not restricted to blacks. Rather, affirmative action is designed to benefit all of society, including women and other racial and ethnic minorities.

Framing of Affirmative Action Cases

Using the earlier research on affirmative action frames as a starting point, Clawson, Strine, and Waltenburg (2003) examine media framing of the 1995 *Adarand v. Pena* ruling in mainstream and black newspapers. The *Adarand* case dealt with affirmative action in government contracting, and the Supreme Court held that strict scrutiny must be used to evaluate all racial classifications imposed by governmental actors. In their analysis, Clawson, Strine, and Waltenburg (2003) identified a "Dramatic Setback" frame as an outgrowth of Gamson and Modigliani's (1987) Remedial Action frame. According to this frame, the Court's ruling was a "dramatic setback to the remedial efforts that had been taking place" (Clawson, Strine, and Waltenburg 2003, 792). As an advocacy press, the black media relied heavily on this Dramatic Setback frame, with two-thirds of the articles using it. In sharp contrast, two-thirds of the mainstream articles emphasized the No Preferential Treatment frame. Due to mainstream reporters' reliance on official sources (Bennett 1996; Gans 1979), in this instance Supreme Court justices, the No Preferential Treatment frame dominated the mainstream coverage.

Richardson and Lancendorfer (2004) analyze newspaper editorials on the 2003 University of Michigan affirmative action cases, *Gratz v. Bollinger* and *Grutter v. Bollinger*. Editorials, of course, are different from straight news coverage in that they are not constrained by the same journalistic norms. Richardson and Lancendorfer (2004) argue that corporations and universities began advancing the diversity rationale for affirmative action in the mid-1980s. As a result, they examine whether editorial writers in the largest newspapers across the country promoted a Diversity frame. The Diversity frame dominated the editorial discourse, whereas the No Preferential Treatment frame "plummeted to relative obscurity" (Richardson and Lancendorfer 2004, 84). The No Preferential Treatment frame, of course, was the more prominent frame in the later years of the Gamson and Modigliani (1987) analysis and in Clawson, Strine, and Waltenburg's (2003) examination of mainstream coverage of *Adarand*. This change is most likely due to several factors: differences between editorials and news articles, differences between education and contracting cases, and perhaps the rhetorical power of the diversity argument in contemporary discussions of affirmative action.

Research Questions and Expectations

We answer two research questions in our analysis of media coverage of the *Ricci v. DeStefano* case. First, what affirmative action frames do the mainstream and black presses use to cover *Ricci*? Richardson and Lancendorfer (2004) find an emphasis on the Diversity frame in mainstream editorial coverage of the University of Michigan cases, but the Diversity frame may be less relevant in employment discussions, particularly in first-responder occupations. Instead, we expect the Remedial Action and No Preferential Treatment frames to be most prominent. Second, do the mainstream and black presses differ in their framing of the *Ricci* case? The different objectives and characteristics of mainstream and black newspapers lead to different expectations for these presses. Because mainstream journalists adhere to norms of objectivity and balance (Bennett 1996; Gans 1979), we hypothesize that both the pro-affirmative action frame, Remedial Action, and the anti-affirmative action frame, No Preferential Treatment, will receive coverage. As discussed in the section that follows, powerful interests staked out different sides on the *Ricci* case so the mainstream media had "official" pro- and anti-affirmative action sources to draw upon. Ultimately, the majority opinion in *Ricci* articulated arguments consistent with the No Preferential Treatment frame, so we expect this frame to receive more coverage in the mainstream press. In contrast, the goal of the black press is to report from an African

American or minority perspective. The black press targets its audience by appealing to its unique background, culture, and interests; moreover, the black press acts as an advocate, casting its coverage as a corrective to incomplete and often erroneous mainstream coverage (Wolseley 1990). Thus, we expect much more attention to pro-affirmative action frames, such as Remedial Action and Diversity, in the black newspapers compared to the mainstream press.

Ricci v. DeStefano

Before we present the research design, a brief review of the *Ricci v. DeStefano* case is in order. The case dealt with employment discrimination claims by "white firefighters" in New Haven, Connecticut.[2] Because of a lawsuit in the 1970s, New Haven took steps to increase the number of minority firefighters serving the city. These efforts dramatically increased the number of minority firefighters, although blacks and Latinos were still underrepresented compared to the proportion of minorities in New Haven. Moreover, despite these efforts, blacks and Latinos were largely absent in senior leadership positions.

Opportunities for promotion in the New Haven fire department were rare. Therefore, when the city offered tests (designed by a private company) to qualify for promotion to lieutenant or captain in November and December of 2003, 118 firefighters took the high-stakes exams. Seventy-seven firefighters, including 43 whites, 19 blacks, and 15 Latinos, completed the lieutenant's exam. Thirty-four passed: 25 whites, 6 blacks, and 3 Latinos. Based on the number of vacancies and a city rule governing the promotion process, the top ten candidates, all white, were eligible for an immediate promotion. Forty-one firefighters took the captain's examination, including 25 whites, 7 blacks, and 8 Latinos. Twenty-two passed: 16 whites, 3 blacks, and 3 Latinos. Nine firefighters, 7 white and 2 Latino, were eligible for immediate promotion to captain, again based on vacancies and a city rule.

City officials were immediately concerned about the test results, with the city's legal counsel, Thomas Ude, arguing the test had a disparate impact on racial minorities and therefore the New Haven Civil Service Board should not certify the results. The head of the New Haven firefighters union supported certifying the results, while Mayor John DeStefano opposed the certification. After a series of meetings, the Civil Service Board voted not to certify the results.[3]

[2] This discussion is based on *Ricci v. DeStefano* (557 U.S. [2009]).

[3] The Civil Service Board voted 2–2, with one member recused. The tie vote resulted in the results not being certified.

Seventeen white firefighters and one Latino firefighter sued the city of New Haven, city officials, the two Civil Service Board members who voted not to certify the results, and a local political activist. The firefighters sued on the basis that their rights under the Equal Protection Clause of the Fourteenth Amendment and under Title VII of the Civil Rights Act (which prohibits disparate treatment) had been violated. The city maintained that they were actually trying to uphold Title VII by ensuring that a disparate impact (also prohibited under Title VII) did not occur. The city feared that promoting the white firefighters would lead to a lawsuit by minority firefighters, and this at least partially drove their decision not to certify the results. The lower courts ruled for the city, but the firefighters successfully appealed their case to the Supreme Court.

On June 29, 2009, Justice Kennedy wrote for the majority in a 5–4 decision that reversed the lower court's judgment and found in favor of the white firefighters.[4] The basic ruling of the Court was that the firefighters' rights guaranteed by Title VII of the Civil Rights Act had been violated when the promotions were not awarded (and therefore the Court did not even need to consider whether their constitutional rights had been violated). The city's concerns about minority firefighters suing for disparate impact did not justify the disparate treatment of the white firefighters, according to the majority opinion. In a sharply worded dissent, Justice Ginsburg argued the majority ignored key facts of the case, including that the test results were rejected based on evidence the tests themselves were flawed, not solely because of the race of the top scoring firefighters.

Research Design

Using Lexis-Nexis and Ethnic Newswatch, we downloaded all the newspaper stories about the *Ricci* case that appeared between January 1, 2009 and January 1, 2010. For this research, we consider mainstream newspapers as commercial outlets that focus on the daily delivery of news in a hard-copy format. A Lexis-Nexis "newspaper" search, using the key words "Ricci," "DeStefano," "white firefighters," and "New Haven," returned nine mainstream newspapers carrying 105 articles covering *Ricci*. Black newspapers are specialized outlets that focus on reporting news from a black perspective on a daily or weekly basis in a hard-copy format. Using the same search terms, an Ethnic Newswatch search returned nineteen black newspapers reporting forty-one relevant stories. See Appendix A for newspaper list.

[4] See the insightful analysis of the *Ricci* ruling on SCOTUSblog: www.scotusblog.com/?p=10110.

APPENDIX A. *Newspapers in Sample*

Mainstream Press	Black Press
Atlanta Journal Constitution	*Afro-American*
Christian Science Monitor	*Afro-American Red Star*
Dallas Morning News	*Bay State Banner*
Denver Post	*Chicago Defender*
Houston Chronicle	*Cleveland Call and Post*
New York Times	*Jackson Advocate*
Philadelphia Inquirer	*Jacksonville Free Press*
San Diego Union-Tribune	*Los Angeles Sentinel*
Washington Post	*Miami Times*
	Michigan Chronicle
	Michigan Citizen
	Mississippi Link
	New York Beacon
	New York Amsterdam News
	Philadelphia Tribune
	Precinct Reporter
	Recorder
	Sun Reporter
	Washington Informer

The selection of our time period, newspaper sources, and content requires some discussion. First, we restrict our content analysis to one year to ensure we capture coverage of the granting of certiorari, oral arguments, and the decision. Second, we compare the coverage of large-circulation, mainstream "papers of record" to a wide variety of black newspapers. This ensures a large number of stories to allow a systematic, quantitative analysis. An alternative would have been to compare and contrast mainstream and black coverage from the same city. A "matched pair" strategy, however, would not have provided us with the desired quantitative leverage. Most importantly, we include the *New York Times* and the *Washington Post*, and their black counterparts, the *New York Amsterdam News* and the *Washington Informer*, in our sample, boosting the generalizability of our results. Last, we rely on news stories, editorials, and opinion pieces.[5]

To investigate the framing of *Ricci*, we content-analyzed mainstream and black press coverage of the case. The unit of analysis is the article itself. We coded for whether each frame and sub-frame was present or absent in each

[5] Wire articles are excluded because many of the newspapers featured the same articles across publications diminishing the variability in content.

article. All frame and sub-frame variables were coded as 1 if present in the article and 0 if not present. This coding procedure allows us to examine what percentage of articles included a particular frame or subframe.[6]

Drawing from previous research on affirmative action frames, we coded for three global framing categories: Remedial Action, No Preferential Treatment, and Diversity. Each of these global frames included a number of subframes. Thus, the Remedial Action frame argues that affirmative action is appropriate to redress discrimination against minorities. In some instances, the frame focuses on the historical oppression of people of color, whereas in other cases it concentrates on current discrimination.

The No Preferential Treatment frame asserts that affirmative action policies are unconstitutional; race-conscious policies constitute racial discrimination regardless of whether they are designed to promote racial inclusion or exclusion. The No Preferential Treatment frame was divided into four subframes: Unearned Advantage, Reverse Discrimination, Harm to Minorities, and Race Neutral Alternatives. The Unearned Advantage subframe states that affirmative action unfairly benefits minorities who are often less qualified than white firefighters denied promotion. The Reverse Discrimination frame argues that affirmative action discriminates against those who do not receive preferences. These preferences are thinly disguised quotas that violate the rights of individuals. Here the goal of a critical mass is simply a veiled attempt at racial balancing. From the Harm to Minorities subframe perspective, affirmative action hurts those whom it is intended to help. For example, unqualified minorities are thrown into firefighting where they are in over their heads. This harms the particular individuals involved and perpetuates stereotypes of minorities as inferior. Finally, the Race Neutral Alternatives subframe asserts that factors other than race should be used in the hiring and promotion process. If building a diverse firefighting department is the objective, then a consideration of firefighters' socioeconomic status or performance-based assessments will accomplish the stated goal without violating the rights of individuals.

The Diversity frame asserts that affirmative action is needed to obtain a mix of people from different races and ethnicities in fire departments. The Diversity category comprises three subframes: Leaders, National Security, and Growth. The Leaders subframe asserts that race-based determinations improve leadership ranks in the fire department and puts role models in

[6] The reliability and validity of the coding scheme are important when conducting content analysis. The first author coded 100% of the articles in the sample. A second coder randomly selected and coded a subset of 40% of the articles in the sample. Our intercoder reliability was 90%.

society. In addition, the Leaders subframe suggests that diversity improves fire service by promoting teamwork and camaraderie among fellow officers and supervisors. We also included a subframe entitled National Security. This frame argues that race-conscious policies improve military readiness by diversifying leadership ranks in relevant fields like firefighting, thus protecting national security and military readiness to deal with natural disasters and national emergencies. The Growth subframe avers that the minority population in the United States is growing, and policies must accommodate that change. American cities are increasingly diverse and firefighters should reflect this reality. See Table 1 for frame descriptions.

Research Findings

As expected, mainstream newspapers devote substantial coverage to the No Preferential Treatment frame. Table 2 shows that the No Preferential Treatment frame is used in 51 percent of the mainstream's articles covering the *Ricci* case, whereas only 31 percent use the Remedial Action frame and 7 percent focused on the Diversity frame. In line with previous research (Entman 1997; Gamson and Modigliani 1987), the Reverse Discrimination subframe is the most prominent among the mainstream's No Preferential Treatment frames, as it is used in 41 percent of the articles. As one example of the Reverse Discrimination frame, *Washington Post* court reporter Robert Barnes wrote, "The case was a victory for conservative groups and the firefighters, who said the city's resolution had amounted to denying promotions based on skin color. The court's conservatives prevailed in a decision that said employers needed a 'strong basis in evidence' that a test is deficient before discarding the results, rather than just 'raw racial statistics' that may indicate a subtle discrimination. 'No individual should face workplace discrimination based on race,' Justice Anthony M. Kennedy wrote for the five-member majority."[7]

When using the Remedial Action frame, the mainstream press focused slightly more articles on the Current frame (26 percent) than the History frame (20 percent). An excerpt from a *New York Times* story illustrates the Remedial Action Current frame: "At other fire stations across the city, firefighters had much to say about the *Ricci* case – but they said they felt uncomfortable expressing their views if their names were going to be used.

[7] Robert Barnes, "Justices Rule for White Firemen in Bias Lawsuit; Sotomayor's Decision is Overturned," *Washington Post*, June 30, 2009.

TABLE 1. *Affirmative Action Frames*

Frame	Theme	Sample Framing Elements
Remedial Action History	Race-conscious policies should be used to redress historical discrimination.	Lingering effects of slavery and segregation require the consideration of race.
Remedial Action Current	Race-conscious policies should be used to offset current discrimination.	Continuing discrimination exists.
No Preferential Treatment: Unearned Advantage	Race-conscious policies unfairly provide benefits to undeserving minorities who have not earned them.	Race-based determinations give unfair advantages to minorities, including less qualified minorities.
No Preferential Treatment: Reverse Discrimination	Race-conscious policies violate individual rights by discriminating against those who do not receive preferences.	Seeking a critical mass of minorities violates the Equal Protection Clause resulting in reverse discrimination.
No Preferential Treatment: Harm to Minorities	Race-conscious policies hurt the minorities they are intended to help.	Unprepared minorities cannot compete, undermining their self-esteem; even prepared minorities are viewed with suspicion.
No Preferential Treatment: Race Neutral Alternatives	Race-conscious programs are not necessary because there are other ways to ensure a mix of people.	Race neutral alternatives are available and have been proven successful.
Diversity: Leaders	Race-conscious policies allow a diverse set of people to become leaders, which is good for everyone.	Diversity benefits everyone and serves the community well; diversity in leadership promotes teamwork and puts role models in society.
Diversity: National Security	Race-conscious policies allow a diverse set of people to become military leaders, which is good for everyone.	Diversity in leadership improves military readiness.
Diversity: Growth	The minority population in the U.S. is growing, and policies must accommodate that growth.	Diversity is required to address increasingly diversified population concerns.
Diversity: Minorities	While all benefit from diversity, minorities in particular benefit.	Diversity provides for a critical mass of minorities, which ensures they are not isolated.

TABLE 2. *Media Coverage of Affirmative Action Frames*

	Articles in Mainstream Press (n = 105)		Articles in Black Press (n = 41)	
Remedial Action	31%	(32)	56%	(23)
History	20	(21)	37	(15)
Current	26	(27)	51	(21)
No Preferential Treatment	51	(53)	17	(7)
Unearned	7	(7)	2	(1)
Reverse Discrimination	41	(43)	10	(4)
Harm Minorities	0	(0)	0	(0)
Race Neutral Alternatives	4	(4)	0	(0)
Diversity	7	(7)	27	(11)
Leaders	4	(4)	5	(2)
National Security	0	(0)	2	(1)
Growth	1	(1)	0	(0)

Note: The first number in each column represents the percentage of newspaper articles in the sample that mention a particular frame. Thus, the entries do not sum to 100%. The number in parentheses represents the number of newspaper articles in the sample that mention a particular frame.

A black firefighter who took the exam in 2003 and did not score high enough to be eligible for a promotion said he thought the test was biased against members of minorities. 'It causes a lot of animosity,' he said of the lawsuit. 'This is almost a daily debate among firefighters.'"[8]

Due to its role as an advocate, we expected the black press to focus more on the Remedial Action and Diversity frames and much less on the No Preferential Treatment frame. As Table 2 indicates, our content analysis provides support for this hypothesis. The black press devotes the most articles to the Remedial Action frame (56 percent) then Diversity (27 percent) and the fewest articles to the No Preferential Treatment frame (17 percent). The Remedial Action Current frame is used in a little over half of the articles (51 percent) in the black press, and 37 percent use the History frame. The *Mississippi Link*, for example, quoted NAACP leader Benjamin Jealous in its story framing the *Ricci* case as Remedial Action Current: "'Monday's ruling, however, did indicate that a majority of the Justices understand that discrimination remains a serious problem in America, and that government and our courts have a responsibility to take measures to address it,' Jealous said. 'Despite today's

[8] Mark Pazniokas and Thomas Kaplan, "Case in Court, New Haven Firefighters Wait and Work," *New York Times*, June 6, 2009.

disappointing ruling, the laws of our Constitution still require employers to avoid policies that are discriminatory in practice,' Jealous said."[9]

Also consistent with our expectations, the black press frames the *Ricci* case in terms of Diversity in 27 percent of its articles, much more than the mainstream (7 percent). As one example, Reverend Jesse Jackson wrote in the *Los Angeles Sentinel*, "Affirmative action is justified on the premise that diversity is good for us as a society, not that diversity rectifies centuries of wrongdoing."[10] In contrast to the mainstream, the black press is much less likely to rely on the No Preferential Treatment frame (17 percent), dedicating only 10 percent of their articles to the Reverse Discrimination subframe.

In sum, this analysis of the *Ricci* case reveals variation in newspaper coverage. Mainstream newspapers are much more likely than the black press to use the No Preferential Treatment frame when covering civil rights, suggesting that the No Preferential Treatment storyline, particularly the Reverse Discrimination subframe, maintains credibility with the traditional media. In contrast to the mainstream press, black newspapers more frequently employ the Remedial Action frame when reporting on affirmative action, followed by the Diversity and No Preferential Treatment frames. Among the Remedial Action frames, the black press relied heavily on the Current subframe, indicating that the black press views contemporary racial discrimination as a compelling perspective in affirmative action coverage. The mainstream press largely ignored the Diversity frame, although it did receive some attention in the black press. Although the Diversity frame is certainly pro-affirmative action, it turns the focus away from helping minorities and puts it on benefitting people in general. For that reason, it is reported less frequently in the black press than the Remedial Action frames.

These differences in media coverage stem from the varying goals of the mainstream and black press. Mainstream journalists, in their quest to uphold norms of objectivity and balance, rely heavily on official sources. Journalists who work for the black press are interested in official voices, but they also cultivate sources representing black interests to ensure they are serving the news needs of their community (Towner, Clawson, and Waltenburg 2006). Furthermore, the mainstream press purports to be neutral, whereas the black press openly proclaims an advocacy role.

[9] Anonymous, "NAACP Statement on New Haven Firefighters Case," *Mississippi Link*, July 2-8, 2009.

[10] Rev. Jesse Jackson, "High Court Ignores the Greater Good," *Los Angeles Sentinel*, July 2-8, 2009.

By comparing affirmative action frames in these two presses, it becomes apparent there is no such thing as neutral news coverage. The No Preferential Treatment frame dominates coverage of *Ricci* in mainstream newspapers, yet black papers rely most heavily on the Remedial Action frame to cover the same case. Such fundamentally different frames belie the impartiality of any news outlet. Journalists must make decisions about which facts are relevant, which sources to use, and what metaphors and analogies best tell the story. These choices result in court cases being framed in vastly different ways. This is important because frames shape public opinion. Clawson and Waltenburg (2009), for example, demonstrate the influence of different media frames of the *Adarand* decision on citizens' support for the ruling. Because the news media play a critical role in conveying information about Supreme Court decisions to the public, further research is needed to examine how cases are framed in different outlets and how those frames influence citizens' attitudes about issues, rulings, and even the Supreme Court itself.

CONCLUSION

In sum, national news coverage of the Supreme Court docket is episodic and fairly limited. Newspapers, especially those with Court reporters, do a better job covering the Court than television, and local and specialized news outlets play a key role in conveying information to the public. Furthermore, the media do not accurately capture the Court's activities. For example, First Amendment, civil rights, and criminal procedures cases receive disproportionate coverage given their share of the docket. Recent scholarship documents the lack of media attention to the vast majority of state supreme court cases as well. Of the limited coverage, the focus is primarily on "civil government" cases, such as First Amendment and privacy cases, and constitutional questions, especially state constitutional issues. Our in-depth review of media coverage of affirmative action cases demonstrates the importance of framing, and our analysis shows that journalists at mainstream and black newspapers relied on very different frames when covering the *Ricci v. DeStefano* case.

REFERENCES

Bennett, W. Lance. 1996. "An Introduction to Journalism Norms and Representations of Politics." *Political Communication* 13:373–84.

Clawson, Rosalee A., Harry C. "Neil" Strine IV, and Eric Waltenburg. 2003. "Framing Supreme Court Decisions: The Mainstream Versus the Black Press." *Journal of Black Studies* 33: 784–800.

Clawson, Rosalee A., Katsuo A. Nishikawa, and Eric. N. Waltenburg. 2004. "Coverage of the Supreme Court's Rulings in the Michigan Affirmative Action Cases: Comparing the Mainstream, Black, and Latino Media." Presented at the Meeting of the Latin American Studies Association, Las Vegas, Nevada.

Clawson, Rosalee A., and Eric N. Waltenburg. 2009. *Legacy and Legitimacy: Black Americans and the Supreme Court*. Philadelphia, PA: Temple University Press.

Collins, Todd A., and Christopher A. Cooper. 2012. "Case Salience and Media Coverage of Supreme Court Decisions: Toward a New Measure." *Political Research Quarterly* 65 (2): 396–407.

Davis, Richard. 1994. *Decisions and Images: The Supreme Court and the Press*. Englewood Cliffs, NJ: Prentice Hall.

2011. *Justices and Journalists: The U.S. Supreme Court and the Media*. Cambridge University Press.

Entman, Robert M. 1993. "Framing: Towards Clarification of a Fractured Paradigm." *Journal of Communication* 43: 51–58.

1997. "Manufacturing Discord: Media in the Affirmative Action Debate." *Harvard International Journal of Press/Politics* 2(4): 39–59.

Epstein, Lee, and Jeffrey A. Segal. 2000. "Measuring Issue Salience." *American Journal of Political Science* 44 (1): 66–83.

Gamson, William A., and Kathryn E. Lasch. 1983. "The Political Culture of the Social Welfare Policy." In *Evaluating the Welfare State: Social and Political Perspectives*, eds. Shimon E. Spiro and Ephraim Yuchtman-Yaar. New York: Academic Press, 397–415.

Gamson, William A., and Andre Modigliani. 1987. "The Changing Culture of Affirmative Action." *Research in Political Sociology* 3: 137–77.

Gamson, Willam A. 1992. *Talking Politics*. New York: Cambridge University Press.

Gans, Herbert J. 1979. *Deciding What's News*. New York: Pantheon Books.

Haider-Markel, Donald P., Mahalley D. Allen, and Morgen Johansen. 2006. "Understanding Variations in Media Coverage of U.S. Supreme Court Decisions." *Harvard International Journal of Press/Politics* 11 (2): 64–85.

Hoekstra, Valerie J. 2003. *Public Reactions to Supreme Court Decisions*. Cambridge University Press.

Johnson, Tyler, and Erica Socker. 2012. "Actions, Factions, and Interactions: Newsworthy Influences on Supreme Court Coverage." *Social Science Quarterly* 93 (2): 434–463.

Nelson, Thomas, and Donald Kinder. 1996. "Issue Frames and Group-Centrism in American Public Opinion." *The Journal of Politics* 58: 1055–78.

O'Callaghan, Jerome, and James O. Dukes. 1992. "Media Coverage of the Supreme Court's Caseload." *Journalism Quarterly* 69 (1): 195–203.

Richardson, John, and Karen Lancendorfer. 2004. "Framing Affirmative Action: The Influence of Race on Newspaper Editorial Responses to the University of Michigan Cases." *The Harvard International Journal of Press/Politics* 9(4): 74–94.

Slotnick, Elliot E., and Jennifer A. Segal. 1998. *Television News and the Supreme Court: All the News That's Fit to Air?* Cambridge University Press.

Spill, Rorie L., and Zoe M. Oxley. 2003. "Philosopher Kings or Political Actors? How the Media Portray the Supreme Court." *Judicature* 87 (1): 22–29.

Towner, Terri L., Rosalee A. Clawson, and Eric N. Waltenburg. 2006. "Media Coverage of the University of Michigan Affirmative Action Decisions: The View from Mainstream, Black, and Latino Journalists." *Judicature* 90 (3): 120–128.
Vining, Jr., Richard L., and Teena Wilhelm. 2010. "Explaining High-Profile Coverage of State Supreme Court Decisions." *Social Science Quarterly* 91 (3): 704–723.
2011. "Measuring Case Salience in State Courts of Last Resort." *Political Research Quarterly* 64 (3): 559–572.
Wolseley, Roland E. 1990. *The Black Press, U.S.A.* Ames: Iowa State University Press.
Yanus, Alixandra B. 2009. "Full-Court Press: An Examination of Media Coverage of State Supreme Courts." *The Justice System Journal* 30 (2): 180–195.

4

The Supreme Court and New Media Technologies

VINCENT JAMES STRICKLER

CASEY AND *SEBELIUS* IN TRADITIONAL MEDIA

On June 29, 1992, the Supreme Court of the United States announced its decision in the case of *Planned Parenthood v. Casey*, which dealt with a Pennsylvania law regulating access to abortions.[1] Twenty years later, on June 28, 2012, the Supreme Court decided the case of *National Federation of Independent Businesses v. Sebelius*, in which the Court considered whether the national government had power to enact the Affordable Care Act.[2] Though these two cases obviously dealt with very different subjects, *Casey* and *Sebelius* were decided under quite similar circumstances. Each decision was the most anticipated of that Supreme Court term,[3] and was announced on the final day of the term.[4] Both were highly controversial, leading to large protests at the Supreme Court building.[5] Both were contested in presidential election years, and the decisions were thought

[1] *Planned Parenthood v. Casey*, 505 U.S. 833 (1992).

[2] *National Federation of Independent Business v. Sebelius*, 567 U.S. ___ (2012).

[3] Ruth Marcus, "At the Court, the Revolution That Wasn't; Opinions So Far Suggest a Majority Balking at Wholesale Change," *Washington Post*, June 28, 1992, A1; Robert Barnes, "Interest In This Ruling Stretches Beyond the Insiders," *Washington Post*, June 27, 2012, A5.

[4] Linda Greenhouse, "The Supreme Court: High Court, 5–4, Affirms Right to Abortion but Allows Most of Pennsylvania's Limits" *New York Times*, June 30, 1992, A1; John H. Cushman, Jr., "Awaiting Ruling on Fairly Simple Questions About a Complex Health Law," *New York Times*, June 28, 2012, A18.

[5] Roberto Suro, "The Supreme Court: Outside Court, Rival Rallies and Heavy Politicking," *New York Times*, June 30, 1992, A15; Kelly Kennedy, "Outside Court: 'This is Free Speech'; Competing Rallies Turn Boisterous on Second Day," *USA Today*, March 28, 2012, A2.

likely to affect the results of those elections.[6] Moreover, both were decided by surprising and complex opinions.[7]

But *Casey* was decided before the Internet had become widely integrated into American life, and *Sebelius* was decided after use of the Internet and social media had become pervasive. Comparing how these two cases were covered in traditional news sources that existed both before and after the rise of the Internet – particularly newspapers and television – may help us understand how the spread of modern media technology has affected the relationship between media and the Supreme Court.

To compare television coverage of the *Casey* and *Sebelius* cases, broadcast network evening news programs, on ABC, CBS, and NBC, were examined for the week before, the day of, and the week after certiorari decisions, oral arguments, and opinion announcements for both cases. These historical broadcasts were accessed via the Vanderbilt Television News Archive.[8] Only story segments that focused primarily on the Supreme Court's resolution of the given case were counted as relevant. Segments that were mostly concerned with the political or social impact of the general issue raised by the case were not included. Forty-seven relevant segments were identified for the two cases, out of 122 segments that initially were selected using date-limited key word searches and then individually coded. The length of time spent on each relevant broadcast discussing *Casey* and *Sebelius*, and the segments' location within each broadcast, were recorded and aggregated in Table 1.

To compare newspaper coverage of these two cases, articles in the *New York Times*, the *Washington Post*, and *USA Today* were examined for the week before, the day of, and the week after certiorari decisions, oral arguments, and opinion announcements for both cases. To locate all relevant articles, date-limited key word searches were conducted in the Lexis-Nexis database.[9] Only articles that focused primarily on the Supreme Court's resolution of the given case were counted as relevant. Articles that were mostly concerned with the political or social impact of the general issue raised by the case were not included. One hundred thirty-one relevant stories were identified in these three newspapers for the two cases, out of

[6] Maralee Schwartz and Ruth Marcus, "Abortion Gains Attention As '92 Campaign Issue; Parties Differ on Effect of Preelection Ruling," *Washington Post*, January 22, 1992, A4; Chris Cillizza, "A Week That Could Decide Obama's Future," *Washington Post*, June 25, 2012, A2.

[7] Ruth Marcus, "5–4 Court Declines to Overrule Roe; But Limits Permitted on Abortion," *Washington Post*, June 30, 1992, A1; Adam Liptak, "Roberts's Delicate Twist" *New York Times*, June 29, 2012, A1.

[8] Vanderbilt Television News Archive, tvnews.vanderbilt.edu/ accessed August 10, 2013.

[9] LexisNexis, www.lexisnexis.com accessed August 10, 2013.

TABLE 1. *Minutes (and lead stories) on broadcast network evening news programs*

	Pre-Cert	Cert Day	Post-Cert	Pre-Oral	Oral Day	Post-Oral	Pre-Opinion	Opinion Day	Post-Opinion
Casey	0:00	9:40	0:00	4:10	15:40	0:00	5:50	29:40	6:50
	(0)	(2)	(0)	(0)	(2)	(0)	(0)	(3)	(0)
Sebelius	0:00	7:00	0:00	3:10	34:00*	8:20	9:40	37:00	6:30
	(0)	(1)	(0)	(0)	(3)*	(1)	(0)	(3)	(1)

TABLE 2. *Words (and articles) in* New York Times, Washington Post, *and* USA Today

	Pre-Cert	Cert Day	Post-Cert	Pre-Oral	Oral Day	Post-Oral	Pre-Opinion	Opinion Day	Post-Opinion
Casey	878	4,508	2,310	11,821	9,138	1,988	4,111	16,173	3,376
	(1)	(6)	(2)	(10)	(7)	(2)	(6)	(13)	(4)
Sebelius	4,407	4,580	2,463	16,324	15,065*	4,547	8,712	13,766	7,847
	(4)	(5)	(3)	(13)	(20)*	(6)	(9)	(13)	(7)

TABLE 3. *Front page words (and articles) in* New York Times, Washington Post, *and* USA Today

	Pre-Cert	Cert Day	Post-Cert	Pre-Oral	Oral Day	Post-Oral	Pre-Opinion	Opinion Day	Post-Opinion
Casey	0	4,125	0	0	4,505	1,207	1,733	6,501	2,435
	(0)	(5)	(0)	(0)	(4)	(1)	(2)	(5)	(2)
Sebelius	2,782	3,248	0	7,808	11,129*	1,166	4,279	8,833	2,838
	(2)	(3)	(0)	(5)	(10)*	(1)	(3)	(6)	(2)

* *Sebelius* oral arguments took place over three days, while *Casey* oral arguments were limited to one day.

hundreds of articles that were initially selected using date-limited key word searches and then individually coded. The number of words in, and location of, each relevant article discussing *Casey* and *Sebelius* was recorded and aggregated in Tables 2 and 3.

As can be seen in Table 1, the amount of coverage, on broadcast-network evening news programs, of the *Casey* and *Sebelius* cases was generally similar – both in the length of time devoted and the situations in which reporting on the cases led off the broadcasts.[10] These network news programs paid comparable attention when the cases were granted writs of certiorari, when they were argued before the Court, and when the Court rendered its decisions. Only in the period between oral arguments and the announcement of the decisions did coverage of *Casey* go silent while these evening news programs continued to report on *Sebelius*.

This divergence in the attention given to *Casey* and *Sebelius* was more pronounced in the coverage that the cases received in newspapers. Table 2 presents data on the number of words devoted to the cases in the *New York Times*, the *Washington Post*, and *USA Today*. On days when the Court acted – to grant writs of certiorari, hear oral arguments, and announce its opinions – the attention given to the two cases was not dramatically different. It was only in the periods between these events that coverage of *Casey* dropped off, compared to coverage of *Sebelius*. Unlike the abortion case, twenty years before, these newspapers continued to pay attention to the Court's handling of the health care case even when the Court was not publically acting on it. When only front-page stories are considered, as shown in Table 3, the differences become more limited, with the more recent case only receiving dramatically more prominent coverage *before* major Court events, and not *after*.

Taken together, the differences between television and newspaper coverage of *Casey* and *Sebelius* show the media of 2012 paying more attention to the actions of the Supreme Court than they did twenty years before – at least for these most noteworthy cases, which were announced, argued, and decided under similar circumstances. This increased attention came in the days between major Court actions (and, particularly, before Court actions).

Not just the volume and location of Supreme Court coverage may be somewhat different from twenty years ago, but the content of coverage may also have changed. The brief examination of traditional media stories about *Casey* and *Sebelius*, engaged in above, suggests so. When *Casey* was argued and decided in 1992, newspapers felt free to quote large excerpts from what

[10] Coverage, by the evening news programs, on the days of oral arguments may appear to be dissimilar – with the health care case receiving far more attention than the abortion case – but this is primarily because *Sebelius* was argued over a three-day period and *Casey* on just a single day. This makes comparison of this stage of litigation problematic. Nonetheless, it can be noted that the total nightly coverage of the *Sebelius* arguments – 12:00, 12:00, 10:00, respectively – was similar (or even less) than that given to the one day of *Casey* argument – 15:40. Therefore, arguably, there was actually a bit more attention paid to the earlier case, not less. Comparing newspaper coverage suffers from the same difficulty, with similar results.

the justices had to say, in multiple stories.[11] Those same newspapers, twenty years later, provided no extensive excerpts from the *Sebelius* arguments or opinions, but instead extensively quoted reactions of political actors to what the Court had done.[12] It is possible that careful examinations of the Court's legal rationales are now moving to "technically oriented websites," catering to narrow audiences, while discussions of emotional impact and political consequences are left to dominate "medium[s] of general circulation."[13]

Therefore, to understand the changing nature of Supreme Court reporting, we must investigate not just how traditional media have changed, but also what new media have arisen to also cover the Court. This might also help us understand what other forces could be motivating traditional media to increase their coverage of major cases, before and after significant Court events.

THE COURT AND MODERN MEDIA

Media coverage of the United States Supreme Court is controlled largely by the Court itself. Since 1935, the Supreme Court has maintained a Public Information Office (PIO) to assist journalists.[14] This office distributes the official documents of the Court – including all petitions, briefs, orders, and opinions – to any interested parties.[15] These official, printed communications are most often the limit of what the Court has to say on a given issue.[16] Unlike the press offices of other governmental institutions, the PIO does not attempt to explain, interpret, or defend the actions of the officials who it represents.[17]

[11] See "The Supreme Court: Excerpts From the Justices' Decision in the Pennsylvania Case," *New York Times*, June 30, 1992, A16; "Our First Obligation Is to Define the Liberty of All," *Washington Post*, June 30, 1992, A8; and "Abortion and the Law: A Day in Court After Years of Skirmishing; Excerpts From Supreme Court Arguments on Pennsylvania Abortion Law," *New York Times*, April 23, 1992, B10.

[12] For example, see "Topic A: Parsing the Supreme Court's Ruling on Health Care; Topic A: What Does the Supreme Court's Health-Care Decision Mean?" *Washington Post*, June 29, 2012, A17.

[13] "Lyle Denniston on Changing Media Coverage of the Supreme Court," C-SPAN, accessed August 10, 2013, supremecourt.c-span.org/Video/Historians/SC_HIST_LyleD_06.aspx.

[14] Lewis Wood, "Press Needs Met by Supreme Court," *New York Times*, January 5, 1936, 7.

[15] Robert Barnes, "A Renewed Call to Televise High Court," *Washington Post*, February 12, 2007, A15.

[16] Mitchell Tropin, "What Exactly is the Court Saying?" *Barrister Magazine*, 68 (Spring 1984): 14.

[17] A former public information officer at the Court proudly explained, "My job is peculiar in Washington because this office doesn't spin, it doesn't flap, it doesn't interpret." "Cameras in the Courtroom," C-SPAN, March 14, 1996.

To quote Justice Anthony Kennedy, the Court wishes to be "judged ultimately by what we write" – and little else.[18]

Modern media innovations have only a limited impact on how the Court does its business, as it stubbornly sticks to routines from an earlier era. Each time the Court hears oral arguments and announces its decisions, it does so in a room where "No Twitter messages will be allowed. No one in the room will be permitted to make a telephone call. There will be no BlackBerrys or laptops or iPads to blog with."[19] While the Court's rules for its courtroom proclaim "NO electronics devices," it does concede that "Note taking only material is allowed in the Courtroom (i.e., pen & pad)."[20] Undoubtedly, these strict measures are a habitual example of the Court's desire to control the delivery of its own message. Former White House Press Secretary Mike McCurry has endorsed the Court's decision to reject live electronic coverage: "The court is right about this. This is not a breaking story where there are 'Aha!' moments. . .They are trying to deliberate and probe and get the answer right. We don't want tweets on every little aspect of this. . .This is a great example of where we want news and media organizations to slow down, give us a comprehensive report."[21] The alternative might be, with instant electronic coverage, that "If Justice Kennedy sneezes, everybody is going to be arguing for ten hours about what that meant."[22]

Journalists covering the Court deal with these restrictions as best they can. Audio of the proceedings in the courtroom is broadcast in the main press room, a floor below. There, reporters listen to the Court in session, or they crowd around a nearby desk, waiting for paper copies of the Court's decisions.[23] Electronic devices are also prohibited in the area where the PIO distributes the Court's written work[24] – forcing journalists to then dash to their phones and computers, in their pressroom cubbyholes, after receiving paper copies of a decision, to report the results.[25] For particularly important cases, members of the electronic media wait outside the Supreme Court

[18] Barnes, "A Renewed Call."

[19] Michael D. Shear, "Neither Phones, Nor Cameras, Nor Tweets in the Court," *New York Times*, March 26, 2012, A12.

[20] Ibid. [21] Ibid. [22] Ibid.

[23] Tom Goldstein, "We're Getting Wildly Differing Assessments," SCOTUSblog, July 7, 2012, accessed August 10, 2013, www.scotusblog.com/2012/07/were-getting-wildly-differing-assessments/.

[24] Jamie Dupree, "Waiting on the U.S. Supreme Court," WSB Radio, June 20, 2012, accessed August 10, 2013, www.wsbradio.com/weblogs/jamie-dupree/2012/jun/20/waiting-us-supreme-court/.

[25] Sarah Kliff, "For SCOTUSblog, A Simple Goal: 'Beat Everybody,'" *Washington Post*, June 28, 2012, A14.

building, ready to broadcast live announcements of the Court's ruling to the world, after they either hear word from associates in the press room or receive their own paper copies from intern runners emerging from the PIO."[26] This antiquated process led one observer, prior to the Court issuing its decision in *Sebelius* case, to predict that: "It's going to be a very weird flashback to the old ways of doing things...It will be like those old-fashioned movie scenes where the reporters fight each other to get into the phone booth to report it in."[27]

One concession that the Court has made to modern technology is to publicly post recordings of oral arguments at the end of each argument week.[28] For a few, very noteworthy cases, the Court will even release these recordings on the same day.[29] However, this is not good enough for news agencies that have repeatedly petitioned the Court to begin televising its public proceedings.[30] Nearly three-fourths of Americans appear to support such a change,[31] but the Court has steadfastly refused, with retired Justice David Souter having famously said that cameras would only enter the courtroom "over my dead body."[32] Other justices have agreed that televising Court proceedings would erode the "public's trust" in the Court.[33]

At the very least, televising the Court in action could distract from its intended messages. When Justice Ruth Bader Ginsburg fell asleep during oral arguments for an important redistricting case, the *Washington Post* noted, "It's lucky for Justice Ginsburg that the Supreme Court has so far refused to allow television cameras in the courtroom, for her visit to the land of nod would have found its way onto late-night shows."[34] But the Court's problems with television go beyond just avoiding embarrassing moments. The medium,

26 Goldstein, "We're Getting Wildly Differing Assessments."

27 Shear, "Neither Phones, Nor Cameras."

28 "Argument Audio," Supreme Court of the United States, accessed August 9, 2013, www.supremecourt.gov/oral_arguments/argument_audio.aspx.

29 Adam Liptak, "Court Announces Early Release of Same-Sex Marriage Arguments," *New York Times*, March 19, 2013, A18.

30 Shear, "Neither Phones, Nor Cameras."

31 Lydia Saad, "Americans Favor Televising Supreme Court Healthcare Case," Gallup, December 9, 2011, accessed August 9, 2013, www.gallup.com/poll/151445/Americans-Favor-Televising-Supreme-Court-Healthcare-Case.aspx.

32 Laurie Asseo, "And Now, the Supreme Court Live?" *San Diego Union-Tribune*, November 26, 2000, G6.

33 "TV and the Supreme Court; The Issue: High Court Denies Coverage of Arguments Friday; Our View: Its Objections Treat Americans Like Children," *Denver Rocky Mountain News*, November 28, 2000, A34.

34 Dana Milbank, "The Justices Look at Some Shapely ... Congressional Districts," *Washington Post*, March 2, 2006, A2.

in many ways, is ill suited to covering the way the Court does its work. As *USA Today* observed, "Covering Supreme Court rulings live on camera is perilous at best: Decisions run to hundreds of pages of dense reasoning not written for people without law degrees."[35] However, television requires news in small, easily digested, chunks. As a result, Brian Lamb, the chairperson of C-SPAN, has said that he hears one primary concern from the justices, regarding TV coverage of their proceedings: "'It's the sound bite,' he said. 'They don't like, in the modern age, that people can sound bite them.'"[36]

Justice Kennedy has pleaded with a United States Senate committee to not try to force television cameras into the Supreme Court courtroom, saying: "Please don't introduce into the dynamic that I have with my colleagues, the insidious temptation ... [of] trying to get a sound bite for the television."[37] Justice Antonin Scalia has further argued that television coverage of Court proceedings would primarily result in "15-second sound takeouts on the network news," which would be "uncharacteristic of what the Court does" and would "misinform the public."[38] Justice Ginsburg humorously explained the Court's concern at length, in a 2011 speech:

> Lawyers and law professors alike pay close attention to the questions Justices pose at oral argument. The 2010–2011 Term was rich in that regard. Questions from the bench ranged from the historical: '[W]hat [did] James Madison th [ink] about video games[?]' to the practical: '[I]sn't ... evidence always ... destroyed when ... marijuana [once possessed by a suspect] is ... smoked? Isn't it being burnt up?' Colleagues have been fearful: 'Does al-Qaeda know all this stuff?', occasionally philosophical: '[W]hy are you here?' '[W]hy are we all here?', and sometimes openly exasperated: 'I know your client doesn't care. But we still have to write [an opinion]. So what['s] the answer?' Queries ran from the natural: 'Is the snake covered?' to the unnatural: '[W]here is the 9,000-foot cow?' to the supernatural: 'What do you think about Satan?' Justice Jackson famously commented that the Court is 'not final because [it is] infallible, [it is] infallible only because [it is] final.' Some musings from the bench last Term bear out that wisdom: 'I don't know what I'm talking about,' 'Is that the best you can find on the other side ... something I once wrote in a case?' You may not be surprised to learn that I uttered none of the

[35] Martha T. Moore, "Court's Complex Ruling Trips Up Media Outlets; CNN, Fox News Wrongly Say Mandate Rejected," *USA Today*, June 29, 2012, A3.

[36] Adam Liptak, "Supreme Court TV? Nice Idea, but Still Not Likely," *New York Times*, November 28, 2011, A18.

[37] "Cameras in the Courtroom," C-SPAN, accessed September 5, 2013, www.c-span.org/The-Courts/Cameras-in-The-Court/.

[38] "Cameras in the Courtroom."

> just-recited lines. For, as the *New York Times* reported, based originally on an empirical study by a former law clerk of mine, when it comes to oral argument, I am – quote – 'the least funny Justice who talks.' From the foregoing samples, you may better understand why the Court does not plan to permit televising oral arguments any time soon.[39]

Though the Supreme Court is unwilling to embrace television, it does dabble in the Internet. In the spring of 2000, the Court launched an official website.[40] The Court's site is very simple and clean in design.[41] Its primary purpose is obviously to convey the same documentary information that the Court has previously made available only in paper, just through an additional mechanism. The home page is dominated by the Court calendar and a menu of documents – such as instructions for submitting cases[42] and Orders of the Court.[43] The home page also has links to pages explaining the operations of the Court – such as the plan for modernizing the Court's building[44] and an explanation of how the public may visit the Court.[45] Current opinions are posted to the Court's website,[46] usually about two minutes after justices begin announcing them from the bench[47] – though sometimes too early,[48] or too late.[49] Recently, the Court's website

39 Ruth Bader Ginsburg, "A Survey of the 2010 Term," Supreme Court of the United States, July 22, 2011, accessed September 5, 2013, www.supremecourt.gov/publicinfo/speeches/viewspeeches.aspx?Filename=sp_07-22-11.html (internal citations and paragraph breaks omitted).

40 "The Scout Report," Internet Scout, April 21, 2000, accessed August 9, 2013, scout.wisc.edu/Reports/ScoutReport/2000/scout-000421.

41 Supreme Court of the United States, accessed August 10, 2013, www.supremecourt.gov/.

42 "Case Handling Guides," Supreme Court of the United States, accessed August 10, 2013, www.supremecourt.gov/casehand/casehand.aspx.

43 "2012 Term Court Orders," Supreme Court of the United States, accessed August 10, 2013, www.supremecourt.gov/orders/ordersofthecourt.aspx.

44 "Supreme Court Building Modernization Project," Supreme Court of the United States, accessed August 10, 2013, www.supremecourt.gov/publicinfo/modernization/home.aspx.

45 "Visiting the Court," Supreme Court of the United States, accessed August 10, 2013, www.supremecourt.gov/visiting/visiting.aspx.

46 "2012 Term Opinions of the Court," Supreme Court of the United States, accessed August 10, 2013, www.supremecourt.gov/opinions/slipopinions.aspx.

47 Goldstein, "We're Getting Wildly Differing Assessments."

48 "The justices' reticence toward the Internet is partly tied to the Court's own Janet Jackson-at-the-Super Bowl moment. After accidentally posting several opinions to the Web about 30 minutes early on December 12, 2011, SCOTUS has since adopted a built-in Web delay, Goldstein says." Dan Diamond, "Regardless of ObamaCare Decision, SCOTUSblog Has Already Won," *Forbes*, June 24, 2012, accessed August 10, 2012, www.forbes.com/sites/dandiamond/2012/06/24/regardless-of-obamacare-decision-scotusblog-has-already-won/.

49 Goldstein, "We're Getting Wildly Differing Assessments."

was updated to automatically detect whether a user is on a mobile device, and then adapt screen size and resolution.[50]

The Court, as an institution, does not maintain a blog, Twitter presence, or a Facebook page[51] – nor do any individual members of the Court.[52] This absence is at least partly intentional, as support personnel at the Court are explicitly discouraged from discussing their duties online.[53] Chief Justice Roberts explained that this prohibition is an outgrowth of the Court's desire to control information about its work:

> I sit down with incoming clerks at the beginning of the year, as soon as we get back, and go through a number of things they have to be aware of, and that's one of them...I tell them that they obviously shouldn't be tweeting about what they're doing, or whether they have websites or whatever. And a lot it is inadvertent. They kind of think 'I'm working very hard on an opinion this week, or getting ready for an argument.' And, you know...discerning people can kind of look at what they're saying and put two and two together and figure out, maybe, what their boss is doing, and all that. So, even unintentionally they could sometimes reveal confidences; and, of course that's very dangerous. So, you know, I advise them, just put all that on hold.[54]

The Supreme Court's official website contains electronic versions of recent decisions, but it does not have a complete opinion archive. The Court's website instead refers users to non-Court sources for historic opinions[55] – such as the LexisNexis[56] and Westlaw[57] subscription services (used mostly by

[50] Dan Diamond, "The Bizarre Way That Millions of Americans, and Even Obama, Will Get the ObamaCare Verdict," *Forbes*, June 27, 2012, accessed August 10, 2012, www.forbes.com/sites/dandiamond/2012/06/27/the-bizarre-way-that-millions-of-americans-and-even-obama-will-get-the-obamacare-verdict/.

[51] A false Supreme Court Twitter account does exist as @USSupremeCourt. "US Supreme Court," Twitter, accessed August 10, 2013, twitter.com/USSupremeCourt accessed August 10, 2013. See also "The Supreme Court on Twitter?" Law Sites, January 21, 2009, accessed August 10, 2012, www.lawsitesblog.com/2009/01/supreme-court-on-twitter.html.

[52] Chief Justice John Roberts has said "[D]ifferent members of the court are more adept at that than others. I don't think any of us have a Facebook page or tweet, whatever that is. But, the technology is making inroads. I mean, we are, we find, when we're traveling, it's easier to have, some of us, briefs on some of the products where you can have them electronically available to carry them around. Different people have a different degree of comfort level." Emil Protalinski, "US Supreme Court: We're Not on Facebook, What's Twitter?" ZDNet, June 28, 2011, www.zdnet.com/blog/facebook/us-supreme-court-were-not-on-facebook-whats-twitter/1756 accessed August 10, 2013.

[53] Protalinski, "US Supreme Court: We're Not on Facebook."

[54] Ibid.

[55] "Where to Obtain Supreme Court Opinions," Supreme Court of the United States, accessed August 10, 2013, www.supremecourt.gov/opinions/obtainopinions.aspx.

[56] LexisNexis, accessed August 10, 2013, www.lexisnexis.com.

[57] Westlaw Classic, accessed August 10, 2013, www.westlaw.com.

lawyers and law students), and the FindLaw,[58] Legal Information Institute,[59] and Oyez websites,[60] which are open to the public.[61] FindLaw, is a comprehensive legal information site,[62] which includes a searchable database of Supreme Court opinions back to 1893.[63] The Legal Information Institute (LII) is maintained at Cornell Law School, providing a variety of core legal materials,[64] and hosting all United States Supreme Court decisions since 1992, along with about 600 selected cases from earlier years.[65] Oyez provides text of Court opinions by linking to Justia.com (another comprehensive legal information website),[66] but it is noteworthy itself because it has an archive of Supreme Court audio recordings.[67]

The Court began taping its oral arguments in 1955, with the audio from one term not available until the next term.[68] These recordings were stored at the National Archives, for use by justices, their clerks, and, later, also academic researchers.[69] The Oyez Project, created in 1989 as pre-Web, HyperCard stacks containing information about the Court,[70] began converting the Court's reel-to-reel recordings to digital format in the mid-1990s to allow

58 "U.S. Supreme Court Opinions," FindLaw, accessed August 10, 2013, www.findlaw.com/casecode/supreme.html.

59 "Supreme Court," Legal Information Institute, accessed August 10, 2013, www.law.cornell.edu/supct/.

60 "Cases," Oyez, accessed August 10, 2013, www.oyez.org/cases/2012.

61 The Supreme Court website also cites the American Bar Association website as a useful source, because it includes all merit case briefs, since the 2007 term. "Preview of United States Supreme Court Cases," American Bar Association, accessed August 10, 2013, www.americanbar.org/publications/preview_home/alphabetical.html.

62 "FindLaw Corporate Information: Company Background," FindLaw, accessed August 10, 2013, http://company.findlaw.com/company-history/findlaw-corporate-information-press-company-background.html#sthash.dWuj8yNQ.dpuf.

63 "US Supreme Court Opinions," FindLaw, accessed August 10, 2012, www.findlaw.com/casecode/supreme.html.

64 "Who We Are," Legal Information Institute, accessed August 10, 2013, www.law.cornell.edu/lii/about/who_we_are.

65 "Supreme Court," Legal Information Institute, accessed August 10, 2013, www.law.cornell.edu/supct/.

66 "US Supreme Court Center," Justia.com, accessed August 10, 2013, http://supreme.justia.com/.

67 "Law School is New Home to Multimedia Archive of U.S. Supreme Court Cases," IIT Chicago-Kent College of Law, November 15, 2010, accessed July 16, 2013, www.kentlaw.edu/news/releases/oyez-project-at-Chicago-Kent.html.

68 "Argument Audio," Supreme Court of the United States, accessed August 9, 2013, www.supremecourt.gov/oral_arguments/argument_audio.aspx.

69 "Once Under Wraps, Supreme Court Audio Trove Now Online," NPR, April 24, 2013, accessed August 9, 2013, www.npr.org/blogs/itsallpolitics/2013/04/25/178660998/Once-Under-Wraps-Supreme-Court-Audio-Trove-Now-Online.

70 "Oyez's Jerry Goldman," Creative Commons, October 1, 2005, accessed August 9, 2013, http://creativecommons.org/weblog/entry/7010.

wider access.[71] (The Court also switched to digital recording in 2005.)[72] Oyez intends to not just provide audio of select cases, but also eventually archive all audio back to 1955.[73] Currently, audio from 1968 to the present is complete and before 1968 is selective.[74] These recordings are even searchable. "If you said, 'I want every instance where Antonin Scalia uses the expression "strict scrutiny,"' you can find it without having to listen to hours of audio."[75] Oyez founder Jerry Goldman believes that Oyez audio is important because "There's so much more information and emotion in the human voice that a transcript can't do it justice."[76] He hopes the audio archive will improve public understanding of the Court and even lead to better oral advocacy and communication by lawyers.[77] Oyez cleaned up the recordings enough, to prepare them for publication, that they have become derivative works, different from the originals – thus allowing Oyez to copyright its versions.[78] Oyez now welcomes almost four million unique visitors per year.[79] Demand has been great enough that Oyez recently launched OyezToday, a smartphone application that allows users to access Oyez materials and share them via Facebook, Twitter, and email.[80]

Other websites, though not mentioned by the Court itself on its official website, are also noteworthy for the additional information they provide about the Court. The C-SPAN site has extensive programming about the Supreme Court and its decisions that is available on-demand online[81] – such as topical documentaries,[82] interviews with Court experts,[83] and interviews

71 Jeffrey Selingo, "Oyez! The Supreme Court, Now on MP3," *New York Times*, August 7, 2003, G3.

72 "About Oyez," Oyez, accessed August 10, 2012, www.oyez.org/about.

73 Katie Zhu, "Man on the Beat: Jerry Goldman, Founder of the Oyez Project," *The Daily Northwestern*, October 7, 2009, dailynorthwestern.com/2009/10/07/thecurrent/artsentertainment/man-on-the-beat-jerry-goldman-founder-of-the-oyez-project/ accessed August 9, 2013.

74 "About Oyez," Oyez, www.oyez.org/about August 10, 2012.

75 Zhu, "Man on the Beat."

76 Phuong Le, "Supreme Court Cases Get a Fresh Hearing," *Washington Post*, August 11, 2003, A15.

77 "Oyez's Jerry Goldman."

78 Ibid.

79 "Users Can Now Tap, Listen, Share U.S. Supreme Court Information via a Free App," IIT Chicago-Kent College of Law, March 29, 2011, accessed July 27, 2013, www.kentlaw.iit.edu/news/2011/the-oyez-project-and-chicago-kent-release-oyeztoday.

80 "Users Can Now Tap."

81 "The Supreme Court," C-SPAN, accessed August 10, 2013, supremecourt.c-span.org/.

82 "C-SPAN's Supreme Court Week Documentary," C-SPAN, accessed August 10, 2013, supremecourt.c-span.org/Video/TVPrograms/SC_Week_Documentary.aspx.

83 "Supreme Court Experts," C-SPAN, accessed August 10, 2013, supremecourt.c-span.org/Historians.aspx.

with sitting justices.[84] The C-SPAN archive does not just include shows about recent cases, such as *Sebelius*, but also hours about historic cases like *Casey* – including participant interviews before oral arguments, reactions to oral arguments, attorney news conferences after oral arguments, call-in programming after oral arguments, interest group news conference after the decision, and call-in programming after the decision.[85]

For opinionated discussions of the Court and its decisions, there are a few widely read group blogs, filled by ongoing, lengthy analysis among law professors. These seem to have even influenced the business of the Court, on occasion. One is the Volokh Conspiracy,[86] a conservative/libertarian blog,[87] whose authors were a driving force behind the *Sebelius* case.[88] Another is Balkinization,[89] a liberal blog,[90] which championed legal challenges to the government's treatment of suspected terrorists.[91] These blogs are important because, as Jack Balkin, the founder of the Balkinization blog explains, they "change[d] the relationship between law professors and journalists because law professors don't need journalists to get their ideas out to the broader public...[L]aw professors can talk about cases the day they come down, driving the discussion forward...It produces a type of legal writing that is more journalistic, more personal, and more driven by current events."[92] Some journalists also regularly write explicitly opinionated posts about the Court and its cases online, such as Linda Greenhouse for the *New York Times* website[93] and Dahlia Lithwick for Slate.com,[94] who champion the views of the political left. As an intentional counterweight, Ed Whelan and others at National Review Online maintain a daily "Bench Memos" blog, evaluating

84 "Justices in Their Own Words," C-SPAN, accessed August 10, 2013, supremecourt.c-span.org/Video/JusticeOwnWords.aspx.

85 "Search Results: 'Planned Parenthood v. Casey'," C-SPAN Video Library, accessed August 10, 2012, www.c-spanvideo.org/search/?keywords=%22planned+parenthood+v.+casey%22.

86 "About," The Volokh Conspiracy, accessed August 10, 2013, www.volokh.com/about/.

87 "Balkin Talks Blogs," *Yale Law Report*, (Winter 2007): 45.

88 Andy Guess, "Blogs and Wikis and 3D, Oh My," *Inside Higher Ed*, May 9, 2008, www.insidehighered.com/news/2008/05/09/blogs#ixzz2bsURa6x4 accessed August 10, 2013.

89 Balkinization, accessed August 10, 2013, balkin.blogspot.com/

90 "Balkin Talks Blogs."

91 "Balkinization (blog)," Wikipedia, accessed August 10, 2013, en.wikipedia.org/wiki/Balkinization_(blog).

92 "Balkin Talks Blogs."

93 "Opinionator: Linda Greenhouse," *New York Times*, accessed August 10, 2013, opinionator.blogs.nytimes.com/category/linda-greenhouse/.

94 "Dahlia Lithwick," Slate, accessed August 10, 2013, /www.slate.com/authors.dahlia_lithwick.html.

news of the Court from the political right.[95] According to Lithwick, not only the interested public follows these online writings: "Justices are really grappling with the Internet right now… There's a sense of being instantly judged… They all have their clerks print out the blogs."[96]

Probably the most important website, in relationship to the Supreme Court, is SCOTUSblog – "the TMZ of the legal world"[97] – a site dedicated to reporting the day-to-day functioning of the Supreme Court of the United States (SCOTUS) in explicit detail, and, in so doing, signaling a sea change in the way the Court is covered. SCOTUSblog began in 2002 as a marketing ploy,[98] funded out of the pockets of a pair of lawyers,[99] to drive business toward their new Supreme Court practice.[100] It failed in that function, but evolved into an institution of pure journalism, with a full-time staff, a team of regular contributors (including Lyle Denniston, the dean of the Supreme Court press corps, who it hired as its lead reporter),[101] a pool of 100 experts to call upon,[102] and even a corporate sponsor.[103]

SCOTUSblog contains a massive amount of information about the Supreme Court.[104] It has a group blog, which includes daily round-ups of Court business.[105] For each merit case, since the 2007 term, the site has a dedicated page, which includes official petitions, orders, briefs, arguments, decisions, and opinions regarding the case, as well as unofficial commentary and explanations.[106] For notable cases, SCOTUSblog provides in-depth

95 "Bench Memos," *National Review Online*, accessed August 10, 2013, www.nationalreview.com/bench-memos.

96 "Journalists Greenhouse and Lithwick Discuss How the Internet Has Affected Supreme Court Reporting," Yale Law School, October 27, 2010, accessed August 10, 2013, www.law.yale.edu/news/12392.htm.

97 Jennifer Steinhauer, "Polarized Over Health Care, United on Drama of Ruling," *New York Times*, June 25, 2012, A1.

98 "About Us," SCOTUSblog, accessed August 10, 2013, www.scotusblog.com/about/.

99 "Silver Gavel Award, Websites: SCOTUSblog," American Bar Association, accessed August 10 2013, www.americanbar.org/content/dam/aba/migrated/publiced/gavel/2010ABASilverGavelAwardsProgramFinalWeb.authcheckdam.pdf.

100 Eric Benson, "New Journalism: SCOTUSblog Publisher Tom Goldstein on Winning the Court Press Wars," *New York*, April 7, 2013, accessed August 10, 2013, nymag.com/news/frank-rich/tom-goldstein-scotusblog-2013-4/.

101 Diamond, "Regardless of ObamaCare." 102 Ibid.

103 "Bloomberg Law and SCOTUSblog Announce Exclusive Sponsorship," Bloomberg Law, September 26, 2011, accessed August 10, 2013, about.bloomberglaw.com/press-room/bloomberg-law-and-scotusblog-announce-exclusive-sponsorship/. Bloomberg Law is an upstart competitor with Lexis-Nexis and Westlaw. See Bloomberg Law, about.bloomberglaw.com/ accessed August 10, 2013.

104 "About Us."

105 "Round-Up," SCOTUSblog, accessed August 10, 2013, www.scotusblog.com/category/round-up/.

106 For example, see "October Term 2013," SCOTUSblog, accessed August 10, 2013, www.scotusblog.com/case-files/terms/ot2013/.

analysis before and after oral arguments and decisions, including through symposiums.[107] For the *Sebelius* case, as an example, SCOTUSblog includes lower court opinions, amicus briefs, merit briefs, oral argument audio, the decision opinions, and explanatory articles.[108] On opinion days, the site hosts a popular live blog – an imbedded feature on a website page that provides rolling textual coverage of an ongoing event, without requiring the user to refresh the page to see updates.

"SCOTUSblog's commentary could best be described as 'spare and balanced.'"[109] SCOTUSblog's founder, Tom Goldstein, explains:

> So often the public learns about the Court from the perspective of disappointed ideologues – liberal and conservatives who believe that the Court is out of control. The Court, of course, doesn't have any way to respond to those attacks. Our job isn't to defend the institution, but, by providing clear and truthful information, hopefully we can improve the public's understanding. Our analysis never takes positions on how the Court ought to decide cases.[110]

Because he still argues cases before the Court, Goldstein's site leaves editorializing to others.[111] This approach has "become exponentially popular with people who want to know what the court has decided."[112] Journalists and lay readers are drawn to the site also because it provides "plain English" explanations of complex legal issues.[113]

SCOTUSblog's work has been well received. It has won an American Bar Association (ABA) Silver Gavel Award,[114] with the editor of the *ABA Journal* declaring that the site "cover[s] the Supreme Court more intensively than any news organization does, and it does a better job, too."[115] It has also received a Sigma Delta Chi Award from the Society of Professional Journalists.[116]

107 "Special Features," SCOTUSblog, accessed August 10, 2013, www.scotusblog.com/category/special-features/.

108 "National Federation of Independent Business v. Sebelius," SCOTUSblog, accessed August 10, 2013, www.scotusblog.com/case-files/cases/national-federation-of-independent-business-v-sebelius/.

109 Diamond, "Regardless of ObamaCare."

110 "Silver Gavel Award."

111 Benson, "New Journalism."

112 Andrew Beaujon, "How SCOTUSblog Prepared for Today's Health Care Ruling," *Poynter*, June 28, 2012, accessed August 10, 2013, www.poynter.org/latest-news/mediawire/179018/how-scotusblog-prepared-its-servers-for-todays-health-care-ruling/.

113 "Plain English / Cases Made Simple," SCOTUSblog, accessed August 10, 2013, www.scotusblog.com/category/plain-english/.

114 "Silver Gavel Award."

115 Al Gibes, "Searching for Truth in Web's Law Blogs," Las Vegas Review-Journal, November 22, 2008, www.reviewjournal.com/business/searching-truth-webs-law-blogs accessed August 10, 2013.

116 "2012 Delta Sigma Chi Award Honorees," Society of Professional Journalists, accessed August 10, 2012, www.spj.org/sdxa12.asp#online.

In addition, it won a Peabody Award for "filling a gap in Supreme Court coverage created by traditional media outlets' staff cutbacks and, in fact, far exceeding it."[117] As other organizations reduce resources dedicated to covering the Court, SCOTUSblog has more than doubled its commitment, to a half-million dollars per year.[118] It has become so proficient at what it does that even staffers within the Supreme Court use it to gather information.[119]

Yet, stunningly, the Supreme Court has not thus far recognized SCOTUSblog as a news outlet, forcing the site to rely on Lyle Denniston's credentials from a Boston-area radio station to gain access.[120] Denied credentialing many times by Court staff,[121] SCOTUSblog has considered suing.[122] The Court is willing to recognize a White House or congressional press pass,[123] but those are issued under very strict and antiquated rules, under which SCOTUSblog was ruled unqualified.[124] The site finally obtained a Senate pass in April 2013,[125] but the Supreme Court has not yet honored it.

Without a Supreme Court press credential of its own, SCOTUSblog developed an alternative procedure for reporting on the Court in real time. Goldstein described it as a "relay race," in which "[i]nformation goes from the Court, to [reporter] Lyle Denniston, to [editor] Amy Howe, to the public. We're mostly concerned with not dropping the baton."[126] After obtaining a written opinion, Denniston will rush to his office in the Court's press area to deliver the information to Howe via phone or Skype, for her to then type into the blog.[127] (Through this process, though "Denniston seldom tweets and has 'no idea how Facebook works,'" he has become an Internet star.[128]) While reporting on the *Sebelius* decision, SCOTUSblog even struck a deal with

[117] "SCOTUSblog (SCOTUSblog.com)," Peabody Awards, accessed August 10, 2013, peabodyawards.com/past-winners/award/?pbaward=1680&pb_search=1&pb_title=&pb_year=&pb_porg=&pb_query=SCOTUSblog.

[118] Benson, "New Journalism."

[119] Mallary Jean Tenore, "Why It's So Hard for SCOTUSblog to Get Supreme Court Press Credentials," *Poynter*, July 11, 2012, accessed August 10, 2013, www.poynter.org/latest-news/top-stories/180581/why-its-so-hard-for-scotusblog-to-get-credentialed/.

[120] Kliff, "For SCOTUSblog." [121] Tenore, "Why It's So Hard." [122] Ibid. [123] Ibid.

[124] Ibid, and David Kupelian, "WND Denied Congressional Pass," WND, February 13, 2002, accessed August 10, 2013, www.wnd.com/2002/02/12759/#OLE8iB12GJPRyT3V.99.

[125] Tom Goldstein, "Press Credential," SCOTUSblog, April 18, 2013, accessed August 10, 2013, www.scotusblog.com/2013/04/press-credential/.

[126] Diamond, "Regardless of ObamaCare." [127] Beaujon, "How SCOTUSblog Prepared."

[128] David Taintor, "SCOTUSblog Is the Talk of the Twitterverse as Court Rules on Major Cases," *Talking Points Memo*, June 25, 2012, accessed August 10, 2013, tpmdc.talkingpointsmemo.com/2012/06/scotusblog-lyle-denniston-obamacare.php.

NBC News and MSNBC, to have one of their runners deliver a copy of the opinions to the SCOTUSblog crew, waiting outside the Court.[129]

The worth of SCOTUSblog is well summed up by Ben Fischer, of the *Washington Business Journal*, who explains that in the "frenetic environment" of decision days, SCOTUSblog grows in importance: "The Court is so maddening with its antiquated attitude toward public access, ... even minor improvements seem like ground-breaking developments. On opinion day, time is of the essence, so that's when [SCOTUSblog's] superior functionality really comes in handy."[130]

How do these changes – in the institutions, resources, and methods dedicated to disseminating information to the public about the Court – impact day-to-day coverage of the Court? Examining how new media reported *Sebelius* can help us find out.

REPORTING *SEBELIUS*

When the case of *National Federation of Independent Businesses v. Sebelius* was argued before the Supreme Court in 2012, the media felt great pressure to provide instantaneous updates, but were constrained by the Court's old–fashioned rules. The Associated Press dealt with this by placing two reporters in the courtroom, one of them with "instructions to leave about halfway through, file a short 'urgent' story for the news service's members, and then post on Twitter whatever is known."[131] The *Wall Street Journal*'s live blog also announced that it had multiple reporters "inside the courthouse and will be rotating in and out with updates, due to the reporting restrictions inside the court."[132]

One small advocacy group even managed to post live updates of the oral arguments on Twitter, despite the Court's strict rules.[133] The Alliance Defense

[129] Andrew Beaujon, "Why SCOTUSblog's Intern Was Running toward MSNBC," *Poynter*, June 27, 2013, accessed August 10, 2013, www.poynter.org/latest-news/mediawire/217002/why-scotusblogs-intern-was-running-toward-msnbc/.

[130] Diamond, "Regardless of ObamaCare."

[131] Shear, "Neither Phones, Nor Cameras."

[132] "Recap: Obama Health Law at the Supreme Court, Day 2," *Wall Street Journal*, March 27, 2012, accessed August 9, 2012, http://www.blogs.wsj.com/washwire/2012/03/27/live-blog-obama-health-law-at-the-supreme-court-day-2/?mod=WSJBlog&utm_source=twitterfeed&utm_medium=twitter. "It is unclear how the newspaper managed that, since the rules provided to reporters said: 'Once you are seated in the courtroom, you are there for the duration of the oral argument. You may not leave the courtroom and return later.'" Michael D. Shear, "Group Manages to Post Live Updates from Health Care Arguments ... for a While," *New York Times*, March 27, 2012, accessed August 9, 2012, thecaucus.blogs.nytimes.com/2012/03/27/group-live-tweets-from-health-care-arguments/?_r=0.

[133] Shear, "Group Manages to Post."

Fund placed a contact, with a cell phone, in the hallway outside the lawyers lounge – an overflow area in the Supreme Court building, with an audio feed from the courtroom and the same rules against electronic devices. They then posted live reports from that person online, until stopped by Court staff.[134] (This breach led the Court to issue a new set of press guidelines before the decision in *Sebelius* was announced.[135]) Though tweeting from the courtroom during oral arguments was prohibited, many journalists posted their impressions, via that platform, immediately after exiting the building.[136] Most infamously, Jeffrey Toobin, a longtime Supreme Court reporter, declared the government's case a "train wreck" one day, and a "plane wreck" the next, on Twitter.[137]

Although Twitter is the favored platform for spreading news about the Court most quickly, SCOTUSblog is the most important source for thorough and up-to-date information on what the Court is doing. Sarah Kliff, of the *Washington Post*, credits SCOTUSblog with becoming "a mainstay for Washington reporters, legislators and lobbyists anxiously awaiting a verdict."[138] Jeffrey Toobin has simply instructed his Twitter followers to "watch @SCOTUSblog" to know what is happening at the Court.[139]

On the day of the *Sebelius* decision, SCOTUSblog anticipated more visitors than in its first five years of operation, combined[140] – as many as two million during the day.[141] To prepare, the site added new servers[142] – including one just for its live blog – and nearly quadrupled its staff for the day.[143] They expected to expend $25,000 in twenty minutes of coverage,[144] and bragged that: "After they hand it to Lyle [Denniston], I expect 25 seconds after that, we'll have [the case outcome] on the live blog. I would be surprised if the Associated Press can beat us."[145] When the Supreme Court justices entered the courtroom to announce the *Sebelius* decision, hackers attacked the blog, trying to shut it down, but failed.[146] On a typical day, SCOTUSblog receives 30,000 visitors,[147] with maybe 3,000 on its live blog;[148] but on the day of the *Sebelius* announcement, the site received 5.3 million hits (ten times its

[134] Shear, "Group Manages to Post." [135] Dupree, "Waiting on the U.S. Supreme Court."
[136] "From the Steps of the Supreme Court," Twitter, accessed August 10, 2012, //dev.twitter.com/media/twitter-moments/news/scotus-healthcare.
[137] "From the Steps of the Supreme Court." [138] Kliff, "For SCOTUSblog." [139] Ibid.
[140] "SCOTUSblog," Twitter, June 28, 2012, accessed August 10, 2012, twitter.com/SCOTUSblog/status/218295540243369985.
[141] Steinhauer, "Polarized Over Health Care." [142] "SCOTUSblog," Twitter.
[143] Steinhauer, "Polarized Over Health Care." [144] "SCOTUSblog," Twitter.
[145] Kliff, "For SCOTUSblog." [146] Goldstein, "We're Getting Wildly Differing Assessments."
[147] Tenore, "Why It's So Hard." [148] Kliff, "For SCOTUSblog."

previous daily high) from 1.7 million unique readers, and had as many as one million people accessing its live blog simultaneously.[149] And the site did not crash. From SCOTUSblog's point of view "[f]or two minutes, they were producing the Olympics" – and they succeeded.[150]

In shocking contrast, when the Supreme Court's technical staff tried to place the *Sebelius* opinions on the Court's official website, they were overwhelmed. SCOTUSblog's Tom Goldstein judged that "[a]t this moment, the [Supreme Court's] website [was] the subject of perhaps greater demand than any other site on the Internet – ever."[151] At one time, the Court supplemented the PIO's paper-document distribution by emailing copies of its opinion to the involved parties when it had announced its decision in a case – but not anymore.[152] It now relies entirely on posting decisions on its official website for electronic distribution. But with so many people trying to access the *Sebelius* decision simultaneously, the Supreme Court's website crashed.[153] SCOTUSblog's Goldstein recounts the result: "In the face of the crushing demand, the Court cannot publish its own decision. The opinion will not appear on the website for a half-hour. So everyone in the country not personally at [the Supreme Court building] is completely dependent on the press to get the decision right."[154] That included the President of the United States.[155]

Meanwhile, Lyle Denniston obtained a paper copy of the Court's decision and, unusually, rushed outside to decipher it with a team of SCOTUSblog experts, rather than just phoning in.[156] Earlier in the morning, an Associated Press reporter had teased that he was in a race with SCOTUSblog to announce the case outcome first. But SCOTUSblog had backed down, with

149 Goldstein, "We're Getting Wildly Differing Assessments."

150 Kliff, "For SCOTUSblog." "'Our lives are completely different for this brief, fleeting solar flare,' said Tom Goldstein, who publishes the blog." Steinhauer, "Polarized Over Health Care."

151 Goldstein, "We're Getting Wildly Differing Assessments." 152 Ibid.

153 Dan Diamond, "Two Key Details in SCOTUSblog's Play-by-Play of ObamaCare Ruling," *Forbes*, July 8, 2012, accessed August 10, 2012, www.forbes.com/sites/dandiamond/2012/07/08/two-key-details-in-scotusblogs-play-by-play-of-obamacare-ruling/.

154 Goldstein, "We're Getting Wildly Differing Assessments."

155 "The Courtroom audio is also piped into the Solicitor General's office at the Court. There, an Administration lawyer is waiting, Blackberry in hand. The White House, fearful that our Live Blog will crash under the load and perhaps unaware that electronic devices are not allowed in that office, has arranged for the lawyer to listen to the proceedings and send email updates every thirty seconds." However, the live audio feed from the courtroom was not helpful, because John Roberts read the critical part of his opinion long after news sources have already reported the result based on their paper copies. Goldstein, "We're Getting Wildly Differing Assessments."

156 Kliff, "For SCOTUSblog."

Tom Goldstein saying, "No one will remember if you move this story first or we do," but the "only thing anyone will ever remember is if we f*** it up."[157] Instead, it would be Bloomberg News who announced first, followed by Reuters, AP and then Dow Jones.[158] This process was actually similar to what had happened twenty years before, when live news anchors struggled to report the decision in *Casey* fastest, and ABC won by seconds (by keeping a man inside the Court to report to the anchor by phone).[159] But now, the race is contested in a new medium.

Despite these early correct reports announcing that the Court had upheld the Affordable Care Act, confusion reigned as other news outlets reported the opposite. CNN failed to read far enough into a complicated opinion, and made the wrong call.[160] FOX News did the same, but their on-air anchor, lawyer and former Supreme Court correspondent Megyn Kelly, immediately questioned it – because she was also monitoring SCOTUSblog's live blog![161] CNN compounded its problem by having its various delivery methods – television, website, and Twitter – integrated, so its mistake immediately appeared in all three platforms.[162] The less integrated FOX News did not fall into the same trap.[163] Individual reporters at other companies began re-tweeting CNN's gaffe.[164] So did entire other news organizations, such as NPR and *Time* magazine.[165] Politicians also ended up passing on the CNN misinterpretation as truth.[166]

157 Goldstein, "We're Getting Wildly Differing Assessments."

158 Scott Hensley, "Supreme Court Health Care Ruling Prompts Foot Race In Press Corps," NPR, June 29, 2012, accessed August 10, 2012, www.npr.org/blogs/health/2012/06/29/155972981/supreme-court-health-care-ruling-prompts-foot-race-in-press-corps.

159 Brian Donlon and Jefferson Graham, "Abortion Ruling Sends the Networks Racing," *USA Today*, June 30, 1992, D3.

160 Chenda Ngak, "Getting It Wrong: Media Rushes to Report on Supreme Court's Health Care Decision," CBS News, June 28, 2012, accessed August 10, 2013, www.cbsnews.com/8301-501465_162-57462787-501465/getting-it-wrong-media-rushes-to-report-on-supreme-courts-health-care-decision/. See Barbara Chai, "Supreme Court Health-Law Ruling Sparks Initial Confusion on Twitter," *Wall Street Journal*, accessed August 10, 2013, blogs.wsj.com/speakeasy/2012/06/28/supreme-court-health-law-ruling-what-theyre-saying-on-twitter/. See also Orangecountyfldems, "Complete Train Wreck: CNN Health Care Ruling Fail, Full Video," YouTube, June 28, 2012, accessed August 10, 2013, www.youtube.com/watch?v=LsjHThZmKrw.

161 Goldstein, "We're Getting Wildly Differing Assessments." 162 Ibid.

163 Ibid. 164 Ibid.

165 "In A Rush To Be First, CNN, FOX, Huffington Post and TIME Get Supreme Court Story Exactly Wrong," *Think Progress*, June 28, 2012, accessed August 10, 2013, thinkprogress.org/media/2012/06/28/508072/in-a-rush-to-be-first-cnn-fox-huffington-post-and-time-get-supreme-court-story-exactly-wrong/?mobile=nc.

166 i.i.cbsi.com/cnwk.1d/i/tim/2012/06/28/deleted-tweets-healthcare.jpg accessed 10 August 2013.

CNN retracted their mistake just minutes later, but, by then, it was too late.[167] David Freddoso, of the *Washington Examiner*, tweeted "Okay, now Twitter has contradictory accounts. Just wait." The *Washington Post*'s Greg Sargent tweeted "BREAKING: Twitter creates mass confusion. Again." The *New York Times*' David Leonhardt tweeted "Be very careful about these one-line instant summaries."[168] Later, when the CNN's big blunder was clear, *Detroit Free Press* editor Brian J. Manzullo tweeted: "Note to CNN: No one would have remembered you posting the #SCOTUS decision first. Now everyone will remember you for having it wrong."[169]

While other outlets rushed to judgment, SCOTUSblog lumbered through for an extra minute or two, making sure they got it right, even commenting about their drawn-out deliberations on their live blog.[170] Other news organizations – including NBC, CBS, ABC, NPR, the *New York Times*, the *Wall Street Journal*, and the *Los Angeles Times* – were along for the ride, having accepted invitations to listen in on SCOTUSblog's conference call among its experts.[171] This was a surprising act of cooperation, and a shining example of Lyle Denniston's observation that "in the blogging community. . .people are mutually supportive, and the dog-eat-dog atmosphere of daily newspaper journalism is blessedly absent. The blogosphere is truly a village."[172] SCOTUSblog's Goldstein briefly muted the conference call, for a final internal consultation, to make sure they had the decision right, before posting their correct conclusion on the website's live blog and announcing it to the other news organizations.[173] Other sites immediately followed SCOTUSblog's lead, with the *U.S. News* live blog and the *Wall Street Journal* live blog simply quoting SCOTUSblog's own live blog post.[174]

167 "CNN Correction: Supreme Court Ruling," CNN, June 28, 2012, accessed August 10, 2013, cnnpressroom.blogs.cnn.com/2012/06/28/cnn-correction/.

168 Patrick Gavin, "Supreme Court Health Care Decision: 10 Top Tweets on SCOTUS Confusion," *Politico*, June 28, 2012, accessed August 10, 2013, www.politico.com/news/stories/0612/77938.html.

169 Ngak, "Getting it Wrong," "Someone needs to tell CNN: There is no such thing as fashioning a scoop over something that's released to the public. . .No one will notice, care or otherwise take heed that your outlet was the first to report on a Supreme Court decision. There's not an outlet that'll own that news. But much heed will be taken of a quick and mistaken interpretation of such a decision." Erik Wemple, "CNN and Fox Get It Wrong on Health-Care Ruling," *Washington Post*, June 28, 2012, accessed August 10, 2013, www.washingtonpost.com/blogs/erik-wemple/post/cnn-correction-on-health-care-ruling-insane/2012/06/28/gJQAg6w78V_blog.html.

170 Goldstein, "We're Getting Wildly Differing Assessments." 171 Ibid.

172 Taintor, "SCOTUSblog Is the Talk."

173 Goldstein, "We're Getting Wildly Differing Assessments."

174 Elizabeth Flock, "LIVE BLOG: The Supreme Court Upholds Affordable Care Act," *U.S. News & World Report*, June 28, 2012, accessed August 10, 2013, www.usnews.com/news/blogs/washington-whispers/2012/06/28/the-supreme-court-health-care-ruling-live-blog and Mark

Not only had other media outlets followed SCOTUSblog's coverage; the White House did, too. When asked how the president would learn of the Court's decision in the *Sebelius* case, White House spokesperson Jay Carney told reporters "We turn on televisions and radios and computers and watch SCOTUSblog. We all will…learn of it at the same time that you do."[175] On decision day, President Obama stepped out of his office to watch CNN and FOX News as the decision was released – and was disappointed when he saw those networks make the wrong call.[176] His staff was not as concerned. The White House also had been invited to listen into SCOTUSblog's conference call, and in both Carney's office and White Counsel Kathryn Remmler's office, they were logged into SCOTUSblog's live blog.[177] But President Obama was not watching or listening to SCOTUSblog, and "for more than five minutes, he had substantially worse information than many Americans."[178] Eventually, Obama learned the truth when Ruemmler told him that CNN got the decision wrong.[179]

After the true decision in *Sebelius* became widely known, the content of most online coverage transitioned. *U.S. News*'s live blog, which had been quoting SCOTUSblog posts, turned to covering reactions to the outcome, not analyzing the opinion.[180] The *New York Times*' live blog also moved immediately to political reaction, not continuing legal analysis.[181] ABC News's live blog continued legal analysis for about a half hour, and then switched to political reactions.[182] In contrast, SCOTUSblog's live blog continued providing legal analysis for almost six more hours.[183] Along the way, Lyle Denniston, by then back in the Court's pressroom listening to the building's audio system, reported on the live blog what he heard as the justices read their opinions in the case from the bench.[184]

Tom Goldstein later summed up what he felt SCOTUSblog had accomplished on the *Sebelius* decision day: "As for the blog, I feel that we showed

Memmott, Eyder Peralta and Korva Coleman, "As It Happened: Supreme Court Upholds Health Care Law," NPR, June 28, 2012, accessed August 10, 2013, www.npr.org/blogs/thetwo-way/2012/06/28/155901105/live-blog-the-health-care-ruling.

175 Kliff, "For SCOTUSblog."

176 Glenn Thrush, "Barack Obama Fooled on Supreme Court Ruling by CNN, Fox News," *Politico*, June 28, 2012, accessed August 10, 2013, www.politico.com/news/stories/0612/77974.html#ixzz1z7CxACgX.

177 Goldstein, "We're Getting Wildly Differing Assessments."

178 Ibid.

179 Thrush, "Barack Obama Fooled."

180 Flock, "LIVE BLOG."

181 "Supreme Court Health Care Decision," *New York Times*, June 28, 2012, accessed August 10, 2013, elections.nytimes.com/2012/live-coverage/scotus-healthcare.

182 "Supreme Court Health Care Decision."

183 Kali Borkoski, "Live Blog of the Health Care Decision," SCOTUSblog, June 28, 2012, accessed August 10, 2012, www.scotusblog.com/?p=147857.

184 Ibid.

that a specialized 'vertical' – a deep team with focused expertise – can contribute to reporting. We helped the traditional media and the White House, and we distributed the information directly to the public."[185]

SCOTUSblog was not the only Internet site dramatically impacted by the *Sebelius* announcement. Politicians, celebrities, and common citizens took to Twitter to express their opinions,[186] with traffic peaking at 13,000 tweets per minute less than ten minutes after the decision was publicly known (more than three times the Twitter traffic compared to when Congress narrowly passed the health care law.).[187] At the same time, the Google search engine saw searches for "Justice Roberts" increase 25,900 percent and searches for "individual mandate" (an important term in the case) jump 12,200 percent.[188] Clearly, Internet media are becoming a significant source for people seeking to understand and communicate about the actions of the Supreme Court.

Not everyone is happy about these developments. SCOTUSblog founder, Tom Goldstein, reports that his relationship with the Supreme Court press corps has grown chilly since the blog's big day covering *Sebelius*: "[T]he mainstream press regards us as an extreme threat. Our external press citations are down. You can see it on Twitter as well. While we'll regularly retweet pieces by other people, and we have the roundup every day of the rest of the press corps, the reverse isn't true at all."[189] He considers this particularly odd since the SCOTUSblog site can track the IP addresses of its users and knows that the press corps, even as they leave the Court's pressroom physically empty, is making use of SCOTUSblog to work from their newsrooms. According to Goldstein, "they make unbelievable use of the blog but really don't want to do anything that promotes it... [T]he newspapers and the wires treat us as competitors."[190]

THE FUTURE OF SUPREME COURT REPORTING

The beginning of this chapter presented evidence that television and newspaper coverage of the *Sebelius* case in 2012 exceeded the attention given by the same news outlets to the *Casey* case in 1992 – at least in the periods between major

[185] Goldstein, "We're Getting Wildly Differing Assessments."

[186] "Supreme Court Health Care Ruling: Twitter Reactions," ABC News, June 28, 2012, accessed August 10, 2013, abcnews.go.com/Politics/supreme-court-health-care-ruling-twitter-reactions/story?id=16670554.

[187] Catalina Camia, "Twitter Use Jumps on Supreme Court's Health Decision," *USA Today*, June 29, 2012, accessed August 10, 2012, content.usatoday.com/communities/onpolitics/post/2012/06/scotus-health-care-ruling-social-media-twitter-google/1#.UggXfxXD-cx.

[188] Camia, "Twitter Use Jumps." [189] Benson, "New Journalism." [190] Ibid.

Court actions. This is, actually, a curious discovery, since Court watchers generally believe that traditional media interest in the Court is declining, with "the Supreme Court press room . . . now, except on decision day, completely empty. . ."[191] Lyle Denniston believes, in fact, that "We are in the early stages of a, perhaps, really profound shift in which the press attention to the Court, the press awareness of the Court. . .is going to be so much smaller over time. . .I can tell you just by my own observation, in the last ten years, the American newspaper scope of coverage of the Supreme Court of the United States has declined markedly."[192]

A possible reason for this perceived decline is the rise of new electronic media, like that discussed in detail earlier, which seem to be drawing time, talent, and energy away from traditional reporting practices and venues. Denniston admits that "much of the raw material with which Supreme Court reporters work is online, so most of the reporters don't [need to] come around to the press room anymore."[193] Yet, even as the Internet makes some aspects of a reporter's labors easier, it also adds new demands. Joan Biskupic explains the "difficult. . .challenging. . .[and] exciting" pace that the Internet has now forced upon the Court's reporters:

> I race down the stairs [after a decision], to the Court press area, where we all have our laptops set up now, and I write a first version of that story so that it can get on our Internet site. This is much different than it was when I first started covering the Court, when you would essentially take all day to digest an opinion, call people, get their reaction, and then file a story around six or seven p.m. that would appear in the next day's newspaper. Now, readers really want to know, as soon as possible, what the Court ruled and potentially what that might mean. . .If I wrote for the next day's paper simply that the Court ruled 5 to 4 in a certain way, who would care? – because everyone would know it by the time they woke up the next morning and got their newspaper.[194]

Notably, Biskupic admits to publishing her just-the-facts stories online, while stories filled with political reactions are saved for the next day's printed paper. Might this explain the difference in printed newspaper stories noticed earlier, wherein justices' opinions in *Casey* were freely quoted at length, but not their *Sebelius* opinions?

[191] Ibid. [192] "Lyle Denniston on Changing Media Coverage."

[193] Liz Goodwin, "Lyle Denniston, Icon of Supreme Court Press Corps, on Health Care Case and Being Older than the Justices," *Yahoo News*, June 25, 2012, accessed August 10, 2013, news.yahoo.com/blogs/ticket/lyle-denniston-icon-supreme-court-press-corps-health-091136289.html.

[194] "Journalists on the Workings of the Supreme Court," C-SPAN, accessed August 10, 2013, /supremecourt.c-span.org/Video/TVPrograms/SC_Week_Monday.aspx.

As Lyle Denniston laments what he perceives as the traditional media's declining interest in the Court, he is compelled to ask, "Who will be the chronicler of the Supreme Court of the future? Who will tell the American people what their Supreme Court is, what it's doing, where it's going, who's on it? Who will be paying attention in other words?"[195] Such coverage will likely still exist in the future, but it may then be found mostly on sites like SCOTUSblog, perhaps with a different audience, different goals, and different content. The unyielding demands of the Internet news cycle already require constant fodder for interested websites, adding to the work that Biskupic, Denniston, and other Court reporters must perform. At least some of this extended coverage is likely bleeding over into traditional media sources, thus possibly explaining the greater attention given to *Sebelius* between Court events, a level of attention not devoted to *Casey*. If a reporter has to be commenting about the Court online in the days before an anticipated Court action, why not just run the story in the printed paper, too?

The increased attention that the press appears to be giving to Supreme Court cases (both in the preceding comparison of *Casey* and *Sebelius*, and in Biskupic's description of her new workload), and the assertion of insiders that media attention to the Supreme Court is in fact declining, are not necessarily contradictory perceptions. First, the small case study results presented earlier, comparing coverage of *Casey* with coverage of *Sebelius*, only gives us a hint of how the traditional media are treating the highest profile cases. What if the coverage of less compelling cases is actually decreasing? Lyle Denniston believes that is the reality – that the press now "ignores lower-profile decisions."[196] Second, it can be true that serious journalistic explanations of the Supreme Court and its actions appear to be declining – if one only looks where it was found before – while it has actually just shifted to new, more specialized venues, like SCOTUSblog, or even The Volokh Conspiracy and Balkinization blogs discussed earlier.[197]

Denniston acknowledges that media interest in the Supreme Court may simply be moving online, but he worries that the quality of the coverage will then suffer, as Internet-attention spans dictate story content:

> To some degree the electronic media, as it is, and as it will develop over time, can take up the slack. But the pressure in the electronic media for constant 24-hour coverage enhances the importance of brevity; and, in covering the

195 "Lyle Denniston on Changing Media Coverage."

196 Goodwin, "Lyle Denniston, Icon of Supreme Court Press Corps."

197 The Volokh Conspiracy, accessed August 10, 2013, /www.volokh.com/ and Balkinization, accessed 10 August 2013, /balkin.blogspot.com/.

> Supreme Court of the United States, brevity can be the enemy of clarity. Brevity can be, actually, a contradiction of the substance of what the Court does, because it takes a little bit of space, a little bit of time, a little bit of language to tell what the Supreme Court's doing when it's deciding issues that are intensely complex...[198]

Longtime Supreme Court correspondent, Linda Greenhouse agrees that the pressures produced by the Internet are counterproductive: "Filing early and constantly is terrible and inimical to thoughtful coverage."[199]

Nonetheless, the Internet does provide lots of room for seriously discussing cases – but that does not mean the public will want to hunt down and read those discussions. For Denniston, "the question becomes, will Americans, themselves, take it upon themselves to find alternative ways to learn about the Court? When it isn't served up as easily as it has been in the American newspaper, will Americans go looking for places to learn about the Supreme Court?...[W]ill people make the effort to do so? I'm not sure that they will."[200] This is not just important for the people who are missing the message, but may be critical for the Court as an institution because "increased awareness of the activities of the Court tends to reinforce legitimacy by exposing people to the powerful symbols of law."[201]

Shifting coverage of the Court to specialty websites, with thoroughly self-selecting audiences may do even more harm than just producing the intellectual isolation that Denniston fears. Consumers tend to choose media outlets based on those sources matching their existing ideological biases.[202] Internet news sites are more segregated (that is, appealing to one ideological position more than another) than any other mass media source, except national newspapers.[203] So, relying on Internet news coverage, rather than, say, television news, can lead to consumers choosing more ideological pure news sources and consequently becoming more ideologically isolated than they otherwise would be. This may then lead to greater political

198 "Lyle Denniston on Changing Media Coverage."

199 "Journalists Greenhouse and Lithwick."

200 "Lyle Denniston on Changing Media Coverage."

201 James L. Gibson, Gregory A. Caldeira, and Lester Kenyatta Spence, "The Supreme Court and the US Presidential Election of 2000: Wounds, Self-Inflicted or Otherwise?" *British Journal of Political Science*, 33 (October 2003): 535. See also James L. Gibson and Gregory A. Caldeira, "Knowing the Supreme Court? A Reconsideration of Public Ignorance of the High Court," *Journal of Politics*, 71 (April 2009): 439.

202 Rebecca Chalif, "Political Media Fragmentation: Echo Chambers in Cable News," *Electronic Media & Politics*, 1 (July 2011): 46.

203 Matthew Gentzkow and Jesse M. Shapiro, "Ideological Segregation Online and Offline," *Quarterly Journal of Economics*, 126 (November, 2011), 1801.

polarization among those who visit isolating websites, where they may expect to encounter only others who think like themselves and drive away those who do not – particularly sites dealing with political issues (like Supreme Court decisions).[204]

Internet isolation may even grow more intense and pure over time, as sites like Google, Yahoo, and Facebook customize our search results to present only those links that we are thought most likely to appreciate.[205] This led prominent law professor, and former member of the Obama administration, Cass Sunstein to conclude, "The market for news, entertainment, and information has finally been perfected. Consumers are able to see exactly what they want. When the power to filter is unlimited, people can decide, in advance and with perfect accuracy, what they will and will not encounter."[206] Online users may then become more vulnerable to what Sunstein calls the "Law of Group Polarization," which claims, "In a striking empirical regularity, deliberation tends to move groups, and the individuals who compose them, toward a more extreme point in the direction indicated by their own predeliberation judgments."[207] In other words, if one talks with people with whom one already agrees, one becomes even more convinced that one is right and those who disagree are wrong.

As a practical reality, one study found that viewers who already have an ideological predisposition, who supplement their television viewing with Internet use, are more extreme in their ideological views, and more interested in niche political issues, than those who only watch television news.[208] Another study, similarly, concluded that:

> blog readers gravitate toward blogs that accord with their political beliefs. Few read blogs on both the left and right of the ideological spectrum. Furthermore, those who read left-wing blogs and those who read right-wing

[204] Eric Gilbert, Tony Bergstrom and Karrie Karahalios, "Blogs Are Echo Chambers: Blogs Are Echo Chambers," University of Illinois at Urbana-Champaign, accessed August 10, 2013, social.cs.uiuc.edu/people/gilbert/pub/hicss09-echo-gilbert.pdf.

[205] Lynn Parramore, "Eli Pariser on the future of the Internet," *Salon*, October 8, 2010, accessed August 10, 2013, www.salon.com/2010/10/08/lynn_parramore_eli_pariser/. See Eli Pariser, *The Filter Bubble: What the Internet Is Hiding from You* (New York: Penguin, 2011).

[206] Cass Sunstein, *Republic.com* 2.0, (Princeton University Press, 2007), 3.

[207] Cass R. Sunstein, "The Law of Group Polarization," John M. Olin Law & Economics Working Paper No. 91 (2nd series), December 7, 1999, page 1, accessed August 10, 2103, www.law.uchicago.edu/files/files/91.CRS_.Polarization.pdf; citing Roger Brown, *Social Psychology*, 2nd ed. (New York: Free Press, 2003), 200–230 for discussion of supporting studies.

[208] Norman H. Nie, Darwin W. Miller, III, Saar Golde, Daniel M. Butler, Kenneth Winneg, "The World Wide Web and the U.S. Political News Market," *American Journal of Political Science*, 54 (April 2010): 428.

> blogs are ideologically far apart. Blog readers are more polarized than either non-blog-readers or consumers of various television news programs, and roughly as polarized as US senators. Blog readers also participate more in politics than non-blog readers.[209]

These results mean that "the necessary conditions for the echo chamber effect are in place; people are using the Internet to expose themselves to opinions similar to their own."[210]

A pessimist might believe we are inevitably moving toward a future in which the media of mass distribution will deny the public comprehensive coverage of the Court. What coverage big media will then provide will focus only on political and social aspects of major cases. Detailed coverage of all the Supreme Court's labors will be relegated to boutique websites, visited by a limited clientele. In addition, public perceptions of the Court will be dominated by polarized discussions found on echoing-opinion websites. Nevertheless, there is hope to be found, too. We have already seen that new media can supply a depth of coverage unknown to traditional sources, with every case, every decision, every argument, and every legal voice available at a mouse click. For those willing to make the small effort to look for themselves, greater understanding of the Court awaits online.

[209] Eric Lawrence, John Sides and Henry Farrell, "Self-Segregation or Deliberation? Blog Readership, Participation, and Polarization in American Politics," *Perspectives on Politics* 8 (March 2010): 141.

[210] Nie, et al, "The World Wide Web," 436.

5

Explaining Intermedia Coverage of Supreme Court Decisions

RICHARD L. VINING, JR., AND PHIL MARCIN

Popular perceptions and knowledge about government are shaped by news content (Brians and Wattenberg 1996; Eveland, Marton, and Seo 2004; Jerit, Barabas, and Bolsen 2006; Page and Shapiro 1992; Tuchman 1978; Zaller 1992). One branch of American government, the judiciary, receives much less coverage than its counterparts (Franklin and Kosaki 1995). Not coincidentally, the public understands the courts less than either Congress or the presidency (Roberts 2007). This lack of understanding can have significant consequences for the judiciary, especially if it is seen as biased or overtly political, because its authority depends largely on public and elite acceptance of its legitimacy. News about courts, including the Supreme Court of the United States, is central to the elite discourse that influences public attitudes about them (see Zaller 1992). When news content about the Supreme Court is present throughout the news media, even individuals with lower levels of cognitive engagement toward legal news are likely to receive it. This is important because the news received and understood by the public influences popular judgments about the legitimacy and performance of the Third Branch.

Scholars have a limited understanding of why judicial activities become news. We examine why news about Supreme Court decisions receives coverage in a greater number and more types of news outlets. We analyze this intermedia coverage by synthesizing the press-Court literature with strands of communication research examining audience fragmentation, defined as the division of the media's audience due to the proliferation of media outlets, and newsworthiness. First, we adapt the gatekeeping theory developed by Shoemaker and coauthors (e.g., Shoemaker and Cohen 2006; Shoemaker and Reese 1996; Shoemaker and Vos 2009) to explain the newsworthiness of Supreme Court decisions. This theory states that the social significance and deviance of an event determine whether it becomes news. Second, we test our theoretical explanation for intermedia news coverage of these rulings. Finally, we present our findings and discuss their implications.

We examine Supreme Court news during the 2008 and 2010 terms in elite newspapers (the *New York Times* and the *Los Angeles Times*), network news broadcasts (*NBC Nightly News* and *ABC World News*), and news curation websites (The Drudge Report and The Huffington Post). By doing so, we can explain intermedia coverage in traditional news outlets and new media. We find that Supreme Court rulings receive coverage that is more widespread when they have characteristics that signify social significance. These include exogenous interest at earlier stages of the judicial process and disagreement among the justices expressed in their signed opinions. Extensive coverage is less likely when a case is decided by a *per curiam* opinion.

AUDIENCE FRAGMENTATION AND REDUNDANCY

The audience for traditional news organizations has shrunk in recent decades (Hindman and Wiegard 2008; Meyer 2009) while the proportion of Americans consuming online news has increased substantially (Ahlers 2006). The emergence of the Internet and greater division of the news audience have revitalized scholarly consideration of audience fragmentation. This concept identifies "a potential relationship between audience and information" (Tewksbury 2005) with news consumers receiving divergent messages from different types of media. Interest in the effects of audience fragmentation flourishes occasionally in response to major innovations in communication technology. These include the growing popularity of television (McLuhan 1964), cable television (Heeter and Greenberg 1985; Katz 1996, 24), and the Internet (Chaffee and Metzger 2001; Havick 2000). Studies of audience fragmentation are motivated by the expectation that media proliferation encourages specialism that disrupts social uniformity and prevents the emergence of a coherent public agenda (McQuail 1997; Merrill and Lowenstein 1979).[1] This hypothesis is supported by studies showing that online news media has different routines than the traditional press (Boczkowski 2004; Lowery 2006) and allows audience members to use websites to acquire specific kinds of information (Tewksbury 2005, 333).

Although concerns about audience fragmentation persist, other scholars argue that intermedia coverage of events should be normal. McCombs (2004,

[1] Chaffee and Metzger (2001) posit that audience fragmentation also presents a challenge to agenda-setting theorists because of its tendency to fracture the agendas of the media and its consumers.

113–117) explains that journalists observe the work of their colleagues, especially those at high status outlets, and mimic their news choices. Gasper (2009, 495) argues that the economic model of news content also predicts homogenous news because rival journalistic organizations compete for similar sets of audience members. Journalists also write for each other and their editors along with their audiences (Shoemaker and Reese 1996); this is likely to result in similar news products given their shared perceptions of newsworthiness. Although they cite different theoretical frameworks to explain newsworthiness, these scholars agree that the content of news outlets is likely to be relatively homogenous – at least with regard to major news items. This duplication unifies the public agenda despite media proliferation (Maier 2010; Riffe, et al. 1986).

There is substantial evidence indicating that the media agenda is unified with regard to the most salient events. Sasser and Russell (1972) found that news items in newspapers, television stations, and radio stations differed *except for the most prominent news items* [emphasis added]. This suggests that variation in news topics is most common for minor news items (also see Shoemaker and Vos 2009, 52). Lee (2007) found similar content in blog posts and mainstream media coverage of the 2004 presidential election. Maier (2010) studied the content of legacy media and news websites and found that their top stories corresponded about 60 percent of the time.

Intermedia coverage increases the likelihood that a message transmitted by elite discourse reaches the public. First, it increases the probability of audience exposure to a news item. Even in the absence of active cognitive engagement with an issue, the reception of elite discourse about a topic is increasingly likely if relevant messages are more plentiful. In addition, even if the news audience is fractured its components will receive similar transmissions if repetition is prevalent among numerous news sources. Second, intermedia coverage is a signal to readers and viewers that an event is salient. News consumers often integrate new information sources into their media diets without abandoning others (Ahlers 2006; Dutta-Bergman 2004). Information from one source supplements data acquired elsewhere.

SUPREME COURT NEWS

The quantity and content of Supreme Court news are correlated with the public mood about the judiciary (Franklin and Kosaki 1995; Johnston and Bartels 2010). However, the judicial branch seldom encourages public scrutiny (Dubeck 2007). In addition, the Supreme Court does not permit live coverage of oral arguments and most of its work takes place behind closed doors. The obscurity of judicial work and proceedings makes it difficult for the media to understand and report (Tuchman 1978, 24). Despite these obstacles, the news media produce Supreme Court news. Why and to what extent information about the Supreme Court is considered newsworthy throughout the news media has received limited attention, especially since the advent of the digital age.

Previous Research on Supreme Court News

Most studies of Supreme Court news focus on a single type of news organization (Katsh 1983; Larson 1985; Maltzman and Wahlbeck 2003; Newland 1964; Slotnick and Segal 1998; Solimine 1980; Spill and Oxley 2003; Tarpley 1984). However, some scholars scrutinize intermedia fragmentation and similarity in coverage of the Court. O'Callaghan and Dukes (1992) analyzed newspaper, newsmagazine, and network television news coverage of the Supreme Court's 1986 term. They show that civil rights cases were frequently featured in all three types of outlets but economic cases were not. Davis (1994) examined Supreme Court news on network television as well as newsmagazines and wire services. He concluded that wire services cover more cases than television or newsmagazines but all of them report social policy cases with greater frequency than others (p. 22).

NEWSWORTHINESS AND NEWS CONTENT

We propose to determine why Supreme Court news is salient enough to receive intermedia coverage in prominent news outlets. We examine content in newspapers, network television broadcasts, and news websites. Because we are interested in which decisions receive widespread coverage we must consider the determinants of news content. We will discuss the concept of newsworthiness and its application to judicial decisions.

Explanations for News Content

It is impossible for the news media to cover all events. Accordingly, some standards of newsworthiness must be applied. Scholars focus on the roles of predispositions, news values, and news routines as factors shaping news content (Oliver and Myers 1999). If events receive coverage in multiple types of news outlets despite media proliferation (Lee 2007; Maier 2010; McCombs 2004; Sasser and Russell 1972) we posit that they have qualities making them newsworthy despite intermedia differences in internal routines, staffing, and audiences.

Although there are no uniform criteria for newsworthiness, scholars identify numerous factors associated with the reporting of news items. Galtung and Ruge (1965) provide a list of "news values" that determine whether an event becomes news. Later scholars provided their own sets of news values (Brighton and Foy 2007, 79; Chibnall 1977; Graber 2009, 85–7; Harcup and O'Neill 2001; Jewkes 2004). There is a consensus among them that potential impact, conflict, geographic proximity, and novelty affect newsworthiness. These studies advance our knowledge of news content but few include rigorous theory development. However, Shoemaker and colleagues (Shoemaker, Danielian, and Brendlinger 1991; Shoemaker and Cohen 2006; Shoemaker and Vos 2009) provide a gatekeeping theory of news content that is parsimonious, generalizable, and falsifiable. In the following sections, we explain this theory and its utility for explaining news coverage of the U.S. Supreme Court.

Gatekeeping Theory

Gatekeeping theory asserts that news items pass through a series of gates or decision points as they progress toward inclusion in news content (Lewin 1951; Shoemaker, et al. 2001). White (1950) introduced gatekeeping theory to the communication literature. He concluded that editors are gatekeepers and their values influence news content, especially for minor news items. Shoemaker and her coauthors focus on the primacy of two concepts, social significance and deviance (whether positive or negative), as indicators of newsworthiness.[2] They assert that these constructs determine how prominently a news item appears in the news media.[3]

Shoemaker and Cohen (2006, 14–15) identify political, public, cultural, and economic dimensions of significance. Political significance, defined as "anything involving the political system, including elections, government activities, the passing of laws, or the breaking of laws" (p. 65), is the strongest and most consistent predictor that an event becomes news content (Skewes and Black 2006, 321). Public significance, which "relates to events that affect the well-being of the citizenry" (Shoemaker and Cohen 2006, 65), is an important but limited predictor of coverage. Cultural significance, generally related to religion, ethnicity, language, and the arts, is strongly related to news

[2] Shoemaker (1996) argues that these traits of news items determine their newsworthiness because of human biological and cultural evolution. People instinctively survey their environments for deviance and pay attention to events that are socially significant or deviate from normal occurrences.

[3] Shoemaker, et al. (2001) examine coverage of congressional bills from 1996 to 1998, concluding that the individual characteristics of journalists were unrelated to coverage.

prominence where cultural activities are frequent and visual elements can accompany the story. Economic significance is only weakly related to the prominence of coverage, if at all; this is likely due to the complexity of business stories and the lack of compelling visuals to accompany them (Skewes and Black 2006, p. 321).

Three types of deviance are related to newsworthiness: social change, statistical, and normative deviance (Shoemaker and Cohen 2006, 49). Social change deviance "refers to threats to the status quo" including civil demonstrations or transformative political or cultural events in hostile environments. Statistical deviance "concerns things that are unusual, odd, or novel, as well as anything that is either above or below average." Normative deviance concerns "violations of law and norms" including crime. Social change deviance is strongly associated with more coverage in the American media. Statistical deviance tends to result in coverage that is more prominent but its impact is inconsistent. However, normative deviance has little influence on news content in the United States (Skewes and Black 2006, 315–18).

Deviance and social significance define newsworthiness in two ways. First, the intensity of deviance or social significance affects news. However, this factor is less important in the United States than other nations (Shoemaker and Cohen 2006, 59–60). Second, newsworthiness is defined by the complexity of the relationships between events and aspects of deviance and significance. Shoemaker and Cohen (2006) define complexity as the number of elements of deviance or significance present, with more resulting in additional coverage (Skewes and Black 2006, 339–40). The greater complexity of an event, the stronger its force on the "gate" it must pass (p. 342). Internal political events are among the most complex possible topics in the universe of news items (p. 345).

GATEKEEPING THEORY AND SUPREME COURT NEWS

We argue that the gatekeeping theory of Shoemaker et al. provides a useful framework to explain intermedia coverage of Supreme Court decisions. Several aspects of legal outcomes indicate either social significance or deviance.

The Social Significance of U.S. Supreme Court Decisions

Several characteristics of Supreme Court decisions indicate their social significance. These include the number of amicus curiae briefs filed, previous coverage of oral arguments, the presence of a civil rights or liberties issue, and opinion authorship by the chief justice.

The filing of amicus curiae briefs indicates exogenous actors' perceptions of the social significance of a case. This is true regardless of which dimension of significance motivates the parties filing briefs. Amicus curiae briefs demonstrate that outside parties believe there are high stakes associated with the outcome. Justices respond to these filings when they construct their discretionary docket (Caldeira and Wright 1988). Studies of both a single newspaper (Maltzmann and Wahlbeck 2003) and multiple television news programs (Slotnick and Segal 1998) find evidence to support the notion that amicus curiae briefs increase the likelihood of news about decisions on the merits. *We anticipate a positive relationship between the number of amicus curiae briefs filed in a case and intermedia coverage of a Supreme Court decision.*

News content about a case prior to the ruling is another indicator of social significance. Interest in earlier stages of the judicial process suggests that the media anticipate a decision with significant consequences for the political system, the populace, popular culture, or the economy. News about further developments is common once an event is reported (Galtung and Ruge 1965, 57). In fact, journalists say explicitly that coverage of case outcomes is more likely if the litigation received media attention at an earlier stage (Davis 1994). After the Supreme Court agrees to decide a case, most of its business takes place in private. The key exception is the oral argument, which is open to the public and press (Franklin and Kosaki 1995, 356; Ginsburg 1998, 280–1). Media attention to oral argument indicates that the case is perceived to be significant. *We hypothesize that the greater the amount of news content about the oral arguments in a case, the greater the intermedia coverage of its outcome.*

Perceived threat to the social system is a strong indicator of newsworthiness. Since at least the rights revolution of the 1950s and 1960s, Supreme Court cases affecting the American social system have focused primarily on citizens' civil rights and liberties (Epp 1998). Examples include First Amendment rights, privacy, and race relations. Jurisprudence in these areas settles questions about the rights and roles of citizens, especially political, racial, and ethnic minority groups. Whether the Court advances or restricts constitutional rights, these cases clarify the relationship between Americans, their fellow citizens, and the government. Media interest in these cases is identified in previous studies as positively associated with news coverage (Collins and Cooper 2011; Maltzman and Wahlbeck 2003; Slotnick and Segal 1998). *We hypothesize that more news organizations and types of news outlets will provide content about Supreme Court decisions addressing civil liberties or civil rights than rulings about other legal issues.*

The status of the majority opinion's author also signifies social significance. The chief justice is the most visible and prestigious member of the Court (Slotnick and Segal 1998; Vining and Wilhelm 2012). He is responsible for choosing the opinion author when he is in the majority and chief justices tend to select themselves disproportionately in politically salient cases (Epstein and Segal 2000). *We expect that there will be greater intermedia coverage of a Supreme Court decision if the chief justice, rather than an associate justice, writes the majority opinion.*

The Deviance of U.S. Supreme Court Decisions

A Supreme Court decision is deviant, whether positive or negative, if it has unusual characteristics. The deviance of a ruling is clear if it voids a law as unconstitutional, is decided with a *per curiam* opinion, or there is stark dissensus within the Court.

Decisions including a declaration of unconstitutionality invalidate definitively actions of the elected branches or state governments. These rulings can exhibit all three types of deviance. They are relatively rare and may result in substantial political or social changes. They often rebuke elected officials, and may be either countermajoritarian or in opposition to the preferences of a mobilized minority of citizens. In addition, these cases result in the type of judicial activism criticized by political elites. *We posit that when a Supreme Court decision includes a declaration of unconstitutionality it will be the subject of news content in a greater number and variety of news outlets in our data set.*

The Supreme Court's treatment of litigation can also be deviant. Most cases are argued orally with a signed opinion issued to explain the decision. In rare cases, the Court issues an unsigned *per curiam* opinion meaning the decision is "by the Court" instead of signed by an individual justice. These opinions are usually short and restricted to uncontroversial matters on the docket. Given the Court's lesser effort in these cases, the media are likely to perceive them as less worthy of news coverage than other cases on the docket. *We expect that a case with a* per curiam *opinion will receive less intermedia news coverage than a case argued orally and decided with a signed opinion.*

Statistical deviance is also apparent when intracourt conflict occurs (Slotnick and Segal 1998; Maltzman and Wahlbeck 2003). Although dissent *per se* is not rare, 5–4 divisions among the justices are more unusual and indicate sharp disagreement. A divided Court allows the media to frame the result as one side against the other. *We hypothesize that narrow majority opinion coalitions will result in more intermedia news coverage of a Supreme Court decision.*

Controls

In addition to predictors associated with social significance and deviance, we expect that the Supreme Court's procedures for releasing opinions affect news coverage. It is routine for the Supreme Court to release many decisions in June shortly before its summer recess. Widespread coverage of these decisions is more likely because the press anticipates their release and is prepared to report them. This reduces the costs of news production. We anticipate that Supreme Court decisions released in June are likely to be covered by a greater number of news outlets, and more types of news outlets, than those issued earlier in the term. On the other hand, the Supreme Court often releases multiple decisions on the same day. Greenhouse (1996) cites the simultaneous release of decisions as an obstacle for the media and Slotnick and Segal (1998) find evidence to support this claim. Even well informed reporters may be constrained by the news hole as well as finite time and resources (see Hamilton 2004).[4] *We expect that as the number of Supreme Court decisions released on a given day increases, fewer news outlets will feature a given ruling.*

EMPIRICAL ANALYSIS AND RESULTS

We investigate intermedia coverage of Supreme Court decisions by a set of prominent news organizations. Specifically, we examine news content in the *New York Times*, the *Los Angeles Times*, *NBC Nightly News*, *ABC World News*, The Drudge Report, and The Huffington Post. We focus on a set of high-profile news sources because they "frequently exert a substantial influence on the agenda of other news media" (McCombs 2004, 113) and are prominent participants in the discourse associated with the formation of public opinion. We examine the October 2008 and 2010 Supreme Court terms due to the availability of complete archives for all news outlets in our data.[5]

4 We also considered whether geographic proximity is likely to influence intermedia coverage of Supreme Court decisions. However, Beam (2003) demonstrates that news organizations with weaker local market orientations are less likely to be sensitive to spatial proximity due to their wider audiences. The national news outlets in our data fit this description. In addition, a consideration of geographic proximity is unwieldy here because the six news organizations we examine are located in several locations.

5 Archives for the 2009 term were not available due to hardware and software failures suffered by the administrators of the Huffington Post Archives and Drudge Report Archives.

We selected the news organizations in our data because of their large audiences and orientations toward national news. The *New York Times* and the *Los Angeles Times* were the third and fourth most circulated newspapers in the United States during 2009 according to the Audit Bureau of Circulations (Zimmerman 2009).[6] The NBC Nightly News and ABC World News have the largest audiences among television news programs according to Nielsen Media Research. The Drudge Report and The Huffington Post are online news curators. They have the largest readership among political websites not affiliated with a newspaper or television network.[7] Each newspaper and television network in our data had a Supreme Court correspondent in Washington, D.C. (Adam Liptak of the *New York Times*, David Savage of the *Los Angeles Times*, Pete Williams of NBC News, and Jan Crawford Greenburg of ABC News); neither website had a legal expert on its staff.

We acquired data about Supreme Court news from online databases. We searched for the term "Supreme Court" in newspapers using Lexis Nexis and in television news using the Vanderbilt Television News Archive.[8] We performed content analysis of the websites by viewing the archives of The Drudge Report and The Huffington Post.[9] These archives include screen captures of each website from throughout the specified day. We derived our list of decisions from the U.S. Supreme Court Database organized by citation.[10] Our data set includes 168 cases from the 2008 and 2010 terms.

The newspapers in our sample provided content about 54.17 percent of Supreme Court decisions during the 2008 and 2010 terms. Television broadcasts and online news sites covered 9.52 and 13.69 percent, respectively. Eleven decisions received coverage in all three types of media. Although these cases were only 6.55 percent of the Court's rulings, they are a substantial proportion of the decisions reported in television (68.75 percent) or online (47.83 percent) news. This is preliminary evidence of intermedia agreement about the Supreme Court's most salient rulings. That said, descriptive statistics do not explain why certain legal outcomes become the subject of coverage throughout the media.

6 *USA Today* and the *Wall Street Journal* have greater total circulation than either the *New York Times* or the *Los Angeles Times*. We omit them from our analysis due to their lesser reputation and focus on economic and financial news, respectively. In addition, we preferred to maintain an equal balance between elite newspapers, television network news programs, and elite news websites in our data.

7 See www.alexa.com/topsites/category/Top/News.

8 See tvnews.vanderbilt.edu.

9 The Drudge Report Archives are available at www.drudgereportarchives.com; The Huffington Post Archives are available at www.huffingtonpost.com/archive.

10 Data available at scdb.wustl.edu/data.php.

We construct regression models to explain intermedia coverage of Supreme Court decisions by elite news organizations. First, we estimate a Poisson regression to explain the number of news outlets reporting a given decision. This is appropriate because the dependent variable is a count of the number of outlets among the six in our data that covered each decision. Second, we estimate a logistic regression explaining why case outcomes were reported in all three types of outlets. The response variable is 1 if a ruling was covered in an elite newspaper, in broadcast news, *and* online, and 0 otherwise. The values of our dependent variables are determined by examining coverage in newspapers on the day after the decision and reporting on television news or online the same day as the decision.[11] Descriptions of our variables are available in Table 1.

The parameter estimates derived from our models are in Table 2. We use robust standard errors for all model specifications. Model 1 identifies relationships between our independent variables and the number of media outlets reporting each decision (range = 1–6).[12] We use a Poisson regression rather than its primary alternative, negative binominal regression, because a likelihood-ratio test reveals that overdispersion is not present ($p = 0.50$).[13]

The results of Model 1 support the hypotheses that social significance and deviance influence intermedia homogeneity in Supreme Court news. Two expressions of social significance, the filing of more amicus curiae briefs and greater media interest in oral arguments, have a statistically significant impact on the number of outlets covering each decision ($p < 0.0001$, two-tailed tests).[14] An increase in one amicus brief corresponds with an increased rate of coverage by a factor of 1.02 holding all other variables constant. Thus, the effect of a single amicus brief is not substantively large. However, when the number of amicus briefs is seventeen, one standard deviation above the mean, the count of outlets in our data reporting its outcome increases by a factor of

[11] We restricted our dependent variable to only the next opportunity for a report by the relevant news outlet. We do not examine prolonged reporting on a case.

[12] The use of a count model is warranted because our dependent variable is discrete and non-negative. Using OLS to interpret event count data may be inaccurate because OLS can render negative predicted counts. Additionally, OLS assumes constant variance, a criterion that is not met. If heteroskedasticity is not accounted for, this can result in underestimated standard errors.

[13] As a robustness check, we also estimated Model 1 with a negative binomial regression model. The results were nearly identical to the output of the Poisson regression.

[14] Poisson regression coefficients represent the log of the expected count and cannot be interpreted in a straightforward manner. To facilitate interpretation we convert the coefficients to incident rate ratios; these are the count model equivalent of odd ratios.

TABLE 1. *Description of variables.*

	Measurement	Expected effect	Mean (s.d.)
Dependent variables			
Number of outlets covering decision (Model 1)	Count of number of media outlets among the six we examine that cover case outcome on day after decision (min. = 0, max = 6).	n/a	1.20 (1.47)
Coverage in all types of outlets (Model 2)	1 if decision received coverage in newspapers, television news, and online news, 0 otherwise.	n/a	.07 (.25)
Independent variables			
Number of amicus curiae briefs	Count of number of amicus curiae briefs filed in case (min. = 0, max. = 64).	+	8.39 (9.26)
Coverage of oral arguments	Number of stories about oral arguments in the *New York Times*, the *Los Angeles Times*, *NBC Nightly News*, *ABC World News*, The Drudge Report, and The Huffington Post (min. = 0, max. = 9).	+	.99 (1.83)
Civil rights/liberties	1 if civil rights or civil liberties issues in case, 0 otherwise.	+	.30 (.46)
Declaration of unconstitutionality	1 if declaration of unconstitutionality in opinion, 0 otherwise.	+	.04 (.19)
Chief Justice author	1 if chief justice wrote opinion, 0 otherwise.	+	.10 (.29)
Per curiam opinion	1 if *per curiam* opinion issued in case, 0 otherwise.	–	.08 (.27)
Split court	1 if justices split 5–4 or 4–4 in vote, 0 otherwise.	+	.25 (.43)
Decisions on same day	Count of number of decisions announced on same day (min. = 1, max. = 6).	–	3.18 (1.46)
June opinion	1 if opinion released in June, 0 otherwise.	+	.33 (.47)

Notes: N = 168. Supreme Court decisions for each model; see text for details. Case characteristics derived from the U.S. Supreme Court Database.

1.40. Figure 1 shows this relationship. Each additional news item about a case at the oral argument stage increases the number of outlets providing decision coverage by a factor of 1.22. An increase in these stories from one standard deviation below the mean (0.84) to one above it (2.82) increases the expected

TABLE 2. *Results of regression models for mass media coverage of Supreme Court decisions, 2008 and 2010 terms.*

	Model 1: Poisson regression for number of outlets covering decision		Model 2: Logit model of coverage in all types of outlets		Model 3: Poisson regression for number of outlets covering decision if oral arguments reported	
	Coeff. (r.s.e.)	Z	Coeff. (r.s.e.)	Z	Coeff. (r.s.e.)	Z
Social significance						
Number of amicus curiae briefs	.02 (.006)	3.22	−.04 (.03)	−1.34	.01 (.007)	2.22
Coverage of oral arguments	.20 (.03)	7.35	.84 (.21)	4.06	–	–
Civil rights/liberties	.18 (.15)	1.21	−.25 (.94)	−.27	.14 (.17)	.86
Chief Justice author	.16 (.22)	.75	−.97 (1.12)	−.87	.28 (.21)	1.38
Deviance						
Declaration of unconstitutionality	−.30 (.37)	−1.04	−.14 (1.56)	−.60	.23 (.40)	.56
Per curiam opinion	−.43 (.40)	−1.07	–	–	−1.01 (.14)	−7.08
Split court	.37 (.16)	2.34	.37 (.96)	.38	.26 (.16)	1.57
Control variables						
June decision	.12 (.24)	.51	1.42 (1.45)	.98	.31 (.19)	1.60
Decisions same day	−.09 (.08)	−1.04	−.33 (.54)	−.60	−.12 (.07)	−1.66
N	168		168		60	
% reduction in error	46.84		45.45		23.73	
McFadden's R^2	.22		.41		.07	
	BIC = −383.71		% pred. corr. = 96.4		BIC = −12.89	

Notes: all standard errors are robust. *Per Curiam Opinion* excluded from Model 2 due to perfect prediction of negative outcome.

number of outlets from 1.18 to 1.76 times greater than when oral arguments failed to be reported. This is consistent with our expectation that once a news event breaches the news gate it is likely to be followed up by the original reporter and her colleagues (Shoemaker and Reese 1996). Our remaining

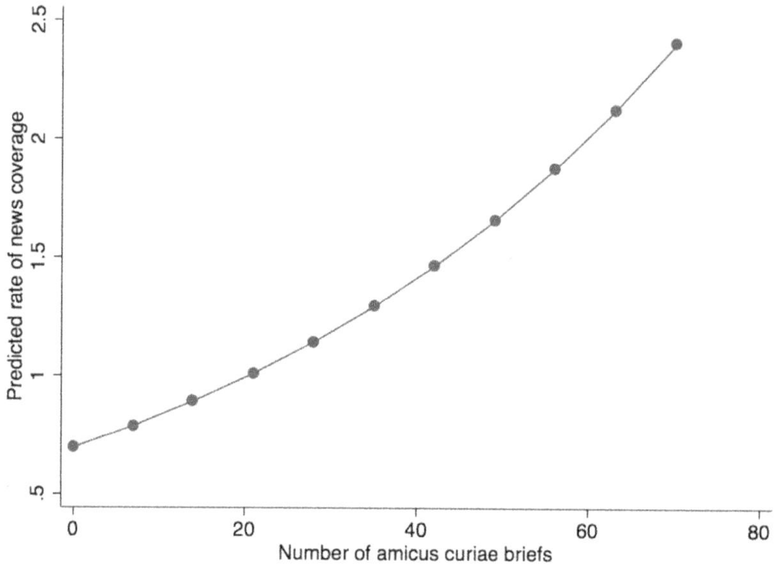

FIGURE 1. Predicted rate of news outlets covering Supreme Court decision by number of amicus curiae briefs filed, 2008 and 2010 terms.
Note: Estimates calculated using estimates from Model 1 and PrGen (Long and Freese 2006) with continuous variables at their means and dichotomous variables at their modal values.

indicators of social significance, civil rights/liberties issues and chief justice authorship, fail to achieve statistical significance.[15]

When the Supreme Court is divided internally about the proper outcome of a case, its decisions are predicted to receive coverage in 1.45 times as many outlets in our data. This is not surprising given expectations that the media is keen to report events that involve conflict or political significance. Twenty-five percent of decisions had tied or minimum winning coalitions, but these decisions are a disproportionate percentage of those reported by newspapers (38.46 percent), television (43.75 percent), and online news (43.48). Neither a declaration of unconstitutionality nor a *per curiam* opinion had a significant effect on the number of outlets providing coverage when controlling for other factors.

[15] We also estimated iterations of Model 1 and Model 3 including economic cases as a separate issue area in order to test their association with intermedia coverage. This variable was not significant in either model ($b = -0.22$, $p = 0.33$ for Model 1; $b = -0.17$, $p = 0.40$ for Model 3). The remaining results were nearly identical.

The results for Model 2 explain the occurrence of intermedia coverage of a decision in newspapers, television news, *and* news websites. We removed the *Per Curiam Opinion* variable from Model 2 because no case with an unsigned opinion received coverage in all three types of news outlets; this is consistent with our expectations. The treatment of cases with *per curiam* opinions signifies their lack of newsworthiness. The only variable to increase significantly the likelihood of intermedia coverage in all three types of outlets is the earlier reporting of oral arguments. This relationship is substantial – the odds of a decision being reported in all three media types are more than two times greater if oral argument was covered. When three stories about oral arguments are observed the odds of intermedia coverage are nearly thirteen times greater than otherwise. To estimate the impact of reporting about oral arguments we generate predicted probabilities with our continuous variables at their means and binary variables at their modal values (King, Tomz, and Wittenberg 2000; Long and Freese 2006). All else being equal, the probability of coverage in all three types of media remains under 0.25 until a third story about oral arguments (one standard deviation above the mean) appears. When a fifth news item about oral arguments is observed the predicted probability reaches 0.55 – better than even odds of extremely widespread coverage in a diverse set of news outlets.

News about oral arguments clearly influences intermedia coverage of Supreme Court decisions. In Model 3 we examine intermedia coverage of only the subset of cases covered at the oral argument stage (N = 60). This allows us to determine why cases that already passed through the news gate receive intermedia coverage at the decision stage. We find evidence that both the social significance of a decision, indicated by the number of amicus curiae briefs, and its deviant treatment, in the form of a *per curiam* opinion, affect intermedia coverage as expected. *Chief Justice Author*, *June Decision*, and *Decisions Same Day* approach but do not meet standard levels of statistical significance using two-tailed tests. We speculate that their narrow failures are due to the smaller sample analyzed using Model 3.

DISCUSSION AND CONCLUSIONS

In this chapter, we have synthesized the press-courts literature with an important theoretical perspective in communication research, gatekeeping theory, to develop and test an explanation for intermedia coverage of Supreme Court rulings in a diverse set of elite news sources. We find that the gatekeeping theory developed by Shoemaker and colleagues provides a useful explanation for news coverage of the Supreme Court. Its rulings receive intermedia coverage if their social significance is established by the filing of multiple amicus curiae briefs and media interest in the oral argument of the case. Prominent news sources are also likely to produce repeated messages about the most significant and divisive items on the Court's docket but little information about cases decided without a signed opinion.

Newspapers provide content about numerous Supreme Court cases. Individuals who learn about the Supreme Court from television and online news are exposed to a smaller segment of the Court's docket. Nonetheless, intermedia coverage of a subset of rulings increases the likelihood of popular awareness of some Supreme Court news. Citizens are most likely to receive elite discourse about cases with high stakes that continue an existing media narrative. When the elite media observe exogenous interest in a case from special interests, politicians, and other journalists, higher levels of intermedia coverage are likely to follow. When this occurs, the public is more likely to receive news about Supreme Court decisions in multiple outlets, including the elite media. No matter the point of view expressed by these news organizations, the existence of intermedia coverage is likely to increase public awareness of a legal ruling and contribute to the store of public affairs information retained by members of the public (Zaller 1992).

This study increases knowledge of the Third Branch and the Fourth Estate and updates the study of courts-press relations. We conclude that Supreme Court news is similar to the remainder of news content. The most important news items, as indicated by their social significance and deviance, receive intermedia coverage regardless of fragmentation. As a result, we expect that the public is likely to have a relatively united public agenda with regard to salient Supreme Court decisions.

REFERENCES

Ahlers, Douglas. 2006. "News Consumption and the New Electronic Media." *The International Journal of Press/Politics* 11: 29–52.

Beam, Randal A. 2003. "Content Differences between Daily Newspapers with Strong and Weak Market Orientations." *Journalism & Mass Communication Quarterly* 80: 368–390.

Boczkowski, Pablo. 2004. "The Processes of Adopting Multimedia and Interactivity in Three Online Newsrooms." *Journal of Communication* 54: 197–213.

Brians, Craig Leonard, and Martin P. Wattenberg. 1996. "Campaign Issue Knowledge and Salience: Comparing Reception from TV Commercials, TV News, and Newspapers." *American Journal of Political Science* 40: 172–193.

Brighton, Paul, and Dennis Foy. 2007. *News Values. Los Angeles*, California: Sage Publications.

Caldeira, Gregory A., and John R. Wright. 1988. "Organized Interests and Agenda Setting in the U.S. Supreme Court." *American Political Science Review* 82: 1109–1127.

Caldeira, Gregory A. 1991. "Courts and Public Opinion." In *The American Courts*, ed. by John B. Gates and Charles A. Johnson. Washington, D.C.: CQ Press.

Chaffee, Steven H., and Stacey Frank. 1996. "How Americans Get Political Information: Print versus Broadcast News." *Annals of the American Academy of Political and Social Science* 546: 48–58.

Chaffee, Steven H., and Miriam J. Metzger. 2001. "The End of Mass Communication?" *Mass Communication and Society* 4: 365–379.

Chibnall, Steve. 1977. *Law and Order News*. London: Tavistock Publications.

Collins, Lauren. 2008. "The Oracle." *The New Yorker*, October 13.

Collins, Todd A., and Christopher A. Cooper. 2011. "*Covering the Constitution: Newspaper Reporting of Supreme Court Constitutional Cases.*" Paper presented at the Annual Meeting of the Southern Political Science Association, New Orleans, Louisiana.

Comiskey, Michael. 1999. "Not Guilty: The News Media in the Supreme Court Confirmation Process." *Journal of Law & Politics* 15: 1–36.

Davis, Richard. 1994. *Decisions and Images: The Supreme Court and the Press*. Englewood Cliffs, New Jersey: Prentice-Hall.

2009. *Typing Politics: The Role of Blogs in American Politics*. New York: Oxford University Press.

2011. *Justices and Journalists: The U.S. Supreme Court and the Media*. New York: Cambridge University Press.

Druckman, James N. 2005. "Media Matter: How Newspapers and Television News Cover Campaigns and Influence Voters." *Political Communication* 22: 463–481.

Dubeck, Leslie B. 2007. "Understanding 'Judicial Lockjaw': The Debate Over Extrajudicial Activity." *New York University Law Review* 82: 569–601.

Dutta-Bergman, Mohan J. 2004. "Complementarity in Consumption of News Types across Traditional and New Media." *Journal of Broadcasting & Electronic Media* 48: 41–60.

Epp, Charles R. 1998. *The Rights Revolution*. Chicago: University of Chicago Press.

Epstein, Lee, and Jeffrey A. Segal. 2000. "Measuring Issue Salience." *American Journal of Political Science* 44: 66–83.

Eveland, William P., Jr., Mihye Seo, and Krisztina Marton. 2002. "Learning from the News in Campaign 2000: An Experimental Comparison of TV News, Newspapers, and Online News." *Media Psychology* 4: 355–380.

Eveland, William P., Jr., Krisztina Marton, and Mihye Seo. 2004. "Moving Beyond 'Just the Facts': The Influence of Online News on the Content and Structure of Public Affairs Knowledge." *Communication Research* 31: 82–108.

Franklin, Charles H., and Liane C. Kosaki. 1995. "Media, Knowledge, and Public Evaluations of the Supreme Court." In Lee Epstein (ed.), *Contemplating Courts*, pp. 352–375. Washington, D.C.: CQ Press.

Galtung, Johan, and Mari Holmboe Ruge. 1965. "The Structure of Foreign News: The Presentation of the Congo, Cuba and Cyprus Crises in Four Norwegian Newspapers." *Journal of Peace Research* 2: 64–90.

Gasper, John T. 2009. "Reporting for Sale: The Market for News Coverage." *Public Choice* 141: 493–508.

Ginsburg, Ruth Bader. 1998. "Informing the Public about the U.S. Supreme Court's Work." *Loyola University Chicago Law Journal* 29: 275–288.

Graber, Doris A. 2009. *Mass Media and American Politics*. Washington, D.C.: CQ Press.

Greenhouse, Linda. 1996. "Telling the Court's Story: Justice and Journalism at the Supreme Court." *Yale Law Journal* 105: 1537–1561.

Harcup, Tony, and Deirdre O'Neill. 2001. "What is News? Galtung and Ruge Revisited." *Journalism Studies* 2: 261–280.

Havick, John. 2000. "The Impact of the Internet on a Television-Based Society." *Technology in Society* 22: 273–287.

Heeter, Carrie, and Bradley Greenberg. 1985. "Cable and Program Choice." In D. Zillman and J. Bryant (eds.) *Selective Exposure to Communication*, pp. 203–224. Hillsdale, New Jersey: Lawrence Erlbaum Associates, Inc.

Hindman, Douglas Blanks, and Kenneth Wiegard. 2008. "The Big Three's Prime-Time Decline: A Technological and Social Context." *Journal of Broadcasting & Electronic Media* 52: 119–35.

Holmes, Lisa M. 2010. "*Media Coverage of Home State Nominees to the U.S. Courts of Appeals.*" Paper presented at the Annual Meeting of the Midwest Political Science Association, Chicago, Illinois. April 22–25.

Jerit, Jennifer, Jason Barabas, and Toby Bolsen. 2006. "Citizens, Knowledge, and the Information Environment." *American Journal of Political Science* 50: 266–282.

Jewkes, Yvonne. 2004. *Media and Crime*. Thousand Oaks, California: Sage Publications.

Johnson, Timothy R., and Andrew D. Martin. 1998. "The Public's Conditional Response to Supreme Court Decisions." *American Political Science Review* 92: 299–309.

Johnston, Christopher D., and Brandon L. Bartels. 2010. "Sensationalism and Sobriety: Differential Media Exposure and Attitudes toward American Courts." *Public Opinion Quarterly* 74: 260–285.

Katsh, Ethan. 1983. "The Supreme Court Beat: How Television Covers the U.S. Supreme Court." *Judicature* 67: 6–11.

Katz, Elihu. 1996. "And Deliver Us from Segmentation." *Annals of the American Academy of Political and Social Sciences* 546: 22–33.

King, Gary, Michael Tomz, and Jason Wittenberg. 2000. "Making the Most of Statistical Analyses: Improving Interpretation and Presentation." *American Journal of Political Science* 44: 341–355.

Kritzer, Herbert M. 2001. "The Impact of *Bush v. Gore* on Public Perceptions and Knowledge of the Supreme Court." *Judicature* 85: 32–38.

Larson, Stephanie Greco. 1985. "How the *New York Times* Covered Discrimination Cases." *Journalism Quarterly* 62: 894–896.

Lee, Jae Kook. 2007. "The Effect of the Internet on Homogeneity of the Media Agenda: A Test of the Fragmentation Thesis." *Journalism and Mass Communication Quarterly* 84: 745–760.

Lewin, Kurt. 1951. *Field Theory in Social Science: Selected Theoretical Papers*. New York: Harper and Row.

Long, J. Scott, and Jeremy Freese. 2006. *Regression Models for Categorical Dependent Variables Using Stata*, 2nd ed. College Station, Texas: Stata Press.

Lowery, Wilson. 2006. "Mapping the Journalism-Blogging Relationship." *Journalism* 7: 477–500.

Luberda, Rachel. 2008. "The Fourth Branch of the Government: Evaluating the Media's Role in Overseeing the Independent Judiciary." *Notre Dame Journal of Law, Ethics, and Public Policy* 22: 507–532.

Maier, Scott. 2010. "All the News Fit to Post? Comparing News Content on the Web to Newspapers, Television, and Radio." *Journalism and Mass Communication Quarterly* 87: 548–562.

Maltzman, Forrest, and Paul Wahlbeck. 2003. "*Salience or Politics: New York Times Coverage of the Supreme Court.*" Paper presented at the Annual Meeting of the Midwest Political Science Association.

McCombs, Maxwell. 2004. *Setting the Agenda: The Mass Media and Public Opinion. Cambridge*. England: Polity Press.

McLuhan, Marshall. 1964. *Understanding Media: The Extensions of Man*. New York: McGraw Hill.

McQuail, Denis. 1997. *Audience Analysis*. Thousand Oaks, California: Sage Publications.

Merrill, John C., and Ralph L. Lowenstein. 1979. *Media, Messages, and Men: New Perspectives in Communication*, 2nd ed. New York: Longman.

Meyer, Philip. 2009. *The Vanishing Newspapers: Saving Journalism in the Information Age*, 2nd ed. Columbia, Missouri: University of Missouri Press.

Newland, Chester A. 1964. "Press Coverage of the United States Supreme Court." *The Western Political Quarterly* 17: 15–36.

O'Callaghan, Jerome, and James O. Dukes. 1992. "Media Coverage of the Supreme Court's Caseload." *Journalism Quarterly* 69: 195–203.

Oliver, Pamela E., and Daniel J. Myers. 1999. "How Events Enter the Public Sphere: Conflict, Location, and Sponsorship in Local Newspaper Coverage of Public Events." *American Journal of Sociology* 105: 38–87.

Page, Benjamin I., and Robert Y. Shapiro. 1992. *The Rational Public: Fifty Years of Trends in Americans' Policy Preferences*. Chicago: University of Chicago Press.

Riffe, Daniel, Brenda Ellis, Momo K. Rogers, Roger L. Van Ommeren, and Kieran A. Woodman. 1986. "Gatekeeping and the Network News Mix." *Journalism Quarterly* 63: 315–321.

Roberts, Keith. 2007. "The Bar's Role in Public Education about the Courts." *Judges' Journal* 46: 27–35.

Sasser, Emery L., and John T. Russell. 1972. "The Fallacy of News Judgment." *Journalism Quarterly* 49: 280–284.

Segal, Jeffrey A., and Albert D. Cover. 1989. "Ideological Values and the Votes of Supreme Court Justices." *The American Political Science Review* 83: 557–565.

Shoemaker, Pamela J., Lucig H. Danielian, and Nancy Brendlinger. 1991. "Deviant Acts, Risky Business, and U.S. Interests: The Newsworthiness of World Events." *Journalism Quarterly* 68: 781–795.

Shoemaker, Pamela J. 1996. "Hardwired for News: Using Biological and Cultural Evolution to Explain the Surveillance Function." *Journal of Communication* 46: 32–47.

Shoemaker, Pamela J, and Stephen D. Reese. 1996. *Mediating the Message: Theories of Influence on Mass Media Content*, 2nd ed. New York: Longman.

Shoemaker, Pamela J, Martin Eichholz, Eunyi Kim, and Brenda Wrigley. 2001. "Individual and Routine Forces in Gatekeeping." *Journalism and Mass Communication Quarterly* 78: 233–246.

Shoemaker, Pamela J., and Akiba A. Cohen. 2006. *News Around the World: Content, Practitioners, and the Public*. New York: Routledge.

Shoemaker, Pamela J., and Tim P. Vos. 2009. *Gatekeeping Theory*. New York: Routledge.

Skewes, Elizabeth A., and Heather Black. 2006, "What's News in the United States?" In Pamela J. Shoemaker and Akiba A. Cohen, (eds.), *News around the World: Content, Practitioners, and the Public*, pp. 309–332. New York: Routledge.

Slotnick, Elliot E., and Jennifer A. Segal. 1998. *Television News and the Supreme Court: All the News that's Fit to Air?* New York: Cambridge University Press.

Solimine, Michael. 1980. "Newsmagazine Coverage of the Supreme Court." *Journalism Quarterly* 57: 661–663.

Spill, Rorie, and Zoe Oxley. 2003. "Philosopher Kings or Political Actors? How the Media Portray the Supreme Court." *Judicature* 78: 22–29.

Tarpley, J. Douglas. 1984. "American Newsmagazine Coverage of the Supreme Court, 1978–1981." *Journalism Quarterly* 61: 801–804, 826.

Tewksbury, David. 2005. "The Seeds of Audience Fragmentation: Specialization in the Use of Online News Sites." *Journal of Broadcasting and Electronic Media* 49: 332–348.

Tuchman, Gaye. 1978. *Making News: A Study in the Construction of Reality*. New York: The Free Press.

Vining, Richard L., Jr., and Teena Wilhelm. 2012. "The Chief Justice as Advocate-in-Chief: Examining the Year-End Report on the Federal Judiciary." *Judicature* 95: 267–274.

White, David M. 1950. "The 'Gate Keeper': A Case Study in the Selection of News." *Journalism Quarterly* 27: 383–390.

Zaller, John R. 1992. *The Nature and Origins of Mass Opinion*. New York: Cambridge University Press.

Zimmerman, Martin. 2009. "Circulation Drops at U.S. Newspapers as Readers Turn to Online News Sources." *The Los Angeles Times* October 29, p. A4

6

Constructing Harry Blackmun

RORIE SPILL SOLBERG AND ERIC N. WALTENBURG

Over much of U.S. history, the Supreme Court has been perceived as an idealized institution responsible for protecting our basic values and constitutional system. The justices preside in a "Marble Temple" and are characterized as "priests of the robe," to paraphrase Perry's poetic title.[1] Or they are described as "Delphic Oracles" who proclaim the Constitution's meaning unaffected by personal biases, preferences, or attitudes.[2] In other words, the justices are above politics, and yet, they are called on to answer the fundamental questions of politics: who gets what and how much.[3] Given their consequential position in our government and the small number of men and women who have been members of the "priestly tribe," one would think the justices would be well known names – perhaps not as well known as the president but certainly more well known than almost any one of the 535 members of Congress. And yet, the justices remain quite anonymous.[4]

Doubtless, much of that anonymity is a function of a conscious effort on the part of the justices and their unwillingness to join other institutions in broadcasting their proceedings.[5] The justices, however, are not wholly to blame. The High Court has always operated under different expectations – it is a political actor that is expected to remain aloof from the political fray.

[1] Perry, Barbara. 1999. *The Priestly Tribe: The Supreme Court's Image in the American Mind.* Westport, CT: Praeger.

[2] Segal, Jeffrey A. and Harold J. Spaeth. 2002. *The Supreme Court and the Attitudinal Model Revisited.* New York: Cambridge University Press, 26f.

[3] Lasswell, Harold D. 1936. *Politics: Who Gets What, When, and How.* New York: Whittlesey House, McGraw-Hill Book Co.

[4] See www.pewresearch.org/2010/08/03/the-invisible-court/ last accessed June 18, 2013

[5] See lawdigitalcommons.bc.edu/lsfp/487/ last accessed June 18, 2013.

Entering the battlefield tends to affect the Court's image and legitimacy.[6] Accordingly, it is not surprising that the Court does not actively attempt to frame public attitudes and reactions to its policy decisions. Instead, the Court leaves the framing and the interpretation of those decisions to the mass media and other interested stakeholders.[7]

As a result, the Court is often at the mercy of the media, and when covering the Court as a political institution, the media operate according to their own modes of behavior. Graber reports that political media coverage tends to be episodic and selective.[8] It is event oriented,[9] and "news pegs" are relied upon to organize stories.[10] All of which might suggest that the Court and its operating procedures are well suited to media coverage. The Court's decisions are unique and episodic. They present the event or "news peg" around which multiple, related stories might be combined. However, the practiced anonymity of the justices and the Court militates against copious media attention. The justices do not hold press conferences to announce and explain decisions; the Court does not provide any advanced notice to the media regarding the timing of decisions[11] nor do the justices grant many interviews. The Court does not provide any guidance on the content or relevance of the decisions; the Court does not forgo issuing multiple important opinions on a single day; the Court does not allow cameras to record its oral proceedings; and the Court does not necessarily issue clear and concise policy decisions. In short, covering the Court is frustrating and difficult for media outlets.

Perhaps this is why the justices are not household names and the Court is not a particularly well-understood institution. Given the consequence and increasing rarity of each Supreme Court opinion, that the justices remain closeted is of great importance in our democracy. After all, as then Governor and later Chief Justice Charles Evans Hughes famously observed, "[w]e are

[6] Gibson, James L. and Gregory A. Caldeira. 2009. *Citizens, Courts, and Confirmations: Positivity Theory and the Judgments of the American Public*. Princeton, NJ: Princeton University Press. The classic example is the *Dred Scott* case (60 U.S. 393 [1857]), and there is academic debate about the long-term effects of *Bush v. Gore* (531 U.S. 98 [2000]) and perhaps *National Federation of Independent Business v. Sebelius* (132 S.Ct. 2566 [2012]).

[7] Clawson, Rosalee and Eric N. Waltenburg. 2001. "The Legitimacy-Conferring Authority of the U.S. Supreme Court." *American Politics Research*. 29:566-607.

[8] Graber, Doris. 1993. *Mass Media and American Politics*. 4th ed. Washington, DC: CQ Press.

[9] Martindale, Carolyn. 1986. *The White Press and the Black Press*. New York: Greenwood Press.

[10] A "news peg" is the topic or event that generates news stories and media attention – for example, a Supreme Court ruling. See Clawson, Rosalee A., Harry C. "Neil" Strine IV, and Eric N. Waltenburg. 2003. "Framing Supreme Court Decisions." *Journal of Black Studies* 33:784-800.

[11] Other high courts will lock reporters in a room with the decisions before release so there is time to read and digest the content.

under a Constitution but the Constitution is what the judges say it is, and the judiciary is the safeguard of our liberty and our property under the Constitution."[12] In forthcoming work, we explore more fully the implications for public knowledge of the interaction of Court and media. Here, we restrict ourselves to analyzing the media's contribution to the anonymity of the justices. Specifically, we focus on the *New York Times*, the paper of national record,[13] and its coverage of Justice Harry A. Blackmun from his nomination to the post mortem release of his personal papers.

Exploration of the *Times*' coverage of Justice Blackmun provides arguably the greatest sample of media attention to the Court or to a justice. The *New York Times*, besides its national reputation and audience, follows the Court and the justices more than other newspapers and certainly more than any broadcast or cable medium.[14] As an object of the *Times*' coverage, Harry Blackmun provides an excellent case study. He served on the Court for a quarter of a century (1970 to 1994). He was present when the Court handed down and/or authored some of the most consequential civil liberties opinions of the late twentieth century. Indeed as we will discuss, his authorship of *Roe v. Wade*[15] and his concomitant association with the abortion issue brought him into sharp focus for the *Times* throughout his tenure on the bench. His ideological drift drew the attention of Court watchers. His personal relationship with Chief Justice Warren Burger ("The Minnesota Twins") and its demise provided one of the more visible personal conflicts between justices. He was more willing than most other justices to discuss "inside baseball" with journalists. He eventually developed a close relationship with Linda Greenhouse, the *Times* Court reporter for much of his tenure, which seems to have resulted in a greater frequency of *Times* coverage of Blackmun than the other justices.[16] Therefore, Blackmun, like the *New York Times*,

[12] Charles Evans Hughes, Speech before the Chamber of Commerce, Elmira, New York, May 3, 1907.—*Addresses and Papers of Charles Evans Hughes, Governor of New York, 1906–1908* (1908): 139.

[13] Althaus, Scott L., Jill A. Edy, and Patricia F. Phalen. 2001. "Using Substitutes for Full-Text News Stories in Content Analysis: Which Text Is Best?" *American Journal of Political Science* 45:707-723.

[14] Spill, Rorie L. and Zoe M. Oxley. 2003. "Philosopher Kings or Political Actors: How the Media Portray the Supreme Court." *Judicature* 87:23-29; Slotnick, Elliot E. and Jennifer A. Segal. 1998. *Television News and the Supreme Court: All the News That's Fit to Air?* New York: Cambridge University Press.

[15] 410 U.S. 113 (1973).

[16] See Davis, Richard. 2011. *Justices and Journalists: The U.S. Supreme Court and the Media*. New York: Cambridge University Press. See Chapter 6: "Becoming Newsworthy." However, in our dataset Linda Greenhouse's byline only appears on about 25 percent of all stories mentioning Justice Blackmun.

provides more fodder and likely "news" than many other justices do. By combining this justice with this newspaper, we give the media the best chance to educate the public about a justice. Using these data, we ask a series of questions: What has been the frequency of the *Times'* coverage of Justice Blackmun? What has been the nature of that coverage? Moreover, based upon that coverage, what can be known about Justice Harry Blackmun?

RESEARCH DESIGN AND ANALYSIS

To answer these questions, we mined the Proquest historical newspaper database for *New York Times* articles that mention Justice Blackmun from one year prior to his nomination to the High Court on April 14, 1970 beyond both his retirement (August 3, 1994) and death (March 4, 1999) through the release of his personal papers on March 4, 2004.[17] Each article was coded according to the nature by which Blackmun was mentioned – including merits votes; whether Blackmun wrote an opinion; his ideological or legal philosophy; and personal attributes or themes (his age, net worth, friends and family).[18] Up to three mentions per story were coded. This resulted in a dataset of 1,697 news stories, about seventy-one stories or eighty-five mentions per year.

The vast majority of the stories mentioning Blackmun during his tenure on the Court appeared while the justices were in session (about 93 percent). There was virtually no attention paid to Blackmun during the summer months, despite the opportunity for greater and easier coverage of the justice's activities off the bench. This pattern is identical to the one Diascro observed when examining broadcast media coverage of Chief Justice Rehnquist.[19] In terms of the number of mentions per story, only 20 percent of the stories have more than one mention and only one percent has three. In other words, whenever Blackmun is mentioned, it is generally in relation to one subject, although a second one is mentioned with some frequency. Given the

[17] We used the following Boolean search phrase: (harry blackmun AND pub (new york times)) AND (justice OR judge) AND ftany (yes) AND NOT (Obituary OR Classified Ad OR Display Ad).

[18] The actual coding categories are: vote on the merits (majority, dissent, or concurrence); opinion author (majority, dissent, or concurrence); oral argument; court "institutional" role; personal attributes; abortion; pre-law/pre-judge career; nomination/appointment/retirement; didn't participate; cert or non-merits decision.

[19] Diascro, Jennifer Segal. 2008. "The Legacy of Chief Justice Rehnquist: A View from the Small Screen." *Judicature* 92:106-117.

distribution of mentions, the following discussion will focus mostly on the first mention with some attention given to the second.

Approaching the categories from the broadest perspective, we find that 62 percent of the discussions focused upon Blackmun's Court work – that is, writing opinions, participation in oral argument, and merits voting. Within this broad category, discussions were dominated by his voting on the merits (60 percent). These mentions could be as minimal as, "In dissent, White was joined by Blackmun, Rehnquist, and Stevens" or as notable as "Justice Blackmun read a 'heated dissent' from the bench," as well as describing the dissenting opinion itself. Breaking this category down further, Blackmun's votes with the majority were mentioned nearly twice as often as his dissenting votes (37 percent versus 19 percent).

Opinion writing also was mentioned with some frequency; almost 32 percent of first mentions concerned Blackmun's role as some type of opinion author. Often, when Blackmun composed an opinion – whether for the Court majority, as a concurrence, or a dissent – the opinion was quoted at length in the *Times* article. More often early in our time period than later, the *Times* would publish long excerpts of major opinions. Not surprising, we find Blackmun is rarely mentioned in connection with oral argument or in his role presiding over his assigned circuit (the Court of Appeals for the Eighth Circuit), at least for the first mention (see Figure 1).[20]

When we observe second mentions at this same coarse level – recall that only 20 percent of news stories (n=198) contained such discussion – we note some differences. Of the second mentions, 62 percent relate to Blackmun's Court work. Mirroring the distribution of the first mentions, his other institutional roles are rarely reported. However, both voting on the merits and opinion authorship are now modal categories.

We turn our attention to a more detailed exploration of mentions unrelated to Blackmun's Court work and find that references to abortion dominate the distribution, accounting for well over 50 percent. As we will discuss in more detail, these mentions are not reports of Blackmun's opinion in *Roe v. Wade* or its progeny.[21] The data also show that when abortion is mentioned, it is discussed first. Of the 122 news stories with a second noninstitutional mention, only 12 percent deal with abortion,

[20] We found one notable exception to this rule: Nebraska Press Association v. Stuart, 427 U.S. 539 (1976).

[21] Reports on his opinions or votes on the merits in *Roe* and later abortion cases would be coded under "Court work."

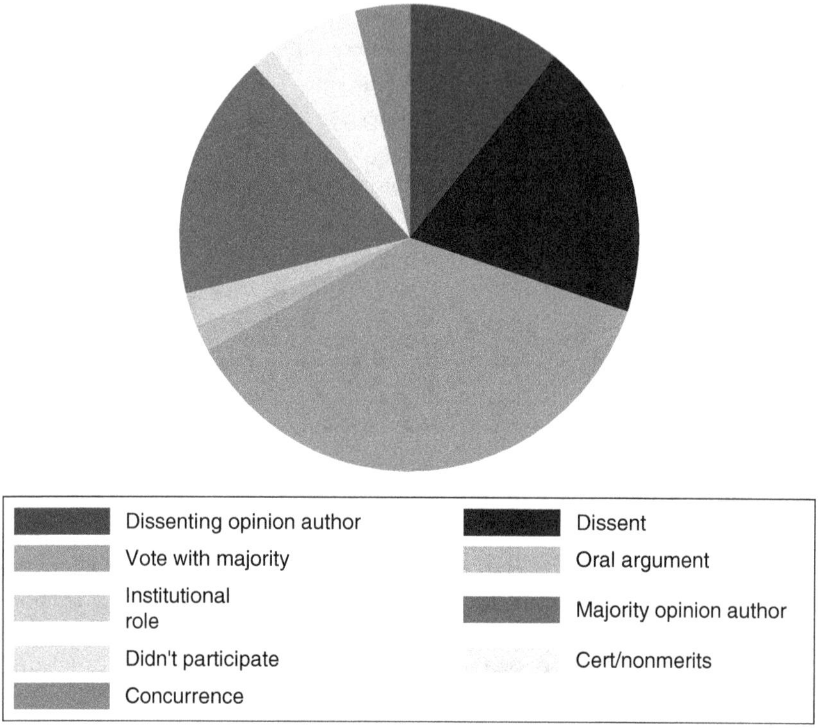

FIGURE 1. Distribution of first mentions, Blackmun's work on the Court.

whereas 43 percent and 29 percent of these second mentions concern ideology or personal stories, respectively. The relatively large presence of ideology and personal stories in noninstitutional second mentions is quite different from their share of first mentions. Ideology accounts for 14 percent and personal matters account for 19 percent of the total noninstitutional first mentions (see Figure 2).

Following abortion, the two largest noninstitutional categories are personal or private life stories (19 percent) and ideology or legal philosophy (14 percent). With respect to references concerning Blackmun's private narrative, Figure 3 shows that the coverage is extremely episodic. There are terms with virtually no discussion of Blackmun as a private citizen interspersed with terms where mentions to this side of the justice hit 100 stories or more. Personal references do seem to dip a bit at the tail end of Blackmun's tenure (see Figure 3). This, however, is a bit deceiving, as the mentions of his personal or private life decreased dramatically between his twenty-second and twenty-third terms on the bench. In reality, the number of mentions in his penultimate term is double that of the median for the full time series (twenty-nine versus sixty-two

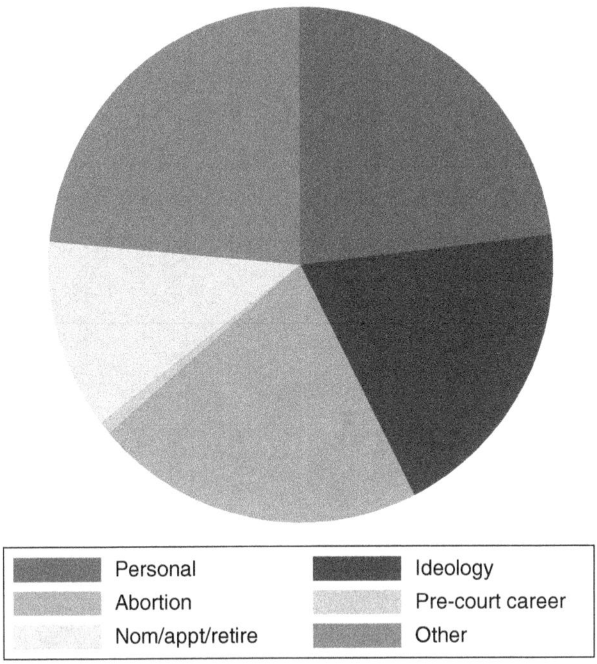

FIGURE 2. Distribution of first mentions, Blackmun's non-work on the Court.

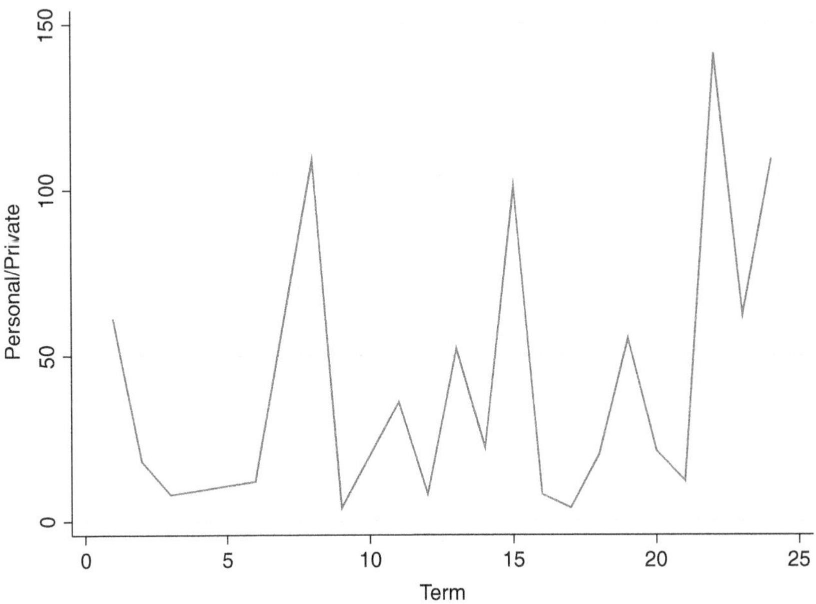

FIGURE 3. Personal or private mentions of Blackmun across terms.

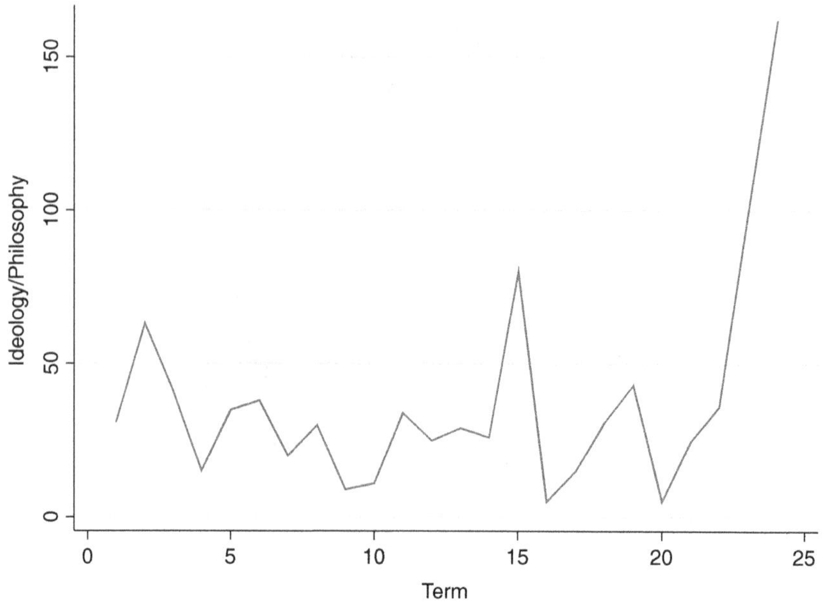

FIGURE 4. Mentions of Blackmun's ideology or legal philosophy.

references). It is also noteworthy (although not surprising) that personal references to Blackmun took on a larger share of the distribution of mentions during summer recesses. Though the total number of stories containing references to Blackmun while the Court was not in session comprise only 6.8 percent of our data, personal references are the modal category comprising 22.6 percent of these mentions.[22]

In terms of ideology, we see a trend similar to initial personal mentions (see Figure 4). It is sporadic and episodic with a similar spike around 1984. The marked upward climb at the end of the figure is a result of Blackmun announcing and then retiring at the end of the October Term 1993. Thus, mentions of Blackmun with respect to phenomena other than his work on the Court topped out at his retirement.

The top three categories switch places a bit in the secondary mentions of noninstitutional attributes. Abortion and ideology/judicial philosophy swap places with personal mentions maintaining its "silver" status. Other coded categories remain practically off the record.

[22] The "personal" references category is followed by our "other" category (17 percent) and "ideology" (13 percent). No other category reaches 10 percent.

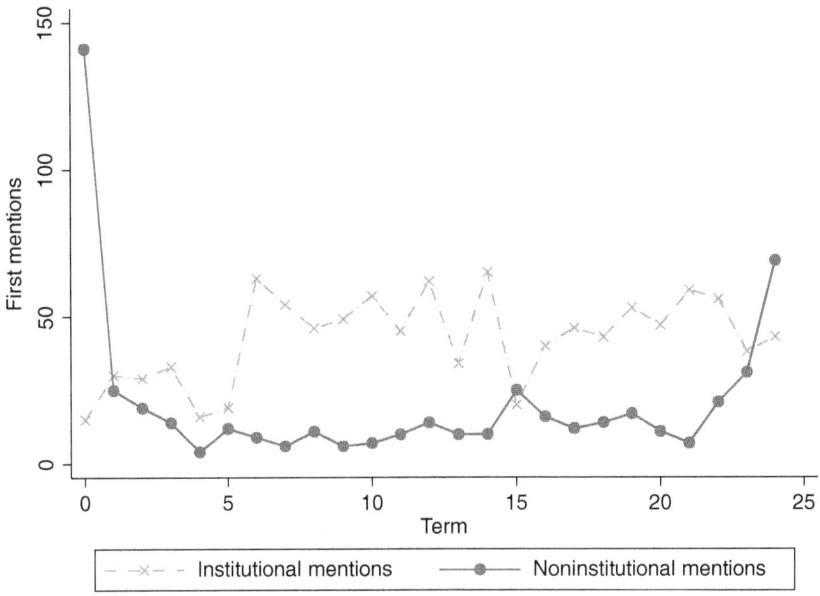

FIGURE 5. Institutional vs. noninstitutional first mentions over time.

Returning to our institutional categories and considering these over time, we do not find any trends similar to the noninstitutional categories. Figure 5 charts institutional versus noninstitutional first mentions over time and illustrates this observation well. For the most part, both first mentions of Blackmun's votes and opinion writing are quite stable over time. The one exception is opinion authorship where there is an initial spike followed by a leveling out. In all likelihood, the initial surge is the result of Blackmun's first published opinions. The press tends to concentrate on a "freshman's firsts."

One additional observation bears note. As expected, the coverage of Blackmun, in general, is bi-modal. There is a great deal of attention paid to Blackmun as a nominee to the Court after President Nixon's announcement. Relatively little attention is paid to the justice throughout his tenure until he begins aging significantly. Then the coverage explodes after Blackmun announces his retirement partway through his twenty-fourth term on the bench (see Figure 6). A t-test of significance shows the difference in coverage between the bookend terms and the bulk of his time on the bench is blindingly significant (t=6.7, p=0.000).

Given the frequency of abortion-related mentions and the conventional wisdom that ties the justice closely to this issue, we now turn to a more systematic exploration of that relationship.

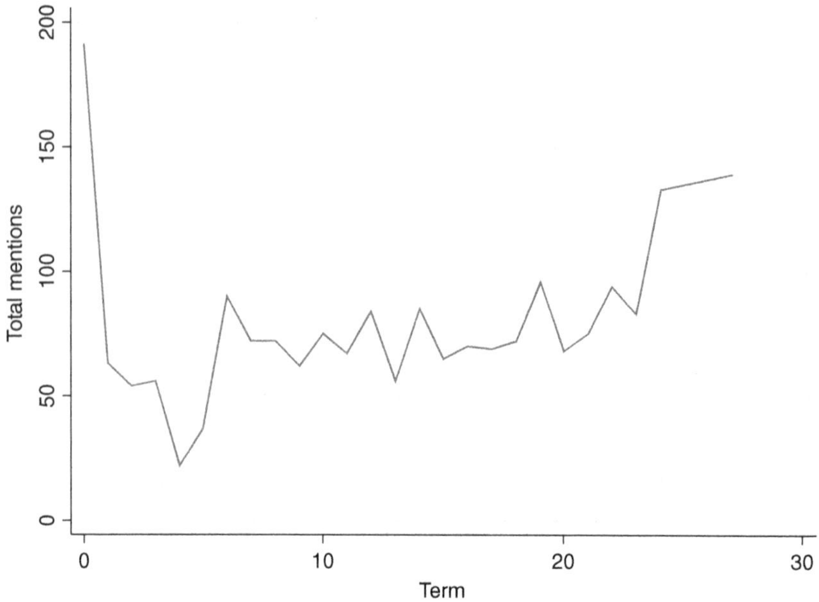

FIGURE 6. Total mentions of Blackmun across terms.

ABORTION AND HARRY BLACKMUN: CONSTRUCTING A LEGACY

Perhaps no other justice besides John Marshall or Roger Taney is as closely associated with a single case and majority opinion as Harry Blackmun. In his third year on the High Bench, Warren Burger, his close friend and Chief Justice, entrusted him with the opinion in *Roe v. Wade*. Many are familiar with Blackmun's struggle while writing this opinion. He took over the Supreme Court library and spent an extended period crafting the opinion. Despite six other members of the Court joining him on the opinion, *Roe v. Wade* is Blackmun's legacy. In his 1982 interview with CNN, Blackmun noted, "I knew it was a no-win case, but I didn't ask for it... I am mildly annoyed with those, law professors included, that personalize it. It was a decision of the court, not my decision. There were seven votes."[23] Yet, he also seemed to acknowledge that decision as his legacy, "even though I think I've contributed a little bit in other areas of law," Blackmun stated off the record.[24]

23 "Blackmun accepts Aftermath of Writing Abortion Opinion," *New York Times* (January 17, 1983): A20.

24 Gorny, Cynthia, "Justice Blackmun, Off the Record," *New York Times* (March 3, 1999): 15. This statement was not published until after the Justice's death. He was speaking at the Aspen Center.

While Justice Blackmun eventually owned his legacy and fought against a steady stream of attacks on the so-called superprecedent at the time of the decision, it was not necessarily clear that this case would define the justice for eternity. After the decision, the *New York Times* published only three articles on the case. One included excerpts of the opinions, a clear indication that the case was not dismissed as inconsequential. However, only twenty-one paragraphs of the opinion were excerpted – fifteen from the majority and six from the dissent. When the Court decided *Webster v. Reproductive Services*[25] in 1989, as a contrast, thirty-four paragraphs of Chief Justice Rehnquist's opinion were published, and the excerpts took up two full pages of the newspaper. Despite Warren Weaver, then Court reporter for the *Times*, calling *Roe* "a historic resolution of a fiercely controversial issue,"[26] Jane E. Brody was more accurate when she wrote, "[t]he full impact of the Supreme Court's sweeping decision on abortion may not be felt for a generation or more."[27] The same could be said for Justice Blackmun; it took some time for the association to escalate and solidify.

According to coverage in the *Times*, the initial negative reaction to *Roe* came from the Catholic Church and some Catholic lay associations. On the other hand, bishops from Blackmun's church, United Methodist, were committed to fighting any amendment to overturn the decision. As corroborated by our data, the decision, and the political fervor surrounding it, took some time to percolate, but by Ronald Reagan's reelection in 1984, *Roe* and Blackmun were significant targets of the emerging New Right. Yet, at the time of the decision, the reaction was minimal. As a comparison, we offer the frenzy of stories accompanying Justice Blackmun's order in the *Nebraska Press Association* case[28] and the subsequent merits decision. Blackmun's stay upholding a gag order on the media during a high profile murder trial was issued in December of October term 1975. Granted, the First Amendment, particularly freedom of the press, was clearly salient to the *Times* for multiple reasons. Free speech and press had been important enough to the Founders to place it in the Bill of Rights. There was copious precedent supporting the liberty, unlike the decision in *Roe*. Moreover, the salience of the case touched both the *Times'* audience and the *Times* as a business venture/media outlet. Still, in comparison to the three stories about the *Roe* decision, there were over twenty stories that reported on Justice Blackmun in connection with the Nebraska gag rule case – many discussing his actions as justice for the circuit. Coverage of a justice's role as circuit justice is exceedingly rare.

25 492 U.S. 490 (1989)

26 Weaver, Warren, "National Guidelines Set by a 7-to-2 Vote," *New York Times* (January 22, 1973): 1.

27 Brody, Jane E., "Landmark Ruling on Abortion," *New York Times* (January 28, 1973): 3.

28 427 U.S. 539 (1976)

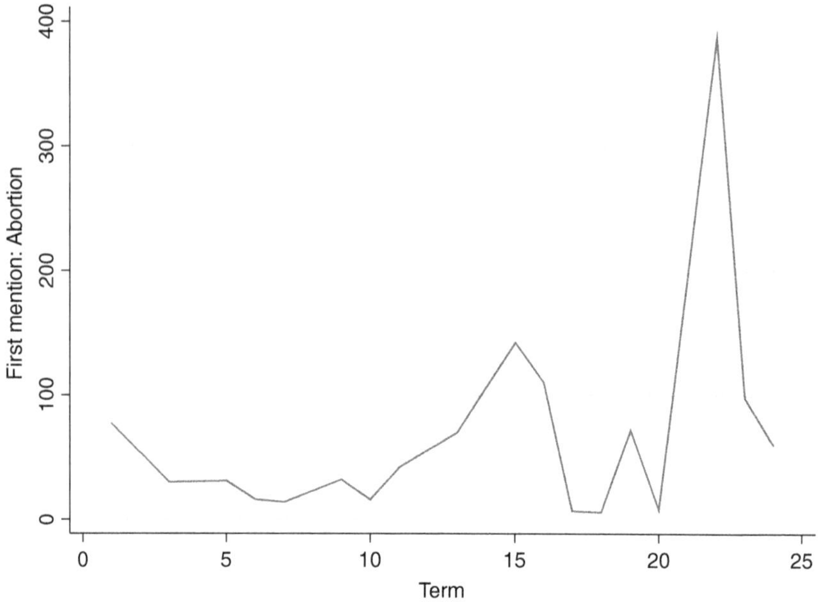

FIGURE 7. Mentions of abortion across terms.

After its slow start, we find the first mentions of abortion skyrocket following the election of Ronald Reagan. In the decade immediately subsequent to the landmark and controversial *Roe* decision, only 35 percent of the noninstitutional first mentions refer to abortion. By the 1980s and beyond, the percentage nearly doubles (62 percent). The relationship is clear: the Rehnquist Court was perceived as a danger to *Roe* and Blackmun's legacy. With each subsequent appointment and decision, references to Blackmun as the author of *Roe* and as its increasingly solitary defender continue. Although the incidence of mentions is small, even after his death (in the 2000s), we see the numbers jump – reaching 76 percent of these mentions relating to abortion. A great deal of the coverage of Blackmun's papers after their initial release also focused upon his role in the development of the abortion debate. Figure 7 displays this general trend nicely. In particular, we find it interesting that the steep monotonic rise of stories with references to Blackmun and abortion between term 10 (October Term 1979) and term 15 (October Term 1984) tracks with Reagan's first election and his reelection campaign. The other drastic and striking spike coincides with the *Planned Parenthood v. Casey*[29] decision in term 21 (October Term 1991) – the last major frontal attack on *Roe* during Blackmun's tenure (see Figure 7).

[29] 505 U.S. 833 (1992).

Overall, from the start of his tenure on the bench through the release of his personal papers, there were 105 stories that mentioned abortion (firstly or secondly) and Justice Blackmun. To engage in a more detailed exploration of the *Times*' mentions of Blackmun with respect to abortion, we further coded these stories for basic content as follows: decision, oral argument, docketing, violence/protests, anniversary of *Roe*, other court processes, commentary/letter, other politics, and other. The olio category of "other" includes stories that covered his 1982 CNN interview. We did that because the content ranged over several of our categories: discussion of Joseph F. Kobylka's biography, Linda Greenhouse's biography (both of which included information on his background, decisions, personal life, and legacy) as well as other information. An excellent example of the "other" category that does not link Blackmun to *Roe* is found in Linda Greenhouse's story "Battle Over; Now, A War"[30] reporting on three more abortion cases coming on the heels of *Webster* that she categorized as "offer[ing] a more direct road map for overturning Roe v. Wade." In the story, she discusses the recent decision, the new cases and summarizes the *Roe* opinion without ever connecting Blackmun to *Roe*. The only mention of Blackmun is in reference to his likely vote on a deadlocked 1987 abortion case from Illinois.

As suggested by our earlier analyses, a plurality of those stories focused on decisions of the Court – 28.5 percent or thirty stories (Recall, only three examined *Roe*, per se). The next two categories were commentary/opinion/letters at 16 percent and "other" at 15 percent. Coming in fourth was reports of violence/protests related to the abortion issue – firebombing of clinics, threats to the justice or others (10.5 percent). If we collapse oral argument stories and docketing stories, they comprise about 10 percent of the total as well. No other categories make up more than 10 percent of the total.

Although we might be slicing the onion a bit thin, we also coded these same categories distinguishing between stories that name Blackmun as the "author of *Roe*" and stories that do not, like the Greenhouse story mentioned above. The categories most likely to identify or connect Blackmun as the author of *Roe* were "other," which makes sense as many of these stories were longer discussions of the justice overall, commentaries, and stories describing violence/protests related to the abortion issue. David Brooks, in a commentary on April 21, 2005, noted that, "Justice Harry Blackmun did more inadvertent damage to our democracy than any other 20th-century American." He went on to blame *Roe* and Blackmun for the "cycle of viciousness and counter-viciousness that has poisoned public life ever since and now threatens

30 Greenhouse, Linda, "Battle Over; Now, a War," *New York Times* (July 4, 1989): A1.

to destroy the Senate as we know it."[31] Next are two examples of coverage of protests or violence, which cite Blackmun as *Roe's* author. In October 1984, just before the presidential election, Justice Blackmun, "author of Roe," received death threats from the Army of God; the guard at the Supreme Court was doubled in response.[32] Or in January 1985, right before Reagan's second inaugural and the anniversary of *Roe*, the *Times* reported on a planned demonstration on the steps of the Supreme Court building. The Pro-life Nonviolent Action Project planned a mock funeral and then hoped to deliver personally a letter to Justice Blackmun, "author of Roe."[33] It is these types of stories that continually connect Blackmun to *Roe*, the abortion issue and women's equality overall *not* the coverage of the barrage of cases challenging *Roe* in the subsequent years. Indeed, only 2 percent or six decision stories covering *Roe's* progeny refer to Blackmun as the author of *Roe*.

Based on this analysis, we suggest that it was not the challenges to *Roe* and Blackmun's continued support of his original decision that gave rise to his legacy – as he put it, "his tag is 'Author of the abortion decision.'"[34] Rather, it was coverage of the increasingly charged political environment surrounding the abortion issue, its prominent place in electoral politics post-Reagan and eventually confirmation politics. As we report in forthcoming work, during the four most recent confirmation hearings, most substantive issues were infrequently the topic of questions. Of the substantive issues, abortion questions were second only to questions regarding discrimination writ large.

We continued to investigate how the *Times* supported Blackmun's legacy as linked to *Roe* by coding each story for whether it included language that suggested the indelible mark *Roe* left on Blackmun and Blackmun left on women's reproductive rights. Twenty-five of the 105 total stories contained such language; not surprisingly, all of them were included in the 66 stories naming Blackmun as author of *Roe*. For example, we can turn to the same David Brooks commentary mentioned previously. On a somewhat lighter note, in a short piece on "interactivity" and technology the *Times* reported on "Oyez Baseball,"[35] an interactive quiz asking Internet visitors to match justices with major league baseball players. Jerry Goldman, originator of the Oyez site, argued that Bobby Thomson best represented Justice Blackmun. "Just as Thomson, as a 1951 New York Giant, smacked the pennant-winning

[31] Brooks, David, "Roe's Birth, and Death," *New York Times* (April 21, 1985): A23.

[32] Barron, James, "Abortion Issue Takes a Violent Turn," *New York Times* (November 25, 1984): E2.

[33] "Abortion Clinic on Special Alert," *New York Times* (January 17, 1985): A14.

[34] *Supra* note 22.

[35] baseball.oyez.org/ last accessed on August 28, 2013.

Shot Heard Round the World, Blackmun will be remembered for a single swing – he wrote the majority opinion in the Roe v. Wade abortion case."[36] As expected, the bulk of these stories (17 or 68 percent) appear in our broad based "other" or commentary/letter categories.

If we examine the legacy stories by date, we find very few news pegs. We operationalize a news peg as a series of stories that fall within four weeks all related to the same topic. Not surprisingly, news pegs that included multiple legacy stories centered on Blackmun announcing his retirement, and his death. Broadening our news peg search to include all abortion-related mentions of Justice Blackmun, we find seven news pegs. These include the two noted previously, retirement announcement and death, and two related to abortion decisions – the only two cases to generate a string of coverage are *Thornburgh v. American College of Obstetricians and Gynecologists*[37] and *Casey*. One news peg occurred at the release of his personal papers five years after his death. The remaining two news pegs relate to the abortion issue but not to a specific case. The earliest peg occurs in early 1985 surrounding threats to the justice and a bullet fired through his window. The other abortion related peg falls at the start of the October Term 1988. At this time, Justice Blackmun publicly stated that he saw a "very distinct possibility that the Court would find a case this term to use as a vehicle for overruling that decision [*Roe*]."[38] In the same article, Linda Greenhouse notes that the three oldest justices are the three staunchest supporters of abortion rights underscoring the fragility of *Roe*. These data, again, support our contention that media coverage and the strident political debate created most of Blackmun's legacy related to abortion.

CONCLUSION

This brief exploration of the incidence and nature of the *New York Times* coverage of Justice Harry A. Blackmun yields several points that warrant greater emphasis and discussion. First, it has become almost commonplace for students of judicial politics to bemoan the anemic quality of the media's treatment of the Supreme Court.[38] Our findings suggest, however, that a mild corrective on this point might be in order. Simply put, it seems fair to say that

36 Mirapaul, Matthew, "Whose Opinions have the Zip of a Fastball?" *New York Times* (October 25, 2001):5.

37 476 U.S. 747 (1986).

38 See, for example, the brief review in Clawson, Rosalee A. and Eric N. Waltenburg. 2009. *Legacy and Legitimacy: Black Americans and the Supreme Court*. Philadelphia: Temple University Press, 68f.

a large amount of information about Justice Blackmun is available, although this information is unlikely to be especially detailed with respect to the substance of Blackmun's (or for that matter, the Court's) decisional behavior or policy outputs.

To be sure, the *Times* reported Blackmun's votes and opinions. Recall that we found that the largest share of mentions of Blackmun were under the category of his institutional role, his work on the Court, and within this cluster of topics, Blackmun's voting and opinion writing loom large. We know from prior research, however, that the media's coverage of the policy and decisional outputs of the Court is inadequate and/or skewed.[39] In particular, certain issues are emphasized over others, and little attention is paid to providing full, meaningful explanations or analyses of the policy ramifications of the Court's decisions. And although we can only offer an impressionistic evaluation,[40] our sense is that the *Times*' coverage of Blackmun is consistent with these earlier findings.

Another point deserving additional comment is the degree to which the prevailing political context affected the media's attention to Blackmun. Blackmun was simultaneously blessed and cursed according to the (purported) ancient Chinese proverb: "May you live in interesting times." From the moment his name was mentioned as a possible Court appointee to his being assigned the responsibility of writing for the majority in *Roe* – arguably the Court's most politically explosive case since *Brown*[41] – to the emergence of the Rehnquist Court from the mid-1980s to the end of his tenure, Blackmun lived in interesting times. The political battles and controversies surrounding his nomination and appointment all but guaranteed the press would revisit it (if even briefly) every time a subsequent vacancy on the High Bench occurred (at least until the dramatic events surrounding the Bork and Thomas nominations trumped Blackmun's ascent in terms of primacy and public interest).

As we have noted, by the end of the 1970s, *Roe* – its preservation or its elimination – had stepped out of legal chambers and into the political arena. It became an issue in presidential campaigns; it became *the* issue in Senate hearings on judicial appointments; organized interests formed around it and propagandized for members and money with respect to it. The presence of

[39] See Franklin, Charles and Liane C. Kosaki. 1995. "Media, Knowledge, and Public Evaluations of the Supreme Court." In *Contemplating Courts*. Ed. Lee Epstein Washington, DC: CQ Books: 352-375; O'Callagahan, Jerome and James O. Dukes. 1992. "Media Coverage of the Supreme Court's Caseload." *Journalism Quarterly* 69:195-203; Shaw, David. 1981. "Media Coverage of the Court: Improving but Still Not Adequate." *Judicature* 65:18-24.

[40] We only coded for mentions, not the quality of those mentions.

[41] *Brown v. Board of Education* (347 U.S. 483 [1954]).

abortion in the nation's ongoing political dialogue, the degree to which it is freighted with emotion and its divisiveness ensures that it is a topic of regular media attention. As the author of *Roe*, this ensured that Harry Blackmun is a subject of regular media attention (or at least mention), too. Blackmun's inevitable aging, as well as the Court's increasing conservatism, made for interesting times as well. With each presidential election, with each Republican victory, with each passing year, Blackmun's legacy as the author of *Roe* and its protection of a woman's right to choose became more uncertain.[42] This too encouraged the *Times* to discuss Harry Blackmun.

Finally, as the association between Justice Blackmun and the abortion issue that we have documented indicates, the media are a powerful force shaping the public's perception of the judiciary – and not just as an institution[43] or toward its policy outputs[44] – but with respect to its members as well. Indeed, the *Times* (and presumably other media outlets) framed Blackmun in terms of *Roe* and abortion, inextricably binding the two together. That this media effect exists for a justice who was far more likely to engage the media and the public than most of his counterparts suggests that, if the media chooses to cover a justice, *how* they cover that justice determines how the public understands that justice. In no small part, then, the "public" justice is a media construction.

42 A point the justice himself raised on occasion.

43 Gibson and Caldeira 2009.

44 Clawson, Rosalee A. and Eric N. Waltenburg. 2003. "Support for a Supreme Court Affirmative Action Decision: A Story in Black and White." *American Politics Research* 31:251-279.

7

On and Off the Supreme Court Beat: Differences in Newspaper Coverage of the Supreme Court and the Implications for Public Support

NICHOLAS LAROWE AND VALERIE HOEKSTRA

INTRODUCTION

The Supreme Court recently has heard a number of high-profile cases that have drawn significant public attention. For example, recent Gallup polls have shown significant awareness of the Court's decision on the *National Federation of Independent Business v. Sebelius* (2012) – commonly referred to as the Affordable Care Act case – and, in fact, that people changed their views specifically toward Chief Justice John Roberts. Moreover, recent research has also dispelled the notion that the public is "woefully ignorant" about the Supreme Court (Gibson and Caldeira 2009). Instead, they find widespread knowledge about the Court. This finding is consistent with other work that found significantly high levels of knowledge in the local communities that generated the court cases (Hoekstra 2000, 2003) as well as knowledge of some national cases (Franklin and Kosaki 1995; Franklin, Kosaki, and Kritzer 1995). Obviously, but importantly, it is the mass media that contribute to this knowledge since the Court remains one of the most reclusive of political institutions. Therefore, understanding the nature of mass media coverage of the Supreme Court is essential to understanding how the public perceives the Court and the decisions it announces.

As important as this link is, the overwhelming majority of research on the impact of Court decisions on public opinion and support for the institution itself overlooks the important role of the news media. In the research that does address some aspect of the media, they still get short shrift in one of two ways. First, much of the research is more interested in understanding the causal links between the Supreme Court and public opinion by comparisons with other institutions or across issues (Hoekstra 1995; Mondak 1991). The ways that media actually cover decisions is not usually central to the analysis. Second, although some research examines the quantity and quality of media coverage of the Supreme Court, it often fails to connect that to public opinion (e.g., Slotnick and Segal 1998; Davis 1987). The research we present in this chapter attempts to look directly at how media coverage influences how the public responds to Court opinions.

PREVIOUS RESEARCH: MEDIA COVERAGE AND THE SUPREME COURT

In one of the first empirical investigations, Ericson (1977) examined newspaper coverage of the Court's 1974 term and found that at most, 112 of 145 of the Court's decisions were covered by the *New York Times* – the paper of record. Of these 112, only 32 received what he considered "complete" coverage. Ericson assesses completeness by examining whether: the decision was even reported, its impact was considered, the coverage was balanced, the process was discussed, the larger context was included, and there was reporting of reactions to the decision. He finds a high correlation between quantity and quality of coverage, meaning that more than three-quarters of the Court's written decisions received less than complete coverage, if they were covered at all (Ericson 1977). Solimine (1980) finds that though newsmagazine coverage is even less frequent than newspaper coverage, the quality of reporting, according to Ericson's rubric, is higher. In her research comparing local versus national coverage of cases and resulting levels of information, Hoekstra (2000, 2003) found that local coverage exceeded national coverage. Moreover, the local media tended to focus more on the impact of the decision than did the national media.

Other scholars have taken a different tack; rather than focusing on quality and quantity, they have asked what explains coverage (or lack thereof) of the Court in the first place. Ura (2009) draws on previous work (e.g., Flemming et al. 1997) to argue that Court rulings that change a policy status quo are more likely to draw attention, and he finds that Court rulings expanding the scope of gay rights draw more coverage than those affirming its current sphere. Sill, Metzgar, and Rouse (2013) employ a multifaceted concept of newsworthiness (case origin, court behavior, issue area, case participants, and case salience) to explain coverage of the Supreme Court. They also investigate to what extent newsworthiness and a case's long-term legal significance intersect. They find significant overlap between a reporter's assessment of newsworthiness and the actual long-term legal significance of a case.

A recent line of research looks at the role of reporters who are specifically assigned to the Supreme Court (beat reporters) and those who only cover the Court occasionally (non-beat reporters) (e.g., Spill and Oxley 2003, Davis

1994). Not surprisingly, beat reporters have a far more sophisticated and nuanced grasp of the legal questions and Court dynamics. Beat reporters tend to use more technical (that is, legal) terms in their writing, but they have also been criticized as being perhaps too deferential in their reporting on the Court (Davis 1994; Segal and Slotnick 1998). Comparing print to broadcast coverage, Spill and Oxley's study (2003) vindicates previous qualitative work (e.g., Davis 1987, 1994), finding that newspaper coverage was generally superior in quality and quantity to television coverage. In addition, they also provide evidence for the claim that television news and non-beat reporters are less deferential to the Court and devote attention to the socio-political implications of a decision, in contrast to a beat reporter's focus on the legal context of a decision – similar to Hoekstra's findings about local versus national coverage (2000, 2003).

A combination of complex rulings, varying reporter expertise, and a lack of interpretive assistance from the justices means the focus is on rulings but not process. It also means that the Court is described as detached from the interbranch process of formulating policy – that is, apolitical – that reporting focuses on the institution rather than individuals, and is deferential, unlike the adversarial stance of reporters covering Congress and the president (Davis 1987; Patterson 1993), and that the framing of a decision varies systematically depending on whether the reporter is on the Supreme Court beat or not.

In a recent content analysis, LaRowe (2010), examined newspaper coverage of the Supreme Court in two large national newspapers, the *New York Times* and *USA Today* from 1997–2004. He analyzes coverage along four dimensions: tone (positive/negative) of coverage, depiction of the Court (political/apolitical), focus (individuals or the Court as an institution), and whether the coverage focuses on the implications of the Court's ruling (yes/no). He also looks to see whether differences in reporting exist between those who cover the Court on a regular basis (beat) and those who do not (non-beat).The results revealed that both groups of reporters depict the Court as apolitical and both groups focus on the institution rather than individual justices. He also finds differences by reporter group: non-beat reporters focus more on the implications of decision and the tone of beat coverage is negative, and significantly more negative than non-beat coverage.

PUBLIC SUPPORT FOR THE SUPREME COURT

When studying public support for the Supreme Court, scholars usually divide the concept into two forms of support, diffuse and specific. Specific support can be usefully conceived as job approval; it is a short- term, rational evaluation of performance, and believed to be relatively fluid. For the Supreme

Court, public approval is often based upon agreement with its rulings (Franklin and Kosaki 1989). However, it can also respond to larger trends like judicial activism and support for other political institutions (Caldeira 1987), or by how the Court conducts its business (Hibbing and Theiss-Morse 1995), or even by controversial nominations (Gibson and Caldeira 2009, Hoekstra and LaRowe 2013).

Broadly speaking, diffuse support is "institutional loyalty" and support for the Court's role in the political system, and is expressed as an unwillingness to make fundamental changes, such as restricting a Court's jurisdiction (Caldeira and Gibson 1992; Gibson, Caldeira, and Spence 2003a, 2003b; Gibson and Caldeira 2009). In studies of institutional loyalty, the most widely applied measurement is an index asking about agreement with the following four propositions: a willingness to do away with the Court, a willingness to limit the Court's jurisdiction, generalized trust in the institution, and whether the Court gets too mixed up in politics.

Diffuse support differs in several ways. Where specific support is short term, diffuse support is durable; where specific support is rational, diffuse support is affective (Easton 1965). Another difference is in the basis for support; specific support is policy-based, and thus often correlates with political attitudes, such as public mood (Durr, Martin, and Wolbrecht 2000), while diffuse support wells up from more fundamental political orientations such as support for a multiparty political system, rule of law, and political tolerance (Caldeira and Gibson 1992).

Furthermore, because specific and diffuse support stem from different sources, changes in one kind of support are thought not to influence levels of the other kind. Thus, one may express dissatisfaction with a court while still supporting its role within the political system (Gibson, Caldeira, and Baird 1998). This is not always the case, however, as sustained disappointment (or, theoretically, pleasure) can lead to changes in institutional support over time. Gibson and Caldeira (1992) find changes in institutional loyalty among blacks over the span of several decades as the liberal civil rights jurisprudence of the Warren Court gave way to the more conservative judging of the Burger and Rehnquist eras (see also Sigelman 1979; Handberg and Maddox 1982).

The main cause of variation in (specific) support for the Supreme Court is, of course, its rulings (Mondak 1991; Hoekstra 2000, 2003; Gibson, Caldeira, and Spence 2003a; Kessel 1966; Grosskopf and Mondak 1998; Johnson and Martin 1998 Durr, Martin, and Wolbrecht 2000; Mondak and Smithey 1997; Brickman and Peterson 2006; Unger 2008, but see Dolbeare and Hammond 1968; Caldeira 1986). And in the studies listed, reaction to the rulings is explained in policy-based terms: those in the public who agree with the Court's ruling reward it with their support, while those who disagree lower their approval accordingly

Recently, however, James Gibson and Gregory Caldeira have advanced a competing model, positivity theory (Gibson and Caldeira 2009). This theory has its intellectual roots in Casey's (1974) findings of a positive correlation between awareness of the Court and a subscription to myths of judicial impartiality and wisdom (see also Scheb and Lyons 2000). Positivity theory holds that the Supreme Court's high and enduring popularity is due in part to an asymmetry in evaluations: it receives credit for popular decisions, while escaping blame for unpopular decisions, which are blamed on "the law" (Gibson, Caldeira, and Baird 1998). Those with the strongest institutional support evince the strongest tendency for a positivity bias in evaluations (Gibson and Caldeira 2009).[1] This presented an apparent puzzle; since exposure to courts is necessary for formation of the "myth," those who paid the most attention to the Court also had the least realistic understanding of how it actually operates, that is, that judicial policy preferences, and not the law, are decisive. However, recent research indicates that Americans have a fairly realistic view of how the Court works, yet this does not harm its legitimacy. People understand that judges exercise discretion, but that they do so in a principled and responsible manner (Gibson and Caldeira 2011).

FRAMING EFFECTS

Central to framing theory is the proposition that there is more than one way to understand an issue or organize facts, and framing theory holds that different understandings or organizations may produce different attitudes or opinions (Gamson and Modigliani 1989). A large portion of the work on framing focuses on the potential for shaping attitudes or attitudinal change, and nearly all the results provide support for the existence of a "framing effect" (e.g., Chong and Druckman 2007a, 2007b; Druckman and Nelson 2003, Kahneman and Tversky 1984).

This does not mean that such effects are inevitable. For such an effect to occur, people must be at least somewhat open to new information. Meaning, for example, that they do not resist messages, are less than certain or are conflicted about how an issue is to be understood (Feldman and Zaller 1992), or have only a dim or elementary understanding of the issues about which they are receiving messages (e.g., Converse 1964).

[1] Like Gibson and Caldeira, we use the terms diffuse support, institutional support, and institutional loyalty interchangeably.

The logical corollary, then, is that several factors, such as attitude strength or political knowledge or sophistication can limit framing effects. Increased political knowledge makes one more capable of independently forming and holding opinions and hence less susceptible to alternative framings (Kinder 1998, 2003). There is an important caveat to this general finding, however. Under certain circumstances political knowledge, especially when combined with cognitive ability can enhance framing effects. High political knowledge and cognitive ability generally allow for an increased ability to absorb information; when the source of information is trusted, normal framing effects are heightened (Price and Zaller 1993; Miller and Krosnick 2000). Attitude strength reduces receptivity to alternative frames (Zaller 1991, 1992). In fact, scholars have found that a backlash can occur. Lodge and Taber (2006) find that, for those with strong attitudes about a given issue, reading a counterargument polarizes and strengthens the previous attitudes, rather than changing or moderating it. A similar effect, described as "counter-arguing," was found when African Americans were exposed to a racially themed crime news script (Gilliam and Iyengar 2000).

NEGATIVE INFORMATION

As a general proposition, negative information matters. Research from psychology and political science tells us that, compared to positive or neutral information, negative information grabs our attention (Fiske 1980), is perceived to be more informative (Skowronski and Carlston 1987, 1989), and tends to be more memorable than positive information (Brians and Wattenberg 1996).

In addition to evolutionary and affective explanations (Lau 1982; Kahneman and Tversky 1984), negative information is also salient for the rather mundane reason that it represents a contrast from a mostly positive world (Lau 1985). The importance of such information helps to explain Carlston and Skowronski's (1987, 1989) finding that negative information has superior diagnostic capability. Social expectations are for good behavior and by and large, (despite how it sometimes seems) people conform to such norms. Therefore, positive information, in the form of good behavior, is not seen as especially informative about a person. Negative information, that is, bad behavior, is less expected and is thus perceived to give us deeper insight into a person's character.

Despite the well-documented salience of negative information, analysts have identified limits to its effectiveness. An important element is the source of criticism. Trust (Miller and Krosnick 2000) is important for information to have an effect, which is perhaps why Fridkin and Kenney (2004) find that press criticisms are influential, particularly for political experts. But the tone and content of criticism matter as well. Research on political campaigns finds that attack ads seen as "shrill" can turn off their audience (Fridkin and Kenney 1999) and result in a "backlash effect" where the ad's sponsor, and not its target, suffers. Thus, to influence opinions, negative information must be seen as reasonable, and is most effective when issuing from a generally respected and trusted source, such as a newspaper.

FRAMING SUPREME COURT DECISIONS

Many studies have chronicled the relationship between Supreme Court policymaking and public support; several of them use and experimental method; a handful attempt to mimic actual media coverage; none model their experimental stimulus on actual patterns documented in a content analysis.

Two recent studies with a similar design provide a kind of immediate foundation for this study, and we a build upon their results. The first was a study of the effects of three framings of *Bush v. Gore* (2000) on both specific and diffuse support for the Supreme Court. Nicholson and Howard (2003) use a telephone survey to test the effects of three explanatory frames – politically based, legally based, or to decide the election – and find that the political framing influences specific support while the "end the election" frame reduces diffuse support.

A second study (Baird and Gangl 2006) investigates whether different portrayals of the Supreme Court's decision-making process – via newspaper coverage – can influence attitudes about the Court's procedural fairness, an attribute considered integral to its institutional legitimacy. They find that a "political wrangling" frame depresses beliefs that the Supreme Court uses fair decision-making procedures.

Both studies provide a welcome focus on the causal relationship between media coverage and opinion change, yet each might be seen as lacking in "mundane realism" critical for the validity of any study purporting to establish a link between media coverage and public attitudes. Nicholson and Howard's approach is to use a phone survey, which differs from how people actually encounter media frames, which, of course, is by media consumption. Baird and Gangl's (2006) article avoids this pitfall, but their experimental stimulus is newspaper coverage which purports to describe the Supreme Court's extremely private decision-making process which is not open to Court clerks, much less the press.

The preceding literature review sets out some fairly clear expectations for how Supreme Court rulings, communicated to the public through newspaper coverage, might influence public opinion. Public reaction generally is thought to be policy-based, and while the focus is on specific support, changes in diffuse support are not inconceivable. Yet a new theory of positivity bias predicts an asymmetry in evaluations for those with strong institutional loyalty, suggesting group differences in reactions. A recent content analysis of newspaper coverage tells us that there are discernible patterns, two of which – differences in tone and framing between reporter types, have relatively well-established implications for public opinion. The negative tone of beat reporting may drive down specific support, as well as institutional trust, an element of diffuse support. In addition, the political framing of non-beat reporting has the potential to undercut another element of the Supreme Court's institutional support, the perception that it is above or removed from politics. We have distilled from this review three two-part hypotheses, each of which anticipates a distinction in reactions dependent upon individual levels of diffuse support.

Hypotheses

1a. Negative Tone Hypothesis – Job Approval: *a negative tone in newspaper coverage will cause a decline in job approval (specific support)*
1b. Positivity Bias Stipulation: *job approval will decline only among those with weak institutional loyalty (diffuse support)*
2a. Negative Tone Hypothesis – Institutional Trust: *a negative tone in newspaper coverage will cause a decline in institutional trust*
2b. Positivity Bias Stipulation: *institutional trust will decline only among those with weak institutional loyalty*
3a. Political Framing Hypothesis – Mixed up in Politics: *politically framed coverage will cause an increase in the belief that the Supreme Court gets too mixed up in politics*
3b. Positivity Bias Stipulation: *an increased belief that the Supreme Court is too mixed up in politics will occur only in those with weak institutional loyalty*

METHODS AND DATA

To test our hypotheses about the effects of different characteristics of newspaper coverage on attitudes toward the Supreme Court, we use a 2(political/legal framing) x 2(mixed/negative tone) factorial experimental design, looking for differences within subjects (pre-test/post-test). We also group subjects by institutional loyalty to see whether pre-test and post-test levels of support for the Supreme Court vary by one's institutional loyalty (discussed below).

Subjects were first asked to fill out our pre-test, which measures variables such as political interest and knowledge as well as measures of both specific and diffuse support. Subjects were then randomly assigned to one of four experimental conditions. After reading the hypothetical Supreme Court decision, subjects were asked to complete an unrelated task. Finally, subjects filled out a post-test where we again measured specific and diffuse support.[2]

Our goal in this experiment is to test the effect of newspaper coverage on two measures of support for the Supreme Court: *specific support* and *diffuse support*. Specific support is measured by the question, "In general, do you approve or disapprove of the way the Supreme Court is doing its job?" Scores ranged from 1 = "approve strongly" to 5 = "disapprove strongly." Diffuse support is a scale of institutional loyalty created by Gibson and Caldeira (2009a).[3] We look at specific support because the measure has been the focus of dozens of studies due to its important connection to subjects including public compliance, policy legitimation, and Supreme Court decision making. We also look at diffuse support because this is the base for the Court's power and relevance as an institution.

To investigate whether effects differ by one's level of institutional loyalty, we use pre-test measurements of Gibson and Caldeira's diffuse support index and use the index median score to divide subjects into strong and weak support groups.[4]

The experimental treatment is a hypothetical newspaper article closely modeled on *USA Today*'s coverage of a Supreme Court ruling *Board of Regents, University of Wisconsin v. Southworth* (2000). The question in

[2] The distracter task is a twenty-item vocabulary quiz. We include this quiz in the questionnaire to increase confidence that any observed effects are genuine as well as to prevent demand effects. Subjects are informed at the outset that they are completing a survey on the relationship between vocabulary skills and media coverage. Students are given the answers to the quiz as part of post-experiment debriefing.

[3] It is composed of answers to the following four statements: "If a Supreme Court justice started to make a lot of decisions that most people disagreed with, it might be better to remove that justice from the bench." "The Supreme Court gets too mixed up in politics." "The right of the Supreme Court to decide certain types of controversial issues should be reduced." "The Supreme Court can usually be trusted to make decisions that are right for the country as a whole." Each item ranges from 1= "agree strongly" to 5= "disagree strongly" and is recoded so that higher scores equal greater institutional loyalty. Diffuse support is rescaled to range from 0–1.0.

[4] All four items of the index are measured on a five-point scale; possible scores thus range from 4–20.

Southworth is whether a mandatory fee used to fund campus student groups violates students' First Amendment right not to speak. To test our hypotheses, we model our hypothetical coverage on the results of LaRowe's (2010) content analysis. To simulate negative coverage, we include three quotes criticizing the decision. To avoid the possibility of framing the criticisms as legal or political, the quotes are non-specific, yet unambiguously critical. Mixed coverage is simulated by one positive comment, one negative comment, and a third comment deferring judgment for twenty years.

Coverage putting the ruling into a legal context focuses on the relation of the ruling to past similar decisions as well as a discussion of the Supreme Court's First Amendment jurisprudence. Coverage putting the ruling into a political context focuses on the likely consequences of the ruling for campus organizations and similar groups. See Appendixes B and C for the original article and for full texts of articles containing each of the four treatments.[5]

SUBJECTS

Subjects were 181 undergraduates at a large state university who participated for extra credit in a political science course.[6] Although it is generally thought that using college students as subjects limits the generalizability of experimental findings (Sears 1986), other research has shown this to be less of an issue when researching framing effects (Druckman and Nelson 2003).

[5] We modeled our experiment on this particular case for several reasons. First, *Southworth* is a typical instance of newspaper coverage: it focuses on the announcement of a final decision, an activity that receives the lion's share of media coverage compared to when the Court adds cases to its docket or hears oral arguments. Second, the case concerns the First Amendment and research shows that civil liberties and civil rights are more likely to receive media coverage than other kinds of issues (Solimine 1980). Third, the topic of student fees is likely to be relevant to our subjects, increasing the relevance of the topic and that they will have meaningful opinions. The actual *Southwarth* decision is now more than nine years old, meaning that a typical senior would have been only thirteen at the time the decision was rendered, yet similar battles are ongoing in lower courts, so matters such as this are still a current controversy.

[6] We drew our subjects from three different courses; two were lower division (100 and 200 level) and one was upper division (300 level). Steps were taken to ensure that no student took the survey twice, and tests uncovered no significant differences among the students of the three classes. In our sample, 56.9 percent were male and 42.5 percent were female (with two missing responses); the average age was 20.4. Politically, 50.3 percent identified as Democrats, 14.5 percent as Independents, and 35.3 percent as Republicans. As a whole, the sample tilts just slightly to the left, with a median ideology score of 3.61 on the seven-point scale. In our sample, 65.1 percent identified as white, 16.7 percent as Latino, 3.3 percent as Asian, 2.7 percent as African American, and 0.55 percent as Native American, with 9.8 percent reporting as other.

TABLE 1. *Characteristics of sample by experimental condition*

Condition	Specific Support	Political knowledge	Political interest	Diffuse Support (pre-test)	Party	Ideology
1: Legal/Negative	3.36	5.48	10.23	.60	3.91	3.80
2: Political/Mixed	3.31	5.68	11.70	.64	3.71	3.47
3: Legal/Mixed	3.42	5.62	10.21	.62	3.91	3.52
4: Political/Negative	3.38	5.77	10.76	.61	3.81	3.61

Note: Cell entries are means for each experimental condition. Difference of means analysis revealed no significant differences among the groups for any measure.

RESULTS

In order to assure that our random assignment produced groups that were as similar as possible to each other, we present a series of difference of means tests in Table 1. Here we present pre-test scores of our dependent variables (specific support and diffuse support) as well as other important individual level characteristics, such as political knowledge, political interest, party identification, and ideology. Political knowledge is measured using Delli Carpini and Keeter's (1993) political knowledge scale and an additional two questions: one asking for the correct number of justices on the Supreme Court and a second asking who the Senate majority leader is. The scale ranges from 0–7. Political interest is a scale measured by the amount of times in the past week the subject has: watched the national news; discussed politics with family, friends, or co-workers; or read the newspaper. Each item ranges from 0–7; the scale ranges from 0–21. Party is measured on a scale ranging from 1–7 where 1 = Strong Democrat and 7 = Strong Republican. Ideology is also measured on a scale ranging from 1–7 where 1 = Very Liberal and 7 = Very Conservative.

The results from this preliminary check suggest that randomization worked. Independent samples t-tests revealed no significant differences for any measure. With pre-test levels of both specific support and diffuse support established, we now test our hypotheses.

Table 2 shows the results of our first hypothesis, that exposure to negative newspaper coverage would depress specific support. Surprisingly, and contrary to our hypothesis, the Court suffered no significant decrease in specific support in either conditions 1 or 4. Though this is contrary to our hypotheses, which are derived from the literature on negative information in the media, what we see here may in fact be consistent with Gibson, Caldeira, and Baird

TABLE 2. *Pre-test/ post-test specific support scores for conditions 1 and 4*

Condition	Pre-test	Post-test
1: Legal/Negative (n=47)	3.36	3.32
4: Political/Negative (n=43)	3.44	3.44

Note: Table shows pre-test and post-test means in specific support for conditions 1 and 4 for hypothesis: a negative tone in newspaper coverage will cause a decline in specific support.

TABLE 3. *Pre-test/ post-test specific support scores for conditions 1 and 4*

	Change in means (low loyalty)		Change in means (high loyalty)	
Condition	Pretest mean	Posttest mean	Pretest mean	Posttest mean
1: Legal/Negative	3.23 n=30	3.13	3.59 n=17	3.65
4: Political/ Negative	3.24 n=25	3.28	3.76 n=17	3.71

Note: Table shows pre-test and post-test means in specific support for conditions 1 and 4 for hypothesis: specific support will decline only among those with weak institutional loyalty (diffuse support).

(1998), who suggested that, while courts gain support from popular rulings they do not lose support for unpopular rulings. The subjects in conditions 1 and 4 were slightly supportive of the Court before reading criticism in the "newspaper" and remained slightly supportive after doing so.

We probe further to test the possibility that the Court is in fact benefitting from an asymmetry in evaluations. Gibson and Caldeira (2009a, 2009b) have argued that those with higher levels of diffuse support (that is, institutional loyalty) evaluate courts and judges differently, while those with lower levels of support view them no differently than the "political" branches of government. If this is so, we should see a drop in specific support among those with low institutional loyalty, while those with high levels of loyalty will not revise their levels of specific support. We divide subjects in conditions 1 and 4 into high and low loyalty groups and test this proposition.

Table 3 shows no apparent pattern of movement in specific support in the face of negative newspaper coverage. No significant changes occur and no patterns emerge. Support drops slightly among those with low loyalty in condition 1 and among those with high levels of loyalty in condition 4.

TABLE 4. *Pre-test/ post-test diffuse support scores for conditions 1 and 4*

Condition	Pre-test mean	Post-test mean
1: Legal/Negative (n=46)	.61	.59
4: Political/Negative (n=41)	.59	.59

Note: Table shows pre-test and post-test means in diffuse support for conditions 1 and 4 for hypothesis: a negative tone in newspaper coverage will cause a decline in diffuse support.

Conversely, support actually increases slightly (though not significantly) among those with low loyalty in condition 4 and among those with high loyalty in condition 1. What we find is puzzling. Contrary to the literature on negativity, specific support did not drop even in the face of criticism from a legal expert. Yet, contrary to positivity theory, we did not witness different reactions from subjects based upon their levels of institutional loyalty. Perhaps, when it comes to the Supreme Court, criticism is not the lever that moves support.

We next test whether negative newspaper coverage can affect levels of diffuse support. This may seem less likely than changes in specific support, given the cumulative nature of diffuse support, yet Gibson and Caldeira chronicled surprising changes in diffuse support for the Court after exposure to a few anti-Alito advertisements (Gibson and Caldeira 2009a). We hypothesize that, as with the anti-Alito ads, negative news coverage will drive down levels of diffuse support. The results of our test are shown in Table 4.

We see, contrary to our predictions that diffuse support does not drop in reaction to negative news coverage. Levels of support dropped a small, non-significant amount in condition 1 and remained unchanged in condition 4. Although this is contrary to our hypotheses, it does fall more into line with much of the literature, which describes diffuse support as a reservoir of goodwill (Easton 1965) and not depleted by exposure to a single negative article.

Perhaps those with low levels of loyalty react differently than those with high levels of loyalty. Again, this is what positivity theory predicts – two separate reactions based upon pre-existing levels of loyalty. We test to see whether positivity theory holds here. Again, we divide our subjects in conditions 1 and 4 into low- and high-loyalty groups. The results appear in Table 5.

Here we do witness a change in levels of diffuse support. Interestingly, though, the results are contrary to our hypothesis but consistent with the unexpected results from the study of Alito's confirmation (Gibson and Caldeira 2009a). Among those with low levels of loyalty in conditions 1 and 4 we see no

TABLE 5. *Pre-test/ post-test diffuse support scores for conditions 1 and 4*

Condition	Change in means (low loyalty)		Change in means (high loyalty)	
	Pretest	*Posttest*	*Pretest*	*Posttest*
1: Legal/Negative	.52 N=29	.52	.76** n=17	.70**
4: Political/Negative	.50 n=25	.51	.74 n=16	.73

Note: Table shows pre-test and post-test means in diffuse support for conditions 1 and 4 for hypothesis: diffuse support will decline only among those with weak institutional loyalty.
** p<.05, * p.<.10, two-tailed hypotheses

TABLE 6. *Pre-test/ post-test diffuse support scores for condition 2, hypothesis 3a*

Condition	*Pre-test*	*Post-test*	Sig. (two-tailed)
2: Political/Mixed (n=46)	.64	.63	.78

Note: Table shows pre-test and post-test means in diffuse support for conditions 2 for hypothesis: politically framed coverage will cause a decline in diffuse support.
** p<.05, * p.<.10, two-tailed hypotheses

movement, as we see no movement for those with high loyalty in condition 4. But we do see movement, *among those with high loyalty*, in condition 1, as levels of support drop from a pre-test .76 to .70. This change is significant at the .05 level. What this means is that, among subjects in condition 1, those with the strongest loyalty were also the most susceptible to negative reporting. At this point, it is unclear why this would be. It is also not clear why support would drop for those in condition 1 but not in condition 4. It may be that small numbers in these groupings lead to varying results.

Our last pair of hypotheses looks at whether politically framed coverage drives down levels of diffuse support. We have no reason for politically framed coverage to affect specific support; such framing is not inherently negative. Yet we do have reason to suspect that newspaper coverage depicting the Court as an "ordinary" political institution may influence levels of diffuse support, as such support is partially based on the belief that courts are "different" from the other branches of government in that they are not politically, but legally motivated actors.

Table 6 shows pre-test and post-test levels of diffuse support condition 2. Condition 4 is not included in the table because pre- and post-test levels

TABLE 7. *Pre-test/ post-test diffuse support scores for condition 2*

Condition	Change in means (low loyalty)		Change in means (high loyalty)	
2: Political/Mixed	.50 n=22	.52	.76 n=24	.74

Note: Table shows pre-test and post-test means in diffuse support for conditions 2 for hypothesis: diffuse support will decline only among those with weak institutional loyalty.

of support were previously examined. As was the case for subjects exposed to negative news coverage, subjects in condition 2 did not significantly change their levels of diffuse support. The mean does drop, to .63 from .64, but this is neither statistically nor substantively significant.

For one last time, we divide our subjects into high and low loyalty groups and put positivity theory to the test; results are shown in Table 7. Again, our expectations as well of those of positivity theory are confounded. The mean level of diffuse support among those with low loyalty increased slightly, but not significantly, to .52 from .50. Among those with high levels of loyalty, mean support dropped to .74 from .76, but this was not significant either. We do note that the change among those with high loyalty was in the same direction as among those in condition 1 with high levels of loyalty. Perhaps the effect was similar, even if statistical significance was not reached.

So far, the results of our study have been largely inconsistent with both the literature on negative news coverage and positivity theory. But there is an alternative theory of specific support we have not tested. As Durr, Martin, and Wobrecht (2000) have shown, specific support for the Court may have a more traditional base – policy agreement. To see whether this is the case for the subjects in our experiment, we looked at pre-test and post-test levels of support among those who disagreed with the Court's ruling. A post-test manipulation check asked subjects, "Overall, do you agree or disagree with the Supreme Court's ruling in this case?" Subjects were given the option of "neither agree nor disagree" as a third choice. Overall, eighty-nine subjects disagreed with the ruling reached by the Supreme Court in their particular experimental condition. In Table 8 we show the pre-test/post-test difference in specific support among all who disagreed. We also divided those who disagreed into low and high loyalty groups, as positivity theory again predicts differing reactions between the two groups.

Among all subjects, there is a decline in specific support, though this decline does not reach statistical significance. Therefore, like others, we see a connection between policy agreement and support. When dividing those who disagree by level of loyalty, the predictions of positivity theory appear to

TABLE 8. *Pre-test/post-test results of difference of means test for changes in Supreme Court job approval for those disagreeing with the ruling overall and by institutional loyalty*

Variable	All subjects	Strong Loyalty	Weak Loyalty
Supreme Court Approval	−.09 (n=89)	.08 (n=38)	−.22** (n=49)

Note: Table shows results of within-subjects difference of means test for changes in specific support among those indicating disagreement with the ruling in a post-test manipulation check. A test for changes in approval among those agreeing with the decision (n=55) found no significant changes either overall or by institutional loyalty. Thirty-seven subjects indicated no opinion in response to the ruling.

** p<.05, * p.<.10, two-tailed hypotheses

be vindicated. Not only did those with strong loyalty not withdraw their support, the direction of change is positive, if small. It appears, then, that a pre-existing well of support may in fact prevent the Court from losing support for unpopular decisions. This inference gains support when we look at the change in support among those with low levels of loyalty. Here, we see a significant drop of .22 in specific support.

DISCUSSION

What to make of these results? We see that negative coverage and political framing seem to do little to affect public support for the Court, whether it be specific support or diffuse support. Yet, when negative coverage does affect support, it affects diffuse support and does so among those with strong institutional loyalty. This is doubly puzzling, as diffuse support is thought to be more resistant to change, and those with strong institutional loyalty were supposed to be among those most resistant to change. Even more intriguing, this finding mirrors that of Gibson and Caldeira's (2009a) study of the Alito confirmation battle. Perhaps it is the case, as they suggest, that expectations are upset, or innocence is shattered. Certainly, there is more work to be done here.

Regarding news coverage casting the Court in a political light, perhaps the public's relatively sophisticated and realistic attitudes about the Court's true political nature nullify the effects of political framing. The American public seems to have a somewhat realistic or even sophisticated view of the intersection of politics and law. When surveyed, people seem comfortable with the idea of a judicial nominee having political or ideological inclinations, so long as they are not extreme or controlling (Gibson and Caldeira 2009). Hoekstra and LaRowe (2013) find that ideological moderation increases support for a (hypothetical) nominee's confirmation, suggesting that the public does consider ideology when deciding whether to lend its support. It bears repeating that strong institutional support means having an idealized, but not unrealistic or caricatured view of the judicial branch. Thus, learning that a Supreme Court ruling will influence events outside of the courtroom may not change attitudes, as this was expected.

Third, and finally, although negative tone did not lower specific support, it appears from further testing that people derive job approval from policy agreement and do not factor criticism into their evaluations. Here the predictions of positivity theory hold true: those with strong loyalty do not change their evaluations, while those with weak loyalty do, on policy grounds. Though contrary to what we would expect, given the campaign effects literature, our findings are consistent with the most current results from studies using positivity theory as well as an older literature on reactions to Supreme Court rulings. In sum, those with strong institutional loyalty seem willing to stand with the Court on individual decisions, but have oddly fragile attitudes about the Court's institutional integrity.

Only recently has research moved from how the news media covers the Supreme Court to how the content of that coverage affects public support. Scholars have often worried about the corrosive effect of negativity: that it may drive down turnout, or, more broadly, lower the overall quality of democracy. The Supreme Court may enjoy high support but it is not immune to the effects of criticism. If the judicial branch continues on its current trajectory – increasingly political campaigns and acrimonious confirmation hearings – its vital legitimacy may be in jeopardy.

APPENDIX A

Table of Full Results for Indicators of Diffuse Support

Master list of pre-test/post-test difference of means test results for all indicators of diffuse support overall and by institutional loyalty for conditions 1, 2, and 4

Condition	Indicator	Overall	Strong Loyalty	Weak Loyalty
1. Legal/ Negative	Institutional Trust	−.15	−.59***	.10
	Should be Removed	.04	−.29*	.23*
	Jurisdiction Reduced	−.13	−.18	−.10
	Too Mixed up in Politics	−.04	.06	−.10
2. Political/ Mixed	Institutional Trust	.04	−.29**	.41***
	Should be Removed	−.06	.00	−.18
	Jurisdiction Reduced	−.15	−.08	−.23
	Too Mixed up in Politics	.13	.04	.23
4. Political/ Negative	Institutional Trust	−.14	−.29*	−.04
	Should be Removed	.14	.06	.20
	Jurisdiction Reduced	.05	−.06	.12
	Too Mixed up in Politics	−.05	.00	−.08

Note: Above are the results of difference means tests for each of the four indicators of diffuse support for conditions 1, 2, and 4. Results are shown by condition and by loyalty groups within conditions. As with other tables, significance levels of .10, .05, and.01 are signified by *, **, and *** respectively. Significant changes are highlighted regardless of whether they were hypothesized.

APPENDIX B

Original Article

Coverage of *Board of Regents v. Southworth* as it appeared in *USA Today* on March 23, 2000:

Supreme Court unanimously upholds required student fees
BYLINE: Richard Willing; Mary Beth Marklein
SECTION: NEWS; Pg. 4A
LENGTH: 641 words
DATELINE: WASHINGTON

WASHINGTON – Students at public universities can be required to pay fees that support campus organizations whose views offend them, a unanimous Supreme Court ruled Wednesday.

The decision, in a lawsuit filed by Christian and conservative students against the University of Wisconsin, has significance for the nation's 1,921 public colleges and universities. At least 70% of them use mandatory fees to finance student organizations. Had the court struck down the fees for violating free speech rights, as the students argued, the universities would have had to drop many activities or find other funding for campus cultural clubs, political forums and advocacy groups.

The court's reasoning: The fees underwrite "dynamic discussions" of a wide range of topics and are thus part of the educational process.

"This is really a landmark in higher education," said Katharine Lyall, president of the University of Wisconsin system. "The court said higher education is a unique thing unto itself and central to its very being is the free expression of ideas."

Scott Southworth, a law student when he sued the University of Wisconsin, challenged the $331.50 charge assessed to all students to support 125 student organizations in the 1995–96 academic year. The student government doled out the money. Organizations unhappy with the amount of their subsidy could ask for a vote by the entire student body.

Southworth said that 18 organizations – including the International Socialist Organization and the Lesbian, Gay, Bisexual and Transgender Center – had views or objectives that clashed with his. Forcing him to subsidize the groups, he argued, violated his First Amendment rights "not to speak."

A U.S. district court and the U.S. Court of Appeals for the 7th circuit agreed. They relied on past Supreme Court decisions that allow members of labor unions and professional associations to withhold fees used to support those groups' political activities.

Such organizations, the court had said, could apply mandatory fees only to activities "germane" to their basic missions, such as organizing workers or training professionals.

On Wednesday, the Supreme Court said that those precedents had been misapplied. The student fees, the court said, were spent not endorsing a particular opinion but the general proposition that on a university campus many views should be heard.

"The speech the university seeks to encourage is distinguished not by discernible limits but by its vast, unexplored bounds," said Justice Anthony Kennedy, author of the main opinion. "Recognition must be given to the important and substantial purposes of the university, which seeks to facilitate a wide range of speech."

Kennedy added that the activity program must be "viewpoint neutral," meaning that funding must be available to all student groups.

All nine justices voted in favor of the decision. But Justices David Souter, John Paul Stevens and Stephen Breyer did not accept Kennedy's contention that student activity programs must be "viewpoint neutral."

Southworth, now a lawyer working for a Wisconsin legislator, was disappointed. "I don't worship the Supreme Court," he said. "Certainly they're humans and they have a right to an opinion, and I have to respect that opinion. But my faith is in God and not the judicial system."

Matt Coles, a lawyer with the American Civil Liberties Union, said the court had applied the "correct analogy" in treating students differently from union members.

"If you enroll at a state university and pay fees, you are more like a taxpayer than a member of an organization," he said. "The court's ruling says that because you don't like picketers, you can't decide not to pay your sidewalk assessment."

APPENDIX C

Experimental Conditions

Examples of hypothetical newspaper coverage. Manipulations of tone are bolded; manipulations of context are italicized.

Condition A: Legal context and with negative tone:
"**Supreme Court upholds required student fees**"
BYLINE: Richard Willing; Mary Beth Marklein
SECTION: NEWS; Pg. 4A
DATELINE: WASHINGTON
WASHINGTON – Students at public universities can be required to pay fees that support campus organizations whose views offend them, the Supreme Court ruled Wednesday.

The decision, in a lawsuit filed by Christian and conservative students against the University of Oregon, is one of several cases the Court will rule on this term which concern 1st Amendment rights on university campuses, as it tries to establish a clear legal doctrine to guide lower courts.

The court's reasoning: The fees underwrite "dynamic discussions" of a wide range of topics and are thus part of the educational process.

Justice Kennedy noted that the activity program must be "viewpoint neutral," meaning that funding must be available to all student groups.

Mark Hughes, a law student when he sued the University of Oregon, challenged the $331.50 charge assessed to all students to support 125 student organizations in the 1995–96 academic year. The student government doled out the money. Organizations unhappy with the amount of their subsidy could ask for a vote by the entire student body.

The Supreme Court's decision was reminiscent of past rulings on laws that allow members of labor unions and professional associations to withhold fees used to support those groups' political activities. Such organizations, the court had said in its opinions, could legally apply mandatory fees only to activities "germane" to their basic missions, such as organizing workers or training professionals.

Julie Licht, a lawyer with the American Civil Liberties Union, said the Court had applied an analogy similar to lower federal Courts. A U.S. district court and the U.S. Court of Appeals for the 9th circuit had also relied on past Supreme Court decisions that allow members of labor unions and professional associations to withhold fees used to support those groups' political activities.

On Wednesday, Kathleen Sullivan, the Dean of Stanford's Law School, said that those precedents had not been correctly applied. She said that the Court had clearly reached the wrong decision, and described herself as very disappointed.

Wallace Lightsey, a former Supreme Court clerk for Lewis Powell, declared the decision to be one of the "worst in recent memory. This was a complicated case, but the Court clearly failed to arrive at a satisfactory conclusion."

And Tony Mauro, a columnist for *Legal Times*, said it was clear that the Court was wrong. "I just can't believe the Court could look at this case and believe this was an appropriate outcome."

The case, *Board of Regents v. Hughes* No. 99–1252, was the Court's only decision handed down on Monday.

Condition B: Political context and with a mixed tone:
"Supreme Court upholds required student fees"
BYLINE: Richard Willing; Mary Beth Marklein
SECTION: NEWS; Pg. 4A
DATELINE: WASHINGTON
WASHINGTON – Students at public universities can be required to pay fees that support campus organizations whose views offend them, the Supreme Court ruled Wednesday.

The impact of the decision, in a lawsuit filed by Christian and conservative students against the University of Oregon will no doubt be felt nationwide, as at least 70% of the nation's public colleges and universities use mandatory fees to help fund campus student organizations.

The court's reasoning: The fees underwrite "dynamic discussions" of a wide range of topics and are thus part of the educational process.

Justice Kennedy noted that the activity program must be "viewpoint neutral," meaning that funding must be available to all student groups.

Mark Hughes, a law student when he sued the University of Oregon, challenged the $331.50 charge assessed to all students to support 125 student organizations in the 1995–96 academic year. The student government doled out the money. Organizations unhappy with the amount of their subsidy could ask for a vote by the entire student body.

The Supreme Court's decision was reminiscent of past decisions regarding labor unions and other organizations. A likely consequence of the court's decision is for student groups on the political fringes, like Students for 9/11 Truth, which has a chapter at the University of Oregon, to increase in visibility and clout on many campuses, while aggravating the financial strain on groups currently receiving funding.

Julie Licht, a lawyer with the American Civil Liberties Union, said the effect would be similar challenges by non-campus organizations. Licht said that high school student groups and local civic organizations would attempt to extend the Court's logic. "We will likely see a sharp increase in efforts by these organizations to argue that this decision should apply to tax revenues, which could indirectly cause dramatic shifts in the makeup of local political leadership."

On Wednesday, Kathleen Sullivan, the Dean of Stanford's Law School, said that those precedents had not been correctly applied. She said that the Court had clearly reached the wrong decision, and described herself as very disappointed.

But Wallace Lightsey, a former Supreme Court clerk for Lewis Powell, declared the decision to be one of the "best in recent memory. This was a complicated case, but the Court did a great job coming to a conclusion."

Tony Mauro, a columnist for *Legal Times*, said it was too early to tell. He said it would be at least "20 years" before a clear assessment could be made on this particular outcome.

The case, *Board of Regents v. Hughes* No. 99–1252, was the Court's only decision handed down on Monday.

REFERENCES

Baird, Vanessa A., and Amy Gangl. 2006. "Shattering the Myth of Legality." *Political Psychology* 27 (4): 597–614.

Brians, C. and Wattenberg, M. 1996. "Campaign Issue Knowledge and Salience: Comparing Reception from TV Commercials, TV News and Newspapers." *American Journal of Political Science* 40: 172–193.

Brickman, Danette, and David A. M. Peterson. 2006. "Public Opinion Reaction to Repeated Events: Citizen Response to Multiple Supreme Court Abortion Decisions." *Political Behavior* 28 (1): 87–112.

Caldeira, Gregory A. 1987. "Public Opinion and the U.S. Supreme Court: FDR's Court-Packing Plan." *American Political Science Review* 81 (December): 1139–1153.

Caldeira, Gregory A. and James L. Gibson. 1992. "The Etiology of Public Support for the Supreme Court." *American Journal of Political Science* 36 (August): 635–691.
Casey, Gregory. 1974. "The Supreme Court and Myth: An Empirical Investigation." *Law and Society Review* 8 (Spring): 385–419.
Converse, Philip E. 1964. "The Nature of Belief Systems in Mass Publics." In *Ideology and Discontent* (Ed. David Apter).
Davis, Richard. 1987. "Lifting the Shroud: News Media Portrayal of the U.S. Supreme Court." *Communications and the Law* 9: 43–59.
1994. *Decisions and Images*. Englewood Cliffs, New Jersey: Prentice Hall, Inc.
Delli Carpini, Michael X., and Scott Keeter. 1996. *What Americans Know About Politics and why it Matters*. New Haven: Yale University Press.
Dolbeare, Kenneth M., and Phillip E. Hammond. "The Political Party Basis of Attitudes Toward the Supreme Court." *Public Opinion Quarterly* 32 (1): 16–30.
Druckman, James N. and Kjersten R. Nelson. 2003. "Framing and Deliberation: How Citizens' Conversations Limit Elite Influence." *American Journal of Political Science* 47 (4): 729–745.
Druckman, James N. 2004. "Political Preference Formation: Competition, Deliberation and the (Ir)relevance of Framing Effects." *The American Political Science Review* 98 (4): 671–686.
Druckman, James N. and Dennis Chong. 2007a. "Framing Public Opinion in Competitive Democracies." *American Political Science Review* 101: 637–655.
2007b. "A Theory of Framing and Opinion Formation in Competitive Elite Environments." *Journal of Communications* 57: 99–118.
Durr, Robert H., Andrew D. Martin, and Christina Wolbrecht. 2000. "Ideological Divergence and Public Support for the Supreme Court." *American Journal of Political Science* 44 (4): 768–776.
Easton, David. 1965. *A Systems Analysis of Political Life*. New York: John Wiley.
Ericson, David. 1977. "Newspaper Coverage of the Supreme Court: A Case Study." *Journalism Quarterly*.
Feldman, Stanley, and John Zaller. 1992. "The Political Culture of Ambivalence: Ideological Responses to the Welfare State." *American Journal of Political Science* 36 (1): 268–307.
Fiske, Susan T. 1980. "Attention and Weight in Person Perception: The Impact of Negative and Extreme Behavior." *Journal of Personality and Social Psychology* 38: 889–906.
Flemming, Roy B., John Bohte, and B. Dan Wood. 1997. "One Voice among Many: The Supreme Court's Influence on Attentiveness to Issues in the United States, 1947 1992." *Journal of Politics* 61: 76–108.
Franklin, Charles and Liane Kosaki. 1989. "Republican Schoolmaster: The United States Supreme Court, Public Opinion, and Abortion." *American Political Science Review* 83 (September): 751–771.
Fridkin, Kim Leslie and Patrick J. Kenney. 2004. "Do Negative Messages Work? The Impact of Negativity on Citizens' Evaluations of Candidates." *American Politics Research* 32 (5): 570–605.
Gamson, William A. and Andre Modigliani. 1989. "Media Discourse and Public Opinion on Nuclear Power: A Constructionist Approach." *American Journal of Sociology* 95: 1–37.

Gibson, James L. and Gregory A. Caldeira. 1992. "Blacks and the United States Supreme Court: Models of Diffuse Support." *The Journal of Politics* 54 (4): 1120–1145.
Gibson, James L., Gregory A. Caldeira, and Vanessa A. Baird. 1998. "On the Legitimacy of National High Courts." *The American Political Science Review* 92 (2): 343–358.
Gibson, James L., Gregory A. Caldeira, and Lester Kenyatta Spence. 2003. "The Supreme Court and the US Presidential Election of 2000: Wounds, Self-Inflicted or Otherwise? *British Journal of Political Science* 33 (4): 535–556.
2003. "Measuring Attitudes Toward the United States Supreme Court." *American Journal of Political Science* 47 (2): 354–367.
Gibson, James L. and Gregory A. Caldeira. 2009a. *Citizens, Courts, and Confirmations: Positivity Theory and the Judgments of the American People*. Princeton: Princeton University Press. 2009b. on knowledge.
2011. "Has Legal Realism Damaged the Legitimacy of the U.S. Supreme Court?" *Law and Society Review* 45 (1): 195–219.
Gilliam, Franklin G. Jr., and Shanton Iyengar. 2000. "Prime Suspects: The Influence of Local Television News on the Viewing Public." *American Journal of Political Science* 44 (3): 560–573.
Grosskopf, Anke and Jeffery J. Mondak. 1998. "Do Attitudes Toward Specific Supreme Court Decisions Matter? The Impact of *Webster* and *Texas v. Johnson* on Public Confidence in the Supreme Court." *Political Research Quarterly* 51 (3): 633–654.
Handberg, Roger, and William S. Maddox. 1982. "Public Support for the Supreme Court in the 1970s." *American Politics Quarterly* 10 (3): 333–346.
Hetherington, Marc J. 2005. *Why Trust Matters: Declining Trust and the Demise of American Liberalism*. Princeton, NJ: Princeton University Press.
Hoekstra, Valerie J. 1995. "The Supreme Court and Opinion Change: An Experimental Study of the Court's Ability to Change Opinion." *American Politics Quarterly* 23 (1): 109–129.
2000. "The Supreme Court and Local Public Opinion." *American Political Science Review* 94 (March): 89–100.
2003. *The Supreme Court and Local Public Opinion*. New York: Cambridge University Press.
Hoeskstra, Valerie J, and Nicholas L, LaRowe. 2013. "Judging Nominees: An Experimental Test of the Impact of Qualifications and Divisiveness on Public Support for Nominees to the Federal Courts." *Justice System Journal* 34 (1): 38–61.
Johnson, Timothy R. and Andrew D. Martin. 1998. "The Public's Conditional Response to Supreme Court Decisions." *American Political Science Review* 92 (June): 299–309.
Kahneman, Daniel and Amos Tversky. 1984. "Choices, Values, and Frames." *American Psychologist* 39 (4): 341–350.
Kessel, John H. "Public Perceptions of the Supreme Court." *Midwest Journal of Political Science* 10 (2): 167–191.
Kinder, Donald R. 1998. "Opinion and Action in the Realm of Politics." In *The Handbook of Social Psychology*. Eds. Daniel T. Gilbert, Susan T. Fiske, and Gardner Lindzey. New York: Oxford University Press.
2003. "Communication and Politics in the age of Information." *In The Oxford Handbook of Political Psychology*. Eds. David O. Sears, Leonie Huddy, and Robert Jervis.

Lau, Richard R. 1982. "Negativity in Political Perception." *Political Behavior* 4 (4): 353–377.

1985. "Two Explanations for Negativity Effects in Political Behavior." *American Journal of Political Science* 29 (1): 119–138.

Lau, Richard R. and Ivy Brown Rovner. 2009. "Negative Campaigning." *Annual Review of Political Science* 12: 285–306.

LaRowe, Nicholas L. 2010. "On and Off the Supreme Court Beat: Differences in Newspaper Coverage of the Supreme Court Beat." Paper presented at the American Political Science Association, Washington, DC.

Miller, Joanne M. and Jon A. Krosnick. 2000. "News Media Impact on the Ingredients of Presidential Evaluations: Politically Knowledgeable Citizens are Guided by a Trusted Source." *American Journal of Political Science* 44 (2): 301–315.

Mondak, Jeffery J. 1991. "Substantive and Procedural Aspects of Supreme Court Decisions as Determinants of Institutional Support." *American Politics Quarterly* 19 (2): 174–188.

Mondak, Jeffery J. and Shannon Ishiyama Smithey. 1997. "The Dynamics of Public Support for the Supreme Court." *The Journal of Politics* 59 (4): 1114–1142.

Nicholson, Stephen P., and Robert M. Howard. 2003. "Framing Support for the Supreme Court in the Aftermath of *Bush v. Gore*." *The Journal of Politics* 65: 676–695.

Scheb, John M. II, and William Lyons. 2000. "The Myth of Legality and Public Evaluation of the Supreme Court." *Social Science Quarterly* 81 (December): 928–940.

Scott, John T., James F. Spriggs II, and James R. Zink. 2006. "Courting the Public: Judicial Behavior and Public Views of Court Decisions." Paper presented at the Midwest Political Science Association, Chicago.

Sears, David O. 1986. "College Sophomores in the Laboratory: Influences of a Narrow Data Base on Social Psychology's View of Human Nature." *Journal of Personality and Social Psychology* 51 (3): 515–530.

Segal, Jeffrey A., and Albert D. Cover. 1989. "Ideological Values and the Votes of U.S. Supreme Court Justices." *American Political Science Review* 83 (2): 557–565.

Sigelman, Lee. 1979. "Black-White Differences in Attitudes toward the Supreme Court: A Replication in the 1970s." *Social Science Quarterly* 60 (1): 113–119.

Sill, Kaitlyn L., Emily T. Metzgar, and Stella M. Rouse. 2013. "Media Coverage of the U.S. Supreme Court: How Do Journalists Assess the Importance of Court Decisions?" *Political Communication* 30:58–80.

Skowronski, John J. and Donal E. Carlston. 1987. "Social Judgment and Social Memory: The Role of Cue Diagnosticity in Negativity, Positivity, and Extremity Biases." *Journal of Personality and Social Psychology* 52 (4): 689–699.

1989. "Negativity and Extremity Biases in Impression Formation: A Review of Explanations." *Psychological Bulletin* 105 (1): 131–142.

Slotnick, Elliot E. and Jennifer A. Segal. 1998. *Television News and the Supreme Court.* Cambridge: University of Cambridge Press.

Solimine, Michael E. 1980. "Newsmagazine Coverage of the Supreme Court." *Journalism Quarterly* 661–663.

Spill, Rorie L., and Zoe Oxley. 2003. "Philosopher Kings or Political Actors: How the Media Portray the Supreme Court." *Judicature* 87: 22–29.

Taber, Charles S. and Milton Lodge. 2006. "Motivated Skepticism in the Evaluation of Political Beliefs." *American Journal of Political Science* 50 (3): 755–769.

Patterson, Thomas E. 1993. *Out of Order*. New York: Alfred Knopf.
Petrick, Michael J. 1968. "The Supreme Court and Authority Acceptance." *The Western Political Quarterly* 21 (1): 5–19.
Price, Vincent, and John Zaller. 1993. "Who Gets the News? Alternative Measures of News Reception and Their Implications for Research." *Public Opinion Quarterly* 57: 133–164.
Unger, Michael A. 2008. "After the Supreme Word: The Effect of McCreary County v. ACLU (2005) and Van Orden v. Perry (2005) on Support for Public Displays of the Ten Commandments." *American Politics Research* 36 (5): 750–775.
Ura, Joseph Daniel. 2009. "The Supreme Court and Issue Attention: The Case of Homosexuality." *Political Communication* 26: 430–446.
Zaller, John. 1991. "Information, Values, and Opinion." *The American Political Science Review* 85 (4): 1215–1237.
1992. *The Nature and Origins of Mass Public Opinion*. Cambridge: Cambridge University Press.

CASES CITED:

Board of Regents, University of Wisconsin v. Southworth 529 U.S. 217 (2000).
Bush v. Gore 531 U.S. 98 (2000).

8

The Placement of Conflict: The Supreme Court and Issue Attention in the National Media

JOSEPH DANIEL URA

In *Democracy in America*, Alexis de Tocqueville famously writes that, "Scarcely any political question arises in the United States that is not resolved, sooner or later, into a judicial question." Indeed, the observation is famous, in part, because scholars of law and judicial politics so often invoke it to highlight the important role that courts, especially the Supreme Court, play in American national politics. Yet, in the past two decades, a small but important body of research in political science has shown that de Tocqueville's observation about the judicialization of political questions is, at best, incomplete.[1] Though issues on the national political agenda often involve legal or constitutional questions that are resolved by the Supreme Court,[2] political scientists have found convincing evidence that Supreme Court decisions can create questions of national political importance. In other words, legal and constitutional questions decided by the United States Supreme Court may resolve into national political issues.

In particular, political scientists have found that Supreme Court decisions which have the effect of disrupting established policy regimes may draw the national media's attention to the issues involved in those cases (Flemming, Bohte, and Wood 1997; Flemming, Wood, and Bohte 1999; Ura 2009). In particular, these studies have found that the Supreme Court has played a significant role in raising the prominence of civil rights, civil liberties, free speech, religious liberty, and gay rights in the national media in recent decades. In turn, the prominence of these issues in the media has often been reflected in the policy agendas of Congress, the president, and the states, with

[1] Graber (2004) also convincingly argues that de Tocqeville substantially overstates the scope of courts' engagement with important political questions in the Jacksonian Era.

[2] The Court's adjudication of constitutional claims arising from the Affordable Care Act (*National Federation of Independent Business v. Sebelius* 2012) is but one recent example.

significant consequences for the development of partisan and electoral politics. Most critically perhaps, the Supreme Court's decision to invalidate state-mandated segregation in public education in *Brown v. Board of Education* (1954) pushed civil rights onto the national agenda (e.g., Flemming, Bohte, and Wood 1997; Klarman 2004), which resulted in the enactment of both the most important civil rights legislation since Reconstruction and the gradual exodus of Southern whites from the Democratic Party to the Republican Party (e.g., Carmines and Stimson 1989; Hetherington 2009; Poole and Rosenthal 1997; Perlstein 2001; McMahon 2011). Although it would be easy to overstate the role of the Supreme Court in shaping the media's issue agenda, it is fair to say that the Court has played an important role in elevating attention to a small number of historically salient issues that have had substantial political consequences. The Supreme Court's role in shaping issue attention in the national media is an important element in American political developments since the middle of the last century.

To address the issues of the Supreme Court's influence on the national media's issue agenda, I begin by outlining the theoretical importance of issue attention or agenda setting in American national politics. Second, I describe the literature that examines the conditions under which the Supreme Court can draw the national media's attention to new issues. Next, I illustrate how the Supreme Court's influence on the media's agenda can have profound effects on American politics by discussing the role of the Supreme Court's decision against segregation in public education in *Brown v. Board of Education* (1954) in catalyzing subsequent federal civil rights legislation. I continue by describing the role of the Supreme Court in American national politics in light of the preceding discussion, and I conclude by offering some thoughts on promising directions for future research in this area.

THE IMPORTANCE OF ISSUE ATTENTION

The political science of issue attention (or agenda setting) in American national politics has developed substantially in the half-century since the critical work of Schattschneider (1960) and Bacharach and Baratz (1962) highlighted the systematic importance of defining the scope of political conflict for making political choices. Schattschneider's (1960) classic statement of the importance of agenda setting for shaping political outcomes remains as apt today as when it was published more than a half-century ago: "There are billions of potential conflicts in any modern society, but *only a few become significant*. The reduction of the number of conflicts is an essential part of politics... As a matter of fact, *the definition of alternatives is the supreme instrument of power.*"(pp. 66–68)

In other words, the process of narrowing the vast space of political conflict to the relatively tiny set of issues that comprise our political discourse at any given time is the crux of political power. Issues or "problems to which government officials, and people outside of government closely associated with those officials, are paying some serious attention to at any given time" may be addressed by changes in policy; those which are excluded from government officials' "agenda" will continue to be structured by prior policy decisions (or non-decisions) (Kingdon 1985, p. 3).

As a result, individuals and groups with interests vested in some existing policy arrangement may serve those interests by attempting to exclude the relevant policy domain from the public agenda. Bacharach and Baratz (1962) describe this "second face of power":

> Of course power is exercised when A participates in the making of decisions that affect B. But, power is also exercised when A devotes his energies to creating or reinforcing social and political values and institutional practices that limit the scope of the political process to consideration of only those issues which are comparatively innocuous to A. To the extent that A succeeds in doing this, B is prevented, for all practical purposes, from bringing to force any issues that might in their resolution be seriously detrimental to A's set of preferences (Bacharach and Baratz 1962, p. 948).

By preventing the consideration of particular issues, current policies may be preserved against any alternative, including those that would have been adopted in place of the status quo were they to be considered. Conversely, moving an issue to the public agenda is a necessary condition for a new policy to be adopted in that area.

These critical theoretical observations are the foundation of a large empirical literature on issue agendas in American national politics. This body of research has addressed both the composition of issue agendas within the branches of government and various media outlets as well as the dynamic interactions between issue attention across and between governmental institutions, the media, and the mass public (e.g., Bartels 1996; Baumgartner and Jones 2009; Canes-Wrone 2010; Cohen 1995; Cook *et al* 1983; Dalton, Beck, and Huckfeldt 1998; Edwards and Wood 1999; Flemming, Wood, and Bohte 1999; Hill 1998; Iyengar and Kinder 1987; Kingdon 1984; McCombs and Shaw 1972; Ura 2009; Yates, Whitford, and Gillespie 2005). Taken as a whole, this body of research emphasizes the complexity of issue attention in the American separation-of-powers system and, often, the important role of the press in mediating agendas across institutions and between the institutions of national government and the American people.

Despite this complexity, the literature persistently identifies the news media as an important element of the system of issue attention in the United States. Various studies show that the national media agenda – the issues chosen to fill pages of print and minutes of broadcast time – strongly affects which proposed policy changes receive serious consideration in the elected branches of government (e.g., Cook *et al* 1983; Dalton, Beck, and Huckfeldt 1998; Kingdon 1984, 1989; Iyengar and Kinder 1987). Other research shows how the media can be a vehicle for government officials to draw public attention to particular issues (Edwards and Wood 1999; Flemming, Wood, and Bohte 1999; Hill 1998; Smith 1980). Understanding issue attention in American national government therefore requires some insight into the processes that shape issue attention in the national news media, and a thorough attempt to outline the influence of the Supreme Court on American national politics should attempt to identify when and how the Supreme Court influences issue attention in the mass media.

DOES THE COURT INFLUENCE THE NEWS MEDIA'S ISSUE AGENDA?

The political science literature that specifically examines whether the Supreme Court shapes the national media's issue agenda is surprisingly small.[3] Most research on issue agendas in American national government has tended to focus of the elected branches of government, excluding the courts. Yet, those studies that address the problem of whether and how the Supreme Court shapes the news media's issue agendas provide a clear picture of the system's basic dynamics.

Rosenberg's (1991) broader study of the ability of Supreme Court decisions to produce social change includes the seminal analysis of the Supreme Court's influence on the national media's issue agenda, which established a basic methodology and baseline result. His method is simple: count the annual number of stories appearing in major news outlets dealing with a salient decision of the Supreme Court and determine whether there is an

[3] This chapter addresses the linkages between Supreme Court decisions and the national media's issue agenda. There are other literatures on the Court and the media. One strand of this scholarship examines the ways in which media cover the court, generally finding that newspapers tend focus on political responses to the Court's decisions rather than the substantive legal issues involved in its cases (Ericson 1977; Newland 1964; but see Larson 1985). Alternatively, other scholars have focussed on understanding when the media turn their attention to the Court, finding that its activities in salient issue domains tend to produce coverage of the Court (e.g., Davis 2011; Sill, Metzgar, and Rouse 2013; Slotnick and Segal 1998).

increase in the number of relevant stories following the Court's decision. Rosenberg counts stories indexed by *The Reader's Guide to Periodical Literature*, which lists all stories appearing in an array of national print publications, organized by topic. Based on the resulting annual data, Rosenberg concludes that neither *Brown v. Board of Education* (1954) nor *Roe v. Wade* (1973) significantly altered the national media's attention to the issues of civil rights or abortion, respectively. In part, this supports his sweeping conclusion that "U.S. Courts can almost never be effective producers of significant social reform" (Rosenberg 1991, p. 338).

Rosenberg's analysis remains the most widely known study of the Supreme Court's influence on the mass media, but subsequent research has sharply challenged his conclusion. Flemming, Bohte, and Wood (1997) investigate the role of the Court in elevating the media's attention to civil rights, free speech, and public displays of religion (See also Flemming, Wood, and Bohte 1999). Flemming and his coauthors find that a small number of the Court's salient decisions in these issue areas had a significant influence on the media's systematic attention to the underlying issues addressed in each case. These agenda-setting cases included three civil rights cases (*Brown v. Board of Education* 1954, *Cooper v. Aaron* 1958, and *Griffin v. County School Board of Prince Edward County*) 1964, one free speech case (*Texas v. Johnson*) 1989, and three Establishment Clause cases (*Illinois ex. rel. McCollum v. Board of Education* 1948, *Engel v. Vitale* 1962, and *Lynch v. Donnelly* 1984). These key cases:

> markedly rearranged the prior distribution of political benefits, either material or symbolic, for various segments of the population. The issues involved in all of these decisions were also highly affective. As a result, the decisions were extremely controversial at the time they were announced. The media participated in expanding the scope of system-wide conflict by publicizing the initial decision and its implications. In each case, the Supreme Court's decisions sparked intense national debates that drew in new participants and expanded the scope of conflict through time...The issues involved in each decision opened wide ideological cleavages among political actors that remain until this day (Flemming *et al* 1997, p. 1247).

Although other Supreme Court decisions may be legally or symbolically important, these decisions so substantially reshaped the nation's policy landscape that the national news media refocused its attention on the issue areas they addressed.

This explanation is, likewise, consistent with the literature in political science and communications showing that disruptive events are more likely to draw media attention to the events that preserve the status quo. The economic forces that shape editorial choices in the media provide strong incentives for media outlets to provide content that attracts as many readers or viewers as possible (Buckalew 1969; Dominick 1975; Esser 1999; Lacy 1987, 1989). Given scarce resources for reporting and limited space for publication and broadcast time, there is an implicit competition among potential news stories for print space, broadcast time, or, in the new media, prominent website placement. Successful news stories are those judged most able to generate attention in competition among various news outlets (Gartner 2004). For coverage resulting from Supreme Court decisions, cases that have the effect of creating substantial changes in public policy are apt to draw media attention to related issue domains.

Among their many results, Flemming, Bohte, and Wood (1997) specifically find that *Brown* significantly and permanently increased media attention to civil rights. This, of course, contrasts sharply with Rosenberg's (1991) result that *Brown* did not draw the media's attention to civil rights. The differing results are principally due to the authors' measurement strategies. Rosenberg measures attention to civil rights by counting news stories indexed by *The Readers' Guide to Periodical Literature* under the heading *Negroes in America*. Flemming and his coauthors base their study on a count of stories indexed in *The Readers' Guide* under the subheadings *Negroes in America – Education*, *Negroes in America – Segregation*, and *Public Education – Desegregation*. As Flemming, Bohte, and Wood's persuasive discussion of the issue indicates, Rosenberg's count includes numerous stories unrelated to civil rights included in the full *Negroes in America* category and excludes a substantial number of relevant stories listed under *Public Education – Desegregation* (1997, p. 1229, n6). It follows that Flemming, Bohte, and Wood's conclusion that *Brown* moved civil rights onto the national media's agenda is the stronger result.

Flemming, Bohte, and Wood's (1997) position on the agenda-setting influence of disruptive Supreme Court decisions is supported by subsequent research. Ura (2009) investigates whether the Supreme Court's decisions in gay rights cases have increased media attention to issues relating to homosexuality. In particular, Ura models whether decisions in *Hurley et al v. Irish-American Gay, Lesbian, and Bisexual Group* (1995), *Romer v. Evans* (1996), *Boy Scouts of America (BSA) v. Dale* (2000), and *Lawrence v. Texas* (2003) increased the frequency of stories in the *New York Times* and *USA Today* that mention a set of key words related to homosexuality. Ura's analysis shows strong support for the idea that the Court can act as an agenda-setting institution when its decisions create substantial changes in public policy.

Ura demonstrates that both the *New York Times* and *USA Today* significantly and persistently increased publication of stories related to homosexuality by more than one-third following *Lawrence v. Texas* in 2003. *Lawrence* substantially expanded the scope of gay rights in the United States. By invalidating state sodomy laws, the decision "markedly rearranged the prior distribution of political benefits, either material or symbolic, for various segments of the population" (Flemming, Bohte, and Wood 1997, p. 1247). *Lawrence* also overturned *Bowers v. Hardwick* (1986), yielding a landmark change in the national legal status of gays – decriminalizing consensual homosexual sexual conduct and offering a symbolic validation of homosexual lifestyle choices. Moreover, the case hinted that the Supreme Court might be amenable to other claims of privacy rights by homosexuals, which have since come to fruition, in part, in the Court's recent decision to invalidate the federal Defense of Marriage Act (*United States v. Windsor* 2013).

These rearrangements of political benefits are not only news in their own rights; they also produced a diverse set of political responses. They include both the mobilization of political resources to further additional same-sex rights claims, such as marriage equality, to conservative countermobilization in support of state and federal action to forestall further expansions of gay rights that were the subject of media attention, as well (Keck 2009). Indeed, *Lawrence* highlights how changes in issue attention related to Supreme Court decisions are closely linked to subsequent political mobilization around relevant issues both positive and negative.

In contrast, *Hurley et al v. Irish-American Gay, Lesbian, and Bisexual Group* (1995) and *Boy Scouts of America v. Dale* (2000) produced no such effects. In these two cases, the Court merely upheld a status quo, affirming the right of private organizations to exclude homosexuals. Because these cases yielded no change in the distribution of political benefits, they yielded less news value and provoked less reallocation of political resources to the issue of homosexuals' political and social status than did *Lawrence*. Likewise, *Romer* (1996), which invalidated a Colorado constitutional amendment prohibiting identifying homosexuals as a protected class in anti-discrimination law that had never gone into effect, produced only a temporary shift in attention to homosexuality in *USA Today*, but not the *New York Times*.

Together, Flemming, Bohte, and Wood (1997) and Ura (2009) provide strong evidence that the Supreme Court can shape the media's issue agenda when its decision has the effect of significantly altering public policy. By disrupting the status quo, the Court creates news directly, catalyzes broader political mobilization, and ultimately draws media attention to the underlying issue involved. Though these disruptive cases may be relatively rare (e.g., Dahl 1957), they may have substantial consequences for American politics and society.

HOW IT MATTERS: THE CASE OF *BROWN*, ATTENTION TO CIVIL RIGHTS, AND CIVIL RIGHTS LEGISLATION

The potential for the Supreme Court to structure the national media's issue agenda and through it to influence decision making elsewhere in the government is evident in the history of *Brown v. Board of Education*. By overturning *Plessy v. Ferguson* (1896) and rejecting its "separate but equal" doctrine in the field of public education, the Supreme Court upended an important pillar of the broader system of institutionalized racial segregation that had marked the South since the end of Reconstruction. This result generated significant new attention to the issue of civil rights in the national media and prompted a series of dynamics changes in the political behavior of white Southerners and the alignment of the national political parties. Though the decision's direct impact on the racial composition of Southern schools was negligible, *Brown*'s influence on the mass media catalyzed the major civil rights legislation of the 1960s and, as I will discuss, led (indirectly) to substantial desegregation in schools in the South.

Brown *and its Effects*

As the Civil War ended, the Republican-controlled Congress embarked on a radical program of constitutional and statutory change to end slavery and to protect the civil rights of former slaves. Between 1865 and 1869, Congress passed the Thirteenth, Fourteenth, and Fifteenth Amendments to the Constitution, which, respectively, prohibited slavery, guaranteed citizenship, due process, and equal protection of the law to former slaves and their descendants, and protected the right to vote without regard to "race, color, or previous condition of servitude." Congress also passed major civil rights legislation in 1866, 1870, 1871, and 1875 to enforce these amendments and to counter Southern whites' efforts to intimidate and disenfranchise black voters. Despite Supreme Court decisions against the constitutionality of important parts of the Civil Rights Acts of 1871 and 1875, federal troops remained in some Southern states until 1877, in part, to protect blacks' civil rights.

Aggressive efforts to extend and protect Southern blacks' civil rights ended abruptly in 1877. As part of a bargain to resolve the disputed presidential election of 1876, Republican leaders agreed to abandon Reconstruction, including withdrawing federal troops from the Southern states where they remained and abandoning civil rights as a national question in favor of states' "home rule" on questions of race (Woodward 1951). Republican Rutherford B. Hayes was inaugurated president in 1877 and ordered the last federal troops to withdraw from the South. Republicans in Congress substantially curtailed legislative efforts on civil rights (Beerman 2001; Gressman 1951), though the party preserved its symbolic support for blacks in the South (Riker 1986, Chapter 2). Southern Democrats established and preserved Jim Crow, a nearly all-encompassing system of legally enforced segregation between blacks and whites, until the late 1960s (Foner 2002; Woodward 1955).

The parties' tacit agreement to avoid the question of civil rights eroded following World War II. For example, President Truman ordered the desegregation of the armed forces in 1948, and, in the same year, the Republican Party adopted a platform calling for federal legislation against lynching and racial discrimination in employment. However, the Democratic Party backed away from support for civil rights after the Dixiecrat Revolt in 1948, and Republicans failed to win the White House or either house of Congress until 1952 (Frederickson 2001; Katznelson 2013).

Then, in 1954, the question of civil rights was thrust onto the national agenda. In that year, the Supreme Court handed down its unanimous decision in *Brown v. Board of Education*, announcing that racially segregated schools are "inherently unequal," that legally mandated segregation of public schools denies minority children the "equal protection of the laws guaranteed by the Fourteenth Amendment," and that "the doctrine of 'separate but equal' [announced in *Plessy v. Ferguson* (1896)] has no place" in public education. Despite the sweeping nature of the Court's decision and its subsequent order for states to desegregate their schools "with all deliberate speed" (*Brown v. Board of Education* 1955), many state and local officials in the South actively delayed or obstructed efforts to end segregation (Rosenberg 1991). As a result, the pace of racial integration in the South's public schools was painfully slow. During the 1963–1964 school year, a decade after *Brown*, only 1.3 percent of black schoolchildren in the South attended racially integrated schools (Rosenberg 2008, p. 94).

Despite a prolonged lack of progress in ending the practice of segregated public education in the South, the Court's decision in *Brown* exploded the exclusion of civil rights from the national agenda. *Brown* prompted a large and enduring increase in the national media's attention to civil right issues (Flemming, Bohte, and Wood 1997; but see Rosenberg 1991) and contributed to increased attention to civil rights issues in Congress and the presidency (Flemming, Wood, and Bohte 1999). These early effects culminated in the Civil Rights Act of 1957, the first national civil rights legislation since the nineteenth century, which passed the House by a vote of 285 to 126 and the Senate with a vote 72 to 18 (Beerman 2001). Congress reinforced this law three years later when it passed the Civil Rights Act of 1960 by a vote of 311 to 109, and the Senate by a vote of 71 to 18.

Brown also radicalized many southern whites in defense of the larger, Jim Crow system of legal segregation in areas far beyond the schoolhouse, prompting support for more extreme candidates for public office and acceptance of violence against advocates for civil rights (Klarman 2004). The growth of southern whites' racial extremism exacerbated tensions between the Democratic Party and white Southerners, which had been growing since the New Deal era (Black and Black 2009; Patterson 1967; Rae 1994). This tension eventually peaked in the mid-1960s, when northern Democrats in Congress made common cause with most Republicans to create the Civil Rights Act of 1964 and the Voting Rights Act of 1965, prompting the start of the mass realignment of southern whites into the Republican Party (Carmines and Stimson 1989; Hetherington 2009; Poole and Rosenthal 1997; Perlstein 2001; McMahon 2011). The passage of the Civil Rights Act ushered in a period of greatly expanded executive and judicial efforts to desegregate public schools in the South (Klarman 2004; Rosenberg 1991, 2008). As a result, in the first decade after the passage of the Civil Rights Act (and the second decade after *Brown*), the desegregation of public schools in the South accelerated dramatically. By the 1973–1974 school year, more than 90 percent of black schoolchildren in the South attended racially integrated schools (Rosenberg 2008, p. 94).

The Role of Issue Attention in Advancing Civil Rights

The Supreme Court's decision in *Brown* catalyzed federal civil rights legislation by putting civil rights on the national agenda. The large, bipartisan majorities of Northern Democrats and Republicans that passed significant civil rights legislation in 1957, 1960, 1964, and 1965 demonstrate that there existed overwhelming operational support for providing increased federal protection for the political, social, and economic rights of southern blacks. The primary obstacle to enacting serious civil rights legislation immediately prior to *Brown* was not, therefore, legislative opposition in the sense of a pivotal number of voters who would have opposed a proposal. Rather, the arrangement of partisan-ideological cleavages in Congress blocked civil rights legislation. By moving civil rights onto the national media's agenda with *Brown*, the Supreme Court injected an issue that cut against the dominant cleavage of liberal-conservative, Democratic-Republican discourse in Congress and American national politics more generally (Poole and Rosenthal 1997).

Given the historic disposition of the Republican Party on black civil rights and scattered evidence of northern Democrats' sympathies with blacks' civil rights claims as early as Franklin Roosevelt's New Deal programs (Katznelson 2013), it seems probable that a precursor of the national majorities that would so forcefully protect blacks' access to the ballot box, public accommodations, and public services in the mid-1960s might have done so earlier – had the issue been moved onto public debate sooner. More darkly, it is at least equally probable that the pro-civil rights supermajority of the mid-1960s would have remained latent had not the judiciary moved civil rights onto the agenda.

On balance, *Brown*'s principal direct influence was on the national political agenda rather than on the racial composition of schools. However, by raising the salience of the race issue and provoking a "backlash" among Southern whites, *Brown* produced a "counterbacklash" in the rest of the country that led to "landmark civil rights legislation" and "transformative racial change" which would not have "occur[red] as rapidly as it did" had the Supreme Court not invalidated legal segregation in public schools (Klarman 2004, p. 442; see also Patterson and Freehling 2001; Lau 2004; Sullivan 2009).

Klarman's (2004) backlash-counterbacklash interpretation of the effect of *Brown* is bolstered by recent political science research. First, studies of more recent Supreme Court decisions suggest that patterns of media coverage of Supreme Court decisions and subsequent attention to related issues may prompt the sort of negative backlash among intense opponents of the Court's decisions that Klarman describes. Haider-Markel, Allen, and Johansen (2006) find that newspapers in states which legally banned sodomy prior to *Lawrence v. Texas* (2003 – and which, therefore, experienced a policy change as a result of the decision – covered the Supreme Court's decision more intensely and more negatively than newspapers in states which had no legal restrictions on sodomy and therefore experienced no change in policy as a result of *Lawrence*. Also, Ura (2014) finds evidence that aggregate public responsiveness to salient Supreme Court decisions is characterized by short-term backlash against the Court in public mood followed by long-run movement in public opinion toward the positions taken by the Court.

WHY IT MATTERS: THE SUPREME COURT, ISSUE ATTENTION, AND COUNTERMAJORITARIANISM

The political consequences of *Brown v. Board of Education* illustrate several important aspects of the Supreme Court's agenda-setting influence and its potential consequences. Perhaps most importantly, the Supreme Court is able to introduce new issues onto the national political agenda by deciding cases that substantially disrupt the established distribution of material or symbolic political benefits (Flemming, Bohte, and Wood 1997; Flemming, Wood, and Bohte 1999; Ura 2009). By introducing new issues, the Supreme Court may disrupt established authority that has been entrenched by the exclusion of some issues from political discourse (Bacharatz and Baratz 1962). This effect indicates a novel way to think about the Court as a countermajoritaran institution. Normative theories of judicial power emphasize the role of the Supreme Court in invalidating laws enacted by Congress or the state legislatures in order to protect the rights of "discrete and insular minorities" against hostile popular and legislative majorities (*United States v. Carolene Products Co.*, n.4, 1938; see also Bickel 1962). This view, however, rests on an implicit view of majority political agency relative to the disadvantaged minority that essentially ignores the problem of agenda setting and the "second face of power."

In classic accounts of judicial countermajoritarianism, a majority creates a law that unjustly injures a minority, which requires redress from a countermajoritarian court. In contrast, agenda-setting theory imagines a multitude of inactive majorities who do not and cannot influence the political process *until they are activated by the definition of political problem* (Bacharach and Baratz 1962; Schattscheider 1960; see also McKelvey 1976). The power to define problems, that is, the power to set the agenda is the power to activate these latent majorities and mobilize them to effect policy change.

There were, for example, at least two relevant majorities surrounding the issue of civil rights in the mid-1950s. There was the prevailing majority who passively ignored the civil rights claims of southern blacks as a national political problem, and there was the latent majority that favored national intervention to end state-sponsored segregation *once the question was on the agenda.*

The Court's decision in *Brown* in favor of the Equal Protection claims of black schoolchildren in the South elevated the issue of civil rights in national political discourse, putting the question of school segregation and broader issues of black civil rights on the agenda. Once on the agenda, national majorities in favor of federal action to end legal segregation in the states and to advance black civil rights more broadly were activated. Majority support of an active civil rights agenda was demonstrated by Gallup Polls showing majority support for the *Brown* decision itself in 1954 and later, and in large congressional majorities that ultimately coalesced behind the Civil Rights Act of 1957 and subsequent federal civil rights legislation. In contrast, prior to *Brown*, no major national survey research organization had polled Americans' attitudes toward racial segregation in public education nor had Congress enacted significant civil rights legislation since Reconstruction.

By finding in favor of the Equal Protection claims of black schoolchildren in the South in *Brown*, the Supreme Court acted as a countermajoritarian institution in two ways. First, and most obviously, the Court worked against southern states' majorities on behalf of their black minorities. Equally as important, though, the Court's decision and its agenda setting consequences acted against a nearly century-long, bipartisan exclusion of black civil rights claims from national political discourse, replacing a passive national majority that tolerated Jim Crown with an active majority supportive of federal intervention on behalf of southern blacks.

More broadly, the alteration of the issue set in the stream of public discourse is not simply an academic curiosity. Changes in the issue agenda in the national media create opportunities for advocates of excluded issues to move proposals for consideration that enjoy majority support but could not be expressed in policy proposals until the shift in issue attention (Schattschneider 1960). This impact may be greatest when these new issues may cut against and disrupt established partisan-ideological cleavages in American national government, as was the case with *Brown*.[4]

However, this more subtle dimension of judicial impact on political outcomes is potentially problematic. First, although the Supreme Court may catalyze media coverage of issues previously excluded from public discourse, the Court has little control over how those issues are ultimately manifest in the media or what policy proposals will emerge in the new issue environment. Of course, the Supreme Court and its justices may work with the press corps to control the public face of its decisions, yet the Court has substantially fewer opportunities to shape coverage of broader issues raised by its decisions (Davis 1994; Davis and Strickler 2000). As a result, the path to social change consistent with Supreme Court decisions may be indirect and uneven. Similarly, when the Supreme Court engages latent majorities, those majorities may be hostile to the Court's decisions. For example, the Supreme Court's

[4] Cleavages over the issue of black civil rights existed in the Democratic Party prior to *Brown*. This is perhaps most evident in the Dixiecrat walkout and presidential campaign of Strom Thurmond in 1948. However, the Democratic Party recovered its national unity by 1952, with white Southern Democrats largely backing Adlai Stevenson and his running mate, Alabama segregationist John Sparkman. The claim presented here is not that *Brown* by itself created the civil rights issue or the divisions that civil rights highlighted within the Democratic Party. Rather, the claim is that *Brown* elevated the issue of civil rights in the national political discourse, allowing a latent national majority to express its support for black civil rights through federal legislation. Once civil rights was an active question on the national agenda, however, the Democratic Party could not sustain the implicit regional bargains that had previously held it together. In this respect, *Brown* cut against existing partisan-ideological cleavages, maximizing the disruption that followed from the case.

decision to invalidate state laws against flag desecration in *Texas v. Johnson* (1989) activated a passionate majority in favor of federal action against flag burning. A Gallup Poll conducted shortly after the decision found that 71 percent of Americans expressed support for "a new constitutional amendment to make flag burning illegal."[5] Goldstein (1996, p. 113) for example, writes:

> [The] *Johnson* decision touched off what *Newsday* characterized as a "firestorm of indignation" and what *Newsweek* termed "stunned outrage" across the United States. Certainly, no Supreme Court decision within recent memory, if ever, was so quickly, bitterly, and overwhelmingly denounced by the American public and political establishment.

Opposition to *Johnson* sparked credible efforts, which have persisted over the intervening decades, to amend the United States Constitution to empower Congress to enact a national ban on flag burning. As recently as 2006, a proposed flag burning amendment passed the House with the required two-thirds majority and failed in the Senate by a single vote.

Over the last half century, Supreme Court decisions on the death penalty, school prayer, campaign finance, and other issues have occasionally sparked sustained political opposition from sizeable portions of the American public. Likewise, recent public remarks by Justice Ruth Bader Ginsberg show that she believes that the Court's decision in favor of abortion rights in *Roe v. Wade* in 1973 set back the cause of reproductive rights by "moving too far, too fast" and catalyzing a backlash against the women's movement (Crary 2012). Like *Johnson*, these cases illustrate the limits of Supreme Court's ability to accurately predict or reliably control political responses to its decisions. Though social and political change may follow from Supreme Court decisions, the Court does not direct such change.

CONCLUSIONS AND DIRECTIONS FOR FUTURE RESEARCH

The small but important political science literature on the Supreme Court's influence on the national media agenda shows that the Court is able to draw the media's attention to new issues when it disrupts prior policy arrangements (Flemming, Bohte, and Wood 1997; Flemming, Wood, and Bohte 1999; Ura 2009). This influence provides the Supreme Court with a powerful but imprecise mechanism for influencing American national politics. By elevating the national media presence of issues that are excluded from political debate by established constellations of power, the Supreme Court creates

[5] Gallup Poll conducted June 23, 1989. N=500 adults.

opportunities for political change. As in the case of *Brown*, the Court's agenda-setting influence may be substantially disruptive and ultimately yield important changes in public opinion and public policy consistent with the Court's decisions (Klarman 2004).

However, the Court has essentially no control over how its decisions are portrayed or how other political actors will react to the novel issue environment and what proposals they will offer (Davis 1994; Davis and Strickler 2000). So, even to the extent that lengthy public debates will tend to resolve themselves in favor of the policy positions reflected in Supreme Court decisions (Ura 2014), the intermediate process between a Supreme Court decision and a positive outcome in public opinion or policy may evolve unevenly and only over the long run. Moreover, even if a typical agenda-setting decision of the Supreme Court ultimately catalyzes positive responses in public opinion and public policy, any given decision may fail to evoke them or, instead, produce a negative public reaction or antagonistic policy responses. Regardless, it is clear that the Supreme Court is a force for change in American politics and that its influence on the mass media is an important pathway by which the Court provokes changes in public opinion and public policy.

Ultimately, though, the literature on the Supreme Court's ability to influence the mass media poses at least as many questions than it answers. On the problem of agenda setting itself, there are numerous opportunities to evaluate whether and how the Supreme Court's salient decisions have influenced media coverage of issues beyond those considered by existing studies, testing their generalizability. Affirmative action, the death penalty, and gun rights are obvious points of departure, but there are many others. Likewise, new agenda-setting studies may consider the Court's role in shaping issue attention in electronic media and social media and the reciprocal influence of agenda setting in traditional media and new media.

Aside from these kinds of studies that extend prior research by examining the generalizability of previous findings of the Supreme Court's agenda-setting influence across issues and media formats, two recent studies point to valuable new directions for research in this area. First, Haider-Markel, Allen, and Johansen's (2006) analysis of heterogeneity in newspaper coverage of the Supreme Court's decision invalidating state sodomy laws in *Lawrence v. Texas* (2003) shows how local political contexts shaped newspapers' coverage of the decision and their subsequent treatment of gay rights issues. By showing that newspapers in states that were more hostile to gay rights prior to *Lawrence* covered the decision more critically, Haier-Markel and his coauthors provide an important missing link between the literature on the Supreme Court's effects on issue attention in the mass media and the literature illustrating varied dynamics in public reactions to Supreme Court decisions (e.g., Brickman and Peterson 2006; Franklin and Kosaki 1989; Hoekstra 2000, 2003; Hoekstra and Segal 1996; Johnson and Martin 1998; Marshall 1989; Ura 2014).

Likewise, Clawson and Waltenberg's (2003) study of the effects of media frames on evaluations of Supreme Court decisions and the larger literature on the role of frames in shaping how individuals connect political information and personal values to form policy attitudes suggest a second new direction (e.g., Brewer 2003, 2008; Iyengar 1990, Jacoby 2000; Kinder and Sanders 1996; Kellstedt 2000; Koch 1998; Nelson, Clawson, and Oxley 1997; Zaller 1992). Another way that the Supreme Court may influence media attention to issues is by introducing new frames or elevating the prominence or acceptability of existing frames in public debates. These types of effects may have profound effects on public opinion that vary cross-sectionally and longitudinally, perhaps helping to account for the complex set of findings in the literature on public reactions to Supreme Court decisions (e.g., Brickman and Peterson 2006; Franklin and Kosaki 1989; Hoekstra 2000, 2003; Hoekstra and Segal 1996; Johnson and Martin 1998; Marshall 1989; Ura 2014).

Finally, as the preceding pair of suggestions indicates, the separate literatures on the Supreme Court's media effects and on public reactions to Supreme Court decisions are due for a more serious integration. Members of Congress and (especially) presidents have opportunities to communicate directly with the American people and utilize an array of political allies in attempts to shape public reactions to their political and policy choices. Supreme Court justices have generally chosen to limit direct public scrutiny of their institution and to interact with the media in much less public ways (e.g., Davis 2011). As a result, the public image of the Supreme Court age and its choices is much more a product of the media than of the elected branches of government. Understanding the processes by which the media filters, frames, and transforms the Supreme Court's decisions into news content is critical for understanding the mechanics of how the Court influences public opinion and policymaking processes, which, by extension, is critical for understanding important dynamics in American national politics.

REFERENCES

Bachrach, Peter, and Morton S. Baratz. 1962. "The Two Faces of Power." *American Political Science Review*. 56(December): 947–952.

Bartels, Larry M. 1996. Politicians and the Press: Who Leads, Who Follows? In *Annual meeting of the American Political Science Association, San Francisco*.

Baumgartner, Frank R., and Bryan D. Jones. 2009. *Agendas and Instability in American Politics*. 2nd ed. Chicago: University of Chicago Press.

Beerman, Jack M. 2001. "The Unhappy History of Civil Rights Legislation, Fifty Years Later." *Connecticut Law Review* 34(4): 981–1033.

Bickel, Alexander. 1962. *The Least Dangerous Branch: The Supreme Court at the Bar of Politics*. Indianapolis, IN: Bobbs-Merrill.

Bowers v. Hardwick. 1986. 478 US 186.

Boy Scouts of America v. Dale. 2000. 530 US 640.

Brewer, Mark D., and Jeffrey Stonecash. 2008. *Split: Class and Cultural Divides in American Politics*. Washington, DC: CQ Press.

Brewer, Paul, R. 2003. "Values, Political Knowledge, and Public Opinion about Gay Rights: A Framing-Based Account." *Public Opinion Quarterly* 67(2): 173–201.

Brickman, Danette, and David A. M. Peterson. 2006. "Public Opinion Reaction to Repeated Events: Citizen Response to Multiple Supreme Court Abortion Decisions." *Political Behavior* 28(March): 87–112.

Brown v. Board of Education II. 1955. 349 U.S. 294.

Brown v. Board of Education of Topeka, Kansas. 1954. 347 US 783.

Buckalew, James K. 1969. "News Elements and Selection by Television News Editors." *Journal of Broadcasting & Electronic Media* 14: 47.

Canes-Wrone, Brandice. 2010. *Who Leads Whom? : Presidents, Policy, and the Public*. Chicago: University of Chicago Press.

Carmines, Edward G., and James A. Stimson. 1989. *Issue Evolution: Race and the Transformation of American Politics*. Princeton, NJ: Princeton University Press.

Clawson, Rosalee A., and Eric N. Waltenburg. 2003. "Support for A Supreme Court Affirmative Action Decision: A Story in Black and White." *American Politics Research* 31(May): 251–279.

Cohen, Jeffrey E. 1995. "Presidential Rhetoric and the Public Agenda." *American Journal of Political Science* 39(1): 87–107.

Cooper v. Aaron. 1958. 358 US 1.

Crary, David. 2012. "Ginsburg Questions 1973 Abortion Ruling's Timing." Boston.com, February 10. www.boston.com/news/education/higher/articles/2012/02/10/ginsburg_questions_1973_abortion_rulings_timing/.

Dahl, Robert. 1957. "Decision-Making in a Democracy: The Supreme Court as a National Policy-Maker." *Journal of Public Law* 6(Fall): 279 295.

Dalton, Russell J., Paul A. Beck, and Robert Huckfeldt. 1998. "Partisan Cues and the Media: Information Flows in the 1992 Presidential Election." *American Political Science Review* 92 (March): 111–126.

Davis, Richard. 1994. *Decisions and Images: The Supreme Court and the Press*. Englewood Cliffs, N.J.: Prentice Hall.

2011. *Justices and Journalists: The U.S. Supreme Court and the Media*. New York: Cambridge University Press.

Davis, Richard, and Vincent James Strickler. 2000. "The Invisible Dance: The Supreme Court and the Press." *Perspectives on Political Science* 29(2): 85–92.

Dominick, James R. 1975. "Televisions Journalism or Show Business: A Content Analysis of Eyewitness News." *Journalism Quarterly* 52(2): 213–218.

Edwards III, George C., and B. Dan Wood. 1999. "Who Influences Whom? The President, Congress, and the Media." *The American Political Science Review* 93(2): 327–344.

Engel v. Vitale. 1962. 370 US 421.
Ericson, David. 1977. "Newspaper Coverage of the Supreme Court: A Case Study." *Journalism Quarterly* 54 (Autumn): 650–607.
Esser, Frank. 1999. "'Tabloidization' of News: A Comparative Analysis of Anglo-American and German Press Journalism." *European Journal of Communications* 14(3): 291–324.
Fay Lomax Cook, Tom R. Tyler, Edward G. Goetz, Margaret T. Gordon, David Protess, Donna R. Leff, and Harvey L. Molotch. 1983. "Media and Agenda Setting: Effects on the Public, Interest Group Leaders, Policy Makers, and Policy." *Public Opinion Quarterly* 47 (Spring): 16–35.
Flemming, Roy B., and B. Dan Wood. 1997. "The Public and the Supreme Court: Individual Justice Responsiveness to American Policy Moods." *American Journal of Political Science* 41(April): 468–498.
Flemming, Roy B., B. Dan Wood, and John Bohte. 1999. "Attention to Issues in a System of Separated Powers: The Macrodynamics of American Policy Agendas." *American Journal of Political Science*. 41 (October): 1224–1250.
Foner, Eric. 2002. *Reconstruction: America's Unfinished Revolution, 1863–1877*. New York: Harper Perennial Modern Classics.
Franklin, Charles H., and Liane C. Kosaki. 1989. "Republican Schoolmaster: The U.S. Supreme Court, Public Opinion, and Abortion." *The American Political Science Review* 83(September): 751–771.
Frederickson, Kari A. 2001. *The Dixiecrat Revolt and the End of the Solid South, 1932–1968*. Chapel Hill, NC: University of North Carolina Press.
Gartner, Scott Sigmund. 2004. "Making the International Local: The Terrorist Attack on the USS Cole, Local Casualties, and Media Coverage." *Political Communication* 21(2): 139–159.
Gressman, Eugene. 1951. "The Unhappy History of Civil Rights Legislation." *Michigan Law review* 50(8): 1323–1358.
Griffin v. County School Board of Prince William County. 1964. 377 US 218.
Hetherington, Marc J. 2009. "Review Article: Putting Polarization in Perspective." *British Journal of Political Science* 39(02): 413–448.
Hill, Kim Quaile. 1998. "The Policy Agendas of the President and the Mass Public: A Research Validation and Extension." *American Journal of Political Science* 42 (4): 1328–1334.
Hoekstra, Valerie J. 2000. "The Supreme Court and Local Public Opinion." *The American Political Science Review* 94(March): 89–100.
2003. *Public reaction to Supreme Court decisions*. New York: Cambridge University Press.
Hoekstra, Valerie J., and Jeffrey A. Segal. 1996. "The Shepherding of Local Public Opinion: The Supreme Court and Lamb's Chapel." *The Journal of Politics* 58 (04): 1079–1102.
Hurley et al v. Irish-American Gay Lesbian and Bisexual Group. 1995. 515 US 557.
Illinois ex rel. McCollum v. Board of Education, District 71. 1948. 333 US 203.
Iyengar, Shanto, and Donald R. Kinder. 1987. *News that Partisan Cues and the Media: Information Flows in the 1992 Presidential Election Matters: Television and American Opinion*. Chicago: University of Chicago Press.
Iyengar, Shanto. 1990. "Framing Responsibility for Political Issues: The Case of Poverty." *Political Behavior* 12(1): 19–40.

Jacoby, William G. 2000. "Issue Framing and Public Opinion on Government Spending." *American Journal of Political Science* 44(4): 750–767.
Jeff L. Yates, Andrew B. Whitford, and William Gillespie. 2005. "Agenda-Setting, Issue Priorities, and Organizational Maintenance: The U.S. Supreme Court, 1995 to 1994." *British Journal of Political Science* 35(2): 357–368.
Johnson, Timothy R., and Andrew D. Martin. 1998. "The Public's Conditional Response to Supreme Court Decisions." *The American Political Science Review* 92(June): 299–309.
Katznelson, Ira. 2013. *Fear Itself: The New Deal and the Origins of Our Time.* New York: W. W. Norton.
Keck, Thomas M. 2009. "Beyond Backlash: Assessing the Impact of Judicial Decisions on LGBT Rights." *Law & Society Review* 43(1): 151–186.
Kellstedt, Paul M. 2000. "Media Framing and the Dynamics of Racial Policy Preferences." *American Journal of Political Science* 44(2): 245–260.
Kinder, Donald R., and Lynn M. Sanders. 1996. *Divided by Color: Racial Politics and Democratic Ideals.* University Of Chicago Press. Kingdon, John. 1984. *Agendas, Alternatives, and Public Policy.* Boston, MA: Little Brown.
1989. *Congressmen's Voting Decisions.* 3 ed. Ann Arbor, MI: University of Michigan Press.
Klarman, Michael J. 2004. *From Jim Crow to Civil Rights: The Supreme Court and the Struggle for Racial Equality: The Supreme Court and the Struggle for Racial Equality.* New York: Oxford University Press.
Koch, Jeffrey W. 1998. "Political Rhetoric and Political Persuasion: The Changing Structure of Citizens' Preferences on Health Insurance during Policy Debates." *Public Opinion Quarterly* 62(2): 209–229.
Lacy, Stephen. 1987. "The Effect of Intracity Competition on Daily Newspaper Content." *Journalism Quarterly* 64(2): 281–290.
1989. "A Model of Demand for News: Impact of Competition on Newspaper Content." *Journalism Quarterly* 66(1): 40–48.
Larson, Stephanie. 1985. "How *The New York Times* Covered Discrimination Cases." *Journalism Quarterly* 47 (Winter): 894–896.
Lau, Peter F. 2004. *From the Grassroots to the Supreme Court: Brown v. Board of Education and American Democracy.* Duke University Press.
Lawrence v. Texas. 2003. 539 US 558.
Lynch v. Donnelly. 1984. 465 US 668.
Marshall, Thomas R. 1989. *Public Opinion and the Supreme Court.* Boston: Unwin Hyman.
McCombs, Maxwell E., and Donald L. Shaw. 1972. "The Agenda-Setting Function of Mass Media." *Public Opinion Quarterly* 36(2): 176–187.
McMahon, Kevin J. 2011. *Nixon's Court: His Challenges to Judicial Liberalism and Its Political Consequences.* Chicago: University of Chicago Press.
Newland, Chester A. 1964. "Press Coverage of the United States Supreme Court." *Western Political Quarterly* 17 (March): 15–36.
Patterson, James T. 1967. *Congressional Conservatism and the New Deal: The Growth of the Conservative Coalition in Congress, 1933–1939.* Lexington, KY: University of Kentucky Press.
Patterson, James T., and William W. Freehling. 2001. *Brown V. Board of Education: A Civil Rights Milestone and Its Troubled Legacy.* Oxford University Press.

Perlstein, Rick. 2001. *Before the Storm: Barry Goldwater and the Unmaking of American Consensus*. New York: Hill and Wang.

Plessy v. Ferguson. 1896. 163 U.S. 537.

Poole, Keith T., and Howard Rosenthal. 1997. *Congress: A Political-Economic History of Roll Call Voting*. New York: Oxford University Press.

Rae, Nicol C. 1994. *Southern Democrats*. New York: Oxford University Press.

Riker, William H. 1986. *The Art of Political Manipulation*. New Haven: Yale University Press.

Roe v. Wade. 1973. 410 US 113.

Romer v. Evans. 1996. US 517 US 620.

Rosenberg, Gerald N. 1991. *The Hollow Hope: Can Courts Bring About Social Change?* Chicago: University of Chicago Press.

Schattschneider, E. E. 1960. *The Semi-Sovereign People: A Realist's View of Democracy in America*. New York: Holt, Rinehart, and Winston.

Slotnick, Elliot E., and Jeffrey A. Segal. 1998. *Television News and the Supreme Court: All the News That's Fit to Air?* Cambridge University Press.

Smith, Tom W. 1980. "America's Most Important Problem—A Trend Analysis, 1946–1976." *Public Opinion Quarterly* 44(2): 164–180.

Sullivan, Patricia. 2009. *Lift Every Voice: The NAACP and the Making of the Civil Rights Movement*. The New Press.

Texas v. Johnson. 1989. 491 US 397.

Thomas E. Nelson, Rosalee A. Clawson, and Zoe M. Oxley. 1997. "Media Framing of a Civil Liberties Conflict and Its Effect on Tolerance." *American Political Science Review* 91(3): 567–583.

Ura, Joseph Daniel. 2009. "The Supreme Court and Issue Attention: The Case of Homosexuality." *Political Communication* 26(4): 430–446.

2014. "Backlash and Legitimation: Macro Political Responses to Supreme Court Decisions." *American Journal of Political Science*. 58 (1): 110–126.

Woodward, C Vann. 1951. *Reunion and Reaction: The Compromise of 1877 and the End of Reconstruction*. Boston: Little, Brown and Company.

1955. *The Strange Career of Jim Crow*. New York: Oxford University Press.

Zaller, John R. 1992. *The Nature and Origins of Mass Opinion*. Cambridge, UK: Cambridge University Press.

9

How Traditional Journalists Cover the Court in the New Media Age

DAVID G. SAVAGE

It was a quiet Tuesday morning in late February 2013, a return to work for most Americans after a long weekend marking Presidents' Day. For the Supreme Court, it meant the return to public sessions after a mid-winter recess.

On that day, the justices would hear arguments in two cases, including one of great interest to agri-business and to the worldwide critics of genetically modified foods. Monsanto was suing an Indiana farmer named Vern Bowman because he had gathered soybeans from a grain elevator and planted them for a late-season crop. Monsanto said some of those soybeans were grown with its special, weed-resistant seeds. The Court had to decide whether the company's patent rights lived beyond the first planting of its seeds.

Before the arguments got underway, however, the Court handed down four decisions. A 9–0 ruling in *Florida v. Harris* said an alert from a trained dog gives a police officer probable cause to search a car, and without further proof of the dog's reliability. "A sniff is up to snuff," wrote Justice Elena Kagan, whenever it is reasonable to believe a search based on dog's alert is likely to reveal illegal drugs.

In a second case, the Federal Trade Commission won more authority to prevent hospital chains from gobbling up small community hospitals and thereby, reducing competition (*FTC v. Phoebe Putney Health System*). And in a surprising criminal law ruling, the Court said the police cannot "seize" a suspect who they saw leave the premises of a home they were about to search. The decision "scrambled the court's usual ideological lines," wrote Jess Bravin in the *Wall Street Journal*. Justice John G. Roberts Jr. and Justice Antonin Scalia were in the majority favoring the criminal defendant, while Justice Stephen Breyer spoke for the dissenters in *Bailey v. United States*.

But the big news that morning was tucked into a twelve-page orders list among several hundred cases that were denied review. Here is what it said in total:

> Appeal—Jurisdiction Noted
>
> No. 12–536. Shaun McCutcheon, et al., Appellants *v.* Federal Election Commission. Appeal from the United States District Court for the District of Columbia. In this case, probable jurisdiction is noted.

Within minutes, the major wire services – Associated Press, Reuters, Bloomberg and Dow Jones – had sent out stories reporting that the Roberts Court was taking on another major campaign finance case in what could be a sequel to its still-controversial Citizens United decision of 2010. Within about an hour, the websites of the major newspapers—including the *New York Times*, the *Wall Street Journal*, the *Los Angeles Times*, the *Washington Post* and *USA Today* – had lengthier stories with more context and explanation. Their print versions included reactions from election-law experts and analysis from both defenders and critics of the election funding laws.

Campaign finance law can be difficult to understand and even harder to explain. In the Court's first and most significant ruling – the *Buckley v. Valeo* decision of 1976 – the justices drew a sharp distinction between a person's spending money to promote his favored candidate and his contributing money to his favored candidate. The theory went like this: A person who spends his own money on election-related ads is just giving voice to his own views. However, if that same person gives millions of dollars to his favored candidate for Congress, that candidate, if elected, might well feel indebted to his wealthy supporter. And certainly, the voters might well suspect their representative in Congress will do the bidding of his big donor. With that theory in mind, the justices sent the law in two directions. Spending on campaign ads is fully protected as free speech under the First Amendment, the Court said in the Buckley decision, so long as it is independent of the candidate and his campaign. However, the law can limit contributions to the candidate or his campaign in order to prevent corruption or the appearance of corruption.

The court's legal theory changed American politics and ushered in an era of fabulously wealthy candidates who campaigned using their own money. Think of presidential candidates like Ross Perot or Steve Forbes or New York Mayor Michael Bloomberg.

All of these candidates were wealthy individuals. The Citizens United decision took the logic of the theory set out in the Buckley case and extended it to campaign spending by corporations. The five conservative justices decided that if independent campaign spending is indeed free speech, the 1947 law that prohibited political "expenditures" by corporations and unions must be unconstitutional. The four dissenters, joined by liberals nationwide, objected and said political spending by huge, profit-making corporations is not in the same category as an individual's free-speech right to spend his own money.

While activists on the left rallied public support for a constitutional amendment to overturn the Citizens United decision, activists on the right went back to court, hoping to chip away at the remaining restrictions on money in politics. In the wake of the Citizens United decision, an appeals court ruling won by a group called "SpeechNow" led to the creation of so-called "SuperPACs."

These groups sought and received huge contributions from wealthy persons and corporations and spent the money on advertising campaigns supporting Republican or Democratic candidates. This was legal, they said, because this money was independent spending blessed by the Court's Citizens United ruling.

Notice, however, that these SuperPACs were taking big contributions to pay for political spending. It looked as though the line separating contributions from spending was blurring.

Many wondered when the next barrier would fall. If the Court's conservatives really believed "money is speech" when it comes to politics, why wouldn't they throw out the limits on how much individuals can give to candidates? That question was presented, if indirectly, by the case of *McCutcheon v. FEC* and *RNC v. FEC*. An Alabama businessperson, Shaun McCutcheon said he wanted to give more to Republican candidates than the $33,000 he gave in 2012, but he was restricted by a cap on total contributions set by federal law (It stood at $123,000 for the 2013–14 election cycle). For its part, the Republican National Committee wanted to receive more from donors like McCutcheon, and it joined in arguing the total contribution limit was an unconstitutional limit on the freedom of speech. That explains why the reporters who cover the Supreme Court were prepared and ready to write on the morning of February 19 when the Court issued its one-sentence notice agreeing to review the McCutcheon case.

This was a surprisingly typical news day for the journalists who cover the Supreme Court. A list of decisions, all coming at the same time, prompted a burst of activity. A reporter trying to make sense of it faced many questions on what to report and what to ignore.

Compared to the mid-1980s, when I began covering the Court, the news coverage these days is richer, deeper, more varied, but most of all, faster. The digital era has sped up the news process and put more pressure on the reporters to respond quickly. No longer can network TV or newspaper reporters focus their attention just on that evening's broadcast or the news story to be filed for the next morning's paper. Their news websites are on all the time, and they are anxious for news – now.

Viewed from inside the pressroom, however, the Court operates much as it did decades ago. Printed copies of decisions are handed out at 10 A.M. In the now-distant era before the Internet, only a handful of people could read them immediately. Law firms often sent someone to the Court to pick up a copy of a decision so it could be read by the lawyers downtown. Linda Greenhouse, the long-time court reporter for the *New York Times*, and I have fondly recalled the times when we would read an entire opinion, including the concurrences, the dissent, and the footnotes, before deciding what to write. We could even take a few hours to talk to lawyers and others who followed the case before we had to file a story.

The basics of writing about the Court have not changed. With each decision comes at least three questions: What did the Court decide? What is the legal basis for the decision? What does it mean? Lawyers and law students tend to focus on the decision and its legal reasoning. News editors, however, want to know whether the decision has significance for the wider world. Should busy readers stop and pay attention to this decision, and if so, why? Does it really change anything? editors often ask. How many people, businesses, or universities might be affected, or how many state laws may change as a result?

These are hard questions, and these days, the answers must come fast. The whole world now can see the Court's opinions at the moment they are released, and anyone who is interested can read them. SCOTUSblog, the first source of court news for many interested readers, posts the decisions instantly, and a smart story from veteran reporter Lyle Denniston usually follows a few minutes later. These days, I am usually writing a story within minutes of a decision being handed down, and yes, before I have finished closely reading the entire text and the dissent. Law professors and other legal experts also weigh in, along with advocates and activists on both sides. Their commentary and analysis enlivens the debate and adds immeasurably to an understanding of the Court's work.

Sometimes, time pressure can be intense. In the last week in June, when the Court was handing down decisions on the fate of President Obama's health care law or on gay marriage, news organizations were determined to post a "breaking news alert" that reported the outcome within seconds of the Court's releasing its decision. Speed can produce errors, and two TV networks briefly reported the health care law had been struck down, rather than narrowly upheld. The pressure to file stories quickly – at least a brief story for the web – is now part of the job for most of the regular reporters who cover the Supreme Court on daily basis, and not just in June. Even on a February morning in the middle of the term, the reporters had to be ready to respond quickly when the Court took action.

To step back a bit, it is important to understand how covering a court is different from covering, say, Congress or the White House. In some respects, writing about the Supreme Court is like covering a specialized field, such as medicine, science, education, or the environment. The reporters who write about the Court are required to do lots of explaining: explaining the law and what is at issue in a case, explaining what the justices are deciding and what it means. Reporters who yearn to "break news" usually find the court beat to be disappointing and disconcerting. True news "scoops" are rare, and leaks rarer yet.

On the other side of First Street on Capitol Hill, members of Congress and their staffs regularly talk to journalists – or at least some of them, and on some topics. When major decisions are being made at the White House or in some agencies, reporters often write in advance about what will be decided. They often do so after a briefing by one of the key players or by a staffer. At the Justice Department, staffers for Attorney General Eric Holder routinely briefed reporters from their favored news outlets before he gave a major speech or made a significant announcement. He apparently thought that was a useful way to shape the news coverage.

The Supreme Court is decidedly different. It does not leak its decisions in advance to favored reporters. The justices and their staffs do not brief reporters on their thinking, either before a decision or afterward. There are no "backgrounders" or hallway talks with unnamed sources. The public information officers at the Court, led by Kathy Arberg, make sure reporters have copies of the Court's opinions, but she and her colleagues do not explain or comment on the substance of the decisions. That is the work of the journalists.

Reporters can and do read the legal briefs that go to the justices. They also can go to the oral arguments in a case and hear the questions and comments from the bench. Over time, they can read enough opinions and dissents from justices to get a good sense of their views on all manner of legal issues. They can even glean a bit from their occasional public speeches and casual conversations at social events.

Unlike fields such as medicine or science, the law as practiced at the Supreme Court also comes with a heavy dose of ideology and politics. The justices are called upon to decide hard legal questions that have divided judges and lawyers and where the correct answer is rarely obvious. A justice's ideological view often tips the scale. Consider the major controversies that divide the Court: abortion or affirmative action, gun rights or gay rights, the death penalty, the role of money in politics, the role of religion in public life or the conflict between environmental protection and private property. All are issues where liberals and Democrats tend to see it one way, while conservatives and Republicans take the opposite view. Since at least the late 1960s, when Richard Nixon ran for the White House by campaigning against the Warren Court, presidents have selected justices they believe share their views on those major issues. In that respect, reporting on the Supreme Court resembles reporting on a political body. If you know which party controls the House or the Senate, you can forecast what bills will pass there. The comparison is not exact, but if you know the ideological and political leanings of the justices, you can correctly forecast the outcome in major cases most of the time.

On days when the Court is in session, the public information staffers will tell reporters that one or more rulings are likely to be handed down. They do not say what case will be decided, let alone what the decision will say. At 10 A.M. when Chief Justice Roberts announces the case to be decided, the staff hands out a copy of the opinion. From there, the journalists are their own.

So, what was the most news worthy development this Tuesday morning in February? The early stories all focused on the upcoming campaign finance case, but there were other competitors for the attention of the press.

The case of *Vern Bowman v. Monsanto* had garnered extraordinary attention on some blogs and in Europe and Asia. It looked to be an epic battle in which a lone farmer takes on the world's biggest agriculture company. Some activists saw the case as a fight over genetically modified foods. In the United States, corporate lawyers saw the case as a major threat to enormously valuable patents in the biotech industry. The justices had been skeptical of patents in recent rulings, and corporate defenders were taken aback when the Court voted to hear the farmer's case. If the patent for a genetically modified seed was "exhausted" after the first planting – as Bowman's lawsuit claimed – farmers could buy one small bag of highly specialized seeds and thereafter, grow new crops with their own seeds. Patents worth billions of dollars would become nearly worthless.

So, a few minutes before 10 A.M., several of the regulars turned off their computers in the pressroom and headed upstairs to listen to the oral argument in *Bowman v. Monsanto*. The courtroom exchanges between the justices and lawyers can supply the drama for a good story. Usually, the comments and questions from the justices reveal how they are likely to rule.

After about an hour, the reporters shuffled back into the pressroom, prepared to write an instant report for their web sites. The consensus was that Vern Bowman was going to lose.

So, what about the decisions in the dog-sniff case, or even the ruling limiting the power of the police to arrest suspects who have left a place about to be searched? As a rule, the Court's decision in a case would be more important and more newsworthy than an oral argument, or a one-line announcement agreeing to review a new case in several months. A ruling is definite and final. A story on an oral argument has to be hedged. Since none of the justices took the farmer's side during the argument, the reporters felt free to predict the outcome that morning. Adam Liptak, writing in the *New York Times*, described a "freewheeling and almost entirely one-sided argument (which) indicated that the justices would not allow Monsanto's patents for genetically altered soybeans to be threatened by an Indiana farmer who used them without paying the company a fee." But even then, the oral argument is just that, an opportunity for the competing lawyers to voice their best claims before the justices. At best, the experienced reporters can give readers a strong clue as to what the Court is likely to decide.

The Florida case involving Aldo, the drug-sniffing dog, had some appeal as a news story. Motorists and passengers at airports are more likely to encounter drug-sniffing dogs than they are likely to run into farmers fighting with seed companies or wealthy donors who want to give more to politicians. The press corps is undoubtedly biased by one measure. The reporters clearly favor the justices whose opinions feature strong, clear, and quotable comments. And on that score, a Kagan opinion rarely disappoints.

In mid-May, Kagan would write the Court's opinion in the Monsanto case, and she rejected what she called farmer Bowman's "blame the bean defense." He had argued the special soybeans from past harvests sprouted in the field and stood up against weed killers. Kagan was not impressed. "Bowman was not a passive observer of his soybeans' multiplication," she wrote. "The seeds he purchased (miraculous though they might be in other respects) did not spontaneously create eight successive soybeans crops" (*Bowman v. Monsanto*, May 13, 2013). All the news stories quoted Kagan's "blame the bean" comment.

But the Florida decision suffered from one major flaw, which Kagan's opinion could not overcome. It did not change much. The Florida Supreme Court had proposed a significant shift in the law. Studies had shown that some dogs alert based on cues from their masters. Voicing skepticism, the Florida justices would have required police and prosecutors to furnish test evidence that would demonstrate that the dog that led the officer to the drug evidence was thoroughly reliable. Otherwise, the search triggered by the dog would be deemed unreasonable, the Florida court said. However, the Supreme Court justices reversed that decision and opted to maintain the status quo. They would continue to allow the police to search cars and seize evidence whenever a canine alerted. The message was, we trust the dogs and their noses. No real news there.

Or at least, no real news on February 19. A pair of Florida cases involving drug dogs had come to the Court, and they were heard on the same day in October. The decision in the other case, *Florida v. Jardines*, was not handed down until March 26, and it made more news. By a 5–4 vote, the Court ruled the police violated the Fourth Amendment when, without a search warrant, they took a drug-detection dog to the front porch of a Miami home so he could sniff for marijuana. Justice Scalia spoke for an unusual majority that consisted of Justices Clarence Thomas, Ruth Bader Ginsburg, Sonia Sotomayor, and Elena Kagan.

This odd split on search cases showed up several times during the 2012–13 term, most notably in the 5–4 decision in *Maryland v. King*, which upheld the growing practice of taking a DNA sample from every person who is arrested for a serious crime. Justices Breyer and Thomas supplied key votes to rule for the government, while Justice Scalia delivered one of his fiery dissents.

This unexpected split was first revealed in the decision in *Bailey v. United States*, handed down February 19. In a 6–3 decision, with Scalia in the majority, the Court curbed the power of the police to arrest people who they had seen leaving a place about to be searched. The decision clarified the law, but it got only a brief mention in most of the news coverage because it arose from an unusual situation.

The journalists working for traditional news organizations face two significant limitations every day: time and space. At 9:30 A.M. that morning, when the weekly "orders list" was released, they could sit before their computers and write stories to be filed on the website reporting the Court was taking on another major campaign finance case. But at 10 A.M., they had to make a choice. They could stay at their computers and write stories on the decision in the case of drug-sniffing dog. If not too rushed, they could add a few sentences on the decision in the Bailey case, since both involved police and crime. Or, they could ignore the decisions for now and sit in the courtroom to listen to the hour-long argument in the Monsanto case. The reporters had to choose how to spend their time, and there is no clearly correct decision. Much depends on their judgment about the relative significance of the cases. In this instance, is the farmer's fight with Monsanto more interesting and potentially more significant than a unanimous ruling that upholds the use of drug-sniffing dogs?

By "space," I mean the amount of newsprint or a website – or, for that matter, broadcast time – that can be devoted to a particular news story.

The major news organizations try to appeal to a mass audience, and they seek to report on the most important and interesting stories of the day, from around the country and around the globe. The Court's decisions, no matter how significant, are not the only news of the day. Whether it is Nina Totenberg at National Public Radio or Pete Williams at NBC or Jess Bravin at the *Wall Street Journal*, the court reporters spend part of their morning talking with their editors about what news should be reported from the Court this day and what "space" does it deserve, whether on the air or in print.

All the major news organizations that cover the Court gave prominent play to the campaign finance case. It was a front-page story in many newspapers on Wednesday, February 20. The Roberts Court appeared poised to knock down another limit on big money flowing into the campaigns for Congress and the White House.

Many news outlets covered the case of the Indiana farmer and his fight with Monsanto. Several of the newspapers with a national audience also covered the rulings on the drug-sniffing dogs, the new limits on the police power to make arrests, and the Federal Trade Commission's victory in its effort to limit mergers by community hospitals. By that evening, the reporters could then look forward to doing it all over the next day. Then, the justices would hear arguments in two more cases and hand down four more decisions.

For a capsule description of how the Court news coverage has changed in recent decades, it is hard to top the career of Lyle Denniston and the rise of SCOTUSblog. When I arrived in 1986, Lyle was the senior print reporter in the pressroom and its most respected authority on the Court. If you were uncertain about a legal doctrine, puzzled by an assertion in an opinion or perplexed by a pending cert petition, Lyle, if asked, would patiently explain it. He was more than a good reporter; he made the rest of the press corps better as well. However, his audience of newspaper readers was quite limited, as was the space in the printed paper. He had worked for the *Washington Star*, the city's afternoon paper before it folded in 1981, and then for the *Baltimore Sun*, where he took a retirement.

But Lyle had no interest in sitting back and relaxing. Washington lawyer Tom Goldstein, like Lyle, has the energy and drive to learn everything about the Court, and he is an innovator and entrepreneur. Goldstein founded SCOTUSblog with his wife Amy Howe with the idea it would help promote his law practice. Instead, he created something entirely new: an all-purpose, online source of news and information about the Court. The site includes everything from monthly calendars of the Court's arguments to legal briefs on pending cases, commentary and statistics on the Court's decisions, and daily news developments.

As SCOTUSblog began to take off, Goldstein hired Denniston as its first full-time reporter. Having reached his early eighties, Lyle had finally found a news-reporting job that could make full use of his vast knowledge and give him a wide and well-informed audience anxious to read what he wrote.

Denniston's postings are substantive and analytical. He focuses on the legal arguments and the precedents that are at issue in a case. He rarely writes about the people involved in a case nor quotes legal commentators, but his postings give readers clear insight into the legal issues before the Court. Here is the opening of Denniston's posting on SCOTUSblog, which went up February 19 at 12:36 P.M.:

> Giving itself the option of changing its mind on government power to limit campaign contributions, the Supreme Court on Tuesday set the stage for review of the constitutionality of a specific donation ceiling set by federal law, but a larger issue looms in the background. Since the Court's landmark opinion in 1976 in *Buckley v. Valeo*, it has always given government more leeway to control contributions to candidates or political organizations than over spending by candidates or by independent political activists. That differing constitutional treatment potentially is at stake in the new case, *McCutcheon v. Federal Election Commission* (docket 12–536).

SCOTUSblog is written mostly for an audience of lawyers, law students, and devoted fans of the Court's work. Journalists for the major news organizations seek to appeal to a different, broader audience that includes intelligent readers who are not lawyers and casual readers who want to keep up with the news of the day. To reach them, the journalists need to digest a Court decision and report it in a way that is clear and understandable. Whenever possible, they drop legal language, including references to "habeas corpus," to "cert petitions," and to doctrines like "Chevron deference." A news story must be written so it can be read and understood by a reader of ordinary intelligence.

On days when the Court issues a major decision, the news coverage may read as though it is much the same. There are only so many ways to report that the Court in a 5–4 decision struck down part of the historic Voting Rights Act. The news stories may differ in their emphasis and depth. Some may feature reactions from the interested parties, while others try to analyze what a particular decision means for future rulings on, say, affirmative action or gay marriage. On the many days when the Court is not in session, the reporters go their own ways and write quite different stories.

Robert Barnes of the *Washington Post* regularly writes features from around the country on people whose cases are before the Court. A story on April 15, 2013 previewed a case called *Adoptive Couple v. Baby Girl*. Here is the opening:

> NOWATA, Okla., and CHARLESTON, S.C. – There are two houses, a thousand miles apart, that each contain a child's play kitchen, a wall of toys and portraits of the same dark-eyed, curly-haired little girl.

In one lives a couple named Matt and Melanie Capobianco, who cared for the girl from the time she drew her first breath until 27 months later, when the courts said she must be returned to her biological father… And in the other house lives the father, Dusten Brown, who once tapped out a text message saying he'd give up rights to his daughter, but now embraces parenthood. His daughter, now 3 ½ , shows off the room that Brown and his new wife have painted pink and purple.

Theirs was a case about the Indian Child Welfare Act, a 1978 law intended to prevent the break-up of Indian families. Brown was part-Cherokee, and he invoked the law to get custody of his daughter. This was a wrenching drama with a child caught in the middle. The biological father would lose in a 5–4 decision handed down June 26, 2013.

Tony Mauro, the veteran reporter for the *Legal Times* and *National Law Journal*, writes regularly about the people around the Court. He has done many stories on the law clerks, including the big bonuses they receive from law firms and the near absence of racial minorities in their ranks. When the Gibson Dunn law firm in Washington, hired Philip Alito, the son of Justice Alito, Mauro wrote about it, noting Alito was joining a firm that practices regularly before the Court and whose partners include Eugene Scalia, the son of Justice Scalia.

Mauro also writes regularly about potential ethical lapses by the justices, including conflicts of interests or a failure to list a spouse's income on a disclosure form. The Court does not welcome these stories. But because the justices wield considerable power while operating behind closed doors, it is important that reporters sometimes raise questions about their actions.

In January of 2004, I learned that Justice Scalia was at private hunting retreat in Louisiana with Vice President Dick Cheney. The two were long-time friends and avid duck hunters, and they had flown there together on a small Air Force jet used by the vice president. This caught my attention because just three weeks earlier, the Court had voted to hear the Bush administration's appeal in a case called "In re Richard B. Cheney." The justices would review a decision requiring the vice president's office to disclose who met with his energy policy task force. I faxed a note to Justice Scalia and asked if he had indeed gone duck hunting with Cheney and whether this raised a question about whether he should step aside from the case. A federal statute says, "Any justice (or) judge … shall disqualify himself in any proceeding in which his impartiality might reasonably be questioned."

Justice Scalia, to his credit, responded directly and said that, yes, he had gone duck hunting with Cheney, but no, he saw no need to step aside because the case involved the office of the vice president, not Dick Cheney personally. When I wrote about this, it set off a wide debate over how the justices exempt themselves from ethical rules that apply elsewhere in the federal judiciary.

A story about a justice – or two of them – can also illuminate a major controversy. Shortly after the Court voted to take up two gay marriage cases, I wrote about Justices Scalia and Kennedy. Here's the opening of the story, which appeared in the *Los Angeles Times* on December 8, 2012.

> WASHINGTON — For more than two decades, the defining battles within the Supreme Court over social and moral controversies have been fought between two devout Catholics appointed by President Reagan.

Justice Antonin Scalia believes the law can and should enforce moral standards, including criminal bans on abortion and on "homosexual conduct" that many "believe to be immoral and destructive."

Justice Anthony M. Kennedy is a libertarian conservative who believes the Constitution protects the freedom of individuals to "make personal decisions relating to marriage, procreation, contraception, family relationships, child rearing and education."

Now the ideological fight between the conservative giants is set for another round. The two 76-year-olds are to some extent likely to be on opposite sides when the court meets in the spring to decide whether the government can refuse marriage and federal benefits to gays and lesbians.

Adam Liptak, a Yale law graduate and a First Amendment lawyer before turning to journalism, writes regularly about academic studies of the Court's work. In a widely quoted *New York Times* story that appeared July 25, 2010, he reported on a statistical analysis of the justices' voting patterns from 1937 forward. The *Times* headline summed it up well. The Roberts Court is "The Most Conservative Court in Decades," it said. In May 2013, Liptak reported on the work of USC Professor Lee Epstein that ranked justices by their votes in business cases. "The study's most striking finding was that the two justices most likely to vote in favor of business interests since 1946 are the two most recent conservative additions to the court, Chief Justice Roberts and Justice Samuel A. Alito Jr.," he wrote ("Corporations Find a Friend in the Supreme Court," *New York Times*, May 5, 2013).

Liptak and the other regular reporters write stories almost every day when the Court is in session. In late June, they may write two or three major stories on the same day, and then follow up with an analysis a day or two later. But the best measure of their work needs to include the many other stories – features, profiles and analysis – that appear throughout the year.

It is surely not news to say that both the media industry and news coverage have been changing rapidly. Newspapers and TV broadcasts that depended on advertising revenue are shrinking as their audiences go online for news and entertainment. At the same time, the limitless capacity of the web has given life and voice to so many more, including those who write and comment on the Court and the law.

On evenings when the Supreme Court is busy, I scan familiar websites to see what has been written and said. Howard Bashman's How Appealing highlights an array of news stories reporting on the courts, with links to their content. The Volokh Conspiracy founded by UCLA's Eugene Volokh, has consistently smart commentary with a libertarian or conservative leaning. To get a smart, liberal perspective, I check Slate to read Dahlia Lithwick or Emily Bazelon, or Garrett Epps and Andrew Cohen at the *Atlantic* or Jeffrey Toobin in the *New Yorker*.

There are excellent blogs devoted to a particular area of law. See, for example, the ElectionLaw blog run by Richard Hasen, a law professor at the University of California at Irvine, or Sentencing Law and Policy run by Ohio State law professor Douglas Berman. Several Washington-based groups turn out thoughtful analysis of legal issues and the Court's work.

Expert commentary on the Court will surely survive and flourish on the web. Readers who lean left or right seek out smart commentary that is in line with their views, and on the Web, they can find it. I am less confident for the future of traditional news reporting, where the goal is to give a fair report that includes both sides of a dispute. Since the mid-twentieth century, big city newspapers and TV networks in the United States have sought a mass audience by playing it down the middle. They did not always succeed, but that was their goal. Now, their audiences have splintered and moved elsewhere, and with them went much of the revenue that supported traditional news reporting.

Most journalists who were at the Court that February morning ready to write about the next battle over campaign funding laws, as well as those who wrote intelligent and balanced stories on the momentous rulings at the term's end, were full-time reporters who had expertise in covering the Court and the law. There are fewer of them than twenty years ago, and there figure to be fewer ten years from now.

Readers and viewers increasingly will go in search of news that fits their perspectives. In doing so, they are likely to miss at least part of the story. Smart commentary usually makes its point by telling part of the story, but not all of it. In the wake of the Supreme Court's ruling that voided part of the Voting Rights Act, the *New York Times* and the *Wall Street Journal* weighed in with editorials. The contrast was stark. The decision was an outrage of the first order, according to the Times, "a dishonest" ruling that "eviscerated enforcement of the Voting Rights Act." The *Journal* saw the ruling as a necessary course correction. It is no longer the 1960s in the South, the *Journal* opined. In reading both editorials, I thought of the old-fashioned radio commentaries by Paul Harvey. After telling a story, he would pause dramatically and say, "Now, for the rest of the story!" Then, he would recount another aspect that put the story in an entirely different light.

In denouncing the Court's decision, the *Times* editorial ignored the fact blacks now register and vote at higher rates in the states of the Deep South compared to blacks in the North. Why then should the South and its voting laws remain under the special scrutiny of Washington? And the *Journal* ignored the fact that the Fifteenth Amendment said, "Congress shall have the power to enforce" its prohibition on racial discrimination in voting. A bi-partisan Congress voted overwhelming to extend the law in 2006. The *Journal* regularly denounces judicial activism and legislating from the bench. Why not this time? My guess is liberal readers finished the *Times* editorial nodding in agreement, and conservative readers did the same after reading the *Journal*'s analysis. Let's hope that at least some of them had read a fuller news report on the decision. It may not have altered their views, but at least they knew the rest of the story.

10

The Supreme Court and New Media

DAHLIA LITHWICK

It is a truism to say that the new media make the current members of the U.S. Supreme Court supremely uneasy. Indeed, one of the great journalistic surprises of the past decade has been the extent to which even the younger justices – notably Elena Kagan and Chief Justice John Roberts – who more or less came of political age in an Internet world – get weird when they talk about it. In a recent speech on the subject, Justice Kagan, who is fifty-three, explained that even as they decide cutting-edge issues of online technology, the nine justices continue to communicate with one another by way of ink on ivory paper.[1] Their mode of intramural communication has not, in fact changed, according to Kagan, since she clerked on the court in 1987. "The justices are not necessarily the most technologically sophisticated people," she said, "The court hasn't really 'gotten to' email." Chief Justice John Roberts mulling the constitutional questions surrounding texting at an oral argument once said: "I thought, you know, you push a button; it goes right to the other thing."[2] Justice Breyer has talked fondly about "the Tweeter."[3] One could go on.

But it goes far deeper than a generalized anxiety about the technology surrounding new media. I have noticed a significant anxiety among several of the justices – unrelated to their relative ages or comfort level with new technologies – about the implications of the new media for privacy and

[1] "Elena Kagan: Supreme Court hasn't 'gotten to' email," *CBS News*, August 21, 2013, www.cbsnews.com/8301-250_162-57599532/elena-kagan-supreme-court-hasnt-gotten-to-email/

[2] Jonathon M. Seidl. "Justice Breyer: SCOTUS Struggles with Technology, Must Adapt to Facebook World," *The Blaze*, November 17, 2010, www.theblaze.com/stories/2010/11/17/justice-breyer-scotus-struggles-with-technology-must-adapt-to-facebook-world/

[3] Maryam K. Ansari. "Justice Roberts Speaks at 4th Circuit Court of Appeals Conference," *FindLaw*, June 30, 2011, blogs.findlaw.com/fourth_circuit/2011/06/justice-roberts-speaks-at-4th-circuit-court-of-appeals-conference.html

harassment.[4] Indeed, I suspect it has begun to have an impact on First Amendment doctrine, with at least some of the judges ever more convinced that online communications have the potential to inflame violent reactions, violate private spaces, and visit uniquely pernicious harms on individuals.

Justice Stephen Breyer, for instance, has suggested that the very nature of online technology and communication might upend the traditional test for speech that incites violence in others, explaining, in a 2010 television interview, that burning a Koran and posting the video online is tantamount to shouting fire in a crowded theatre.[5] Breyer seems more and more persuaded that the Internet makes new and ominous violence and threats possible, and he would have decided *Snyder v. Phelps*[6] quite differently had the Court reached the issue of online communications. I have argued elsewhere[7] that Justices Thomas and Alito have been burned by online incursions into their privacy – by way of "gotcha" videos and embarrassing online revelations, and that it is thus probably no accident that the two of them have become quite determined to assess online speech in ways that are roundly different from speech published in other fora. Dissenting in *Doe v. Reed*, a case about whether signatories to a petition that would have put a marriage equality question to a state referendum had a privacy interest in their names, Justice Thomas memorably wrote that "the state of technology today, creates at least *some* probability that the signers of every referendum will be subjected to threats, harassment or reprisals if their personal information is disclosed. [T]he advent of the internet enables rapid dissemination of the information needed to threaten or harass every referendum signer."[8]

Justice Samuel Alito, concurring in the opinion in *Doe*, nevertheless expressed his own profound worries about the perils of Internet communication: once the names of petition signers were posted online, "then anyone with access to a computer could compile a wealth of information about all of those persons."[9] Alito went on to worry that by aggregating information about where petition signatories live, where their children attend school, their

[4] Dahlia Lithwick. "Their Own Private Hell," *Slate*, March 8, 2011, www.slate.com/articles/news_and_politics/jurisprudence/2011/03/their_own_private_hell.html

[5] Kate McCarthy. "Justice Stephen Breyer: Is Burning Koran 'Shouting Fire in a Crowded Theater?'" *ABC News*, September 14, 2010, abcnews.go.com/blogs/politics/2010/09/justice-stephen-breyer-is-burning-koran-shouting-fire-in-a-crowded-theater/

[6] *Snyder v. Phelps.*, 580 F. 3d 206 (2011)

[7] Dahlia Lithwick. "Supreme Court Breakfast Table: Kagan's hat trick," *Slate*, June 28, 2010, www.slate.com/articles/life/the_breakfast_table/features/2010/supreme_court_breakfast_table/freud_and_the_first_amendment.html

[8] *Doe v. Reed.*, 586 F. 3d 671 (2010)

[9] *Doe v. Reed.*, 586 F. 3d 671 (2010)

other private information and the amount of their mortgages, the potential that such information could be used for harassment is vast."[10]

That same deep anxiety about the potential of the new media to foster a culture of harassment and even violence pervaded the Court's 2010 *per curiam* opinion in *Hollingsworth v. Perry*[11] determining that California's marriage equality case would not be televised, despite the existence of a pilot project that would have permitted it. That same language was echoed in a Clarence Thomas dissent in the *Citizens United*[12] case that same year, as the justices fretted about witnesses concerned for their security, "Internet blacklists" and the Internet's unique potential to incite and foment harassment.

The same trio of Justices – Breyer, Alito, and Thomas – also showed deep concern over the potential for violent videogames to engender more violence in children than other forms of media, largely as a result of new technology, in a 2011 challenge to a California ban on the sale of violent video games to minors.[13] Again Thomas and Breyer dissented in the case and again the subtext of both appeals was that in the rough-and-tumble world of new media, speech just ain't what it used to be, and need not be protected as such.

The question of whether the Court's anxieties about social media will begin to be reflected in First Amendment doctrine is only part of the puzzle confronting a Court that is attempting to understand a medium that changes too rapidly to be fully understood. The second part of the equation is whether the Court's refusal to fully embrace the new media is coming at a cost to the institution. Reasonable people will differ on this matter. The justices maintain that barring access to television cameras, same-day audio, all but a handful of bloggers, and anyone else with a device that connects to an outlet from the High Court, maintains the integrity and gravitas of the institution. Many of us who cover the Court believe that the opposite is true; that barring new forms of media and technology from the Court harms both the judicial branch and the reporters attempting to cover the Court in a new age. The question going forward, is does it matter that the court has frozen itself in another century when it comes to new media access?

A lot of ink has been spilled on the question of whether there should be television cameras in the Supreme Court, and I will not belabor the matter here. Suffice to say it seems that most of the arguments advanced have more to do with protecting the privacy and personal space of the justices as individuals,

[10] Id. [11] *Hollingsworth v. Perry.*, 558 U.S (2010)

[12] *Citizens United v. Federal Election Commission.*, 558 U.S. 310 (2010)

[13] Adam Liptak. "Justices Reject Ban on Violent Video Games for Children," *New York Times*, June 27, 2011, www.nytimes.com/2011/06/28/us/28scotus.html?pagewanted=all&_r=1&

and the institution in general, than with any substantial objection to the right of access of the American public. It defies logic for the same jurists who grumble about the editorializing, slanting, and interpretation by journalists who mediate the daily news from inside the Court,[14] to complain about the possibility of televising the Court's daily proceedings, which would obviate the need for journalistic commentary and interpretation. If the justices have a better argument for barring cameras from the premises than their fear of Jon Stewart and the Snippet Effect (the fear of out-of-context audio or video quotations being used to spoof the justices on the late-night comedy shows), they have yet to advance it. That one of three branches of government conducts its public affairs in a virtual cone of secrecy – and that citizens stand in line for days if not hours[15] to watch landmark cases – is an execrable state of affairs in a democracy.

To be sure, the Court's recent move to release transcripts a mere hours after oral argument has improved the quality of same-day press reports immeasurably. Reporters no longer spend time after argument checking handwritten quotes against one another, hoping to offer reasonably accurate reports of what was said at argument. Today, journalists have access to online transcripts a few scant hours after the session has concluded and the result has been much more consistent and thorough coverage. Indeed, where the transcripts once declined to identify the various justices by name – referring to all questions as emanating from "the Court" – the transcripts also identify explicitly which justice has asked what question, again contributing immeasurably to the clarity and accuracy of subsequent reports. But even the printed transcript policy is strange, with journalists asked not to quote more than a few lines from the early versions of the transcript, and errors are frequent, often making their way into print. The same-day release of written transcripts, in short, has significantly improved the caliber of daily journalism, but it is not a substitute for live television cameras, which would capture the arguments, and whose transcripts are reviewable for accuracy.

The Court's experiment with same-day audio reflects the same generalized confusion about whether the Court wishes to provide access and transparency or shield its daily affairs from public scrutiny. Virtually every argument that can be advanced for barring televisions from the Supreme Court's ceremonial

[14] Dahlia Lithwick. "Scalia, Alito, and Kennedy take on the Fourth Estate," *Slate*, October 24, 2006, www.slate.com/articles/news_and_politics/jurisprudence/2006/10/the_supreme_press_critics.html

[15] Sarah Kitt. "To hear health care oral arguments, a three day camp-out," *Washington Post*, March 23, 2012, www.washingtonpost.com/blogs/wonkblog/post/to-hear-health-care-oral-arguments-a-three-day-camp-out/2012/03/23/gIQAnBeYWS_blog.html

courtroom break down when one is contemplating same-day release of audio. So much so, that the U.S. Court of Appeals for the District of Columbia Circuit, often characterized as the second most important court in the country, has just authorized the posting of audio recordings of oral arguments on its website within hours of the event.[16]

The U.S. Supreme Court has declined to release same-day audio and continues to post a week's worth of arguments every Friday. On twenty-three occasions since arguments in *Bush v. Gore*, the Court has released same-day audio of "blockbuster" cases, however, including the arguments in the Affordable Care Act challenges in 2012, and in the same-sex marriage cases in 2013.[17] The result is an inexpressibly bizarre outcome in which the Court as an institution declines to afford the public same-day access to its proceedings, except for those cases in which the justices are most likely to say partisan and inflammatory things, and later divide by along perfectly ideological 5–4 lines, thus confirming the American public's (and mainstream media's) pervasive sense that this is how the Court behaves all of the time.[18]

The Court has not been much more consistent when it comes to credentialing bloggers. The sad story of SCOTUSblog's legendary Lyle Denniston stands as a cautionary tale for any new media journalist seeking to cover the high court's daily proceedings. For complicated reasons, only twenty-six journalists have permanent Court credentials, all of them employed by print, radio, or television. A few online journalists are given day passes to cover oral arguments. But to have any credentials to cover the Court requires having an active White House and congressional credential. SCOTUSblog has neither, so Denniston is still credentialed based on his historic affiliation with WBUR.[19] Blame is routinely shifted for this state of affairs, among the various credentialing entities, including the Court, the Senate Press Gallery, and SCOTUSblog itself, but the fact of the matter is that SCOTUSblog is among the most vital resources for Court experts both inside and outside the Supreme

[16] Michael McGough. "An audio example for the Supreme Court," *Los Angeles Times*, September 12, 2013, www.latimes.com/opinion/opinion-la/la-ol-audio-supreme-court-scalia-20130912,0,7530886.story#axzz2jzbBdTHY

[17] Adam Liptak. "Court Announces Early Release of Same-Sex Marriage Arguments," *New York Times*, March 19, 2013, www.nytimes.com/2013/03/20/us/court-announces-early-release-of-same-sex-marriage-arguments.html

[18] Dahlia Lithwick. "The Supreme Court's hot/cold audio-casting policy," *Slate*, November 28, 2006, /www.slate.com/articles/news_and_politics/jurisprudence/2006/11/listen_up.html

[19] Mallary Jean Tenore. "Why it's so hard for SCOTUSblog to get Supreme Court press credentials," *Poynter*, July 11, 2012, www.poynter.org/latest-news/top-stories/180581/why-its-so-hard-for-scotusblog-to-get-credentialed/

Court building.[20] That this online entity cannot obtain a daily press pass to attend oral arguments, despite millions of readers and a decade-long history of impeccable journalism, is nothing short of a journalistic scandal, which is why journalistic watchdogs such as Poynter continue to cover the story with a permanently dropped jaw.

Bloggers have been on the frontlines of reporting on everything from the U.S. Attorney scandal to the Arab Spring to the National Security Agency (NSA) surveillance leaks. They have long ago established that at least some of them are as good as – if not better than – their print and broadcast colleagues in terms of accuracy, fairness, and substantial legal knowledge. Bloggers who have attended oral arguments in the healthcare cases, the marriage equality cases, and other landmark cases on a day pass have often proven themselves to be as knowledgeable and well prepared as their colleagues in print. Yet the Court has been slow to grant them permanent press access and even slower to grant access to the very things – like contemporaneous audio and video – that make for a compelling report in the new media. The Court seems unwilling to realize that by treating online journalists like rude interlopers, they may well be encouraging a form of journalism marked by rude interloping. There is no principled reason to draw a line between new and old media at the Court; it is a credentialing policy rooted more in fear than in reality.

In addition to matters of credentialing and coverage, the most significant ongoing barrier to the practice of effective online journalism at the Court remains the ban on electronic devices in the courtroom. Because reporters can bring only a pen and a notepad into the proceedings, it has become a joke of the trade that one can now cover the sessions in which cases are handed down more quickly and effectively at home in one's pajamas, than from the ceremonial courtroom. This is one of the ways the Court itself reinforces the stereotype of bloggers as a tribe of "pajama-jockeys." Any blogger on a tight deadline (and all bloggers are on a tight deadline) would do better to stay home and watch the news unspool on SCOTUSblog, than find herself unable to leave a public session, in which lengthy opinions, concurrences, and dissents are read from the bench.

Again, the Court has made important moves toward correcting this odd state of affairs. It has created a sort of three-tiered system in the major cases, such as the ACA challenge, in which reporters may choose between sitting in the courtroom for the entirety of the hand-down session and filing late (but reporting on atmospherics that – because there are no cameras – they will

[20] Id.

otherwise miss entirely); sitting in another room and listening to the session without access to electronic devices, but with the option to leave and file at any time; or sitting in the press room with electronic devices at the ready, with the caveat that someone can race out of the room with an audio feed and report news as it unfolds. The system works well for huge news organizations that can afford to put three reporters on a single story.

Large news organizations can seat someone in the courtroom, assign someone else to listen to the audio feed, and have a third person tweet or blog the news. But it puts online journalists and bloggers in the unenviable position of having to choose whether they would like to see history being made, hear it being made, or miss all of it being made but still be able to report it. Again, the sheer oddity that the Court has created a system in which the incentive is to participate in this convoluted game of telephone – with reporters racing to and fro and hoping to convey news accurately – is paradoxical, given the Court's ongoing complaints about the news media's tendency to misreport what has occurred in a session.

Journalistic complaints about the ways in which cases are handed down are as old as the hills, and in no way are these problems specific to the new media. But as bloggers and online journalists are pressed to report court news as it breaks and to tweet hundred-page opinions a mere seconds after they come down, the opportunities for massive and consequential reporting errors increase exponentially. Misreporting of the ACA decision by two major networks and several other media sources earned the Court's usually scrupulous press corps a well-publicized slap on the wrists.[21] But such errors will continue as long as the Court stands by its position that it will not assist journalists attempting to report breaking news. Simple fixes like the Canadian Supreme Court's grant of a lockup[22] – reporters are given advance copies of an opinion before it is released, so long as they don't transmit their stories until the session opens – could save the media from persistently misreporting important, complex, or lengthy opinions, and would save the Court the embarrassment of flawed initial reports. The Court's longstanding position – that it is the responsibility of the press to take as much time as it needs to get the story right, regardless of the demands of their editors, producers and bosses – sounds lovely. It in no way correlates to the reality of the practice of journalism in the modern era.

[21] Tom Goldstein. "We're getting wildly differing assessments," *SCOTUSblog*, July 7, 2012, www.scotusblog.com/2012/07/were-getting-wildly-differing-assessments/

[22] Thaddeus Pope. "Cuthbertson v. Rasouli – Supreme Court Media Lock-up," *Medical Futility Blog*, July 12, 2013, medicalfutility.blogspot.com/2013/07/cuthbertson-v-rasouli-supreme-court.html

If I have sounded critical up to this point, it is simply because so much of the current friction between the Court and the new media strikes me as utterly unnecessary. Where one might have argued fifteen years ago that blogging and online journalism were passing fads, it's now clear that they are here to stay. Indeed, even the stodgiest online publications now demand real-time online updates from their Supreme Court correspondents, confirming, as if any confirmation were needed, that We Are All Bloggers Now. Given the choice between helping reporters get it right and get it wrong, the Court has pretty consistently opted for door number two, possibly with the view that erroneous reporting that reflects poorly upon the press in no way colors the public view of the Court. I have yet to see an empirical study of whether mistakes about the Court affect the institution's prestige and dignity, although certainly the justices themselves are quick to point out that reporter error does affect the way in which the public sees the Court. In the absence of much data confirming the fact, it seems intuitively clear that whenever the media misreport a Court decision, a quote, or a colloquy that occurred at oral argument, it can reflect poorly on the Court itself. This is not – as some justices have argued – because the press is forever apt to sensationalize and slant the day's events. It is largely because we are working on extremely tight deadlines with limited technological support. It would seem to be in the mutual interest of both parties then to do everything possible to aid the press in getting the story as straight as possible.

This brings us of course to the nub of the problem: the widespread perception, both within the Court and outside it, that online journalism is a kind of latter-day muckraking, devoted chiefly to slandering and shaming the institutions we cover. At first blush, there is merit to some of these claims, as the new media certainly have been responsible for some of the worst intrusions on judicial privacy – from the coverage of judicial speeches and appearances that can sometimes be quite inflammatory in tone, to the often purely silly coverage of the justices' extracurricular activities. Websites such as Above the Law enjoy twitting judicial egos, and others, including Think Progress on the left and The National Review Online can be zealous advocates during confirmation hearings and major cases. All of the justices undoubtedly have been burned once or twice by an intrusive piece of reporting that appeared online. But the question is not whether online journalism embarrasses the court, but whether Supreme Court Justices are entitled to some kind of special immunity from what can be the rough-and-tumble tone of the new media.

There are valid arguments to suggest that they should be immune. Several of the justices have taken the position that the only real power that inheres in the U.S. Supreme Court is the authority and dignity of the judicial office, which is compromised when there is closer scrutiny.[23] Images of Supreme Court justices in situations that are embarrassing or compromising certainly undermine the gravitas of the institution. But it has always seemed to me that the cure for this possibility is not to ensure that the doings of the Court remain shrouded in opaque mystery. Barring cameras, audio, and recording equipment of any kind doesn't guarantee that the justices won't do or say something that will prove embarrassing to the institution. In my experience, the "gotcha" quotes, the questionable public appearances, and the inflammatory off-the-bench speeches tend to be reported whether or not there are cameras. Only the justices themselves can ensure that they are not portrayed in ways that might embarrass or demean the institution, and they can do so by holding themselves to the highest standards of judicial conduct.

The refusal to allow judicial speeches to be filmed (and even, in some cases, the institutional refusal to publish the schedule of judicial speeches) strikes me as the most classic instance of shooting the messenger. The press is not responsible for covering the justices' questionable conduct. The justices are responsible. It's worth noting that, as press corps go, the Supreme Court's press corps tends to be the most respectful, circumspect, and generally laudatory in the professional media.[24] That behavior occurs much to the chagrin of journalists outside the family.[25] It has long been a convention in Washington that the Supreme Court press corps generally avoids reporting on leaks, scandals, and gossip (This may have changed somewhat following the reports of leaks about deliberations in the healthcare challenges).[26] Many of the justices have thus come to believe that any media scrutiny of their extracurricular or off-bench activities is inappropriate and intrusive.[27] But this all seems to be a vestige of a lost era that has no real correlation to the rise of online journalism. Indeed, with the advent of camera phones, "citizen journalism" and the pervasive possibility of "gotchas," it's clear that there is no

[23] "Justice Kennedy: Cameras at Court Would be 'Insidious,'" *Wall Street Journal*, March 14, 2013, blogs.wsj.com/law/2013/03/14/justice-kennedy-cameras-at-court-would-be-insidious/

[24] Emily Bazelon and Dahlia Lithwick. "Nine Ways to Read The Nine," *Slate*, September 21, 2007, www.slate.com/articles/news_and_politics/jurisprudence/2007/09/nine_ways_to_read_the_nine.html

[25] Edward Lazarus. "The Supreme Court's Excessive Secrecy: Why It Isn't Merited," *FindLaw*, September 30, 2004, writ.news.findlaw.com/lazarus/20040930.html

[26] Jan Crawford. "Roberts switched views to uphold health care law," *CBS News*, July 1, 2012, www.cbsnews.com/8301-3460_162-57464549/roberts-switched-views-to-uphold-health-care-law/

[27] Lee Fang. "Exclusive: Supreme Court Justice Sam Alito Dismisses His Profligate Right-Wing Fundraising As 'Not Important'," *ThinkProgress*, November 10, 2010, thinkprogress.org/politics/2010/11/10/129395/sam-alito-republican-fundraiser/

longer any safe place for a justice to speak casually, or off the record,[28] and not even a facial expression will go unobserved.[29] Paradoxically, if the justices want to avoid masses of online chatter speculating about whether their conduct was appropriate, churlish, or juvenile,[30] probably the best way to let the public decide would be to allow them to see the conduct on videotape, as opposed to having it mediated by the press.

Ultimately, the great irony underlying the Court's ongoing resistance to the new media is that it seems to be rooted in a belief that there is some ironclad directive among online journalists to embarrass and humiliate the justices, and possibly even to aggressively encourage harassment and incursions upon their privacy. And this leads some of the justices to fight back even more aggressively. Some of them seem more and more apt to respond to the roller derby quality of the modern media age by simply rolling up their sleeves and jumping into the fray. In a 2008 interview with C-SPAN,[31] Justice Antonin Scalia explained that "[i]t's no use, I'm going to be a public spectacle whether I come out of the closet or not, beyond T-shirts and bobblehead dolls and what-not. So if, you know, if I am going to be a public figure, I guess the public may as well get their notion of me firsthand rather than filtered through people such as [C-SPAN's] Brian Lamb, you know." It seems beyond dispute that some of the justices – paradoxically some of the oldest among them – have become more comfortable with the possibility that to be a Supreme Court jurist in a "Real Housewives" age is to be constantly on display. They seem more inclined to talk to reporters and to audiences in a way that is unfiltered, yes, but also likely to raise public hackles.

Despite irreversible changes in the nature of the media, there are many jurists, and I'd venture to say most of them, who believe that the Internet is a cesspool of violence and danger, and that to allow even a rivulet of Internet coverage into the decorous life of the Court is to open the faucet on an open sewer of hate, violence, and incivility. Certainly, the Internet has given them reason to fear this possibility. But the same concerns raised about the new

[28] Dean Schabner. "Clarence Thomas Speaks Out in Support of His Wife," *ABC News*, February 27, 2011, abcnews.go.com/blogs/politics/2011/02/clarence-thomas-speaks-out-in-support-of-his-wife/

[29] Ryan Rainey. "Samuel Alito Rolls Eyes While Ruth Bader Ginsburg Reads Dissent," *The Huffington Post*, June 24, 2013, www.huffingtonpost.com/2013/06/24/samuel-alito-rolls-eyes_n_3492704.html

[30] Garrett Epps. "Justice Alito's Inexcusable Rudeness," *The Atlantic*, June 24, 2013, www.theatlantic.com/national/archive/2013/06/justice-alitos-inexcusable-rudeness/277163/

[31] Ashby Jones. "Next Stop on Nino's Book Tour: A Riveting Talk with C-SPAN's Brian Lamb," *Wall Street Journal*, May 7, 2008, blogs.wsj.com/law/2008/05/07/next-stop-on-ninos-book-tour-a-riveting-talk-with-c-spans-brian-lamb/

media were once voiced over print newspapers. Moreover, as justices continue to cite legal blogs, online articles, and government documents in their opinions,[32] it becomes increasingly clear that they are not shying away from the Internet – they're just shying away from the parts of it that worry them. The days of ink on ivory-colored paper are clearly numbered at the Court, even if, in the most formal sense, the Court wants to cling to them.

To paraphrase Dickens, when it comes to online reporting – as was the case for every new technology from the printing press to the television – the medium brings about both the best of times and the worst of times. That will continue until the next medium comes along to add both heat and light, probably in about equal amounts, to the working of the Court. Gossipy and sneering coverage of judicial activities was not born with the advent of the new media. But the ability to link directly to precedent on a page certainly was. Snippy tweets about unfortunate comments made at oral argument are a new thing. But so is the specialized academic law blog, which I would hazard has added more to the general public understanding of what the Supreme Court does than the century's worth of law review articles that came before. The new media can, in short, be silly and trivial, personality-focused, sensationalist, and small. They can also be lofty and coherent, useful and accurate, brilliant and inspiring. That duality is not surprising. The Court itself is similarly capable of both extremes.

[32] Pamela A. MacLean. "Judges Cite More Blogs in Rulings," *The National Law Journal*, September 12, 2006, www.law.com/jsp/article.jsp?id=900005551064&Judges_Cite_More_Blogs_in_Rulings&slreturn=20131007154045

11

What the Justices Think of the Press

LAURA MOYER AND MATTHEW THORNTON

At first, I thought that was a wonderful idea, until I found out that they then unlock the door and let them out.

- Justice Samuel Alito, on the Canadian Supreme Court's practice of announcing their decisions to the press in a locked room with no recording devices.[1]

What exactly do Supreme Court justices think of the press, not in terms of the First Amendment, but rather as an institution?

This chapter approaches our question in two ways. We begin by discussing major themes in the justices' comments about the press, focusing primarily on the Rehnquist and Roberts courts. Although the norm professed by the justices is that they speak only through their opinions, this is not, strictly speaking, accurate. Justices write books, which they actively promote through the news media, and they give numerous speeches to legal and civic groups. With respect to the latter, the Supreme Court Public Information Office publishes the text of selected speeches on the Supreme Court website (dating back to 2000), and journalists frequently cover speaking engagements and other public appearances.

In their written and spoken comments, we find that the justices often reveal their sometimes-contradictory attitudes toward journalists and the news media. Although there may be good reason to be skeptical about taking judges' statements at face value when investigating other research questions (Segal and Spaeth 2002), we argue that, for our purposes, a close examination of the justices' remarks can tell us something about the underlying motivations for engaging the world outside the Supreme Court building. How does each

[1] As reported by Justin Katz for The Ocean State Current live blog on September 14, 2012. Accessed April 5, 2013. /oceanstatecurrent.com/liveblog/091412-supreme-court-justice-samuel-alito-roger-williams-law-school/

justice view his or her public role? Moreover, what do their comments about the press suggest about a justice's view of the Supreme Court in our political system?

In the latter half of the chapter, we examine our question from a broader vantage point in order to assess whether there are trends with respect to when and how often the justices engage the press. Do justices engage the press strategically in response to public opinion about the Court? Is their engagement better explained by their book tours and nothing more? This, too, sheds light on how the justices think about the news media and how those attitudes have changed over time.

We believe these are important questions to understand, particularly as the landscape of journalism continues to evolve away from more "traditional" news outlets. The extent to which justices embrace these changes (or reject them) may affect how the public understands both the Supreme Court as an institution and the decisions that affect their lives.

WHAT JUSTICES THINK ABOUT THE PRESS: MAJOR THEMES

In his book *Judges and Their Audiences*, Baum (2006, 25) argues that judges, like ordinary people, are motivated by a desire "to be liked and respected by others who are important to them." As such, he speculates that judges may view the press as important for several reasons (135–36). First, the press can act as an intermediary between judges and other audiences that judges want to reach, such as ideologically similar interest groups, political actors, and other elites in the legal profession. Relatedly, out of a concern for legitimacy, judges may desire public approval for their decisions and thus see press coverage as a way to influence public perception. Finally, Baum suggests that judges care about how the media view their work. Justice Stevens, for instance, hinted at Chief Justice Warren Burger's desire to be more positively reviewed in the press than his colleagues: "I had the impression that Chief Justice Burger liked to write opinions in which the Court favored First Amendment claims and to assign Byron [White] the task of writing opinions that members of the press could be expected to criticize" (Stevens 2011a).

The discussion that follows is an overview of major themes expressed by Supreme Court justices in their written and spoken remarks. In order to identify justices' comments about the press, we downloaded all publically available speeches given by the justices from 2000 to 2012 and conducted Internet searches for interviews and news stories about the justices. We then searched within those sources for statements by the justices about the press, eliminating sources that were not clearly relevant. Finally, we sorted the comments into thematic categories. Although the comments highlighted are by no means exhaustive, they provide important insights about the relationship between justices and journalists.

The Press is Inaccurate and Focuses Too Much on Politics When Covering the Court

A prominent and recurring theme in the justices' comments is criticism of the press. This criticism tends to fall into two general categories: complaints about inaccuracy and complaints about the media focusing too much on the "politics" of the Court. Beginning with inaccuracy, some justices express concern about the press giving too much emphasis to unimportant aspects of the Court's work. For instance, comedian Jon Stewart (*The Daily Show*) asked Justice Sotomayor whether the term "judicial activism" held any significance for members of the Court or whether it was mostly a phrase used by outsiders (Sotomayor 2013). "'Activism' is a term, I'm sorry to say, that mostly journalists are fond of," Sotomayor replied. She went on to express her desire that more members of the public read the Court's decisions for themselves, presumably to get a more accurate picture of the Court's rulings. Other justices apparently share this sentiment. Adam Liptak, the *New York Times* Supreme Court correspondent, noted one common complaint he hears from current justices is that "many articles start with which side won rather than the rule of law announced."[2]

Other complaints about perceived inaccuracies are more serious. Thurgood Marshall recounted an experience he had as a lawyer, in which a journalist had interviewed him for an entire afternoon about a pending case only to misquote him in the article's headline. Marshall concluded his recollection by observing wryly, "That's been my experience with the press" (Retirement of Justice Marshall 1991). Similarly, Justice Stevens and Justice Alito have publicly taken issue with the press' characterization of opinions they wrote or joined. Both were fairly direct in their criticism. A retired Stevens identified a journalist by name (Damon W. Root at www.reason.com) and asserted that one reason why the *Kelo v. New London* decision was unpopular was because "popular commentary mis-described the motivation for the City's plan" (Stevens 2011). He then went on to quote verbatim from Root's post. FOX News covered Alito's speech to the Federalist Society in November 2012, particularly his criticism that detractors of the *Citizens*

[2] Liptak, Adam. 2013. Personal correspondence with the author.

United decision had "mounted an effective, but misleading, public relations campaign" (Justice Alito Defends 2012).

In several instances, justices have gone so far as to accuse the press of publishing unsubstantiated rumors or of actually lying. Justice Marshall called a *New York Times* story that suggested he had retired because he was "angry and frustrated" a "double-barreled lie" (Retirement of Justice Marshall 1991). More recently, several justices have disputed the accuracy of coverage in the Affordable Care Act case. One target was a *60 Minutes* story by CBS correspondent Jan Crawford that claimed, through an anonymous source, that Chief Justice Roberts had switched his vote after conference, upholding the individual mandate and greatly angering his conservative colleagues on the Court. Justice Scalia was especially blunt in his assessments, as evidenced by this 2012 interview with Chris Wallace of FOX News: "[Y]ou shouldn't believe what you read about the internal court proceedings, because the reporter who reports that is either: A, lying, which can be done with impunity, because as you know, we don't respond . . .or B, that reporter had the information from some [person] who was breaking the oath of confidentiality, which means that's an unreliable person." In a separate interview on the CBS program *Face the Nation*, Justice O'Connor also noted her skepticism about the reliability of Crawford's *60 Minutes* report. Justice Ginsburg took a lighter tone, joking in a speech to the American Constitution Society that press sources who published "a steady stream of rumors and fifth-hand accounts" about when the Court would announce its healthcare ruling got their "just desserts" when the day in question turned out to be the announcement of a real estate decision (2012).

Another common category of complaints, according to Adam Liptak (2013b), stems from the fact that "the justices sure don't like to be described in political terms. . .They don't like to think of themselves as political actors." Justices chafe at any characterization of the Court as "political," including labeling decisions and justices as "liberal" or "conservative" and emphasizing narrowly divided decisions. "I don't think the Court is political at all," Justice Scalia told FOX News' Chris Wallace. Scalia attributed 5–4 decisions along party lines to differences in judicial philosophies favored by Democratic and Republican presidents. Similarly, Justice Ginsburg (2009) downplayed the significance of divided Court decisions in comments to the Second Judicial Conference: "The press tends to focus on splits with the Chief Justice, and Justices Scalia, Kennedy, Thomas, and Alito arranged on one side; Justices Stevens, Souter, Ginsburg, and Breyer on the other. It is not always so. True, nine of the seventeen 5–4 decisions already released shaped up that way. But in five of the 5–4's, Justices Stevens, Kennedy, Souter, Ginsburg, and Breyer composed the majority. There were unusual lineups as well." In other appearances, Ginsburg has emphasized the collegiality of the Court and the support she received from all of her colleagues during difficult periods in her personal life.

Concern with Lack of Public Understanding and Trust

Although accuracy for its own sake is important, other comments made by the justices suggest their criticisms about accuracy in coverage often relate to other concerns, particularly a lack of both public understanding and trust in the Supreme Court. Two justices in particular, Stephen Breyer and Sandra Day O'Connor, often voice this view.

Justice Breyer's concern with dropping levels of public confidence in governmental institutions and the Court appears as a frequent theme in his speeches and books. In 2000, Breyer told attendees at a conference on the legal profession and public service: "I am not concerned when I read that fewer Americans can name three Supreme Court justices than can name the Three Stooges. But it does bother me that more teenagers can name the Three Stooges than can name the three branches of government... It worries me even more that 'trust in government' as measured by statistical surveys has headed steadily downward since 1964" (Breyer 2000, 11–12).[3] Eight years later, Breyer bemoaned public opinion data that showed a decline in the percentage of respondents who believed that judges decide cases impartially based on the rule of law: "This trend is alarming not least because it bears absolutely no resemblance to how judges believe they approach their work... A serious discrepancy between our own view of our own efforts and the view of a large segment of the public is cause for concern in a democracy" (2009). While not specifically naming the media as the source of this problem, Breyer also does not assign fault to the Supreme Court for, say, writing dense, complex decisions that are difficult for the average American to understand.

In her retirement, Justice O'Connor has busied herself with several civic education projects, which she has promoted through venues as diverse as *The Daily Show with Jon Stewart*, *The Today Show* and *Time* magazine. O'Connor (2011) told journalist Cokie Roberts in a PBS interview that she felt the public was "not sufficiently well educated" about the role of the judge or the Court, which was why she had started her own educational website for middle-school children. Earlier interviews by O'Connor also voiced alarm

[3] Breyer (2001) voiced similar concerns over declining trust in government in a post-9/11 context.

about public misunderstanding, particularly in the face of criticisms about judges from elected officials. "I have felt that the public concern has followed the concerns expressed by various legislators both in Congress and state legislatures, concerns about so-called activist judges," O'Connor said in a *Time* magazine interview. "I suspect when people hear legislators so often publicly denounce activist, godless judges that people start thinking that's the situation. It's very much a concern to me" (O'Connor 2006). She echoed similar comments three years later in an interview on *The Daily Show* (O'Connor 2009). In the same interview, O'Connor went on to cite an Annenberg poll that found only a third of Americans could name the three branches of government, "let alone say what they do." The implications of declining public understanding and trust are potentially troublesome for the Court, especially as it is lacks the power to enforce its own decisions (Davis 2011; Rosenberg 2008).

The Media as a Promotional Vehicle

As discussed above, Justice O'Connor's concerns about public understanding of the Supreme Court have resulted in her proactive use of the media to publicize her educational initiatives. Other justices have used the media to promote a particular understanding of the Constitution; for instance, William Rehnquist, an advocate of original intent, frequently gave speeches (with the press in attendance) that were heavy in historical content. We have just discussed how certain justices appear to use the press to promote messages about the apolitical nature of judicial decision making. However, on a more practical level, the justices seek out the press as a vehicle to promote the books they publish in their spare time, as a supplement to their judicial salaries.[4]

As of November 2012, the legal blog SCOTUSblog had catalogued 353 books authored or co-authored by Supreme Court justices since the beginning of the Court (Collins 2012). On the Roberts Court (2012–13), every justice except John Roberts and Elena Kagan has at least one book to their name. Some justices are especially prolific, like Stephen Breyer (ten books) and Ruth Bader Ginsburg (six). The late William Rehnquist wrote six books (plus two shorter publications) while retired; Justice Sandra Day O'Connor has penned seven. The content of these books ranges from jurisprudential philosophy to memoirs and even children's books (for example, O'Connor's book *Chico*).

[4] Certainly, justices promote their views about jurisprudence or other matters without having a book to promote, though having published a book does give them additional incentives to promote its message through press appearances.

On the other side, journalists learn to take advantage of these rare efforts by the justices to reach out to the press on the record. *New York Times* journalist Adam Liptak observes that, in spite of the fact that he regularly sees and interacts with justices, they "very seldom come on the record – almost exclusively when they have a book to promote" (2013b). Nina Totenberg (2013), Supreme Court correspondent for National Public Radio, points out that "Even if the book is boring, it is a good opportunity to engage the justice in an interview" where other topics might be broached.

Justices are likely aware of what journalists hope to ascertain in these book promotion interviews, and consequently, some justices are more selective than others in choosing particular media outlets for interviews. This selectivity (or lack thereof) tells us something about how different justices view the media as a whole, but also that they perceive particular outlets as "friendly" or perhaps worthwhile for book promotion purposes. For instance, *The Charlie Rose Show* has been a popular venue for Supreme Court justices. The PBS program has featured hour-long interviews with at least six justices since 2004 (Rehnquist, Stevens, Breyer, Scalia, O'Connor, and Sotomayor), suggesting that justices across the ideological spectrum view the outlet as "friendly."

On the other hand, Liptak observes that Justice Clarence Thomas is "perhaps more comfortable with conservative outlets."[5] Indeed, in 2007, Thomas appeared on Rush Limbaugh's radio program in a special extended interview to talk about his new memoir, *My Grandfather's Son*. In 2008, Thomas granted another television interview to conservative columnist and talk show host Armstrong Williams. However, Thomas also promoted his memoir through more traditional venues as well, going on both C-SPAN and *60 Minutes*.

When Justice Sotomayor's memoir *My Beloved World* was published, her ubiquitous appearances in the press to promote her book were the subject of a *New York Times* profile. The article noted that Sotomayor (who is of Puerto Rican heritage) had "salsa danced with Univision anchor Jorge Ramos in her chambers," had excerpts of the book published in *People en Español*, and had even moved up the time for swearing in Vice President Joe Biden to 8:15 A.M. "rather than just before noon as guided by the Constitution" so that she could appear at a Barnes and Noble book promotion event that day (Kantor 2013).

In contrast, Samuel Alito highlighted his distaste for engaging the press when he told a group of law students at a legal symposium: "All of my

[5] Liptak, Adam. 2013. Personal communication with author.

colleagues have been going on *Charlie Rose* or *The Daily Show*, but this is about as close as I get" (Katz 2012). Despite early comparisons of Alito to Scalia and the moniker "Scalito" that emerged during Alito's confirmation hearings (Ververs 2005), the two men do not share the same views about the press and the utility of engaging journalists. Unlike Alito, Scalia appears to enjoy engaging the press, participating in interviews with Piers Morgan (CNN), Chris Matthews (FOX News), Charlie Rose (PBS), and Nina Totenberg (National Public Radio), to name only a few.

Televising the Work of the Court

A favorite question of journalists for the justices is whether the Court should televise its proceedings. Sitting Supreme Court justices uniformly oppose it, even those like Scalia, Kagan, and Sotomayor, who previously stated their support for televising oral arguments in their confirmation hearings (Liptak 2013a). In testimony before the House Appropriations Committee, former Justice David Souter famously responded, "I can tell you the day you see a camera come into our courtroom, it's going to roll over my dead body" (On Cameras in Supreme Court 1996). The primary concerns voiced by the justices reflect themes we have encountered earlier: concern for accuracy in media coverage and a dislike of the press' tendency to characterize the Court in political terms.

In a 2012 interview with C-SPAN, Justice Scalia elaborated on why he now opposes allowing cameras in the courtroom: "Your outfit [C-SPAN] would carry it all, to be sure, but what most of the American people would see would be 30 second, 15 second take-outs from our argument, and those take-outs would not be characteristic of what we do" (Cohn 2012). Of newspaper articles, Scalia argued, "People read that and they say, 'Well, it's an article in a newspaper, and the guy may be lying, or he may be misinformed... But somehow when you see it live ... it has a much greater impact" (Cohn 2012). Speaking in 2012 at the University of Michigan law school, Justice Kagan echoed Scalia's comments, confessing that she too had changed her mind on this question. Kagan argued televising proceedings would make the institution "work less well" because clips could be taken out of context (Vloet 2012).

Justices have also dismissed the idea by suggesting much of their work is not interesting to the public. Justice Ginsburg, in a speech reviewing the prior term, offered several examples along these lines. First, she recalled an opinion announcement by Justice Kagan, where the justice began by telling those gathered, "If you understand anything I say here, you will likely be a lawyer, and you will have had your morning cup of coffee." Ginsburg then rattled off a series of humorous questions asked by justices during oral arguments, noting that according to the *New York Times*, she was the "least funny justice who talks." She then concluded, "From the foregoing samples, you may better understand why the Court does not plan to permit televising oral arguments any time soon" (Ginsburg 2011).

Justice Sotomayor also has made similar comments. In an interview with Charlie Rose (as reported by the *New York Times*), she argued the general public lacked the appropriate background to get much out of oral arguments: "I don't think most viewers take the time to actually delve into either the briefs or the legal arguments to appreciate what the court is doing. . .Very few of them understand what the process is, which is to play devil's advocate" (Liptak 2013a). Overall, there appears to be a strong norm opposing televising the Court's proceedings, a position ironically at odds with the justices' professed interest in educating the public.

The Press as a Conduit to Send and Receive Messages to and from the Public

Although most justices oppose cameras in the Supreme Court, speeches and public comments suggest at least some of the justices deliberately engage the press in order to serve a public education function. Chief Justice Rehnquist, for example, routinely gave speeches about the history of the Court, often mentioning the legacy of John Marshall in his comments (e.g., Rehnquist 2001). More recently, Justice Breyer (2009) told an audience of lawyers and judges assembled for the sesquicentennial anniversary of the Massachusetts Superior Court: "I think judges must do more than simply undertake our own jobs as best we can. We must also, in this day of speedy communication, try to explain or to teach why that institution and independence are important, not simply to the judges or to the lawyers, but to ordinary Americans whom ultimately our institution seeks to serve."

In 2010, Diane Sawyer interviewed both O'Connor and Ginsburg and asked them what they would like the public to know about how the Court functions. O'Connor replied that "that the Court is a place where decisions are made and people are persuaded by reasoning and explanation, not logrolling" (Ginsburg and O'Connor 2010). Ginsburg added that, unlike other political institutions, the Court must provide extensive reasons for its decisions. She went on to praise her colleagues for their support during her battles with cancer and after the death of her husband.

More evidence of using the press to educate the public can be found in the decision of the Roberts Court to cooperate with C-SPAN's 2009 documentary,

The Supreme Court: Home to America's Highest Court. In the documentary, all of the then-current justices explained something about how the Supreme Court works, or offered their impressions of the job. There are still camera shots of each room in the Supreme Court building, sometimes narrated by the justices. The decision to allow unprecedented access to the justices and their workspace, underscores the value placed on educating the public about the work of the Court – and using a "trusted" media outlet to disseminate that civic message.

At the same time, some justices see media as beneficial to educate the justices themselves on public sentiment. Sotomayor told Jon Stewart of *The Daily Show*, "We're not monks. We don't sit in a cave. Hopefully, most of us are involved citizens so we do read the newspapers… Being aware [of public opinion] is simply part of being in a society and knowing what is going on around you" (Sotomayor 2013). Similarly, Ginsburg has attributed change in the Supreme Court's understanding of gender-based discrimination to the fact that justices "read the newspapers…and are affected…by the climate of the era" (Ginsburg 2006). She has also noted justices can learn much from "all manner of commentary," including "any number of legal blogs" (Ginsburg 2009). These comments are generally consistent with other reports of justices keeping and annotating newspaper clippings about the Court and their decisions (Davis 1994 and 2011; Baum 2006).

Taken as a whole, anecdotal evidence suggests that the justices generally view the press in a utilitarian manner: as a means to some end. Indeed, the practices and comments of many justices suggest they value media as a promotional tool or, at times, educational conduit. Alternatively, the practices and comments of some justices likewise appear to reflect a genuine concern regarding public perception and trust in the Court. Given such variance in practices and comments, we now shift to a quantitative analysis of newspaper coverage to ascertain what can be gleaned from the timing and frequency with which justices engage the press.

If, as indicated, justices are concerned about public understanding and perception of the Court, is it beneficial for justices to engage the press in an attempt to influence public perceptions of the Court? Conversely, if justices merely engage the press as a means to promote their writings, as some journalists argue, does news coverage simply reflect the frequency with which justices publish books? To the extent that such questions can be answered through a quantitative analysis of press coverage, we feel this approach provides a more nuanced understanding of what justices think about the press.

ANALYZING NEWS COVERAGE OF THE JUSTICES

Our second line of inquiry begins with a discussion of the relationship between news coverage of the justices and public perception of the Court. We then examine the connection between news coverage of the justices and book publications. Finally, we discuss what our findings suggest for understanding what the justices think about the press.

Media Engagement as News Coverage

We model news coverage by specifically examining articles referencing Supreme Court justices published in the *New York Times* and the *Washington Post* from 1980–2012. We selected both papers as they enjoy large national circulation (Alliance 2013), prominently cover national politics, and are commonly read by political elites and policy makers (Grau 1976; Weiss 1974). Moreover, scholars have long noted the tendency of such elite papers, particularly the *New York Times*, to set the news agenda for other papers and news organizations, what has been termed intermedia agenda setting (e.g., Golan 2006; McCombs 2005; Reese and Danielian 1989). Hence, to the extent Supreme Court justices are likely to engage the media, news coverage is most likely to appear in one or both newspapers.

As *LexisNexis* provides full transcripts of both papers beginning in 1980, our analysis covers a thirty-two-year span of news coverage from January 1, 1980 to December 31, 2012. We began our analysis by compiling all articles in each paper that reference the Supreme Court and one or more justice from the Burger through Roberts courts. As we were principally concerned with ascertaining what justices specifically think about the press, we further limited our searches to include only articles mentioning media-related terms. That is, we sought to isolate articles wherein justices were likely to be referencing the media. Specifically, searches were conducted on the following combination of terms: "Supreme Court" and "Justice (followed by the name of each justice)" and the media terms "news" or "media" or "journalist" or "reporter" or "press."

As news coverage necessarily reflects interaction of the justices with the press, we argue article counts serve as a reasonable proxy for press engagement by the justices.[6] The results of our searches of the *New York Times* and the

[6] Admittedly a noisy measure, raw article counts nonetheless capture the extent to which justices engage the press in lieu of in-depth analysis of approximately 15,000 individual articles over the 32-year period.

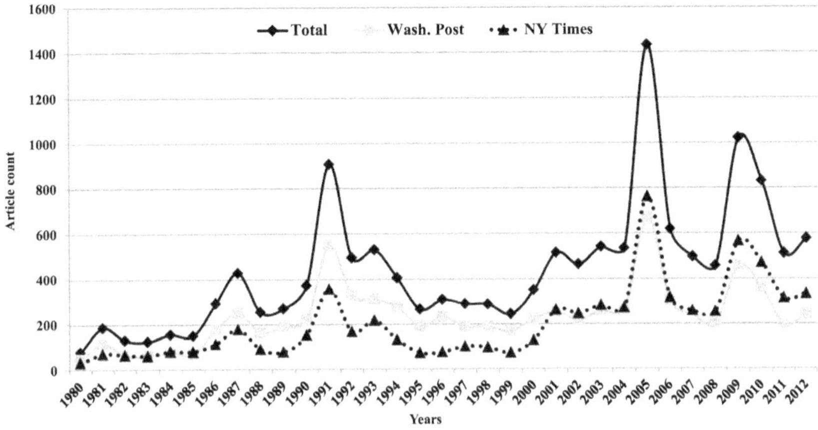

FIGURE 1. Annual newspaper coverage of U.S. Supreme Court Justices, 1980–2012.
Note: Coverage data obtained from LexisNexis searches of the *Washington Post and* the *New York Times. Article counts exclude unclassified documents and blog entries.*

Washington Post appear in Figure 1. As is evident, news coverage for justices has tended to increase over time, with periodic spikes in coverage in both papers. What remains to be seen, however, are factors that may explain such trends in news coverage – factors that may illuminate what the justices think of the press.

Examining News Coverage and Public Perceptions of the Court

As scholars have noted, in contrast to the presidency or Congress, the Supreme Court lacks the power to enforce its decisions, and is therefore heavily dependent on public trust and confidence in the institution (Davis 2011). Indeed, as discussed earlier, justices have openly voiced concern over public understanding and trust in the Court (Breyer 2000, 2001, 2009; O'Connor 2006). Given such comments and the importance of public confidence to the Court, justices may view the press as a method of influencing coverage of the Court and thereby public perceptions of the institution. To that end, we pair the results of news coverage searches above with public opinion measures of confidence in the Court to determine whether identifiable relationships exist between the level of press engagement by the justices as indicated by news coverage and the level of public confidence in the Court. The presence of relationships between news coverage and public opinion measures offers the opportunity to examine whether press engagement of the justices is potentially beneficial in terms of promoting greater confidence in the Court and, likewise, whether evidence suggests justices may be strategically engaging the press to combat declining confidence in the Court.

To establish the relationship between our news coverage variable and public perception of the Court, we utilize data from the General Social Survey regarding public confidence in the Supreme Court. Since 1972, the GSS has routinely measured public confidence in governmental institutions. The measure is drawn from responses to the following question: "As far as the people running (the Supreme Court) are concerned, would you say you have a great deal of confidence, only some confidence, or hardly any confidence at all in them?" Although results for all thirty-two years under study were not available, eighteen years of results between 1980 and 2006 were available, thus offering a consistent measure of public confidence we could pair to news coverage. As "only some confidence" and "hardly any confidence" could be interpreted similarly depending on the view of the respondent, for parsimony we opted to collapse results for these two response categories into a single measure. Hence, we compare those responding they have "a great deal of confidence" in the justices relative to those responding "only some" or "hardly any" confidence in the justices, which we then model against news coverage.

To illustrate the relationship between public confidence in the Court and "media-focused" news coverage, we created index variables scaled from 0 to 1 corresponding to the level of annual news coverage and the measure of public confidence in the Court. Figure 2 presents the relationship between

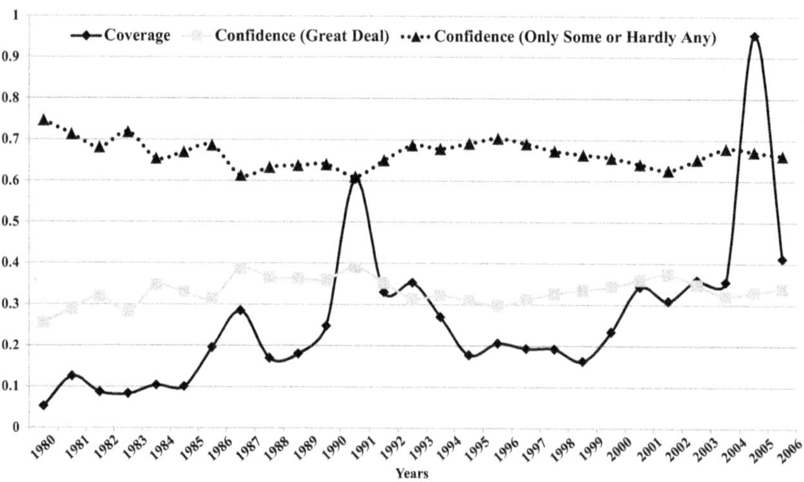

FIGURE 2. Trends in newspaper coverage and confidence in the U.S. Supreme Court, 1980–2006. *Note: Coverage data obtained from LexisNexis searches of* the *Washington Post and* the *New York Times. Confidence data obtained from General Social Survey, which is available through 2006.*

news coverage and confidence in the Court. If media coverage and public confidence in the Court were related, we would expect to observe clear trends corresponding to shifts in news coverage and public opinion. Moreover, if news coverage reflects press engagement of the justices, which has the potential to favorably influence public perception of the Court, there should be a positive relationship between press coverage and confidence in the justices. As Figure 2 illustrates, such a pattern exists. Consider the period from 1980 to 1991. The increase in news coverage during this period corresponds to an increase in adults possessing a "great deal" of confidence in the Court and a decline in respondents offering less favorable evaluations of the justices (represented by the dotted triangle line). This pattern, however, reverses after 1991 and continues through the mid-1990s such that a decline in news coverage corresponds to a drop in confidence in the Court.

As Figure 2 makes evident, an increase in news coverage of the justices tended to correspond to a complementary increase in confidence in the Court. Likewise, a decline in news coverage corresponded to a similar decline in confidence in the Court. Moreover, the correlation observed between news coverage and public perception of the Court proves statistically significant over the period of study. News coverage and those expressing a "great deal" of confidence in the Court was positively correlated ($r = .537$, $p < .05$), while news coverage was negatively correlated to those expressing "only some" or "hardly any" confidence in the Court ($r = -.534$, $p < .05$). Such trends suggest increased media engagement by the justices to be beneficial in producing greater confidence in the Court. But do justices strategically engage the press to combat declining confidence in the Court?

If justices were strategically responding to declining perceptions of the Court, we should observe a significant lag between news coverage and public opinion such that justices would increasingly engage the press following a decline in public perceptions of the Court. We tested for this effect by lagging public confidence in the Court to news coverage one year, in essence examining the relationship between confidence in the Court in a given year and news coverage the following year. News coverage, however, was not significantly associated with greater confidence in the Court ($r = .186$) or lower confidence in the Court ($r = -.186$). Such results call into question the premise of justices actively engaging the press to combat declining perceptions of the Court, at least based upon our measures of public opinion and news coverage.

If justices do not appear to view the press in strategic terms as a means to favorably influence public perceptions of the Court, do the justices nonetheless embrace the press as a promotional tool to promote their writings, as has been suggested by members of the press (Liptak 2013b; Totenberg 2013)? To assess whether the justices view the press in more utilitarian terms (as advancing their own interests), we now examine the extent to which news coverage of the justices reflects book-related content, and is thus a function of the frequency with which justices publish books.

The Press as Promotional Agent?

To determine if justices engage the press to promote their books, we compared newspaper coverage of the justices in years when justices published books to years in which no justices published books. We additionally accounted for news articles that specifically referenced books. Examining both aspects permitted us to establish whether overall news coverage increased during book publication years, and whether the percentage of book-specific coverage spiked during years when justices published books relative to years when they did not. As scholars, journalists, and pundits routinely publish books about the Supreme Court, we would likely observe book-specific news coverage of the justices in years even when the justices produced no books. If, however, the justices actively engage the press to promote their books, we should observe a notable rise in the percentage of book-specific news coverage during years when justices publish their own works.

Consistent with procedures described earlier, we used annual article counts obtained from *LexisNexis* searches of the *New York Times* and the *Washington Post* as our measure of news coverage. Specifically, we used the search terms "Supreme Court" and the series of justice names (e.g., "Justice Samuel Alito" or "Harry Blackmun") for each year beginning with 1980 and continuing through 2012 to create a total news coverage variable. We then conducted a series of searches using the same terms with the addition of the search term "and book" to identify articles containing book-specific news coverage. In essence, the second series of searches effectively parsed the total coverage figures to permit comparison between book-specific news coverage and non-book news coverage of the justices.

Figure 3 presents the annual article counts for total news coverage and book-specific coverage for each of the thirty-two years under study. In general, justices published fewer books in the 1980s; only in 1987 and 1988 were books written by a justice. In contrast, at least one book written by a justice has been published every year from 1997 to 2012. As Figure 3

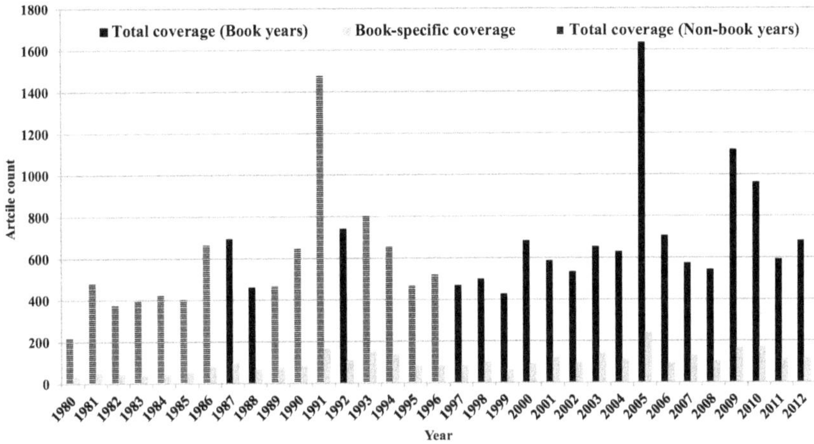

FIGURE 3. Total and book-specific annual newspaper coverage of U.S. Supreme Court Justices (1980–2012).
Note: Solid black lines indicate total news coverage of justices in book publication years, while hatched lines represent total new coverage in non-publication years. Small solid gray lines indicate book-specific coverage in each year. Coverage data obtained from LexisNexis searches of the Washington Post and NY Times. Article counts exclude unclassified documents and blog entries.

illustrates, total annual news coverage tends to be higher during years when justices write books. Moreover, book-specific coverage is generally greater in book publication years.

Consider, for example, news coverage coinciding with books by Justice Sandra Day O'Connor. O'Connor wrote five books in the period under study. In years when O'Connor did not publish a book, her name appears in 106 articles on average across both papers. Conversely, her name appears in 212 articles on average in years when she authored a book – a 99 percent increase in overall news coverage. Moreover, articles specifically referencing O'Connor and "book" jumped 132 percent, from 13.6 articles on average in non-book years to 31.6 stories on average across the two papers in years when O'Connor wrote a book.[7] A similar, although less-pronounced effect, emerged in news coverage of Justice Stephen Breyer, who wrote six books in five different years. Overall news coverage mentioning Breyer jumped 41 percent in years when he wrote a book.

[7] O'Connor authored a book in 2005, the year she announced her retirement, and thus the large increase in overall news coverage coinciding with book publications for O'Connor is likely driven, to some degree, by the announcement of her retirement. As noted, however, coverage referencing books experienced a marked increase as well.

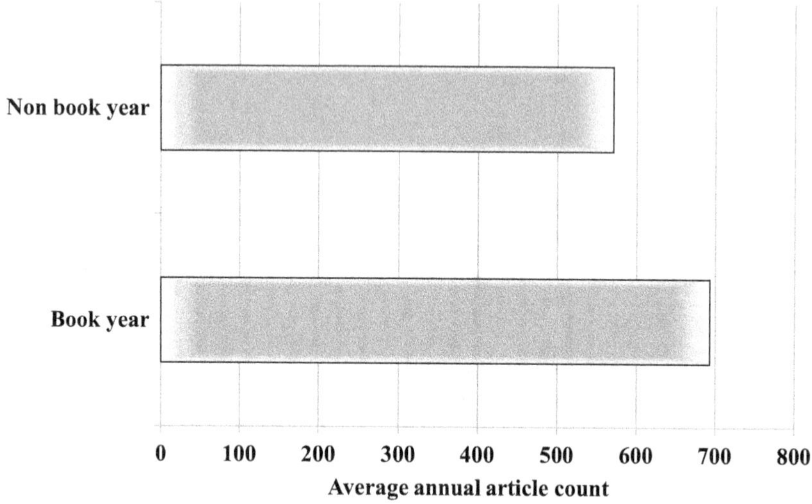

FIGURE 4. Average annual total newspaper coverage for non-book and book publication years. *Note: Coverage data obtained from LexisNexis searches of* the *Washington Post and* the *New York Times. Article counts exclude unclassified documents and blog entries.*

To better illustrate the overall effect that book publication by justices has on news coverage, Figure 4 presents the average article count for book publication years and non-publication years. In comparison, Figure 5 shows the same information for book-specific coverage in book publication and non-publication years. As Figure 4 illustrates, total news coverage in years when justices produce no books averages approximately 570 stories across the *Washington Post* and the *New York Times*. However, in years when a justice publishes a book, total annual news coverage increases to approximately 690 articles per year – a substantive 21 percent increase over non-publication years. But does the increase reflect news coverage devoted to discussion of books, or is it simply an artifact of increased general news coverage of the Court in recent years?

Simply put, the data show that a focus of news organizations on books written by the justices partly drives the increased coverage of the Court. Not only is there an overall increase in news coverage in book publication years (see Figure 4), there is also a notable increase in book-specific coverage (see Figure 5). While there are approximately seventy-eight stories on average specifically referencing books in non-publication years, book-specific coverage jumps 48 percent to 116 articles in a typical year when justices write a book. In other words, both overall coverage and book-specific coverage increases in years when justices publish books. Moreover, the percentage increase in

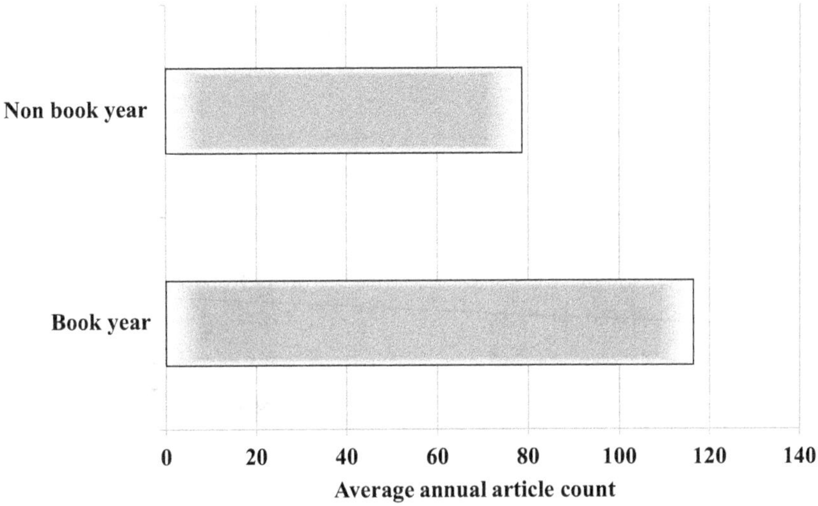

FIGURE 5. Average annual book-related coverage for non-Book and book publication years. *Note: Coverage data obtained from LexisNexis searches of* the *Washington Post and* the *New York Times. Article counts exclude unclassified documents and blog entries.*

book-specific coverage is greater than the increase in total news coverage. This suggests that stories that mention books written by justices disproportionately drive the increase in coverage. Such a pattern is consistent with the observation by journalists that justices tend to engage the press more frequently when promoting their books.

As justices engage the press to promote their books, we should not conclude that book-specific news coverage dominates coverage of the Court in general. In spite of an increase in book-related news coverage in years when justices likely promote their writings (see Figure 6), book-specific coverage continues to represent a relatively modest percentage of overall news coverage of the justices. Indeed, even in years when justices write books, book-related coverage only accounts for 17 percent of total news coverage; coverage of the justices continues to reflect primarily non-book related content.

As the analysis of book-related news coverage indicates, the notion that justices more frequently engage the press to promote their books appears to ring true. In essence, not only does the overall news coverage pie increase during book publication years, so too does the slice of pie devoted to book-specific news coverage. Such findings lend persuasive evidence that justices embrace the media as a means to advance their own interests – in the present case, to promote their books.

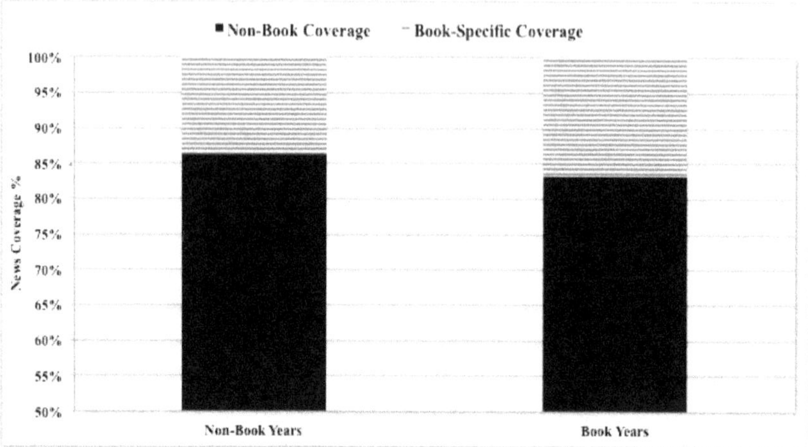

FIGURE 6. Newspaper coverage by subject for non-book and book publication years.
Note: Coverage data obtained from LexisNexis searches of the *Washington Post and* the *New York Times and exclude unclassified documents and blog entries.*

To the extent that justices engage the press with the intent of self-promotion, it is worth noting once again that such occasions nevertheless provide the opportunity for journalists to pose questions to the justices on additional newsworthy issues. For instance, *60 Minutes* used its interview with Sonia Sotomayor, who was promoting her memoir, as the basis for an additional segment that contrasted her views on affirmative action with those of Justice Thomas, linking them to the broader debate about affirmative action.[8] Charlie Rose used a similar interview with Sotomayor to ask about her views on "making history" with opinions, questions that were highly relevant given the same-sex marriage cases pending before the Court.[9] From this perspective, the recent trend for justices to increasingly churn out books proves beneficial, not only for the educational and informative value of the books, but for journalists who wish to provide news consumers a better glimpse into the relatively secluded lives of Supreme Court justices.

[8] "How Affirmative Action Divides Two Justices." January 13, 2013. *60 Minutes Overtime*. Accessed July 28, 2013. www.cbsnews.com/8301-504803_162-57563699-10391709/how-affirmative-action-divides-two-justices/

[9] Sotomayor, Sonia. "Supreme Court Justice Sonia Sotomayor, Part 2." February 7, 2013. Interview with Charlie Rose. www.bloomberg.com/video/supreme-court-justice-sonia-sotomayor-part-2-9yOhWEHVREKG3ZXOxKotBw.html.

CONCLUSION

This chapter sought to establish what Supreme Court justices think about the press, a challenging proposition given the lack of access granted journalists who cover the Court. Nevertheless, we examined scores of speeches, interviews, and lectures given by current and former justices, alongside three decades of news coverage patterns of the justices in two prominent national newspapers. What emerged was a contrasting picture – an image of justices often critical of the press, yet willing to engage the press to promote their own works.

In spite of such mixed observations, however, general themes among the justices nonetheless emerged. Our review of speeches, lectures, and interviews suggests that justices generally view press coverage of the Court critically, with the exception of a handful of outlets deemed "friendly." Indeed, justices at times have characterized news coverage of their institution as inaccurate or too focused on painting an overly political picture of the Court. Justices are worried about how coverage of the Court affects public understanding of and support for the institution, and they oppose changes (like televising oral arguments) that they think would undermine public confidence even further.

Given the justices' expressed concerns about how they are portrayed, we examined whether justices respond to such concerns through increased engagement of the press as indicated by news coverage of justices. Although we find evidence that increased news coverage of the Court is associated with greater confidence in the justices, it does not appear that justices respond to declining public opinion by strategically courting media outlets.

In spite of concerns about inaccurate and overly political portrayals of the Court, justices nonetheless appear amicable to news organizations when it comes to promoting their books. Consistent with the observations of Court correspondents, we find persuasive evidence that justices provide more access to journalists when they have a book to promote. There is a notable increase in overall coverage of the justices as well as book-specific coverage of the Court in years when justices write books. Just as justices use the press as a means to generate interest in their writings, we also find evidence that the justices view media as a means to promote greater interest in and understanding of the Court.

From such a perspective, the opinions that justices voice about the press are not unlike the perceptions held of the public at large. Like justices who have a critical view of press coverage, the public tends to view the media, and news organizations in particular, with a healthy dose of skepticism (Pew Research 2011). At the same time, just as justices value the utilitarian aspects of media, be it of a promotional or educational nature, the public likewise values the press for serving the interests of citizens through informing society and monitoring government (Pew Research 2011). Such similarities illustrate that when it comes to what Supreme Court justices think about the media, their views are not much different from those of Main Street. Ambivalent views of the press appear the same, even from the lofty perch of the bench.

REFERENCES

Alliance for Audited Media. April 30, 2013. Accessed July 1, 2013. www.auditedmedia.com/news/blog/top-25-us-newspapers-for-march-2013.aspx.

Baum, Lawrence. 2006. *Judges and Their Audiences*. Princeton: Princeton University Press.

Breyer, Stephen. October 10, 2000. "The Legal Profession and Public Service." Accessed July 1 2013. http://www.supremecourt.gov/publicinfo/speeches/

October 22, 2001. "Fall 2001 James Madison Lecture." Accessed July 1, 2013. http://www.supremecourt.gov/publicinfo/speeches/

September 22, 2009. "An Independent Judiciary: In Honor of the Sesquicentennial Anniversary of the Massachusetts Superior Court." Accessed July 1, 2013. www.supremecourt.gov/publicinfo/speeches/

"Chamber Endorses Samuel Alito as Supreme Court Associate Justice." June 1, 2006. Accessed July 8, 2013. www.uschamber.com/node/6237/%252Fjune.

Cohn, Alicia M. July 26, 2012. "Scalia: Cameras in Supreme Court Would 'Miseducate' Americans." *The Hill*. Accessed July 1, 2013. thehill.com/video/in-the-news/240519-justice-scalia-cameras-in-supreme-court-would-miseducate-americans

Collins, Ron. 353 *books by Supreme Court Justices (UPDATED 11/7/12)*, SCOTUSblog (Mar. 12, 2012, 10:13 AM), www.scotusblog.com/2012/03/351-books-by-supreme-court-justices/

Davis, Richard. 1994. *Decisions and Images: The Supreme Court and the Press*. Prentice-Hall.

2011. *Justices and Journalists: The U.S. Supreme Court in the Media Age*. New York: Cambridge University Press.

Ginsburg, Ruth Bader. February 10, 2006. "Advocating the Elimination of Gender-Based Discrimination." University of Cape Town, South Africa. Accessed July 1, 2013. www.supremecourt.gov/publicinfo/speeches/

July 25, 2011. "A Survey of the 2010 Term." Cooperstown, NY. Accessed July 1, 2013. http://www.supremecourt.gov/publicinfo/speeches/

June 12, 2009. "Remarks for the Second Circuit Judicial Conference, Bolton Landing, NY." Accessed July 1, 2013. www.supremecourt.gov/publicinfo/speeches/

June 18, 2012. "Remarks to the American Constitution Society." Accessed July 1, 2013. http://www.supremecourt.gov/publicinfo/speeches/

Ginsburg, Ruth Bader and Sandra Day O'Connor. 2010. Interview with Diane Sawyer. "Sawyer Interviews Ruth Bader Ginsburg and Sandra Day O'Connor." Accessed July 1, 2013. abcnews.go.com/WNT/video/sawyer-interviews-ruth-bader-ginsburg-sandra-day-oconnor-11983364.

Golan, G. 2006. "Inter-media agenda setting and global news coverage: Assessing the influence of the *New York Times* on three network television evening news programs." *Journalism Studies*, 7(2), 323–333.

Grau, C. H. 1976. "What publications are most frequently quoted in the *Congressional Record*." *Journalism Quarterly*, 53, 716–719.

"Justice Alito Defends High Court's 2010 Decision in Citizens United Case." November 17, 2012. Accessed July 1, 2013. www.foxnews.com/politics/2012/11/17/justice-alito-defends-high-court-2010-decision-in-citizens-united-case/

Kantor, Jodi. February 3, 2013. "On Book Tour Circuit, Sotomayor Sees New Niche for a Justice." *New York Times*. www.nytimes.com/2013/02/04/us/politics/book-tour-rock-star-sotomayor-sees-an-even-higher-calling.html?pagewanted=all&_r=0

Katz, Justin. September 14, 2012. "09/14/12 – Supreme Court Justice Samuel Alito – Roger Williams Law School." Accessed July 1, 2013. oceanstatecurrent.com/live-blog/091412-supreme-court-justice-samuel-alito-roger-williams-law-school/.

Liptak, Adam. February 18, 2013. "Bucking a Trend, Supreme Court Justices Reject Video Coverage." *The New York Times*. Accessed July 1, 2013. www.nytimes.com/2013/02/19/us/bucking-trend-supreme-court-still-rejects-video-coverage.html?ref=adamliptak.

Interview with Max Mallory. 2013b. *Scotusblog on Camera: Adam Liptak*. www.scotusblog.com/media/scotusblog-on-camera-adam-liptak-interview/

McCombs, M. 2005. "A look at agenda-setting: Past, present and future." *Journalism Studies*, 6(4), 543–557.

O'Connor, Sandra Day. September 28, 2006. "Q & A with Sandra Day O'Connor." *Time Magazine*. http://www.time.com/time/nation/article/0,8599,1540702,00.html

March 3, 2009. Interview with Jon Stewart. *The Daily Show with Jon Stewart*. Television program.

September 30, 2011. Interview with Cokie Roberts. *To the Contrary*. Television program. http://video.pbs.org/video/15262766/.

August 5, 2012. Interview with Bob Schieffer. *Face the Nation*. www.cbsnews.com/8301-3460_162-57487020/face-the-nation-transcripts-august-5-2012-mcdonnell-rendell-strickland-diaz-balart/?pageNum=7&tag=contentMain;contentBody.

Pew Research. September 22, 2011. Public Perception of Media Bias Hits Historic High. Accessed July 2, 2013. www.people-press.org/2011/09/22/press-widely-criticized-but-trusted-more-than-other-institutions/

Reese, S. D., & Danielian, L. H. 1989. "A closer look at intermedia influences on agenda setting: The cocaine issue of 1986." Shoemaker, Pamela (Hg): *Communication Campaigns about Drugs*, 47–66.

Rehnquist, William. June 4, 2001. "Remarks of the Chief Justice, Supreme Court Historical Society 2001 Annual Lecture." Accessed July 1, 2013. www.supremecourt.gov/publicinfo/speeches/

"Retirement of Justice Marshall." June 28, 1991. C-SPAN. Available at: www.c-spanvideo.org/program/18624-1. Television.

Rosenberg, Gerald. 2008. *The Hollow Hope: Can Courts Bring About Social Change?* 2nd ed. Chicago: University of Chicago Press.

Segal, Jeffrey and Harold Spaeth. 2002. *The Attitudinal Model Revisited*. Cambridge: Cambridge University Press.

"On Cameras in Supreme Court, Souter Says 'Over My Dead Body.'" Associated Press. March 30, 1996. www.nytimes.com/1996/03/30/us/on-cameras-in-supreme-court-souter-says-over-my-dead-body.html

Sotomayor, Sonia. January 21, 2013. Interview with Jon Stewart. *The Daily Show with Jon Stewart.*

Stevens, John Paul. September 22, 2011. "Byron White: Hero and Scholar." Available at: www.supremecourt.gov/publicinfo/speeches/

November 16, 2011. "Kelo, Popularity, and Substantive Due Process." Available at: www.supremecourt.gov/publicinfo/speeches/

"The Supreme Court: Home to America's Highest Court." 2009. *C-SPAN* documentary.

Totenberg, Nina, interview with Max Mallory. 2013. *Scotusblog on Camera: Nina Totenberg Interview.* www.scotusblog.com/media/scotusblog-on-camera-nina-totenberg-interview/

Ververs, Vaughn. November 1, 2005. "You Say Scalito, I Say Alito." Accessed July 17, 2013. www.cbsnews.com/8301-500486_162-999542-500486.html

Vloet, Katie. September 8, 2012. "Justice Kagan Highlights South Hall Dedication Weekend." Available at: www.law.umich.edu/newsandinfo/features/Pages/kagan_SHdedication.aspx

Wallace, Chris. July 29, 2012. "Justice Antonin Scalia on issues facing SCOTUS and the country." www.foxnews.com/on-air/fox-news-sunday/2012/07/29/justice-antonin-scalia-issues-facing-scotus-and-country#p//v/1760654457001

Weiss. C. H. 1974. "What America's leaders read." *Public Opinion Quarterly* 38, 1–22.

12

Justice Brennan and the Press

SETH STERN

On March 9, 1964, Associate Justice William J. Brennan, Jr. announced the landmark *New York Times v. Sullivan* decision, which established a high bar for libel suits against public officials and provided the press new latitude to make some errors.[1] Yet, when an Ohio college student asked Brennan to participate in a press conference during a campus visit two years later, he was quick to say no, explaining that he, as a policy, rejected all media requests. "There is just too much risk of being misquoted or misunderstood," Brennan explained in a letter to a college official.[2]

Brennan's fear of being misquoted by the very journalists his decisions protected reflects the ambivalence this champion of press freedoms felt about the media. Brennan read at least two newspapers every morning, watched the evening news on television each night, and genuinely believed reporters played a vital role in a democratic society. "As money is to the economy, so the press is to our political culture; it is the medium of circulation," Brennan said in a 1979 speech.[3] He could not escape from the press even if he tried: two of his three children married newspaper reporters during the 1960s.[4]

Journalists, however, managed to infuriate Brennan like no one else during his thirty-four terms on the Court between 1956 and 1990. The genial justice known for being as warm to the Court's elevator operator as to his colleagues once shoved an Associated Press reporter who asked him a question he didn't

[1] New York Times Co. v. Sullivan, 376 U.S. 254 (1964).

[2] William J. Brennan Jr. to Marietta College, October 1966, William J. Brennan Jr. Papers, Library of Congress.

[3] William J. Brennan Jr., "Dedication of the Samuel I. Newhouse Law Center" (speech, Rutgers University, Newark, NJ, October 17, 1979).

[4] Tim Phelps, his daughter's first husband, would have a distinguished career at the *St. Petersburg Times*, *Newsday* and the *Log Angeles Times*. His son Bill's wife, Georgie, was a reporter for the *Newark Star Ledger*.

like. He refused to speak to Fred Graham, who covered the Court for the *New York Times* and CBS for grievances both real and imagined. The mere mention of the *Washington Post*'s Bob Woodward, who wrote *The Brethren*, could prompt a fusillade of obscenities.

Press freedom wasn't the only issue about which Brennan exhibited a striking disconnect between his judicial decisions and private opinions.[5] He refused to hire female clerks in the early 1970s even as his decisions expanded women's rights. Moreover, he remained uneasy about abortion long after he had quietly helped craft the *Roe v. Wade* decision.[6] As with female clerks, his views about the press evolved over time. In the 1980s, he lifted his longstanding prohibition on interviews. He developed a warm friendship with National Public Radio correspondent Nina Totenberg, after having tartly rebuffed her efforts to curry favor with him a decade earlier. Perhaps most surprisingly, Brennan granted unprecedented access to Stephen Wermiel, the *Wall Street Journal*'s Supreme Court reporter, who he had selected to be his biographer.

PRE-COURT ATTITUDES

Brennan's distrust of the press dates back to his childhood in Newark, New Jersey where he grew up reading newspaper coverage of his father, William Brennan Sr., a prominent local union leader turned politician. The elder Brennan was elected to Newark's city commission in 1917 when his son was eleven years old. Brennan's father was a diligent and popular public servant, who nevertheless found himself harshly criticized as director of public safety for how the city's police department enforced Prohibition during the 1920s. As a teenager, Brennan read accounts in Newark's newspapers of Protestant church groups and the local chapter of the Anti-Saloon League lambasting the elder Brennan for lax enforcement, insinuating that he was a drunk.[7] Brennan took these attacks to heart, turning away from politics for good.[8] He also developed a life-long sensitivity to press coverage of his family.

His father's prominence explains why Brennan attracted an outsized amount of press attention as a young Newark corporate lawyer. When Brennan, at the age of 27, delivered a series of campaign speeches on behalf of one of

[5] Seth Stern and Stephen Wermiel, *Justice Brennan: Liberal Champion* (Boston: Houghton Mifflin Harcourt, 2010)

[6] *Roe v. Wade*, 410 U.S. 113 (1973).

[7] *Newark Evening News*, "Asserts 'Higher Ups' Balk Newark Police," January 23, 1925.

[8] William J. Brennan Jr., interview by Stephen Wermiel, May 30, 1990.

his father's political allies, the *Newark Ledger* praised him as "the worthy son of a worthy sire, who, we believe, is destined to play a big role in Newark's official life."[9] Brennan never ran for office himself, but he continued to attract newspaper headlines within New Jersey after becoming a state judge, and ultimately a member of the state's highest court.

Brennan still was little known outside his home state when President Dwight Eisenhower on September 29, 1956 announced his recess appointment to the U.S. Supreme Court. He discovered how much life had changed that night when his train returned from Washington to Newark's Penn Station and hordes of photographers jostled to take pictures of him.[10] Reporters interrupted his wife Marjorie's dinner preparations and photographers camped out on the lawn outside their Rumson, New Jersey home.[11]

Brennan's nomination generated glowing coverage, although many of the stories inaccurately portrayed his rise as an Irish rags-to-riches tale.[12] Brennan did his best to knock down the myths of a hard-knocks childhood. "I'm no Horatio Alger," Brennan told *Life* magazine shortly after his nomination.[13] It was harder to dislodge stereotypical portrayals of him as a happy leprechaun, which would infuse press coverage throughout his tenure. *Time* magazine headlined its profile of Brennan "The Ninth Justice: A Happy Irishman;" the article described him as "an affable, storytelling Irishman."[14]

EARLY YEARS AS JUSTICE

At the end of his first term, one of Brennan's earliest opinions generated an unexpected public backlash fed by what he considered inaccurate press coverage. The case of *Jencks v. United States* involved the president of a New Mexico local union charged with falsely filing an affidavit swearing he was not a communist.[15] Clinton Jencks' conviction depended largely on the testimony of two paid FBI informers, one of whom had confessed to lying and fabricating information. Brennan concluded the government had to share its agents' prior statements in order to prove the witness had previously given a different account. In the midst of the Red Scare, Brennan's June 1957 decision

9 Editorial, "Another William J. Brennan!" *Newark Ledger*, May 6, 1933.
10 William J. Brennan Jr., interview by Stephen Wermiel, October 28, 1986.
11 *Newark Evening News*, "Brennan Dinner Party Becomes Celebration," September 30, 1956.
12 Associated Press, "Justice Brennan, Son of Irish Immigrants, Came Up the Hard Way to Highest Tribunal," William J. Brennan Jr. personal scrapbook.
13 *Life*, "A Fine Judge Ready for His Biggest Job," October 29, 1956.
14 *Time*, "The Ninth Justice: A Happy Irishman," October 8, 1956.
15 *Jencks v. United States*, 353 U.S. 657 (1957).

sparked furious condemnation and alarmist media coverage about the Court granting communists access to government secrets. A typical cartoon in the *Fort Wayne News Sentinel* depicted the justices digging an escape route for communist prisoners.[16]

Unlike some of his colleagues, Brennan thought it best to let his opinions speak for themselves, rather than try to respond publicly to critics. For instance, when the Court's 1962 *Engel v. Vitale*[17] school-prayer decision sparked widespread public outrage, Justice Tom Clark defended the decision at an appearance before the San Francisco Commonwealth Club.[18] Clark blamed the media for presenting the public with an incomplete version of the Court's decision. Brennan too, thought the press coverage was ill informed, but he didn't try to rebut it publicly. "The tradition that judges do not debate decisions or the reasoning on which they rest has roots in history, and I think its discard would be more unfortunate and undesirable," Brennan told *Look* magazine later that year.[19]

Brennan did vent some frustration publicly about how the press covered another school prayer case a year later.[20] Brennan thought reporters and commentators did not take enough time to read the Court's opinions – including his own carefully crafted concurrence – or to understand the justices' reasoning before criticizing the result. "There were four majority opinions which filled 109 printed pages," he later complained in a speech. "Yet within two hours the critics were in print saying the Court was wrong. It was obvious they could not have read the explanations."[21]

Brennan was the subject of occasional newspaper and magazine stories in the early 1960s, including a profile in *Look* magazine published in December 1962, which portrayed him as "a man at peace with himself, in love with his family and his work."[22] His central role on the Court was a focus of Sidney Zion's five-part 1965 series in the *New York Post*, which described Brennan as "the most important man in the majority bloc."[23] A friend back in New Jersey mailed Zion's article to Brennan, who had not seen it yet himself.

[16] Arthur E. Sutherland Jr., Foreward: The Citizen's Immunities and Public Opinion, 71 *Harv. L. Rev.* 85, 86 (1957).

[17] *Engel v. Vitale*, 370 U.S. 421 (1962).

[18] James E. Clayton, *The Making of Justice: The Supreme Court in Action* (New York: E. P. Dutton, 1964), 21–22.

[19] *Look*, "A Visit with Justice Brennan," December 18, 1962.

[20] *Abington School District v. Schempp*, 374 U.S. 203 (1963).

[21] Associated Press, "High Court Found Imperiled by Foes, "*New York Times*, August 30, 1963.

[22] *Look*, "A Visit with Justice Brennan," December 18, 1962.

[23] Sidney Zion, "The Supreme Court," *New York Post*, February 4, 1965.

Brennan objected to Zion's conclusions. "Mr. Zion is very flattering but I am appalled at the idea that the Chief Justice and Justices Black, Douglas, and Goldberg goose step to my tune," Brennan wrote back. "Believe me, Bill, it just ain't so."[24]

Brennan was happy to maintain a low media profile and immediately regretted the one time he had given an impromptu press conference during a 1962 visit to Puerto Rico. Reporters asked him whether a new statute that directed the U.S. Supreme Court to review directly the judgments of Puerto Rico's highest court – just as it did with each state's highest court – meant that Puerto Rico was a de facto state. Brennan offered a complicated answer about Puerto Rico's status as a territory. But front-page headlines in the island's newspaper the next day heralded his comments as an important endorsement of statehood. "I did put my foot in my mouth didn't I?" Brennan wrote one member of Puerto Rico's Supreme Court after returning to Washington. "Apparently, I should have followed my general practice of keeping quiet on such matters."[25] That is what he did in subsequent years, declining all interview requests during campus speaking engagements.

In Washington, Brennan generally avoided getting close to reporters, but he made an exception for Anthony Lewis, the *New York Times*' Supreme Court correspondent. Lewis began covering the Court during Brennan's second term in 1957 at the age of thirty after completing a Nieman Fellowship at Harvard Law School.[26] Lewis's reporting impressed both Brennan and Justice Felix Frankfurter, the prickly former Harvard Law School professor, who said Lewis had as good a grasp of cases as some of the justices themselves.[27] Brennan sent Lewis a congratulatory note when he won journalism's highest award for his Court reporting. "I can't sufficiently express my enthusiasm for the so richly deserved Pulitzer Prize for your coverage of the Court. You have been, and are, performing a truly distinguished public service."[28] When Lewis moved off the Supreme Court beat to become the *Times*' London bureau chief, Brennan wrote to say, "We'll all miss you, officially and personally."[29]

[24] William J. Brennan Jr. to Luis Blanco Lugo, February 21, 1962, William J. Brennan Jr. Papers, Library of Congress.

[25] Ibid.

[26] Adam Liptak, "Anthony Lewis, Supreme Court Reporter Who Brought Law to Life, Dies at 85," *New York Times*, March 25, 2013.

[27] James Reston, *Deadline: A Memoir* (New York: Random House, 1991), 204.

[28] William J. Brennan Jr. to Anthony Lewis, 1963, William J. Brennan Jr. Papers, Library of Congress.

[29] William J. Brennan Jr. to Anthony Lewis, November 7, 1964, William J. Brennan Jr. Papers, Library of Congress.

Their correspondence continued after Lewis settled in London. "I can be unqualified in expressing the sentiment that all of us miss you greatly," Brennan wrote Lewis in 1966. "I follow your pieces from London and obviously you are as perceptive about England's problems as you were about ours. But I only wish you were still giving all your attention to us."[30]

BRENNAN'S WITHDRAWAL: THE 1970S

Brennan's relations with the press soured as the liberal voting bloc led by Chief Justice Earl Warren, which had dominated the Court during the 1960s, came under conservative attack. In May 1969, soon after Justice Abe Fortas resigned from the Court under pressure, several Washington papers, as well as the *New York Times* and *Chicago Tribune*, published stories detailing Brennan's investments in a series of real estate partnerships with fellow judges.[31] Hoping to head off further controversy, Brennan took the drastic step of withdrawing from all outside activities. He quit law school visiting committees, canceled every future speaking engagement, and resigned from both the American Bar Association and New Jersey Bar Association.[32]

Brennan had hoped the controversy over his real estate deals had died down three weeks later, when fellow justices, members of his family, friends, and some journalists gathered in the Court's East Conference Room for a ceremony at which he received a medal from the University of Notre Dame. Brennan wanted to use the ceremony as an occasion to honor Warren publicly on the eve of his retirement. That morning, however, the *New York Times* published a story by Fred Graham about Brennan's decision to cut back on most off-the-bench activities.[33] Afterward, Barry Schweid, who covered the Court for the Associated Press, approached Brennan and asked about the *Times* article. Brennan cut him off by saying, "Go ahead . . . beat it," and then nudged Schweid in the chest. Schweid recounted the incident in a story he filed that day for the Associated Press.[34]

[30] William J. Brennan Jr. to Anthony Lewis, 1966, William J. Brennan Jr. Papers, Library of Congress.

[31] Philip Warden, "Dealings of 2 Court Members Keep Ethics Issue Boiling," *Chicago Tribune*, May 17, 1969; *New York Times*, "Court to Let Brennan Hear Case Despite Real Estate Partnership," May 27, 1969.

[32] Associated Press, "All Activities Outside Court Given Up by Justice Brennan," *Bridgeport* (CT) *Telegram*, June 12, 1969.

[33] Fred Graham, "Justices Curbing Off-Bench Roles," *New York Times*, June 9, 1969.

[34] Barry Schweid, e-mail message to author, May 1, 2007.

Schweid wasn't the only reporter on the receiving end of Brennan's wrath over the issue. Graham said Brennan was so "livid" about his *Times* article that the justice stopped returning his phone calls. "By the time I learned of my role in triggering this, it was too late," Graham wrote in his memoir. "The justice had gone to ground and would not return my calls."[35] Brennan also blamed Graham for the *Times'* coverage of an earlier controversy involving his son, William J. Brennan III, even though Graham hadn't even written any of the offending stories.[36] In December 1968, Brennan's son, then an attorney in the New Jersey state attorney general's office, gave a speech to the local chapter of a society of journalists in New Jersey, warning that organized crime had infiltrated every facet of life in the state.[37] The resulting controversy made headlines in both New Jersey and New York and prompted calls for Brennan's son to be fired. "I think young Mr. Brennan is done here," one New Jersey state legislator was quoted as saying in the *New York Times*.[38] Reading the harsh criticisms leveled against his son might have reminded Brennan of the way his father was treated during Prohibition.

Brennan held onto his grudge. When Graham later moved to CBS and requested an interview, Brennan responded with a two-sentence-long rejection letter.[39] Several of Brennan's clerks remembered the usually gregarious justice openly disparaging Graham in their presence. But reporters who hadn't angered Brennan fared no better during the 1970s and early 1980s, a time when he was preoccupied with his wife's failing health. He rejected almost all interview requests, whether from Court beat reporters, such as Fred Barbash at the *Washington Post*, or prominent television journalists, such as Dan Rather of CBS' *60 Minutes*.

Brennan made a rare exception for one home-state media outlet. He answered by mail a series of innocuous questions posed by a *Trenton Times* reporter in October 1976 about his daily schedule and his contact with judges back in New Jersey. "You doubtless are aware that I've had a policy for several years not to have interviews," Brennan wrote the *Trenton Times* reporter. "Were I to make any exceptions to that policy I'd necessarily have to discontinue it.

35 Fred Graham, *Happy Talk: Confessions of a TV Newsman* (New York: W.W. Norton & Company, 1990), 140.

36 William J. Brennan Jr., interview by Stephen Wermiel, December 14, 1987.

37 Associated Press, "Organized Crime Said to Infiltrate Jersey Legislature," *New York Times*, December 12, 1968.

38 Sidney Zion, "Brennan Recital Is Called Flimsy," *New York Times*, December 31, 1968.

39 Graham wrote Brennan a lengthy letter on June 19, 1978, requesting an interview, and Brennan replied with a curt rejection two days later.

I prefer to adhere to it." Nevertheless, Brennan said he decided to reply in this instance "since you have indicated the questions you would like to ask."[40]

During this period, Brennan could be uncharacteristically sharp when reporters attempted even simple gestures of good will. Nina Totenberg had sent Brennan a note with a free subscription to her publication, the *National Observer*, when she started covering the Court. He replied tartly that he did not accept gifts. Brennan was no more receptive when Totenberg sent a copy of a 1974 article she wrote for another publication, *New Times*, about the status of the Court's minority employees and requested an interview in the accompanying handwritten note.[41] He even avoided photojournalists trying to take his picture. A photographer on assignment for *Time* magazine in 1973 approached him as he left for his morning walk and asked whether he was Justice Brennan. "No," Brennan said, "Never heard of him." Only when Brennan was out of camera range did the photographer realize he had been fooled.[42]

The press, in turn, portrayed Brennan as bitter about how the four conservative justices appointed by President Richard Nixon had rolled back the Warren Court precedents he helped shape. "Justice Brennan now appears to be angry, and lately has had trouble containing his hot feelings," Lyle Denniston wrote in the *Washington Star* in April 1971.[43] Graham singled out Brennan in the *Times* when he noted "the increasingly vinegary statements by justices who were mainstays of the Warren Court's liberal wing."[44]

Brennan continued to stay in touch with Lewis, who moved back to the U.S. and began writing a column for the *Times* in 1969. Lewis occasionally wrote Brennan to compliment his decisions or speeches and stopped by the Court to see Brennan once a year or so. Brennan wrote Lewis praising his columns and at least once, invited Lewis to have tea at his Washington apartment with him and his wife.[45] When Brennan was diagnosed with throat cancer in 1977, Lewis called to express his concerns. "I am deeply touched by your interest," Brennan wrote Lewis in a thank you note.[46]

[40] William J. Brennan Jr. to T.R. Reid, October 20, 1976, William J. Brennan Jr. Papers, Library of Congress.

[41] Nina Totenberg, "The Last Plantation," *New Times*, July 1974; Totenberg, interview with author, August 21, 2007.

[42] Donald M. Morrison, "Apostle of Justice," *Pennsylvania Gazette*, October 1977.

[43] Lyle Denniston, "Angry Justice Brennan," *Trenton Times*, April 2, 1971.

[44] Fred Graham, "Justices Are Losing Their Cool," *New York Times*, April 11, 1971.

[45] William J. Brennan Jr. to Anthony Lewis, April 13, 1977, William J. Brennan Jr. Papers, Library of Congress.

[46] William J. Brennan Jr. to Anthony Lewis, May 12, 1977, William J. Brennan Jr. Papers, Library of Congress.

THE BRETHREN

Lewis came to Brennan's defense after the 1979 release of *The Brethren*, coauthored by Scott Armstrong and Bob Woodward, whose reporting on Watergate for the *Washington Post* had helped bring down President Richard Nixon.[47] *The Brethren*'s behind-the-scenes account of Warren Burger's first seven terms as chief justice infuriated Brennan more than anything else published about the Court during his tenure.

Excerpts began appearing in newspapers around the country, including in the *Washington Post*, where Woodward was now an editor, on Sunday, December 2, 1979.[48] Brennan was shocked to read in the accompanying news story in the *Post* that among the "unprecedented accumulation of secret court materials" obtained by Woodward and Armstrong were some of his own term histories. Each term, Brennan had his clerks write an account of key cases as a reference tool within his chambers. The *Post* described the term histories as Brennan's "private journals."[49] *The Brethren* quoted Brennan as privately calling Burger a "dummy" and suggested Brennan refused to overturn a prison sentence in 1972, even though he believed the defendant "Slick" Moore, was unfairly convicted in order to win over Justice Harry Blackmun in unrelated cases.[50]

That night, Woodward and Armstrong appeared on *60 Minutes*. When asked whether Brennan was *The Brethren*'s "Deep Throat," a reference to Woodward's secret Watergate source, Armstrong replied, "I think we'd rather not answer that." Armstrong later explained that he was simply trying to avoid questions about their sources.[51] But that answer enraged Brennan, who thought it intentionally left the impression that he had helped the authors. Pounding his hand on the table, Brennan yelled, "I will never vote for the First Amendment again!" His angry response shocked Tim Phelps, his daughter's ex-husband, who was a journalist himself and happened to be watching the program with Brennan that night. Phelps had known Brennan for more than a decade, but had never seen him so angry.

This was not the first time something published in the *Post* infuriated Brennan. Peter Harkness, who grew up next door to Brennan in Georgetown,

[47] Bob Woodward and Scott Armstrong, *The Brethren: Inside the Supreme Court* (New York: Simon & Schuster, 1979).

[48] Bob Woodward and Scott Armstrong, "Inside the Supreme Court: Burger's First Test," *Washington Post*, December 2, 1979.

[49] Fred Barbash, "Author's View: No True Leader," *Washington Post*, December 2, 1979.

[50] *Moore v. Illinois*, 408 U.S. 786 (1972).

[51] *Oakland Tribune*, "Woodward, Armstrong and the Court," January 24, 1980.

remembered attending a dinner where the justice exploded about an article that had appeared in the paper. "Here is the icon of the First Amendment and he is just lambasting this newspaper," said Harkness, who went on to a career in journalism. "I'm certain he'd rule in their favor the next day if the case was presented but I was shocked at the anger."[52]

Publication of *The Brethren* proved particularly traumatic for Brennan. He resented how the book fed the public perception that he operated in the Court like a savvy Irish politician. The conflict–averse justice was mortified that Burger would read how he talked about the chief justice in private. Brennan certainly did not welcome the book's depiction of him as a key behind-the-scenes player in the *Roe* case after intentionally trying to distance himself from abortion cases. He was galled by how columnists mischaracterized and condemned his case histories as some sort of sordid diary or "gossip file."[53] William Safire, in his *New York Times* column, accused Brennan of misusing federal employees "to edify or enrich his posterity."[54] He was stung the most by lawyer-author George V. Higgins's column in the *Boston Globe*'s Sunday magazine, which characterized his behavior as "contemptible."[55] Brennan confided in a letter to a professor, "My daughter and granddaughter live in Boston and this has hurt them deeply."[56]

He was outraged by the suggestion that he might have traded his vote in a case to curry favor with Blackmun, which he labeled a "damnable lie" and "canard" in a letter to one law professor.[57] Four clerks who served during the term of the case at issue wrote a letter to the editor of the *Post* denouncing *The Brethren*'s account as false.[58] Lewis followed up with an investigation of his own that ran in the *New York Review of Books* in February 1980. Lewis accused Woodward and Armstrong of "hit-and-run journalism."[59] Woodward and Armstrong stood by their story in a lengthy rebuttal.[60] Brennan privately thanked Lewis for his efforts. "I can't adequately tell you how much your response means to me," Brennan wrote Lewis.[61]

[52] Peter Harkness, interview by author, November 9, 2007.
[53] For a full discussion of Brennan's term histories, see Stern and Wermiel, 465–67.
[54] William Safire, "Our Brethren's Keepers," *New York Times*, December 10, 1979.
[55] George V. Higgins, "The Court's Curveball," *Boston Globe Magazine*, December 30, 1979.
[56] William J. Brennan Jr. to Walter Murphy, January 7, 1980, William J. Brennan Jr. private papers.
[57] Ibid. [58] Unpublished letter, December 11, 1979.
[59] Anthony Lewis, "Supreme Court Confidential," *New York Review of Books*, February 7, 1980.
[60] Bob Woodward and Scott Armstrong, "The Evidence of 'The Brethren': An Exchange," *New York Review of Books*, June 12, 1980.
[61] William J. Brennan Jr. to Anthony Lewis, May 19, 1980, William J. Brennan private papers.

Shortly before the publication of *The Brethren*, Brennan scolded the press publicly during a speech at Rutgers University.[62] Brennan said that "in the heat of the controversy the press may be misapprehending the fundamental issues at stake, and may be consequently failing in its important task of illuminating these issues for the court and the public." The comments were prompted by the Court's decision a few months earlier in *Gannett Co. v. DePasquale* holding that the Sixth Amendment's guarantee of public trials did not protect a right of trial access for the public or reporters.[63] In response, dozens of judges closed proceedings and newspaper editorial pages across the country decried the decision's impact. A *Minneapolis Star Tribune* columnist condemned the justices for giving trial judges "a free hand to lock courtroom doors against the public and journalists who are the citizens' surrogates."[64] Four justices offered rare public rebuttals to the press backlash, insisting the decision held no such thing.

Brennan distinguished in his Rutgers speech between two different ways of thinking about the role of the press. He contrasted the "speech" model under which the press "requires and is accorded the absolute protection of the First Amendment" with a "structural" model in which "the press' interests may conflict with other societal interests and adjustment of the conflict on occasion favors the competing claim." Brennan argued that the press' tendency to confuse these two models explained much of the acrimony triggered by the Court's decision. "The press has reacted as if its role as a public spokesman [was] being restricted, and as a consequence, it has on occasion overreacted," Brennan said. "The press can be of assistance only if bitterness does not cloud its vision, nor self-righteousness its judgment."

Given Brennan's status as a protector of free speech, his comments attracted serious press consideration. A *Washington Post* editorial noted Brennan's "harsh words" should have "sent quivers through" newsrooms around the country, since they came "from a friend on whose support, in judicial circles, the press has come to depend." The *Post* said Brennan had provided "a fascinating and highly useful analysis of what the Court has been doing in recent years." "Unlike most criticisms of the press, it provides a theory whose wisdom the press and the judges can debate without engaging in outrageous rhetoric."[65]

[62] William J. Brennan Jr., "Dedication of the Samuel I. Newhouse Law Center" (speech, Rutgers University, Newark, NJ, October 17, 1979).

[63] *Gannett Co. v. DePasquale*, 443 U.S. 368 (1979).

[64] Austin C. Wehrwein, "An Eloquent Dissent in the Closed-trial Case," *Minneapolis Star*, July 11, 1979.

[65] *Washington Post*, "Justice Brennan Tells Off the Press," October 22, 1979.

Brennan's anger about *The Brethren* – and its authors – did not fade. Woodward later approached a friend of Brennan's in an effort to arrange a meeting with the justice after hearing how furious the book had made the justice. Brennan said he would think about a meeting, but he never raised the subject again.[66] He labeled the book "pure fiction" when asked about it by a law student visiting the Court in March 1990. He used less delicate language when his biographer referred to the book while asking about a case. "I don't want anything [from] that Goddamn shit sheet," Brennan said. "We'll have to rely on what I can remember."[67]

BRENNAN REENGAGES: THE 1980S

Brennan emerged from his self-imposed exile from public life in the early 1980s following his wife's death. After marrying his longtime secretary, Mary Fowler, Brennan began traveling again and started accepting public speaking invitations, which attracted newspaper coverage about his reemergence. "Brennan is his ebullient former self – working the crowd at a reception, dancing the night away at a party, traveling to Europe and around the country," the *Washington Post* noted in 1985.[68] Brennan decided to raise his public profile further in the months leading up to his eightieth birthday. He agreed to speak with the many journalists who requested interviews timed to his birthday.

He began his media blitz during a trip to Alabama in February 1986 to celebrate the hundredth anniversary of the late Justice Hugo Black's birth. Brennan was following a precedent set by Black, who had sat for a CBS television interview after completing thirty years on the Court, a milestone Brennan would reach in the fall of 1986. While in Alabama, Brennan was interviewed by NBC News Supreme Court reporter Carl Stern. For the sake of fairness, Brennan believed that if he agreed to one interview he should grant them all.[69] Therefore, in the months to come, he spoke to virtually every major news organization in the country.[70] "When he

66 Miriam Kellner Bazelon Knox, *A Salute to Life: Mickey's Memoir* (Washington, DC: K2 Pub., 2002), 128.

67 William J. Brennan Jr. interview by Stephen Wermiel, May 8, 1989.

68 Al Kamen, "Justice's Renaissance," *Washington Post*, October 28, 1985.

69 William J. Brennan Jr. to United Press International, February 4, 1986, William J. Brennan Jr. Papers, Library of Congress.

70 Lyle Denniston, "At 80, Brennan Has No Plans to Retire," *Baltimore Sun*, May 2, 1986; Al Kamen, "Brennan: Tipping the Scales of Justice at 80," *Washington Post*, April 25, 1986; Philip Hager, "Brennan, Near 80, Holds Firm to Court Post," *Los Angeles Times*, April 19, 1986; Stuart Taylor Jr., "Brennan: 30 Years and the Thrill is Not Gone," *New York Times*, April 16, 1986.

thawed, he thawed completely," recalled Richard Carelli, who covered the Court for the Associated Press from 1976 to 2000.[71]

The resulting articles revealed how Brennan's views about press coverage of the Court had evolved. He praised the media for doing a "much better job" in an interview with the *New Jersey Law Journal*. "But I still wish more space could be given, particularly on major cases that are decided. I appreciate that there's only so much space competing with all the other news items. In that sense, I'm disappointed. Because we'd like a better understanding of the court's functioning and the way the court operates."[72]

Brennan thought the Court should do its part to facilitate press coverage, by opening up its proceedings to television cameras, an idea he had earlier opposed. By 1986, he had come to believe it was both "inevitable" and the right thing to do. "Ours is a public proceeding," Brennan told the *New York Times*. "And there's no reason in my judgment why only those who can gain entrance to the courtroom should be able to witness those proceedings."[73] His view remained a minority one at the time. In April 1986, Brennan was among four justices who voted in favor of allowing live radio broadcast of the oral argument on the constitutionality of the Graham-Rudman-Hollings Act mandating a balanced federal budget.[74] But Burger, who called television cameras in the courtroom "the most destructive thing in the world," strongly opposed the idea and four colleagues voted with him.[75]

Nothing better symbolized Brennan's growing comfort with journalists than his choice of Wermiel, a *Wall Street Journal* reporter, to be his biographer. Brennan had his legacy in mind as he quietly began working with Wermiel on the biography in the months leading up to his thirtieth anniversary as a justice. He purposely chose to collaborate with a journalist, rather than one of his many admirers in legal academia. A few years earlier, he had opened up his files – including his term histories – to a law professor working on a biography of Earl Warren. Brennan was disappointed by the biography, which he thought was too dense and inaccessible.[76] For his own biographer,

[71] Richard Carelli, interview with author, January 30, 2009.

[72] Bruce S. Rosen, "Brennan on the Record," *New Jersey Law Journal*, June 26, 1986.

[73] Stuart Taylor Jr., "Brennan: 30 Years and the Thrill is Not Gone," *New York Times*, April 16, 1986.

[74] *Bowsher v. Synar*, 478 U.S. 714 (1986).

[75] James H. Rubin, "Burger Rejects Radio Coverage of Balanced-Budget Court Arguments," Associated Press, March 13, 1986; Stuart Taylor Jr., "Supreme Court Says No to Radio Coverage," *The Times-News* (Hendersonville, NC), April 21, 1986.

[76] Bernard Schwartz, *Super Chief: Earl Warren and His Supreme Court: A Judicial Biography* (New York: New York University Press, 1983); William J. Brennan, Jr. to Ruggero J. Aldisert, June 11, 1984, William J. Brennan Jr. Papers, Library of Congress.

Brennan wanted a journalist well versed in the Court, who could write a book aimed at a general audience. Brennan's friend and fellow judge Abner Mikva, suggested Wermiel, who had covered the Court since 1979.[77]

Brennan's willingness to work with a *Wall Street Journal* reporter was particularly noteworthy. He disliked the *Journal's* conservative editorial page so much that he refused to read it.[78] He remained angry about a 1981 *Journal* article, which had mischaracterized his role in a case involving a New Jersey real estate sale in which his son was involved as an attorney.[79] Brennan had written a letter to the editor taking issue with the article. "Is it too much to expect that this letter . . . will receive prominence in a forthcoming issue of the Journal equal to that given the untrue statement in the issue of February 27?," Brennan wrote to the paper's editor.[80] (He forwarded the letter to his son with a cover note in which he wrote, "The mail provoked by that Wall Street Journal Switlik article has come from all over the country and with a common threat of viciousness. I ignored it, but finally decided I ought to do something about it. Hence the enclosure to the Journal."[81]) Years later, Brennan was still angry that no *Journal* editor acknowledged receiving his letter. "And worse, when he finally, grudgingly, published a retraction, buried it where nobody could possibly have seen it, after the big-front page story he had on it," Brennan complained to Wermiel in one of their first interviews in 1986.[82]

Brennan didn't hold the *Journal's* editorial page or its past news coverage against Wermiel. In the summer of 1986, they began the first of what proved to be more than sixty recorded interviews conducted in Brennan's chambers over the course of the next five years. The project remained a secret at first, since Brennan said he didn't want it to affect his working relationship with his colleagues. Brennan allowed Wermiel to sift through tens of thousands of pages of records in the justice's office and occasionally sit in on his private meetings with clerks when he prepared for oral arguments. Brennan granted Wermiel unrestricted access to his case files, including draft opinions and memos exchanged among the justices. He encouraged members of his family

77 For an account of the book's origins, see Stern and Wermiel, 549–51; Adam Liptak, "Brennan Book, Many Years in Making," *New York Times*, October 5, 2010.

78 William J. Brennan Jr., interview by Stephen Wermiel, November 23, 1987.

79 Jonathan Kwitny, "How A New Jerseyite Stands to Lose Fortune Over His Sale of Land," *Wall Street Journal*, February 27, 1981.

80 William J. Brennan Jr. to Editor, *Wall Street Journal*, March 24, 1981, William J. Brennan Jr. private papers.

81 William J. Brennan Jr. to William J. Brennan III, March 26, 1981, William J. Brennan Jr. private papers.

82 William J. Brennan Jr. interview with Stephen Wermiel, October 24, 1986; *Wall Street Journal*, "Corrections & Amplifications," April 27, 1981.

and law clerks to cooperate. Remarkably, the justice who for decades had assiduously avoided reporters now granted a journalist carte blanche to examine every aspect of his life, a level of access without precedent in the history of the Court.

Wermiel kept an arms-length approach to his personal relationship with Brennan and compartmentalized his roles as *Journal* beat reporter and biographer. He didn't write newspaper stories about what he learned about pending cases while working on the biography inside Brennan's chambers. On at least one occasion, however, he shifted from observer to participant. Wermiel helped Brennan draft a retirement letter and statement in July 1990 after he suffered what his doctors believed was a mild stroke.[83]

The line between Brennan's friendship and professional relationship with another journalist, Nina Totenberg, blurred on the day he announced his retirement. Brennan had decided to retire on Friday, July 20, but hoped to keep his decision secret for a few days so he had time to tell his four new clerks the news personally. But that afternoon, a *Washington Post* reporter called the Court's public information director asking about Brennan's plans and then Totenberg called his home and reached his wife Mary.[84]

Brennan had become friendly with Totenberg, whose outreach efforts he had rebuffed in the early 1970s. Totenberg kept trying after she became National Public Radio's legal affairs correspondent. Brennan began speaking informally to Totenberg in the early 1980s and she was among the reporters who interviewed him in 1986. Their friendship extended outside the Court. Brennan and his second wife Mary had dinner at Totenberg's house several times.[85] When Washington's elite Cosmos Club voted to admit women for the first time in June 1988, Brennan wrote a letter to the admissions committee on her behalf ten days later. "I have been a long-time listener of her 'All Things Considered' broadcasts covering legal matters," Brennan wrote. "She has been unfailing in the accuracy and thoroughness of her radio broadcasts covering the work of the Supreme Court. Indeed, I know of no other in the press, television, or radio, who does as effective and able depiction of the Court's work in its decisions."[86]

As Totenberg later wrote in a tribute to Brennan, "It's not an easy friendship because each of you must recognize that the other has a job to do that may well be at odds with yours."[87] That Friday, Mary thought she was talking

83 Stern and Wermiel, 550.

84 *See* Stern and Wermiel, 536–38 for a full account of Brennan's retirement day.

85 Nina Totenberg, interview with author, August 21, 2007.

86 William J. Brennan Jr. to Admissions Committee of the Cosmos Club, June 29, 1988, William J. Brennan Jr. Papers, Library of Congress.

87 Nina Totenberg, "A Tribute to Justice William J. Brennan Jr., 104 Harv. L. Rev. 1, 34 (1990).

to Totenberg as a friend when she told her about Brennan's fall, his meetings with his doctor, and his retirement decision. Mary was upset when Totenberg indicated she was going to report his retirement, even after they asked her to wait until Monday. Brennan then moved up his announcement and his clerks scrambled to find someone at the White House willing to accept a signed copy of his resignation letter.

Their friendship survived his resignation day. Brennan later wrote letters of recommendation for Totenberg's sister when she sought to become a judge.[88] Totenberg remained a loyal friend long after Brennan was a useful source. She visited him every couple of weeks after he was confined to a nursing home in 1996 where, Totenberg recalled, he "loved to have me sing to him."[89] On the night Brennan died in July 1997, Totenberg paid tribute during an appearance on Charlie Rose's television show alongside two of Brennan's former clerks. "One of the great benefits of being a reporter is that every once in a while you get to meet somebody who is called great and if you're very lucky, you get to be that person's friend," Totenberg said. "And in this case, I kept finding out all the time that he was a really great man."[90]

Brennan's relationships with Totenberg and Wermiel show how much his attitude towards the press had evolved during his time on the Court. It is inconceivable that he would have developed the same kind of close friendship he had with Totenberg or granted a reporter the kind of access to his chambers he gave Wermiel earlier in his tenure.

Becoming more accessible to reporters late in a justice's tenure is not a phenomenon unique to Brennan. As noted earlier, Black had granted a rare television interview in 1968, on his thirtieth anniversary on the Court. Harry Blackmun did his own series of press interviews, including with a brand new television news channel called CNN, in the early 1980s. As Ruth Bader Ginsburg would prove again in 2013, when she gave multiple interviews around the time of her eightieth birthday and twentieth anniversary as a justice, such milestones seem to make some justices more amenable to press attention.[91]

[88] Amy Totenberg was later nominated by President Barack Obama for a seat on the U.S. District Court for the Northern District of Georgia and was confirmed by the U.S. Senate on February 28, 2011.

[89] Totenberg, interview by Charlie Rose, *Charlie Rose*, PBS, July 24, 1997.

[90] Totenberg, interview by Charlie Rose, *Charlie Rose*, PBS, July 24, 1997.

[91] *See* Adam Liptak, "Court Is 'One of Most Activist,' Ginsburg Says, Vowing to Stay," *New York Times*, August 24, 2013; Richard Wolf, "Ginsburg's Dedication Undimmed after 20 Years on Court," *USA Today*, August 1, 2013; Greg Stohr, "Ginsburg Embraces Gay-Marriage Rulings as Court Shuns Bold Moves," Bloomberg News, August 26, 2013; Joan Biskupic, "Supreme Court's Ginsburg Vows to Resist Pressure to Retire," Reuters, July 4, 2013.

Brennan had other motivations for making himself more accessible to the press. He felt particularly out of step with the times in the 1980s during Ronald Reagan's presidency. Press attention made Brennan feel relevant. As he reached what he knew was the end of his tenure, Brennan also had a longer term strategic goal in mind. He was seeking to influence how journalists, and historians, wrote about his legacy. Brennan maintained a modest public posture about his accomplishments, but was more candid in his private conversations with Wermiel. He was well aware of his own legacy and that of his liberal allies on the Warren Court and wanted to make sure they got their due, even as he saw the pendulum swinging towards the ascendant conservatives.

13

Justice John Paul Stevens and the Press: Extra! Extra! Read All About It!

BILL BARNHART

INTRODUCTION

Supreme Court justices have had problems dealing directly with the press. Justice Antonin Scalia replied to a *Boston Herald* reporter who confronted him outside a church with a hand gesture that her newspaper described as obscene.[1] Seated with *Chicago Tribune* reporters and their bosses at an annual black-tie White House Correspondents' Association dinner, Justice William O. Douglas silenced dinner-table chatter about current cases with a pointed dig: "Have you *read* the Constitution?"[2]

Douglas's successor, Justice John Paul Stevens, avoided press relations problems by not having relations with the press until near the end of his more than three decades on the bench. He simply followed the rule that he and his co-clerk learned decades earlier in the chambers of Justice Wiley Rutledge.

"It was perfectly clear that we weren't supposed to talk," he recalled from his clerkship in the October 1947 term. "We never did… The clerks all ate together in the [Court's] cafeteria, and either we were smart enough or someone told us to be aware of reporters sitting at the next table trying to overhear us. We were conscious of keeping Court business within the Court."[3]

In his own chambers, Justice Stevens never granted interviews until he was near retirement from active service at the end of the October 2009. Unlike

[1] "Bada Zing! Feisty Scalia rips critics with 'Sicilian' flick of the wrist," *Boston Herald*, Mar. 27, 2006, at 4.

[2] Thanks to the late Glen Elsasser, who covered the Supreme Court for the *Chicago Tribune*, for this account. Thanks also to George Condon of the *National Journal* for confirming the year of the incident.

[3] Interview with Justice John Paul Stevens, in Wash., D.C (April 21, 2011), on file at Nw. U. L. Rev.

many justices these days, he didn't publish a book while in active service and have a publisher arrange book tours that could have exposed him to media questions.

Stevens did not keep a press-clipping file. "I have a friend in Los Angeles who sends me clippings, but it's totally random," he said in my 2011 interview.[4] "I read the paper myself, of course." On rare occasions, one of his law clerks would bring his attention to media coverage of his work. But when I asked him to assess the Supreme Court press, I began my question with the comment that I probably was asking him to respond to something he didn't think about much. "You're right," he said.

"Honestly, I never really had any contact with him," said Stephen Wermiel, who covered the Court for the *Wall Street Journal* from 1979 to 1991.[5] "Justice Stevens was quite elusive when I was there," said Linda Greenhouse, who covered the Court for the *New York Times* from 1978 to 2008, almost the entire span of Stevens's tenure. "I never had any interaction with him that could be called an interview."[6] "He was the most polite and remote and one of the few justices I never met," said Dahlia Lithwick, legal correspondent for *Slate* magazine. "I think he was neutral on the press... He just kind of didn't seem to care much either way."[7]

Of course, being press-shy is not unusual on the Supreme Court. But Stevens's jurisprudence in cases involving the free press clause of the Constitution suggests he might have been more accessible than he was. Stevens, both on the bench and in speeches about the Court's work, viewed reporters as partners with judges in advancing the national dialog. He regarded the press and the Court in terms of a division of labor in the marketplace of ideas.

"For the most part, the press has done a good job covering the Court," he told me. "I think in [my] very first few years with the Court, it wasn't quite as good." Nevertheless, he did not expect the press to do the Court's work. "Read what I've written," he would say to anyone curious about his job performance.[8]

Stevens nonetheless on occasion tacitly guided, not to say prodded, the press in the role for which he is best known – a dissenter. Occasionally,

[4] Interview with Justice John Paul Stevens, *supra* note 3.

[5] E-mail from Stephen Wermiel, fellow in law and government, American University Washington College of Law (Nov. 29, 2010, 2:50 PM CDT) (on file with author).

[6] E-mail from Linda Greenhouse, senior research scholar in law, Yale Law School (Nov. 29, 2010, 11:15 AM CDT) (on file with author).

[7] E-mails from Dahlia Lithwick, senior editor and legal correspondent for *Slate* (Dec. 1, 2010, 1:12 PM and 2:24 PM CDT) (on file with author).

[8] Conversation with Justice John Paul Stevens at 13:25 (C-SPAN television broadcast July 19, 2007), available at www.c-spanvideo.org/program/PaulSte#.

the press took the hint. Stevens regarded dissenting and concurring opinions as vital components of the Court's output. Dissents and concurrences, he believed, inform the judicial system's professional constituents – litigants, lawyers, legislators and regulators – about the full range of thinking on an evolving controversy.

The press, as the eyes and ears of ordinary people, is a different constituent. Lani Guinier, in a law review analysis, said dissents and concurrences by Supreme Court justices "can spark a kind of deliberation that is not the same as partisan politics, but is rooted in the deeply democratic practices of constitutional governmental institutions."[9] A well-delivered dissent can make "conflict on the Court transparent to non-legal actors and open a new window on pathways toward ... democratic accountability... Dissenting judges may educate, inspire and mobilize citizens."

Stevens never would admit to being a news tipster, but he was never sorry when his dissents had that effect. Dissents were his version of newspaper extra editions, intended to attract an audience to something special.

VILLAGE IDIOT

Stevens of course had his frustrations with the news media. In 2007, the *New York Times* declined to publish his letter to the editor that listed biographical errors he found in a positive Sunday magazine profile of him by Jeffrey Rosen.[10] After he instructed a law clerk to push his complaint, the newspaper ran a single correction, regarding the name of his undergraduate college, but did not correct what Stevens said was an erroneous account of his World War II service. "I was really not happy with it," he said.[11]

After the death of President Gerald Ford in 2007, Stevens agreed to his first network television interview on the condition that it would be about Ford, who had nominated him to the high court. ABC-TV reporter Jan Greenberg sought the interview. "She asked me if I would answer a few questions about President Ford," Stevens said. But more than half of the nearly three-minute interview ABC aired[12] concerned Crawford's questions about Stevens's "liberal

[9] Lani Guinier, "The Supreme Court 2007 Term, Foreword: Demosprudence through Dissent," 122 *Harv. L. Rev.*, 4, 12 (2008), available at www.law.harvard.edu/faculty/guinier/publications/foreword.pdf.

[10] Jeffrey Rosen, "The Dissenter," *NewYork Times Magazine*, Sept. 23, 2007, at 50, available at query.nytimes.com/gst/fullpage.html?res=9C0CE3DE123DF930A1575AC0A9619C8B63

[11] Interview with Justice Stevens, *supra* note 3.

[12] *Nightline*: Justice Stevens' First TV Interview at 0:10 (ABC television broadcast Jan. 2, 2007), available at abcnews.go.com/Nightline/video/justice-stevens-tv-interview-10334251.

leanings" on the Court. "I had no interest whatsoever in being asked the questions she asked me. It was a very unsuccessful event. I thought it was a departure from what I agreed to do."[13]

Perhaps his biggest gripe concerns what he says was the failure by reporters either to understand or to convey the precise issue on which he ruled against President Bill Clinton in the 1997 case, *Clinton v. Jones*.[14] Seasoned Court reporters called Stevens naïve and "epically incorrect" in deciding that Clinton, despite being President of the United States, could not delay a trial in Paula Jones's civil suit against him for sexual harassment years earlier.[15] Clinton himself called Stevens's opinion for a unanimous court "one of the most politically naïve decisions the Supreme Court had made in a long time."[16] In my 2011 interview, Stevens said he became "the village idiot" in the eyes of many commentators simply by affirming Jones's right as a private citizen to have her case proceed.[17]

None of these disputes reflected Stevens's news media jurisprudence. As in most areas of the law, Stevens reached decisions based on the particulars of a news media-related case, not what he called "glittering generalities." He was not always press friendly. On one issue, however – the media's access to information about government – he broke new ground. In two cases, *Houchins v. KQED*,[18] limiting press access to jails, and *Richmond Newspapers Inc. v. Virginia*,[19] concerning public and press access to criminal trials, Stevens used a dissent in *Houchins* and a concurring opinion in *Richmond Newspapers* to assert a First Amendment right of the press to gather, not just convey, information about government.

"WHO?"

Congressman Thomas ("Tip") O'Neill's one-word initial reaction in 1975 to President Gerald Ford's nomination of U.S. Circuit Judge Stevens of Chicago to become an associate justice[20] was typical on Capitol Hill and in the press. There was little press curiosity about the nominee, even though it was the only

[13] Interview with Justice Stevens, *supra* note 3. [14] 520 U.S. 681 (1997).

[15] Interview with Nina Totenberg, Legal Affairs Correspondent, Nat'l Public Radio, in Wash., D.C. (Oct. 8, 2003); Jeffrey Toobin, *The Nine*, 118 (2007).

[16] Bill Clinton, *My Life*, 762 (2004). [17] Interview with Justice Stevens, *supra* note 3.

[18] 438 U.S. 1 (1978). [19] 448 U.S. 555 (1980).

[20] *Judge John Paul Stevens/Congressional Reaction*, Memorandum from Max L. Friedersdorf, to Gerald R. Ford, Congressional Relations Office Files, Nov. 28, 1975, Gerald R. Ford Presidential Library; see also Bill Barnhart and Gene Schlickman, *John Paul Stevens: an Independent Life*, 194–196 (2010).

time in the nation's history when a president who had never stood in a national election exercised the power of a Supreme Court selection.

He was the last nominee whose confirmation hearing before the Senate Judiciary Committee was not televised. It was the first nomination since the Court's 1973 *Roe v. Wade*[21] decision. But no senator asked about abortion at the confirmation hearing.[22] The Ford White House sought to avoid more controversy than it already had, with women's groups and First Lady Betty Ford lobbying the president to name the first woman to the Supreme Court. Stevens's sex was apparent, but when a reporter asked Ford's press secretary Ron Nessen to reveal the nominee's religion and political party affiliations, Nessen said he didn't know. "You will have to ask Judge Stevens."[23] There is no record that any reporter did so before Stevens was confirmed.

In his early years on the bench, Stevens expressed bemusement about articles that attempted to characterize the junior justice. Handicapping a new justice as liberal or conservative is standard operating procedure. Stevens, it seems, was hard to peg. Stephen Wermiel, covering the Court in 1978 for the *Boston Globe*, wrote one such profile, with words such as "the Supreme Court's dissenter," "outspoken," "independent," and "content to state his views on his own, rather than seeking support for his position from other justices."[24] A *New York Times* profile by Lesley Oelsner called Stevens a "wild card."[25]

Despite the early consensus among reporters that Stevens was, as political science professor Bradley Canon would later put it, "the lone ranger in a black robe,"[26] Wermiel recalled, "I heard from a Stevens law clerk that he saw the story and asked the clerk if it were true, that he was a maverick."[27] Stevens's question to his clerk was not unfounded. In his first term, while reporters were pinning a "maverick" tag on him, he was meeting with two senior justices, Potter Stewart and Lewis Powell, to write a series of jointly authored opinions,

[21] 410 U.S. 113 (1973).

[22] *Nomination of John Paul Stevens to be a Justice of the Supreme Court: Hearings before the Committee of the Judiciary, United States Senate*, 94th Congress, Dec. 8 – 10, 1975.

[23] White House news conference transcript, Nov. 28, 1975, Office of the Counsel to the President files, Gerald R. Ford Presidential Library; see also Barnhart & Schlickman, *supra* note 21 at 194 – 195.

[24] Stephen Wermiel, "The Supreme Court's Dissenter," *Boston Globe*, Dec. 24, 1978, at 25.

[25] Lesley Oelsner, "John Paul Stevens is Proving to Be 'Wild Card' in High Court Rulings," *N.Y. Times*, Feb. 6, 1977, at L22.

[26] Bradley C. Canon, "Justice John Paul Stevens: The Lone Ranger in a Black Robe," in *The Burger Court: Political and Judicial Profiles*, 343 (Charles M. Lamb and Stephen C. Halpern, eds., 1991).

[27] E-mail from Stephen Wermiel to author (Nov. 29, 2010, 2:50 PM CST) (on file with author).

led by *Gregg v. Georgia*,[28] which reinstated capital punishment in many states. The press largely overlooked Stevens's part in this inter-chamber teamwork, which is rare in the Court's history.

Stevens wasn't always detached from press reports. Near the end of the Court's 1983–1984 term, *Baltimore Sun* Supreme Court correspondent Lyle Denniston reported that drawings of Stevens by news media illustrators, part of a display of press caricatures of justices that had stood in the Court's exhibit hall since late February, mysteriously had vanished. Denniston quoted an unnamed source who claimed that Stevens had requested that the drawings of himself be removed.[29] Internal Court correspondence, disclosed much later in the papers of Justice Harry Blackmun, reveal that Denniston's article reflected comments by justices during one of their secret deliberations and triggered a flutter of memos by Stevens and Chief Justice Warren Burger.[30]

In took a while, but more than three months after Denniston's article, Stevens's side of the story appeared in the *Washington Post*, again without attribution. The *Post* reported that Stevens simply had asked Chief Burger and his fellow associate justices in a closed-door conference why the caricatures had been on display so long. "Stevens apparently never asked that any sketches be removed and was embarrassed when word circulated that he had."[31]

Stevens occasionally reacted to media comments about the justices' work in speeches he gave to law audiences.[32] In October 1985, he cited "at least one television network commentator" who had remarked that on the first Monday of October the Court by tradition returns to work "after completing their

[28] 428 U.S. 153 (1976).

[29] Lyle Denniston, "Case of the vanishing justice: sketches disappear," *The Baltimore Sun*, June 29, 1984.

[30] In a memo to his fellow justices, Stevens noted the breach of Court secrecy and said, "The only request I ever made to anyone at the Court concerning the exhibit was the discussion that we had in the Conference on Monday." In his reply memo to the justices a few days later, Burger essentially confirmed Denniston's story, that Stevens had asked that the sketches of himself be removed. Burger blamed Stevens for the controversy: "We can hardly expect that the removal of some part of an exhibit, in which media people are involved, would not draw some attention from the media." Burger added, "No inquiry on this subject was made to me or my office, but if any request had been addressed to me, I would have declined any comment." In a separate memo to Burger, Stevens shot back: "just for the purpose of clarifying a matter that is hardly worth our attention, let me say that I intended to make the point that the entire exhibit should come down. Obviously, I did not express myself as clearly as I should have." John Paul Stevens, memorandum to the conference, June 29, 1984; Warren E. Burger, memorandum to the conference, July 3, 1984; John Paul Stevens, memorandum to the Chief justice, July 3, 1984. Harry A. Blackman Papers, Library of Congress.

[31] Fred Barbash, Column, "Insider: The Judiciary," *Washington Post*, Sept. 9, 1984 at A19.

[32] John Paul Stevens, "The Supreme Court of the United States: Reflections After a Summer Recess," 27, *S. Texas L. Rev.*, 447 (1986).

three months vacation."[33] Stevens then described summer work of the Court, including appearances to law conferences. The most prolific dissenter on the Court then took a swipe at what he saw as the failure of press to spot news.

"Typically these talks rehash material that has either been included in previous addresses or has been stated with great gusto in dissenting opinions. Nevertheless, I still find it remarkable that a statement [by a justice] critical of the Court will usually be ignored by the news media when it is included in a written dissent but will be treated as a dramatic news story when it is repeated several weeks later in a talk to a small audience of federal judges at a judicial conference."

"SOMETIMES YOU CAN'T TRUST REPORTERS."

Stevens's background[34] helped make him press-shy. As a teenager in the early 1930s, his family suffered censorious, front-page headlines in the Chicago newspapers after the family's substantial insurance business failed and policyholders alleged fraud by Stevens's grandfather, father and uncle. A local prosecutor indicted all three. The grandfather became too ill to stand trial. The uncle committed suicide. A jury convicted his father, Ernest J. Stevens, of embezzlement, but the Illinois Supreme Court overturned the verdict.[35]

Ten years later, as a communications analyst for the Navy in Pearl Harbor after the Japanese attack, young Stevens worked under the tight secrecy rules of Allied code-breaking operations – rules that apparently had been broken when the *Chicago Tribune* reported on a U.S. code-breaking success before the Navy's victory at the Battle of Midway in June 1942.[36]

In 1969, private attorney Stevens served pro-bono as a special counsel investigating charges of corruption against two Illinois Supreme Court justices. He mostly avoided the press as he and a team of volunteer lawyers uncovered the facts of the scandal, which led the justices to resign. Near the end of public hearings, he agreed to provide off-the-record background to a newspaper reporter concerning upcoming witness testimony. He told what happened in the 2011 interview:

> I invited [the reporter] to come to the office the night before the day of testimony so that I could explain to him some of the stuff that was going

[33] Ibid., see also John Paul Stevens, speech to Chicago Bar Association and Chicago Bar Foundation Fifth Annual Justice John Paul Stevens Awards Luncheon, Chicago, Ill., Sept. 15, 2004, courtesy of the chambers of Justice John Paul Stevens.

[34] This section is drawn from Barnhart & Schlickman, *supra* 21, Chapters 1 – 6.

[35] *People v. Stevens*, 193 N.E. 154 (Ill. 1934). See Barnhart & Schlickman, *supra* note 21 at 31 – 35.

[36] "Navy Had Word of Jap Plan to Strike at Sea," *Chicago Tribune*, June 7, 1942, at 1. See Barnhart & Schlickman, *supra* note 21 at 44 – 51.

into the public record at the hearing, for fear he might not be able to follow it. I thought it would be fair to give him a hand on the understanding he definitely wouldn't publish anything until after the hearing. He published it the next morning. It taught me a lesson that sometimes you can't trust reporters.[37]

"A GREAT POTENTIAL MEDIUM"

Such experiences by a teenager, a young Navy officer and a private lawyer help explain Justice Stevens's distance from reporters. They don't bear on his abstract kinship with journalists as instruments of democracy.

A valuable piece of biographical evidence on this theme is a law review comment Stevens wrote as a twenty-six-year-old Navy vet and Northwestern University Law School student.[38] The comment concerned Justice Department antitrust action against major motion picture studios. Stevens concluded that the motion picture industry, like the news media, might deserve especially strict antitrust scrutiny because of its role in informing the public.

To that end, he cited a 1945 Supreme Court ruling against a news wire service, *Associated Press v. United States*.[39] The Court found that AP violated the Sherman Act by allowing its member news media companies to blackball competitors from AP's service. In his concurring opinion, Justice Felix Frankfurter declared: "In addition to being a commercial enterprise, [AP] has a relation to the public interest unlike that of any other enterprise pursued for profit. A free press is indispensable to the workings of our democratic society... Truth and understanding are not wares like peanuts or potatoes. And so, the incidence of restraints upon the promotion of truth through denial of access to the basis for understanding calls into play considerations very different from comparable restraints in a cooperative enterprise having merely a commercial aspect."

Noting that newsreels were part of the movie-going experience, law student Stevens extended Frankfurter's analysis to Hollywood: "There is reason for saying that the public interest in this powerful industry is somewhat unique... Motion pictures are a great potential medium for the distribution of propaganda; they play an important role in the education of the people. It is possible

[37] Interview with Justice Stevens, *supra* note 4. See Barnhart & Schlickman, *supra* note 21 at 141 – 144.

[38] "Price-Fixing in the Motion Picture Industry," 41 *Illinois Law Review*, 631 (1947). Justice Stevens acknowledged authorship of the anonymous comment in Introductory Comment, 75 *Nw. U. L. Rev* 977 (1981).

[39] 326 U.S. 1 (1945).

that a few producer-distributors could achieve dominant political as well as economic power through monopoly. Granting this possibility, it does not seem unreasonable to conclude that the public has a greater interest in free competition in this industry than in others."

Like Justice Frankfurter, Stevens's embrace in 1946 of the media as an important public institution reflected America's revulsion toward the totalitarian regimes of Germany and Japan in the World War II era. But the scourge of tyranny played an identical role in motivating the Court's dissenters who sided with the AP. "The tragic history of recent years demonstrates far too well how despotic governments may interfere with the press and other means of communication in their efforts to corrupt public opinion and to destroy individual freedom," wrote Justice Frank Murphy in dissent. "Experience teaches us to hesitate before creating a precedent in which might lurk even the slightest justification for such interference by the Government in these matters."

In choosing Frankfurter's "promotion of truth" over Murphy's "interference by the government" in the AP case, law student Stevens aligned his future judicial philosophy with the liberal side of First Amendment law, aimed at maximizing public participation in political speech rather than shielding the owners of printing presses.

Professor Gregory Magarian, in a law review essay on the "pragmatic populism" of Stevens's free speech jurisprudence, stated the opposing, conservative view: "In a trend that gradually developed under Chief Justice Warren Burger and took firm hold under Chief Justice William Rehnquist, the Court has treated expressive freedom not as a means to an end of inclusive democratic discourse but rather as a negative right that shields individual autonomy against government interference... [Under this view] the First Amendment does more for rich and powerful political speakers than for poor and politically marginal speakers."[40]

"PUSHY TV PEOPLE"

Chief Justice Burger, Justice Stevens's first chief, kept tight control over the authorship of opinions affecting the news media, he recalled in my 2011 interview: "Whenever there was a First Amendment case in which the Court was going to uphold the right of the press, [Burger] wrote the opinion himself.

[40] Gregory P. Magarian, "The Pragmatic Populism of Justice Stevens' Free Speech Jurisprudence," 74 *Fordham L. Rev* 2201 (2006).

When there was a case in which they were going to rule against the interest of the press, he assigned it to [Justice Byron White]."[41]

Stevens's chance to publish his own press-friendly decision during Burger's tenure fell short after one of his colleagues, Justice Potter Stewart, withdrew his support for Stevens's position and flipped the result to the opposing side, led by Burger.[42] Stevens was left with a lengthy dissent, which bucked long-standing judicial precedent and championed a First Amendment right of reporters covering government to gather information.

In *Houchins v. KQED*, a plurality opinion of seven judges written by Burger – a decidedly anti-press decision by the press-conscious chief – ruled that a television station in San Francisco had no special right to film or conduct interviews in a county jail beyond the access that the county sheriff might grant to the public at large. KQED's demand for camera access arose after the station reported a prisoner suicide in the jail and quoted an independent psychiatrist who said jail conditions led to prisoner illnesses.

Burger sided with the sheriff: "The public importance of conditions in penal facilities and the media's role in providing information afford no basis for reading into the constitution a right of the public or the media to enter these institutions, with camera equipment, and taking moving and still pictures of inmates for broadcast purposes..." The First Amendment does not grant the press any special right of access to government information or

[41] Interview with Justice Stevens, *supra* note 4. Justice White biographer Dennis Hutchinson cites three Burger-era opinions that, as Hutchinson put it, concentrated journalists' bile against White. Burger joined all three opinions (Dennis Hutchinson, *The Man Who Once Was Whizzer White: A Portrait of Justice Byron R. White*, 382 (1998)). In 1972, White wrote for a 5–4 majority that a reporter cannot claim a First Amendment shield against responding to a subpoena and giving evidence to a grand jury in a criminal investigation (*Branzburg v. Hayes*, 408 U.S. 665 (1972)); in 1978, with Stevens dissenting, White wrote that the Fourth Amendment did not protect a student newspaper from being search by law enforcement for evidence against demonstrators who had clashed with police (*Zurcher v. Stanford Daily*, 436 U.S. 547 (1978)); in 1978, joined by Stevens, White ruled that someone suing for libel may seek information about the editorial decision-making process (*Herbert v. Lando*, 441 U.S. 153 (1979)). Charles Lamb, in a profile of Burger, cites three press-friendly decisions by the chief justice, all joined by White (Charles M. Lamb, Chief Justice Warren R. Burger: A Conservative Chief for Conservatives Times, in *The Burger Court: Political and Judicial Profiles* 144 (Charles M. Lamb and Stephen C. Halpern, eds., 1991): a unanimous opinion finding that disallowed a Florida law that forced newspapers to print replies by political candidates to newspaper reporting and opinion (*Miami Herald Publishing Co. v. Tornillo*, 418 U.S. 241 (1974)); a unanimous opinion barring a press gag order by a Nebraska state court judge in a criminal case (*Nebraska Press Association v. Stuart*, 427 U.S. 539 (1976)); a ruling restating the constitutionality of public and press access to criminal trials (*Richmond Newspapers Inc. v. Virginia*, 448 U.S. 555 (1980)).

[42] Bernard Schwartz, *The Unpublished Opinions of the Burger Court* 372 (1988).

sources of information under government control, he said. In a private memo to his fellow justices about the case, reported years later by Professor Bernard Schwartz, Burger was more explicit. He ridiculed "pushy TV people interested directly in the sensational."[43]

After Stewart changed his vote, Stevens, then in his second term on the Court, turned his majority opinion draft into a dissent. He attacked Burger on three points:

- KQED's cameras and reporters, as agents for the public in a matter of public concern, had been granted access to other jails and prisons in the San Francisco area. Its request in this case "does not rest on the premise that the press has a greater right to access information regarding prison conditions than do other members of the public."
- The First Amendment power and duty of the press to convey information about government is hollow when information is denied. "Without some protection for the acquisition of information about the operation of public institutions such as prisons by the public at large, the process of self-governance contemplated by the Framers would be stripped of its substance," Stevens wrote. "Admittedly, the right to receive or acquire information is not specifically mentioned in the Constitution." But, extending Justice Oliver Wendell Holmes's famous admonition, Stevens said the marketplace of ideas imagined by the writers of the First Amendment would be barren if the marketplace "had willing buyers and sellers but no meaningful information to exchange."
- The Sixth Amendment requires "a speedy and public trial." The constitutional requirement for a public trial extends to post-conviction incarcerations as an element of a holistic criminal justice system. Thus, the request by KQED carries special constitutional weight, Stevens argued. "That public interest survives the judgment of conviction and appropriately carries over to an interest in how a convicted person is treated during his period of punishment and hoped-for rehabilitation," Stevens wrote.

Stevens's dissent, joined by Justices William Brennan and Lewis Powell, was represented well in newspaper coverage. Morton Mintz's report in the *Washington Post* quoted more extensively from Stevens's opinion than from Burger's, as did coverage with no byline in the *New York Times*.[44]

[43] *Id.*

[44] Morton Mintz, "Press Access to Data Is Same as Public's, High Court Rules," *Wash. Post*, June 27, 1978, at A4; Court Rules Press Has No Right of Access to Prisons, *NewYork Times*, June 27, 1978, at B5.

Jim Mann's account of the decision for the *Los Angeles Times*, quoted from Stevens's dissent.[45]

The dissent became an enthusiastic concurrence two years later when the Court moderated its press access rule.

"A WATERSHED CASE"

In a 1979 law school speech about press access to criminal trials, Stevens said journalists were overreacting to a Supreme Court ruling earlier that year in *Gannett Co. v. Pasquale*[46] that upheld a judge's order to bar reporters and the public from a pretrial evidence hearing in a murder case. Stevens was in the majority, sanctioning the discretion of the judge and lawyers for both sides who approved the restriction. "I have heard the prophets of doom argue that the Watergate scandal would not have been exposed if Gannett and other cases had been decided a few years ago," he said.[47]

But he gave the press a left-handed compliment that embodied his pragmatism regarding the Court and the news media. "Although much of the debate is unpersuasive, it is all constructive," he said. "It maximizes the likelihood that legislatures and other lawmakers will make constructive changes in rules relating to access to government proceedings."

Just a year later, the justices themselves were the "other lawmakers." Led by Burger, the Court established the right of the press to cover criminal trials under the First Amendment's guarantees of a free press and the right to assemble. The case, *Richmond Newspapers Inc. v. Virginia*, concerned a trial judge's decision to close the fourth trial of a murder suspect to the press and public. As in *Gannett*, the closure was requested by defense counsel, and was not opposed by the prosecutors or by reporters present in the courtroom. Burger wrote that the trial judge erred.

In concurrence, Stevens cheered. He noted that Justices Thurgood Marshall and Harry Blackmun, who concurred in Burger's ruling, had not participated in *Houchins*. "This is a watershed case," he said. "Until today the Court has accorded virtually absolute protection to the dissemination of information or ideas, but never before has it squarely held that the acquisition of newsworthy matter is entitled to any constitutional protection whatsoever."

45 Jim Mann, "Supreme Court Rules Prisons May Bar Press and Public: Decision Appears to Permit Banning Media From Other Government Institutions Also," *Los Angeles Times*, June 27, 1978, at B6.

46 443 U.S. 368.

47 John Paul Stevens, "The Gannett Case in Perspective," 5 *B. Leader* 2, Nov. – Dec. 1979.

MAXIMUM ATTENTION

Justices, including Stevens, frequently assert that press and public access to information is a hallmark of the Supreme Court's work – despite its secret conferences, its closing of files other than published orders and opinions, and its denial of live electronic media access to public Court sessions.

"I think it's entirely appropriate that we stay out of the limelight, because, after all, we do say an awful lot in our opinions, much more than most of you are willing to read," he told a judicial conference in 2007. "You try to explain your decisions as carefully as you can. That is a characteristic of the judiciary. It's not a characteristic of other branches of government."[48]

In an era of cable television and 140-character tweets, publishing judicial texts that are "more than most of you are willing to read" is hardly a heads-up for press coverage of the Supreme Court. As Professor Guinier writes, a well-crafted dissent, especially one delivered aloud by a Justice in open court, can make "the work of judicial interpretation accessible to a larger audience."[49]

When he investigated the conflicts of interest of two Illinois Supreme Court justices, Stevens became convinced that written opinions by appellate judges beyond the deciding opinion should be published as part of the "awful lot" that judges say. He concluded that the scandal's damage to the state's high court would have been reduced if the public knew of dissents by two other justices in the underlying case.[50]

"The fact that a justice disagrees with his colleagues is a matter of sufficient importance that the public is entitled to know it..." he told Kenneth Manaster, who worked with him on the investigation and published a book about it. "So that's why I've followed that practice ever since. It's because of this incident."[51]

This view remains controversial. In becoming the Court's leading dissenter, Stevens in effect overruled his former Northwestern law school dean, Leon Green. In 1978, Green warned the new justice that published dissents "will destroy the court and the law. To save them both, written dissents should be destroyed and simply noted."[52] After his first year as chief justice, John Roberts Jr. urged his colleagues to curb their separate opinions: "I think that every justice should be worried about the Court acting as a Court and

48 Conversation with Justice John Paul Stevens, *supra* note 5.

49 Guinier, *supra* note 6, at 13.

50 People v. Isaacs, 37 Ill. 2d 205, 226 N.E. 2d 38 (1967), See Kenneth A. Manaster,*Illinois Justice: The Scandal of 1969 and the Rise of John Paul Stevens* (2001).

51 *Id.* at 274.

52 Leon Green Papers, 1904 – 1979, Tarlton Law Library, University of Texas School of Law.

functioning as a Court, and they should all be worried when they are writing separately, about the effect on the institution."[53]

Stevens wrote more than 600 dissents.[54] He was "fierce in dissent," wrote Jeffrey Rosen in his 2007 *New York Times* profile.[55] Two planks in Stevens's legacy are his oral dissents from the bench against the Court's *Bush v. Gore* decision, which awarded the presidency to George W. Bush in 2000, and his 2010 dissent against *Citizens United v. Federal Election Commission*,[56] which upended decades-old legal barriers to corporate money in politics. In *Citizens United*, his halting speech while reading his words prompted speculation about Stevens's health, even by Stevens himself.[57] But he persevered. "I wanted to give it the maximum attention, because it was such an outrageous case," he said later.[58]

Yet Stevens's tendency to dissent, often energetically and alone, did not make him a media star. Adjusting for the number of years of the justice's service, Stevens's dissents yielded less coverage in the *New York Times* and NBC News than dissents by justices who, unlike Stevens, granted press interviews, according to Professor Richard Davis.[59] Still, Stevens believed that dissents – especially expressed aloud from the bench – helped elevate the news value of his work. "You feel so strongly about it you kind of want to get it off your chest, too," he added.[60]

Indeed, his most effective dissents, in terms of sparking media coverage, have the justice, in effect, taking off his black robe, displaying emotion and speaking past the elites of constitutional law to ordinary people. Here is a sample.

At the end of the October 1988 term, Stevens read aloud his dissent to a majority opinion that overturned a Texas criminal law against desecrating the U.S. flag.[61] Stevens thought the Texas veneration of the flag was constitutional and appropriate. "I never heard in his voice that amount of emotion," his secretary Nellie Pitts recalled years later.[62] Lawrence Marshall,

[53] Jeffrey Rosen, "Roberts's Rules," TheAtantic.com (Jan. 1, 2007, 12:00 PM), available at www.theatlantic.com/magazine/archive/2007/01/robertss-rules/305559/

[54] Adam Liptak, "The End of an Era, for Court and Nation," *New York Times*, April 9, 2010, at A1.

[55] Rosen, *supra* note 6, at 53.

[56] 558 U.S. 310 (2010).

[57] In my interview, Justice Stevens said his doctor gave him a clean bill of health after the episode of halting speech. But the incident convinced him to retire.

[58] Interview with Justice Stevens, *supra* note 3.

[59] Richard Davis, *Justices and Journalists: The U.S. Supreme Court and the Media*, 164 – 165 (2011).

[60] Interview with Justice Stevens, *supra* note 4.

[61] *Texas v. Johnson*, 491 U.S. 397 (1989).

[62] Interview with Nellie Pitts, secretary to Justice John Paul Stevens, in Wash., D.C. (Sept. 15, 2004) (Gene Schlickman participated in the interview). See also Barnhart & Schlickman, *supra* note 21, at 18 – 20

a Stevens law clerk at the time, remembered, "I had not ever seen him like that, visibly angry, red in the face."[63]

The American flag "is a symbol of freedom, of equal opportunity, of religious tolerance, and of good will for other people who share our aspirations," said the decorated World War II veteran. "If those ideas are worth fighting for – and history demonstrates that they are – it cannot be true that the flag that uniquely symbolizes their power is not itself worth of protection from unnecessary desecration."

Stevens's words received next-day coverage and helped shape *Washington Post* columnist William Raspberry's op-ed article on the case a few days later.[64] Raspberry supported the majority but cited Stevens to draw an odd distinction between the American flag and "replicas of the America flag," a distinction Stevens did not make. Suggesting that the American flag involved in the Texas case was not a real flag, "such as those in the National Archives, for instance," Raspberry seemed to be agreeing with Stevens and the Court majority. He had no problem with burning the flag at the center of the case but "wouldn't allow the desecration of particular flags." The national dialogue is not always logical.

On the final day of a "tumultuous term"[65] of the Court, Justice Stevens looked directly at reporters in the Court while he delivered a twenty-minute rebuttal to Justice Scalia's decision that gutted initial enforcement of background checks for gun buyers under the new Brady Handgun Violence Protection Act.[66] In the absence of television coverage of the Court's public business, Linda Greenhouse of the *New York Times* provided an unusually pictorial newspaper account of justices speaking to the press, not just to elites of the legal profession:

> The courtroom was surprisingly empty for the final day of the term, perhaps because members of the Washington bar, knowing that only the Brady law case was due for decision, decided not to come. But the tourists, the Court staff and [Clinton] Administration lawyers who showed up were treated to a riveting and unusual display as Justice Scalia summarized his opinion and Justice Stevens responded. Side by side the two justices sat, the bearded, dark-haired justice Scalia, youthful at 61, and the grandfatherly Justice Stevens, at 77 the Court's oldest member, both men deeply committed to opposing

[63] Interview with Lawrence C. Marshall, law clerk to Justice John Paul Stevens, in Chicago, Ill. (June 20, 2003) (Gene Schlickman participated in the interview).

[64] William Raspberry, Column, "Protecting a Hateful Act," *Washington Post*, June 26, 1989, at A11.

[65] Joan Biskupic, "Court Voids Background Check of Gun Buyer under Brady Law," *Washington Post*, June 28, 1997, at A1.

[66] *Printz v. United States*, 521 U.S. 898 (1997).

> visions of constitutional structure they have devoted their professional lives to interpreting. Justice Stevens at time read from a memorandum that contained excerpts from his dissenting opinion. But often he spoke off the cuff.[67]

"The Brady Act was passed in response to what Congress described as an 'epidemic of gun violence,'" Stevens said in his written dissent. "There is not a clause, sentence, or paragraph in the text of the Constitution of the United States that supports the proposition that a local police officer can ignore a command contained in a statute enacted by Congress pursuant to an express delegation of power enumerated in Article I."

In a 2011 interview with Stevens, George Stephanopoulos of ABC News cited his dissents in *Bush v. Gore* and *Citizens United v. Federal Election Commission* to say that Stevens's pen "got mightier" late in his tenure. Stevens replied that his dissents were "received, perhaps more favorably" near the end of his career but said earlier dissents, such as in the Brady law case, contained "some pretty strong language."

Stevens's strongest dissent, in terms of press coverage and likely impact on public policy, came in a concurrence he wrote to a death penalty case.[68] Stevens could find no way in judicial precedent or in his respect for state authorities to oppose the majority's decision to uphold Kentucky's lethal injection program for capital cases. Only the last paragraph of his opinion, however, presented his formal concurrence. The remainder was his announcement that, after thirty-two years of justifying and modifying the death penalty, he was no longer willing to go along.

He borrowed his most effective statement from his former colleague Justice White: "The imposition of the death penalty represents 'the pointless and needless extinction of life with only marginal contributions to any social or public purpose. A penalty with such negligible returns to the State would be patently excessive and cruel and unusual punishment.'"[69]

Stevens opened his dissent by stating his belief that the case would "generate debate … about the justification for the death penalty itself." Professor Guinier commented, "The debate Justice Stevens seeks to spark goes beyond sparring with his colleagues on the bench." She noted the widespread news and editorial coverage of Steven's solo concurrence – and Justice Scalia's

67 Linda Greenhouse, "Justices Limit Brady Gun Law as Intrusion on States' Rights," *New York Times*, June 28, 1997, at A1. In a July 15, 2012 e-mail, Greenhouse recalled that the practice of justices talking "off the cuff" in announcing dissents from the bench was more common in 1997 then now and that Justice Stevens often did it.

68 *Base v. Rees*, 553 U.S. 35 (2008).

69 Justice Stevens quotes Justice White in *Furman v. Georgia*, 408 U.S. 238 (1972).

intense reaction to it – in major papers and in smaller papers, such as an editorial in the *Providence Journal Bulletin*. "The editorial transformed Justice Stevens's attempt to 'generate debate' on the death penalty into a demand for legislatures and courts to 'face the matter squarely' and 'put the death penalty to rest.' The editorial pages of other newspapers also helped translate Justices Stevens's careful words into a clarion call."[70]

CONCLUSION

Stevens expected that announcing his dissents and concurrences from the bench occasionally would help make them newsworthy, an oblique press relations strategy that is arms-length but sometimes effective. Of course, it didn't always work. "On my very last day on the bench, I made an announcement in a patent case that nobody noticed," Stevens said in my interview. The case[71] concerned whether patents can protect methods of operating a business. "It was a terribly important patent issue. I wrote an opinion almost as long as *Citizens United*," Stevens said. He even spiced up his brief oral from the bench on the arcane topic with a metaphor from his favorite spectator sport – baseball. If business methods are patentable, "a process for deciding whether to pitch a curve ball or change-of-pace could be patented," he said. But, he recalled later, "Nobody paid any attention to it."

Dissents and concurrences, especially when announced from the bench, inform intensely interested audiences – judges, legislators and advocates – as well as the public. They may foreshadow future Court rulings. They may motivate political activists. In a different but no less weighty context, no credible financial journalist would fail to report every detail he or she could find about dissents by members of the Federal Reserve's Open Market Committee to the committee's monetary policy decisions.

It would be a stretch to suggest that Stevens's use of separate opinions in dissent or concurrence was a concerted media strategy. As we have seen, his engagement with the media began only near the end of his active service. Still, it appears that some members of the Court are picking up where Stevens left off, summoning reporters to pay attention. The closing days of the October 2012 term featured extraordinary dramatics as several judges announced majority opinions and dissents from the bench.

In one incident, according to Garrett Epps of TheAtlantic.com, Justice Samuel Alito "pursed his lips, rolled his eyes to the ceiling, and shook his head

[70] Guinier, *supra* note 6, at 65, 67.

[71] *Bilski v. Kappos*, 130 S.Ct. 3218 (2010)

'no'" as Justice Ginsburg was announcing her dissent in two related employment discrimination cases.[72] "Because Alito's mini-tantrum was silent, it will not be recorded in the transcript or audio; but it was clear to all with eyes, and brought gasps from more than one person in the audience," Epps wrote.[73] In the WashingtonPost.com, Dana Milbank commented, "Typically justices state their differences in words – and Alito, as it happens, had just spoken several hundred words from the bench. But he frequently supplements words with middle-school gestures."[74]

Such theatrics by justices help upend the Stevens-era rule of keeping the Court's business within the Court and advance the cause of cameras in the Court's public sessions. However, it seems that at least Justice Stevens's faith in separate opinions as a prompt for news coverage will be part of his legacy.

[72] Justice Ginsburg on June 24, 2013, read from her dissents in an affirmative action case, *Fisher v. University of Texas at Austin* (570 U.S. ___ (2013)), and gave a single reading of her dissents in two related employment discrimination cases, *Vance v. Ball State University* (570 U.S. ___ (2013)) and *University of Texas Southwestern Medical v. Nassar* (570 U.S. ___ (2013)). The next day, she read from her dissent in a voting rights case, *Shelby County v. Holder* (570 U.S. ___ (2013)).

[73] Garrett Epps, "Justice Alito's Inexcusable Rudeness," TheAtlantic.com (June 24, 2013, at 2:22 PM EST), www.theatlantic.com/national/archive/2013/06/justice-alitos-inexcusable-rudeness/277163/.

[74] Dana Milbank, "Justice Alito's middle-school antics," WashingtonPost.com (June 24, 2013), articles.washingtonpost.com/2013-06-24/opinions/40162827_1_justices-elena-kagan-high-court.

Index

For EU product safety concerns, contact us at Calle de José Abascal, 56–1°,
28003 Madrid, Spain or eugpsr@cambridge.org.

www.ingramcontent.com/pod-product-compliance
Lightning Source LLC
LaVergne TN
LVHW011523200926
848484LV00001B/132

* 9 7 8 1 1 0 7 0 5 2 4 5 1 *